The
Bible Knowledge
Commentary

MINOR PROPHETS

The
Bible Knowledge
Commentary

MINOR PROPHETS

John F. Walvoord and Roy B. Zuck
GENERAL EDITORS

DAVID C COOK

transforming lives together

THE BIBLE KNOWLEDGE COMMENTARY: MINOR PROPHETS
Published by David C Cook
4050 Lee Vance Drive
Colorado Springs, CO 80918 U.S.A.

David C Cook U.K., Kingsway Communications
Eastbourne, East Sussex BN23 6NT, England

The graphic circle C logo is a registered trademark of David C Cook.

The website addresses recommended throughout this book are offered as a resource
to you. These websites are not intended in any way to be or imply an endorsement
on the part of David C Cook, nor do we vouch for their content.

Unless otherwise noted, all Scripture quotations are taken from the Holy Bible, New
International Version®, NIV®. Copyright © 1973, 1978 by Biblica, Inc.™ Used by
permission of Zondervan. All rights reserved worldwide. www.zondervan.com.
The authors have added italics to Scripture quotations for emphasis.

LCCN 2017955605
ISBN 978-0-8307-7266-7
eISBN 978-0-8307-7293-3

Cover Design: Nick Lee
Cover Photo: Getty Images

Printed in the United States of America
First Edition 2018

1 2 3 4 5 6 7 8 9 10

010818

CONTENTS

PREFACE

The Bible Knowledge Commentary series is an exposition of the Scriptures written and edited solely by Dallas Seminary faculty members. It is designed for pastors, laypersons, Bible teachers, serious Bible students, and others who want a comprehensive but brief and reliable commentary on the entire Bible.

Why another Bible commentary when so many commentaries are already available? Several features make this series a distinctive Bible study tool.

The Bible Knowledge Commentary series is written by faculty members of one school: Dallas Theological Seminary. This commentary interprets the Scriptures consistently from the grammatical-historical approach and from the pretribulational, premillennial perspective, for which Dallas Seminary is well known. At the same time, the authors often present various views of passages where differences of opinion exist within evangelical scholarship.

Additionally, this commentary has features that not all commentaries include. (a) In their comments on the biblical text, the writers discuss how the purpose of the book unfolds, how each part fits with the whole and with what precedes and follows it. This helps readers see why the biblical authors chose the material they did as their words were guided by the Holy Spirit's inspiration. (b) Problem passages, puzzling Bible-time customs, and alleged contradictions are carefully considered and discussed. (c) Insights from modern conservative biblical scholarship are incorporated in this series. (d) Many Hebrew, Aramaic, and Greek words, important to the understanding of certain passages, are discussed. These words are transliterated for the benefit of readers not proficient in the biblical languages. Yet those who do know these languages will also appreciate these comments. (e) Throughout the series, dozens of maps, charts, and diagrams are included; they are placed conveniently with the Bible passages being discussed, not at the end of each book. (f) Numerous cross references to related or parallel passages are included with the discussions on many passages.

The material on each Bible book includes an *Introduction* (discussion of items such as authorship, date, purpose, unity, style, unique features), *Outline, Commentary,* and *Bibliography*. In the *Commentary* section, summaries of entire sections of the text are given, followed by detailed comments on the passage verse by verse and often phrase by phrase. All words quoted from the New International Version of the Bible appear in boldface type, as do the verse numbers at the beginning of paragraphs. The *Bibliography* entries, suggested for further study, are not all endorsed in their entirety by the authors and editors. The writers and editors have listed both works they have consulted and others which would be useful to readers.

Personal pronouns referring to Deity are capitalized, which often helps make it clear that the commentator is writing about a Member of the Trinity. The word LORD is the English translation of the Hebrew YHWH, often rendered *Yahweh* in English. *Lord* translates *'Adōnāy*. When the two names stand together as a compound name of God, they are rendered "Sovereign LORD," as in the NIV.

The consulting editors—Dr. Kenneth L. Barker and Dr. Eugene H. Merrill on the Old Testament, and Dr. Stanley D. Toussaint on the New Testament—have added to the quality of this commentary by reading the manuscripts and offering helpful suggestions. Their work is greatly appreciated. We also express thanks to Lloyd Cory, Victor Books Reference Editor, to Barbara Williams, whose careful editing enhanced the material appreciably, to Production Coordinator Myrna Jean Hasse, to Jan Arroyo, and other people in the text editing department at Scripture

7

Press, who spent many long hours keyboarding and preparing pages for typesetting, and to the several manuscript typists at Dallas Theological Seminary for their diligence.

This commentary series is an exposition of the Bible, an explanation of the text of Scripture, based on careful exegesis. It is not primarily a devotional commentary, or an exegetical work giving details of lexicology, grammar, and syntax with extensive discussion of critical matters pertaining to textual and background data. May this commentary deepen your insight into the Scriptures, as you seek to have "the eyes of your heart … enlightened" (Eph. 1:18) by the teaching ministry of the Holy Spirit.

This book is designed to enrich your understanding and appreciation of the Scriptures, God's inspired, inerrant Word, and to motivate you "not merely [to] listen to the Word" but also to "do what it says" (James 1:22) and "also … to teach others" (2 Tim. 2:2).

John F. Walvoord
Roy B. Zuck

Editors

John F. Walvoord, B.A., M.A., TH.M., Th.D., D.D., Litt.D.
Chancellor Emeritus
Professor Emeritus of Systematic Theology

Roy B. Zuck, A.B., Th.M., Th.D.
Senior Professor Emeritus of Bible Exposition
Editor, *Bibliotheca Sacra*

Consulting Editors

Old Testament
Kenneth L. Barker, B.A., Th.M., Ph.D.
Writer, Lewisville, Texas

Eugene H. Merrill, B.A., M.A., M.Phil., Ph.D.
Distinguished Professor of Old Testament Studies

New Testament
Stanley D. Toussaint, B.A., Th.M., Th.D.
Senior Professor Emeritus of Bible Exposition

Series Contributing Authors

Walter L. Baker, B.A., Th.M., D.D.
Associate Professor Emeritus of World
Missions and Intercultural Studies
Obadiah

Craig Blaising, B.S. Th.M., Th.D., Ph.D.
Professor of Christian Theology Southern
Baptist Theological Seminary Louisville,
Kentucky
Malachi

J. Ronald Blue, B.A., Th.M.
President Emeritus CAM International
Dallas, Texas
Habakkuk

Sid S. Buzzell, B.S., Th.M., Ph.D.
Professor of Bible Exposition Colorado
Christian University Lakewood,
Colorado
Proverbs

Donald K. Campbell, B.A., Th.M., Th.D.
President Emeritus
Professor Emeritus of Bible Exposition
Joshua

**Robert B. Chisholm, Jr., B.A., M. Div.,
Th.M., Th.D.**
Professor of Old Testament Studies
Hosea, Joel

Thomas L. Constable, B.A., Th.M., Th.D.
Chairman and Senior Professor of Bible
Exposition
1 and 2 Kings

Jack S. Deere, B.A., Th.M., Th.D.
Associate Senior Pastor Trinity
Fellowship Church Amarillo, Texas
Deuteronomy, Song of Songs

Charles H. Dyer, B.A., Th.M., Th.D.
Provost and Senior Vice-President of
Education
Moody Bible Institute Chicago, Illinois
Jeremiah, Lamentations, Ezekiel

Gene A. Getz, B.A., M.A., Ph.D.
Senior Pastor
Fellowship Bible Church, North Plano,
Texas
Nehemiah

9

Donald R. Glenn, B.S., M.A., Th.M.
Chairman and Senior Professor of Old Testament Studies
Ecclesiastes

John D. Hannah, B.S., Th.M., Th.D.
Chairman and Distinguished Professor of Historical Theology
Exodus, Jonah, Zephaniah

Elliott E. Johnson, B.S., Th.M., Th.D.
Senior Professor of Bible Exposition
Nahum

F. Duane Lindsey, B.A., B.D., Th.M., Th.D.
Former Registrar, Research Librarian, and Assistant Professor of Systematic Theology
Leviticus, Judges, Haggai, Zechariah

John A. Martin, B.A., Th.M., Th.D.
Provost
Robert Wesleyan College
Rochester, New York
Ezra, Esther, Isaiah, Micah

Eugene H. Merrill, B.A., M.A., M.Phil., Ph.D.
Distinguished Professor of Old Testament Studies
Numbers, 1 and 2 Samuel, 1 and 2 Chronicles

J. Dwight Pentecost, B.A., Th.M., Th.D.
Distinguished Professor Emeritus of Bible Exposition
Daniel

John W. Reed, B.A., M.A., M.Div., Ph.D.
Director of D.Min. Studies
Senior Professor Emeritus of Pastoral Ministries
Ruth

Allen P. Ross, B.A., M.A., M.Div., Ph.D.
Professor of Old Testament Studies
Trinity Evangelical Episcopal Seminary
Ambridge, Pennsylvania
Genesis, Psalms

Donald R. Sunukjian, B.A., Th.M., Th.D., Ph.D.
Professor of Christian Ministry and Leadership
Talbot School of Theology La Mirada, California
Amos

Roy B. Zuck, B.A., Th.M., Th.D.
Editor, Bibliotheca Sacra
Senior Professor of Bible Exposition
Job

*Authorial information based on original edition of the Bible Knowledge Commentary set. At the time of the commentary's first printing, each author was a faculty member of Dallas Theological Seminary.

Abbreviations

A. General

act.	active	n., nn.	note(s)
Akk.	Akkadian	n.d.	no date
Apoc.	Apocrypha	neut.	neuter
Aram.	Aramaic	n.p.	no publisher, no place of
ca.	*circa*, about		publication
cf.	*confer*, compare	no.	number
chap., chaps.	chapter(s)	NT	New Testament
comp.	compiled, compilation,	OT	Old Testament
	compiler	p., pp.	page(s)
ed.	edited, edition, editor	par., pars.	paragraph(s)
eds.	editors	part.	participle
e.g.	*exempli gratia*, for example	pass.	passive
Eng.	English	perf.	perfect
et al.	*et alii*, and others	pl.	plural
fem.	feminine	pres.	present
Gr.	Greek	q.v.	*quod vide*, which see
Heb.	Hebrew	Sem.	Semitic
ibid.	*ibidem*, in the same place	sing.	singular
i.e.	*id est*, that is	s.v.	*sub verbo*, under the word
imper.	imperative	trans.	translation, translator,
imperf.	imperfect		translated
lit.	literal, literally	viz.	*videlicet*, namely
LXX	Septuagint	vol., vols.	volume(s)
marg.	margin, marginal reading	v., vv.	verse(s)
masc.	masculine	vs.	versus
ms., mss.	manuscript(s)	Vul.	Vulgate
MT	Masoretic text		

B. Abbreviations of Books of the Bible

Gen.	Ruth	Job	Lam.	Jonah
Ex.	1, 2 Sam.	Ps., Pss. (pl.)	Ezek.	Micah
Lev.	1, 2 Kings	Prov.	Dan.	Nahum
Num.	1, 2 Chron.	Ecc.	Hosea	Hab.
Deut.	Ezra	Song	Joel	Zeph.
Josh.	Neh.	Isa.	Amos	Hag.
Jud.	Es.	Jer.	Obad.	Zech.
				Mal.

Matt.	Acts	Eph.	1, 2 Tim.	James
Mark	Rom.	Phil.	Titus	1, 2 Peter
Luke	1, 2 Cor.	Col.	Phile.	1, 2, 3 John
John	Gal.	1, 2 Thes.	Heb.	Jude
				Rev.

C. Abbreviations of Bible Versions, Translations, and Paraphrases

ASV	American Standard Version
JB	Jerusalem Bible
KJV	King James Version
NASB	New American Standard Bible
NEB	New English Bible
NIV	New International Version
RSV	Revised Standard Version

Transliterations

Hebrew

Consonants

א – '	ד – ḏ	י – y	ס – s	ר – r
ב – b	ה – h	כ – k	ע – ʿ	שׂ – ś
ב – ḇ	ו – w	כ – ḵ	פ – p	שׁ – š
ג – g	ז – z	ל – l	פ – p̄	תּ – t
ג – ḡ	ח – ḥ	מ – m	צ – ṣ	ת – ṯ
ד – d	ט – ṭ	נ – n	ק – q	

Daghesh forte is represented by doubling the letter.

Vocalization

בָּה – bâh	בָּ – bā	בֹּ – bo[1]	בְּ – bĕ
בוֹ – bô	בֹּ – bō	בֻּ – bu[1]	בּ – b
בוּ – bû	בֻּ – bū	בֶּ – be	בָּה – bāh
בֵּ – bê	בֵּ – bē	בִּ – bi[1]	בָּא – bā'
בֶּ – bè	בִּ – bī	בֲּ – bă	בֵּה – bēh
בִּ – bî	בַּ – ba	בֳּ – bŏ	בֶּה – beh

[1] In closed syllables

Greek

α, ἀ – a	ξ – x	γγ – ng
β – b	ο – o	γκ – nk
γ – g	π – p	γξ – nx
δ – d	ρ – r	γχ – nch
ε – e	σ, ς – s	αἰ – ai
ζ – z	τ – t	αὐ – au
η, ἠ – ē	υ – y	εἰ – ei
θ – th	φ – ph	εὐ – eu
ι – i	χ – ch	ηὐ – ēu
κ – k	ψ – ps	οἰ – oi
λ – l	ω, ὠ – ō	οὐ – ou
μ – m	ῥ – rh	υἱ – hui
ν – n	ʽ – h	

An Overview of Old Testament History

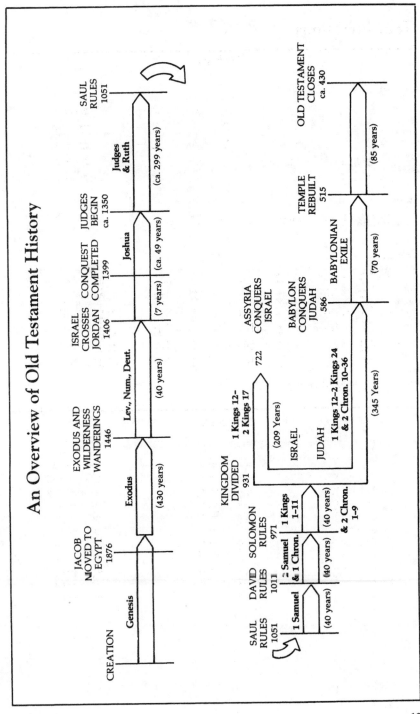

CREATION

Genesis

JACOB MOVED TO EGYPT
1876

Exodus

(430 years)

EXODUS AND WILDERNESS WANDERINGS
1446

Lev., Num., Deut.

(40 years)

ISRAEL CROSSES JORDAN
1406

(7 years)

CONQUEST COMPLETED
1399

Joshua

(ca. 49 years)

JUDGES BEGIN
ca. 1350

Judges & Ruth

(ca. 299 years)

SAUL RULES
1051

SAUL RULES
1051

1 Samuel

(40 years)

DAVID RULES
1011

2 Samuel & 1 Chron.

(40 years)

SOLOMON RULES
971

1 Kings 1–11

(40 years)

KINGDOM DIVIDED
931

1 Kings 12– 2 Kings 17

ISRAEL

(209 Years)

ASSYRIA CONQUERS ISRAEL
722

JUDAH

1 Kings 12–2 Kings 24 & 2 Chron. 10–36

& 2 Chron. 1–9

BABYLON CONQUERS JUDAH
586

(345 Years)

BABYLONIAN EXILE

(70 years)

TEMPLE REBUILT
515

(85 years)

OLD TESTAMENT CLOSES
ca. 430

Biblical Weights and Measures

BIBLICAL UNIT		AMERICAN EQUIVALENT	METRIC EQUIVALENT
WEIGHT			
talent	(60 minas)	75 pounds	34 kilograms
mina	(50 shekels)	1 1/4 pounds	0.6 kilogram
shekel	(2 bekas)	2/5 ounce	11.5 grams
pim	(2/3 shekel)	1/3 ounce	7.6 grams
beka	(10 gerahs)	1/5 ounce	6 grams
gerah		1/50 ounce	0.6 gram
LENGTH			
cubit		18 inches	0.5 meter
span		9 inches	23 centimeters
handbreadth		3 inches	7 centimeters
CAPACITY			
Dry Measure			
cor [homer]	(10 ephahs)	6 bushels	220 liters
lethech	(5 ephahs)	3 bushels	110 liters
ephah	(10 omers)	1/2 bushel	22 liters
seah	(1/3 ephah)	7 quarts	7.3 liters
omer	(1/10 ephah)	2 quarts	2 liters
cab	(1/18 ephah)	1/2 pint	0.3 liter
Liquid Measure			
bath	(1 ephah)	6 gallons	22 liters
hin	(1/6 bath)	4 quarts	4 liters
log	(1/72 bath)	1/3 quart	0.3 liter

The information in this chart, while not being mathematically precise, gives approximate amounts and distances. The figures are calculated on the basis of a shekel equaling 11.5 grams, a cubit equaling 18 inches, and an ephah equaling 22 liters.

HOSEA

Robert B. Chisholm, Jr.

INTRODUCTION

Authorship. According to Hosea 1:1 the author of this prophecy was Hosea, son of Beeri. But several commentators have attributed some of the material in the book to later editorial activity. According to these scholars, the present form of the book is the product of an evolutionary process whereby original material by Hosea was reworked and supplemented (cf., e.g., William Rainey Harper, *A Critical and Exegetical Commentary on Amos and Hosea*, pp. clix-clxii; Hans Walter Wolff, *Hosea*, pp. xxix-xxxii). In particular, references to Judah and parallels to the language and theology of Deuteronomy have been offered as examples of redactional additions. However, it is unnecessary to deny the Judean passages to Hosea. Though his main target was the Northern Kingdom, his message encompassed the entire people of God. Like Hosea, other eighth-century B.C. prophets spoke to both kingdoms in the course of their prophecies (for a detailed discussion of the Judean passages in Hosea, see R.K. Harrison, *Introduction to the Old Testament*. Grand Rapids: Wm. B. Eerdmans Publishing Co., 1969, pp. 868-70). Hosea's parallels to Deuteronomy cannot be labeled later additions if Deuteronomy is correctly dated before, not after, Hosea.

Date. Hosea's ministry spanned several decades, beginning near the end of the reigns of Uzziah of Judah (ca. 790–739 B.C.) and Jeroboam II of Israel (ca. 793–753 B.C.) and concluding in the early years of Hezekiah's reign. The latter's rule began around 715 B.C. after a period of vice-regency with his father Ahaz. Since Israel was Hosea's primary audience, it seems strange that four Judean kings, but only one Israelite king, are mentioned in 1:1. The reason for the omission of the six Israelite kings who followed Jeroboam II is uncertain. Perhaps it suggests the legitimacy of the Davidic dynasty (cf. 3:5) in contrast with the instability and disintegration of the kingship in the North (cf. 7:3-7).

Historical Background. The events in the reigns of the kings mentioned in 1:1 are recorded in 2 Chronicles 26–32. Hosea began his ministry near the end of a period of military success and prosperity for both Israel and Judah (cf. 2 Kings 14:25-28; 2 Chron. 26:2, 6-15). During the first half of the eighth century Assyrian influence in the West had declined, allowing the kingdoms of Jeroboam II and Uzziah to flourish. However, the situation soon changed. As foreseen by Hosea the Assyrians under Tiglath-Pileser III (745–727 B.C.) revived their expansionist policy in the West. In 733-732 B.C. the Northern Kingdom was made a puppet state within the Assyrian Empire (2 Kings 15:29). After plotting revolt, Israel was defeated in 722 B.C. by the Assyrians and Israel's people were deported (2 Kings 17:1-6; 18:10-12). Also Judah was incorporated as a vassal state into the Assyrian Empire during Hosea's time (cf. 2 Kings 16:5-10).

Purpose and Message. The primary purpose of Hosea's prophecy, like that of his eighth-century contemporaries Amos, Isaiah, and Micah, must be understood against the background of the message and theology of Deuteronomy. The latter records the covenantal agreement between the Lord and Israel. Israel was to maintain loyalty to the Lord by worshiping Him alone and by obeying His commandments. Obedience to the covenant would result in blessing (cf. Deut. 28:1-14). Disobedience would bring judgment and eventually exile (cf. the covenant curses listed in Deut. 28:15-68). Hosea's role as a prophet was to expose the nation's breach of covenant and announce God's intention to implement the covenant curses. At the same time Hosea affirmed the Deuteronomic promise of Israel's ultimate restoration (cf. Deut. 30:1-10).

The major themes of Hosea's message can be summarized in three words: sin, judgment, and salvation. In exposing Israel's sin, Hosea emphasized its idolatry (e.g., Hosea 4:17; 8:4, 6; 10:5; 11:2; 13:2). He compared Israel's covenant relationship to the Lord with marriage and accused Israel (the Lord's "wife") of spiritual adultery. She had turned to Baal, the Canaanite storm and fertility god (cf. 2:8, 13; 11:2; 13:1), in an effort to promote agricultural and human fertility. To illustrate Israel's infidelity Hosea married a woman who would, like the nation, prove unfaithful to her husband. Many other sins are mentioned in the book, including social injustice (12:7), violent crime (4:2; 6:9; 12:1), religious hypocrisy (6:6), political revolt (7:3-7), foreign alliances (7:11; 8:9), selfish arrogance (13:6), and spiritual ingratitude (7:15).

Though Hosea's prophecy contains some calls to repentance, he did not expect a positive response. Judgment was inescapable. In implementing the curses, the Lord would cause the nation to experience infertility, military invasion, and exile. Several times Hosea emphasized the justice of God by indicating that His divine punishment fit the crimes perfectly.

However, the Lord would not abandon Israel totally. Despite its severity, each judgment was disciplinary and was intended to turn Israel back to God. Hosea's own reconciliation with his wayward wife illustrated Israel's ultimate restoration. The very structure of the book reflects this positive emphasis. One is able to discern five judgment-salvation cycles throughout the prophecy:

	Judgment	Salvation
1.	1:2-9	1:10–2:1
2.	2:2-13	2:14–3:5
3.	4:1–5:14	5:15–6:3
4.	6:4–11:7	11:8-11
5.	11:12–13:16	chap. 14

OUTLINE

I. Hosea's Times (1:1)
II. Hosea's Experience: A Portrayal of God's Dealings with Israel (1:2–3:5)
  A. The symbolism of Hosea's family (1:2–2:1)
    1. Hosea's marriage: Israel's unfaithfulness (1:2–3a)
    2. Hosea's children: Israel's judgment (1:3b–9)
    3. The symbolism reversed (1:10–2:1)
  B. Restoration through punishment (2:2-23)
    1. The Lord's punishment of Israel (2:2-13)
    2. The Lord's restoration of Israel (2:14-23)
  C. The restoration of Hosea's marriage (chap. 3)
    1. The divine command (3:1)
    2. Hosea's obedient response (3:2-3)
    3. The illustration explained (3:4-5)
III. Hosea's Message: God's Judgment and Restoration of Israel (chaps. 4–14)
  A. The Lord's case against Israel (4:1–6:3)
    1. Israel's guilt exposed (chap. 4)
    2. Israel's judgment announced (5:1-14)
    3. Israel's restoration envisioned (5:15–6:3)
  B. The Lord's case against Israel expanded (6:4–11:11)
    1. Israel's guilt and punishment (6:4–8:14)
    2. Israel's guilt and punishment reiterated (9:1–11:7)
    3. The Lord's compassion renewed (11:8-11)
  C. The Lord's case against Israel concluded (11:12–14:9)
    1. A concluding indictment (11:12–13:16)
    2. A concluding exhortation (chap. 14)

COMMENTARY

I. Hosea's Times (1:1)

1:1. In Hebrew the name **Hosea** ("salvation") is the same as Hoshea, Israel's last king (2 Kings 17:1). Hoshea was also Joshua's original name (Num. 13:8, 16). Nothing is known of Hosea's family background except that he was a son of Beeri.

Hosea's ministry extended for a number of decades in the second half of the eighth century B.C. Four kings of Judah (Uzziah, Jotham, Ahaz, and Hezekiah) reigned when Hosea prophesied. Only one king of the north (Jeroboam II), is mentioned though Hosea's message was directed primarily to the Northern Kingdom. Six kings of Israel followed Jeroboam II during the reigns of the four Judean kings mentioned. Perhaps Hosea omitted those six (as stated under "Date" in the *Introduction*) to point up the legitimacy of the Davidic dynasty in Judah.

II. Hosea's Experience: A Portrayal of God's Dealings with Israel (1:2–3:5)

The message of the first three chapters (and of the entire book) oscillates between judgment and salvation. Hosea's marital experiences, which included the heartbreak caused by his wife's unfaithfulness and the joy of their renewed relationship, provide the framework for this message.

A. The symbolism of Hosea's family (1:2–2:1)

This opening section sets forth the major themes of the entire prophecy: Israel's unfaithfulness, the certainty of judgment, and the ultimate restoration of the nation. These ideas are introduced within the context of the Lord's command to Hosea to marry and have children.

1. HOSEA'S MARRIAGE: ISRAEL'S UNFAITHFULNESS (1:2-3A)

1:2-3a. At the outset of Hosea's ministry **the Lord** instructed him to marry **an adulterous woman.** This relationship, characterized by infidelity on the wife's part, was to portray Israel's unfaithfulness to its covenant with the Lord (cf. 2:2-23). In response to the divine command **Hosea. . . . married Gomer,** a **daughter of Diblaim.**

Much debate has centered on the circumstances of Hosea's marriage. Some have held that the marriage was only visionary or allegorical, not literal. This

proposal was motivated by a desire to sidestep the supposed moral difficulty of the holy God commanding His servant to marry a woman of disreputable character. However, the account is presented as a straightforward narrative, not as a report of a vision or as a purely symbolic act (cf. chap. 3). The Lord sometimes required His prophets to carry out orders that many would consider over and above the call of duty (e.g., Isa. 20:1-4; Ezek. 4:1–5:4).

Those who hold to a literal marriage disagree over Gomer's status at the beginning of her relationship with Hosea. Some argue that Gomer was a prostitute at the time she was married. A modification of this is the view that she was a typical young Israelite woman who had participated in a Canaanite rite of sexual initiation in preparation for marriage (Wolff, *Hosea*, pp. 14-5). Others contend that Gomer was sexually pure at the time of marriage and later became an adulteress. The Book of Hosea does not provide information concerning Gomer's premarital sexual experience. The expression "adulterous wife" (lit., "wife of adultery") does not describe her condition at the time of marriage, but anticipates what she proved to be, a wife characterized by unfaithfulness. Any knowledge of Gomer's status at the time of marriage is thereby precluded.

Both the language of Hosea 1:2 and the following context support this interpretation. The expression is similar to others in Hebrew that describe a married woman's character (e.g., "wife of one's youth," "a quarrelsome wife" ["a wife of quarrelings"], "a wife of noble character"; for these and other examples see Francis I. Andersen and David Noel Freedman, *Hosea: A New Translation, Introduction and Commentary,* p. 159). The Hebrew word $z^e n\hat{u}n\hat{i}m$ (trans. here "adulterous") refers elsewhere in Hosea to the activity of Israel under the figure of a married woman (cf. 2:2, 4; 4:12; 5:4). Also the emphasis in the following context (1:2b; 2:2–3:5) is on the unfaithfulness that characterized both the Lord's and Hosea's marriages, not on the brides' premarital experiences. Thus the Lord's command should be understood as follows, "Go, take to yourself a wife who will prove to be unfaithful."

The Lord also told Hosea to **take . . .**

17

children of unfaithfulness. This does not refer to children born from another father before Gomer's marriage to Hosea. The Hebrew expression is elliptical with the second verb omitted. The command could be paraphrased, "Go, take to yourself an adulterous wife and have (NASB) children of unfaithfulness." The children are those mentioned in 1:3-9. "Unfaithfulness" does not necessarily imply they were the products of Gomer's illicit relationships. The fact that Hosea is not specifically mentioned in verses 6 and 8 as the children's father need not point to their illegitimacy. In Genesis 29:32-35 the same phrase which appears in Hosea 1:6, 8 ("she conceived again and gave birth") is used with no mention of the father (Jacob) because he is identified in the preceding context (as in Hosea, v. 3; cf. Andersen and Freedman, *Hosea*, p. 168). "Children of unfaithfulness" may simply point to their being born in the context of (but not as a direct result of) Gomer's infidelity. Also the phrase emphasizes the mother's character, not that of the children. Andersen and Freedman understand the phrase as elliptical: "children of (a wife of) promiscuity" (*Hosea*, p. 168). It is similar to other Hebrew expressions in which the descriptive term points primarily to a quality of the parent not of the offspring (cf. $b^e n\hat{e}$ $hann^{e^c}\hat{u}r\hat{i}m$, lit., "sons of youth," i.e., "sons born to a youthful parent," Ps. 127:4; and ben $z^e q\bar{u}n\hat{i}m$, lit., "son of old age," i.e., "a son born to an aged parent," Gen. 37:3).

In Hosea 1:2 **the land,** which stands for those living in it (cf. 4:1), is personified as a wife who **is guilty of the vilest adultery.** This Hebrew verbal expression is emphatic, highlighting the extent to which Israel had departed **from the LORD.**

2. HOSEA'S CHILDREN: ISRAEL'S JUDGMENT (1:3B-9)

The divinely chosen names for Hosea's three children served as reminders of the broken relationship between the Lord and Israel and pointed ahead to judgment. Each section on the children (vv. 3b-5, 6-7, 8-9) contains a birth notice (vv. 3b, 6a, 8), a divine word of instruction concerning the child's name (vv. 4a, 6b, 9a), and an explanation of the meaning of the name (vv. 4b-5, 6b, 9b). God's words (v. 7) are unique in that they quali-

fy the announcement of judgment given (v. 6).

a. Jezreel (1:3b-5)

1:3b. The first child (**a son**) was named Jezreel. At this point the significance of his name was not in its meaning ("God sows"), but in its association with past and future events at the place Jezreel (cf., however, v. 11; 2:22-23). Jezreel was the site of Jehu's ruthless massacre of the house of Ahab (1:4; cf. 2 Kings 9–10). In the future it would be the scene of Israel's military demise (Hosea 1:5).

1:4. The reason for the Lord's coming punishment on Jehu's dynasty (lit., **house**) was **the massacre** (lit., "bloodshed") **at Jezreel** (ca. 841 B.C.). Jehu's slaughter of Jezebel and Ahab's descendants had been prophesied by Elijah (1 Kings 21:21-24), commanded by Elisha (2 Kings 9:6-10), and commended by the Lord Himself (2 Kings 10:30). So many think the attitude expressed by the Lord (Hosea 1:4) contradicted that in the accounts in 1 and 2 Kings. But a closer examination of the historical record suggests a resolution to the problem. **Jehu** also killed Joram (2 Kings 9:24), Ahaziah, king of Judah (2 Kings 9:27-28), 42 of Ahaziah's relatives (2 Kings 10:12-14), and several functionaries of the Baal cult (2 Kings 10:18-28). Though the execution of Baal's servants was certainly in accord with the Lord's will (cf. 1 Kings 18:40), Jehu's attack on the house of David went too far. Despite the fact that Ahaziah's assassination could be attributed to God's providence (2 Chron. 22:7), it demonstrated an underlying lack of regard for the Lord's commands. This disregard subsequently came to the surface in other ways (cf. 2 Kings 10:29-31). So Hosea 1:4 probably refers to the slaughter of Ahaziah and his relatives. Though their deaths did not actually occur in Jezreel (cf. 2 Kings 9:27; 10:12-14), they were associated with the wholesale slaughter at that place.

The fulfillment of this prophecy came in 752 B.C. when Shallum assassinated Zechariah, the fourth of Jehu's descendants to rule the Northern Kingdom (2 Kings 15:10), thereby cutting off Jehu's dynasty forever.

1:5. God told Hosea that the demise of Jehu's dynasty was to be accompanied by the downfall of the Northern Kingdom. In a display of poetic justice the Lord would **break Israel's bow in the Valley of Jezreel,** the site of Jehu's sin. Breaking the bow refers to the destruction of the nation's military might (cf. 1 Sam. 2:4; Ps. 46:9; Jer. 49:35).

The general fulfillment of this prophecy came in 734–722 B.C. when the Assyrians overran Israel and reduced it to a province within their empire (2 Kings 15:29; 17:3-5). The Jezreel plain in particular was probably conquered in 733 B.C. by Tiglath-Pileser III. This valley, which had been the scene of a great military victory under Gideon (Jud. 6:33; 7), again became a symbol of national disgrace and defeat, as it had been after Saul's death (1 Sam. 29:1, 11; 31).

b. Lo-Ruhamah: "Not loved" (1:6-7)

1:6. The second child received the name **Lo-Ruhamah,** which means "she is not loved." Her name indicated that the Lord's **love** for **Israel** would be cut off for a time. "Ruhamah," from the verb *rāḥam*, describes tender feelings of compassion, such as those expressed by a parent for a child (cf. 1 Kings 3:26; Ps. 103:13; Isa. 49:15) or by a man for his younger brother (cf. Gen. 43:30). At Sinai the Lord described Himself (Ex. 34:6) as "the compassionate . . . God" (*'ēl raḥûm*) who is willing to forgive iniquity (Ex. 34:6). However, despite His gracious character, times come when He will no longer "leave the guilty unpunished" (Ex. 34:7). Such a time had come for the Northern Kingdom.

1:7. The light of God's grace shines through the gloom of impending judgment. **Judah,** the Southern Kingdom, in contrast with Israel, would experience the Lord's **love** in the form of deliverance from the Assyrians. This would **not** be accomplished through human military might (symbolized by the **bow, sword,** etc.), **but by the** Lord's intervention. This promise was fulfilled in 701 B.C. when God supernaturally annihilated 185,000 soldiers in the powerful Assyrian army in one night thereby ending its campaign against Judah (2 Kings 19:32-36).

c. Lo-Ammi: "Not My people" (1:8-9)

1:8-9. The third child, a **son,** was named **Lo-Ammi,** which means **not My people.** In the ancient covenant formula God declared, "I will walk among you

and be your God, and you will be My people" (Lev. 26:12; cf. Ex. 6:7; Deut. 26:17-18). But now that relationship was to be severed. The last clause of Hosea 1:9 (**I am not your God**) is literally, "and I [am] not I AM (*'ehyeh*) to you." The statement probably alludes to God's words to Moses, "I am (*'ehyeh*) who I am (*'ehyeh*). This is what you are to say to the Israelites: I AM (*'ehyeh*) has sent me to you" (Ex. 3:14). "I AM," which is closely related to the divine name Yahweh, points to God as the covenant LORD of Israel who watches over and delivers His people (cf. Ex. 3:16-17). However, through Lo-Ammi the Lord announced that Israel would no longer experience His special saving presence.

3. THE SYMBOLISM REVERSED (1:10–2:1)

In a remarkable shift of tone the Lord declared that the effects of judgment would someday be reversed. He promised a time of rich blessing accompanied by restoration of the covenant relationship and national unity.

1:10. Despite the demise of the Northern Kingdom (vv. 4-5), **the Israelites will** again **be like the sand on the seashore** in fulfillment of the Lord's irrevocable promise to Abraham (Gen. 22:17; 32:12). **In the** same **place where** Israel heard the words **not My people** (cf. Hosea 1:9) **they will be called sons of the living God.** The sonship reference points to restoration of the covenant relationship, pictured under the figure of a family setting (cf. 2:1-5). The divine title "living God" was used in Joshua 3:10 in reference to the Lord's mighty presence with Israel during the Conquest of the land. In the future Israel will again experience the benefits of a relationship with the living God as they reoccupy the Promised Land.

1:11. At the time of national restoration the two kingdoms (**Judah and . . . Israel**), which had divided under Solomon's son Rehoboam (1 Kings 12), **will be reunited** under **one Leader** (cf. Ezek. 37:22), the ideal Davidic Ruler of the Kingdom Age (cf. Hosea 3:5; Isa. 9:6-7; Amos 9:11; Micah 5:2). The promise to David of an everlasting throne will be fulfilled (cf. 2 Sam. 7:11b-16).

The united nation also **will come up out of the land.** This statement may refer to a return from exile, the "land" being

19

Egypt (cf. Hosea 2:15), which serves as a symbol of the future place(s) of captivity (cf. 8:13; 9:3, 6; 11:5; Deut. 28:68). However, "land" ('ereṣ) elsewhere in the Book of Hosea refers either to the land of Israel (cf. Hosea 1:2; 2:18, 23; 4:1, 3) or to the literal surface of the ground (cf. 2:21-22; 6:3) when used with the definite article and without a qualifying geographical term. The land of Egypt is specifically designated as such when mentioned in Hosea (2:15; 7:11, 16; 8:13; 9:3, 6; 11:1, 5, 11; 12:1, 9, 13; 13:4). So it is better to understand this as a comparison between Israel and a plant which grows up from the soil. "Land" can refer to the ground (as just noted), as "come up" ('ālâh) is used elsewhere of plant life sprouting forth from the soil (cf. "grow up," 10:8; "growing" Deut. 29:23). The following context also supports this view. According to Hosea 2:23, the Lord promised that He would "plant" (zāra', the same word used in the name Jezreel) the nation in the land as one sows seed on the ground (cf. 2:22, where the name Jezreel, "God sows," appears). Because the Lord Himself will be the One who sows, Israel will sprout forth and grow luxuriantly.

The day of Jezreel probably alludes to this time when God will plant His people in the land. If so, the literal meaning of the name Jezreel ("God sows") takes on significance at this point. It is also likely that it alludes to Gideon's victory over the Midianites in the Valley of Jezreel (Jud. 7). The future day of restoration will be ushered in by a great military triumph like that of Gideon (cf. Isa. 9:4-7; see also Isa. 41:8-16; Amos 9:11-12; Joel 3:9-17). Those who oppose the Lord's theocratic rule through the messianic King will be defeated (cf. Rev. 19:11-21). The greatness of this eschatological "day of Jezreel" will reverse the shame and defeat which Israel experienced there at the hands of the Assyrians (cf. Hosea 1:5).

2:1. These words were spoken to a segment of the restored nation of the future (cf. v. 23), viewed as a group of children (**say** and **your** are pl. in Heb.). They were told to proclaim to their **brothers** and **sisters** (other Israelites) that the nation's relationship with the Lord had been reestablished. The Lord then addressed them as **My people** ('ammî; cf. 1:9) and **My loved one** (ruḥāmâh; cf. 1:6). Long before Hosea, Moses had predicted such a change in the Lord's attitude (Deut. 30:1-9). After describing the nation's future exile (Deut. 30:1), Moses promised that their repentance would result in a renewal of the Lord's compassion (Deut. 30:2-3, rāḥam) and a return to the land (Deut. 30:4-9). Long after Hosea, the Apostle Paul also foresaw this time of Israel's restoration (Rom. 11:25-32).

In summary, Hosea 1:10–2:1 contains a marvelous prophecy of Israel's future restoration, in which the effects of the Lord's judgment will be totally reversed. The nation that suffered defeat at Jezreel and was called "not loved" and "not My people" will take part in the great "day of Jezreel" and hear the Lord say, "My people" and "[My] loved one." The covenant promises to Abraham (of numerous descendants) and David (of eternal kingship) will be fulfilled when the covenant ideal predicted by Moses will be realized.

B. Restoration through punishment (2:2-23)

Hosea's relationship with Gomer was designed to reflect the Lord's experience of being rejected by His covenant people Israel (cf. 1:2). In 2:2-23 the Lord described this rejection in detail, comparing Israel to an unfaithful wife who chased after lovers. In the process of confirming the nation's guilt, the Lord announced coming punishment. This judgment, however, would not be final, for God intended to draw Israel back and restore the broken covenantal relationship. Thus this section, like the preceding one (1:2–2:1) progresses from judgment (2:2-13) to salvation (2:14-23, along with chap. 3).

1. THE LORD'S PUNISHMENT OF ISRAEL (2:2-13)

Included in this section are an introductory summons (v. 2a), an appeal for repentance (v. 2b) accompanied by a threat of punishment (vv. 3-4), and two judgmental speeches (vv. 5-7, 8-13), each containing an accusation (vv. 5, 8) and an announcement of punishment (vv. 6-7, 9-13).

a. Punishment threatened (2:2-4)

2:2. The section opens with the Lord calling for a formal accusation to be brought against Israel. The covenant relationship is likened to marriage, the Lord being the husband and Israel the wife. The children addressed (cf. **your mother**) need not represent any specific group within Israel. They are included for rhetorical effect and add to the realism of the figurative portrayal. The word translated **rebuke** (*rîḇ*) is used here of a formal legal accusation. A related noun often refers to a lawsuit (cf. Ex. 23:2-3, 6). In Hosea 4:1 this same noun is translated "charge." The reason for the accusation was the disrupted relationship between the covenant partners. The Lord, speaking as the Husband who had been severely wronged, declared, **She is not My wife, and I am not her Husband**. Some have interpreted this statement as a formal declaration of divorce, which is unlikely in this context. The Lord's ultimate purpose was to heal the relationship, not terminate it (cf. 2:2b, 6-7, 14-23). Thus the statement was probably an acknowledgment that "no reality remained in the relationship" (Derek Kidner, *Love to the Loveless*, p. 27). The Lord's wife, by her unfaithful behavior, had for all practical purposes severed the relationship with her Husband.

Rather than exercising His legal prerogative by having His wayward wife executed (cf. Lev. 20:10; Deut. 22:22), the Lord issued a call for repentance, urging the nation to abandon its **adulterous** activity (Hosea 2:2b).

2:3. The Lord's appeal (v. 2b) was strengthened by a severe threat containing three solemn warnings to Israel (**I will** occurs three times in vv. 3-4). First, the Lord threatened to **strip her naked,** making her an object of shame and ridicule (cf. v. 10; Ezek. 16:35-43). The punishment fit the crime. She who had exposed her nakedness to her lovers would be exposed publicly for all to see. This public act apparently preceded the execution of an adulteress (cf. Ezek. 16:38-40).

Second, the Lord threatened to **make her like** an arid **desert,** deprived of water (cf. **slay her with thirst**), incapable of producing or sustaining life. All her powers of fertility would be removed. Again the punishment fit the crime. She who had engaged in illicit sexual behavior would become incapable of reproduction.

2:4. The third threat involved the rejection of the wife's **children.** The reason was that **they** were **children of adultery.**

This may mean they were products of their mother's illicit relationships, though probably it simply indicates they were covered with shame by reason of their association with such a mother (cf. v. 5 and comments on 1:2). At any rate, the Lord announced they would not receive His **love** (*rāḥam*; cf. 1:6-8; 2:1), implying they would be disowned and become orphans. In this way any reminder of the relationship with their mother would be eliminated.

The harsh punishment threatened in verses 3-4 seems to imply complete termination of the marriage. The wayward wife would be executed and her children disowned. However, the context clearly demonstrates that this would not occur. This same anomaly occurs in Ezekiel 16 where Israel is executed as an adulteress (Ezek. 16:35-42) only to be eventually restored to favor (Ezek. 16:59-63). Apparently the harsh language was intended to emphasize the severity of the punishment without implying the absolute termination of the Lord's relationship with Israel.

b. Punishment initiated (2:5-13)

The Lord's judgment, instead of bringing His relationship with Israel to a complete end, was designed to effect restoration. The first step in this process was to deprive the nation of its false gods and the prosperity it erroneously attributed to them.

(1) Israel deprived of her lovers. **2:5-7.** In verse 5 Israel's unfaithfulness is vividly pictured. She resolved to pursue her **lovers** (the Baals; cf. vv. 13, 17; 11:2) because she believed they supplied her physical nourishment (**food . . . water**), protection (**wool and . . . linen**; cf. 2:9), and pleasure (**oil and . . . drink**). In response the Lord declared that He would soon eliminate all means of access to these lovers. Israel would find familiar paths blocked with thorns and stone walls (v. 6). Her frantic efforts to find her **lovers** would be thwarted (v. 7a). As a last resort, she would resolve to return to her **Husband,** the Lord, opening the way for restoration. The reality behind this figurative portrayal of judgment probably included drought, invasion, and exile (cf. vv. 9, 11-12; Lev. 26:18-22).

(2) Israel deprived of the Lord's blessings (2:8-13). **2:8.** Israel's guilt was

established as the basis for her punishment. She had failed to acknowledge the Lord as the Source of her produce and wealth. Instead she used **silver and gold** to manufacture **Baal** idols (cf. 8:4; 13:2), for it was this Canaanite deity to whom she attributed her agricultural (**grain . . . new wine and oil**) and economic prosperity (2:5, 12-13).

Baal was the Canaanite god who supposedly controlled storms and was responsible for both agricultural and human fertility. The Canaanite "Legend of Keret" associated Baal's rain with agricultural blessing in the form of grain, bread, wine, and oil (cf. J.C.L. Gibson, *Canaanite Myths and Legends.* Edinburgh: T. & T. Clark, 1978, p. 98). By looking to Baal for these things Israel broke the first of the Ten Commandments (cf. Ex. 20:3; Deut. 5:7), rejecting one of the main principles of the Mosaic legislation. Moses taught that the Lord provided grain, wine, and oil (Deut. 7:13; 11:14). Each Israelite, when presenting his firstfruits in the harvest festival, was to recite the following words in the presence of the priest, "I bring the firstfruits of the soil that You, O LORD, have given me" (Deut. 26:10).

2:9a. In response to Israel's unfaithfulness, the Lord said He would deprive the nation of agricultural produce (**grain** and **new wine**), leaving it destitute. The Mosaic Law made agricultural prosperity dependent on loyalty to the Lord. Obedience to the covenant stipulations would result in the Lord's blessing in the form of plentiful harvests, numerous offspring, and security (cf. Lev. 26:3-13; Deut. 28:1-14). Disobedience would bring drought, pestilence, war, death, and exile (Lev. 26:14-39; Deut. 28:15-68). Thus the announcement in Hosea 2:9 revealed the Lord's intention to implement the covenant curses against Israel. Drought, blight, insect swarms, and invading armies would destroy the land's produce (cf. Deut. 28:51; Joel 1:4-12; Amos 4:6-9; 7:1).

2:9b-10. The figurative portrayal of Israel as the Lord's wife is carried along in these verses. Without **wool** and **linen** (cf. v. 5), which were used to make clothing (Lev. 13:47, 59; Deut. 22:11; Prov. 31:13; Ezek. 44:17), she would have no means of covering **her nakedness.** Through this deprivation the Lord would **expose her lewdness.** Her shameful behavior would become known to all through this public demonstration (cf. Hosea 2:3; Ezek. 16:36-37). "Lewdness" (*naḇlûṯ,* which occurs only here in the OT) refers to a blatant breach of covenant which disgraces the entire community. A related term (*neḇālâh*) is used of Achan's sin (Josh. 7:15), as well as various prohibited sexual acts, including fornication (Deut. 22:21), incest (2 Sam. 13:12), rape (Jud. 19:23; 20:6), and adultery (Jer. 29:23). During this exhibition Israel's **lovers** would be forced to stand by helplessly, being unable to deliver her from the Lord's powerful grip. Then the Lord's superiority and the lovers' weakness (or apathy) would become apparent to her.

2:11. The coming judgment would also bring the cessation of Israel's joyous religious **celebrations,** including the great **yearly festivals** (Ex. 23:14-17), the monthly **New Moons** (i.e., New Moon sacrifices; Num. 10:10, 28:11-15), and the weekly **Sabbath** observances. These **feasts** had been corrupted by Baal worship (cf. Hosea 2:13) and were no longer desired by the Lord.

2:12-13. The themes in verses 5-9 are repeated in verses 12-13. In implementing the covenant curses the Lord would destroy the produce (**her vines and her fig trees**; cf. Deut. 28:38-42; Joel 1:7; Amos 4:9), which Israel erroneously regarded as the **pay** given by **her** paramours in exchange for her services (cf. Hosea 9:1; Micah 1:7). The vineyards would be reduced to an overgrown **thicket** inhabited by **wild animals.** This would be an effect of the depopulation which would accompany the nation's military defeat and exile (cf. Ps. 80:12-13; Isa. 5:5-6; 7:23-25; 17:9; 32:9-14; Micah 3:12).

In burning **incense to the Baals** Israel had, as it were, seductively chased **after her lovers** (cf. Hosea 2:5). The **rings and jewelry,** though sources of delight and signs of prestige in the proper context (cf. Prov. 25:12; Ezek. 16:12-14), here represent the unfaithful wife's efforts to attract her lovers. The plural "Baals" (cf. also Hosea 2:17; 11:2; Jud. 2:11 [see comments there]; 1 Sam. 7:4; Jer. 2:23; 9:14) in this context probably refer to various local manifestations of the one Canaanite deity (cf. the singular Baal in Hosea 2:8; 13:1), who was represented by images in Baal shrines scattered throughout the land (cf. 13:1-2). The plurality of idols naturally suggested the comparison to many lovers (cf. James Luther Mays, *Hosea: A Commentary*, p. 43).

The final statement in this section (2:2-13) summarizes Israel's basic sin and the reason for the coming judgment: she had forgotten (*šāḵaḥ*) **the Lord**. The verb here does not refer to a mental lapse or loss of knowledge; it describes a refusal to acknowledge the Lord's goodness and authority (cf. 8:14; 13:6). Moses had repeatedly urged the nation not to forget the Lord's gracious deeds (Deut. 4:9; 8:11) and His demand for exclusive worship (Deut. 4:23; 6:12; 8:19; cf. 2 Kings 17:38). However, in fulfillment of Moses' prediction (cf. Deut. 31:27-29 with Deut. 32:18) Israel throughout her history **forgot** the Lord and worshiped false gods (cf. Jud. 3:7; 1 Sam. 12:9-10; Ps. 78:9-11; Jer. 23:27).

2. THE LORD'S RESTORATION OF ISRAEL (2:14-23)

Having brought Israel to a place of desperation in which she would again look to Him (cf. v. 7), the Lord said He would take the next steps in restoring the relationship. Israel's positive response would lead to covenant renewal and blessing.

a. Renewed love (2:14-15)

In these verses the Lord described His overtures of love and Israel's future positive response.

2:14. The Lord promised to initiate reconciliation with His wayward wife by **alluring her. Allure** refers here to tender, even seductive, speech. Elsewhere the term describes a man's seduction of a virgin (Ex. 22:16) and a lover's attempt to entice a man (Samson) into divulging confidential information (Jud. 14:15; 16:5). The Lord said He **will lead** Israel **into the desert,** where she will be completely separated from past lovers and will be able to concentrate totally on His advances. The reference to the desert recalls Israel's 40 years of wandering in the wilderness after the Exodus. This was sometimes pictured as a time when Israel experienced the Lord's care in a special way (cf. Hosea 13:5) and when she, in return, loved Him with the devotion of a new bride (Jer. 2:2-3). The allusion to the wilderness also represents a remarkable reversal in the use of the desert motif in

this chapter. For the Lord had threatened to make Israel "like a desert" (Hosea 2:3). According to verse 14 the desert will become the site of His romantic overtures to her. There He will **speak tenderly to her** (lit., "speak to her heart"; cf. Isa. 40:2). This Hebrew idiom refers to gentle, encouraging words, such as a man speaks to his desired bride (cf. Gen. 34:3; Ruth 2:13). As Mays states, the boldly anthropomorphic language "is astonishing" especially in light of the Bible's "studied aversion for speaking of God in any sexual terms." He adds, "it is in this daring kind of portrayal that the passion of God becomes visible—a passion that does not hesitate at any condescension or hold back from any act for the sake of the beloved elect" (*Hosea*, pp. 44-5).

2:15. When the Lord leads Israel out of the desert back into the Promised Land, He will restore **her vineyards.** The words **There I will give** misinterpret the elliptical Hebrew text (which reads lit., "from there") by implying that vineyards will grow in the wilderness where Israel had wandered. The agricultural prosperity envisioned here will be in Israel (cf. vv. 22-23; Deut. 30:4-5, 9; Amos 9:13-15), not in the desert. When Israel enters the land she will again pass through **the Valley of Achor** (lit., "Valley of trouble"), the site of Achan's heinous sin which jeopardized the success of the Conquest (Josh. 7). However, this time the valley will be a symbol of better things to come, **a door of hope** leading to repossession of the Promised Land (cf. Isa. 65:10). The effects of the trouble caused by Israel's past unfaithfulness will have disappeared. Instead she will respond favorably to the Lord **as in the** days immediately after the Exodus (cf. Jer. 2:2). Admittedly this earlier period is idealized here, as even a cursory reading of the narratives in Exodus and Numbers reveals.

b. Renewed marriage (2:16-20)

2:16-17. In that day, when Israel is restored to the land, she will acknowledge **the Lord** as her husband. She will address Him as *'îšî,* **my Husband,** rather than *ba' ălî,* **my Master.** These two Hebrew words are essentially synonymous. They are used interchangeably in 2 Samuel 11:26, "Now when the wife of Uriah heard that Uriah her husband (*'îš*) was dead, she mourned for her husband (*ba'al*; NASB; cf. also Deut. 24:3-4). However, the word *ba'al* would be a reminder of Israel's former Baal worship. Therefore God will prohibit its use, and Israel will no longer use **the names of the Baals** (cf. the pl. "Baals" in Hosea 2:13; 11:2).

2:18. Israel's return to the land will be accompanied by peace. The Lord will mediate **a covenant** between the nation and the animal kingdom. **The** harmful **beasts of the field,** which had earlier devoured the vines and fig trees (v. 12; cf. Lev. 26:22), will no longer be hostile (cf. Ezek. 34:25). Isaiah also portrayed the Kingdom Age as one of harmony between man and animals (Isa. 11:6-8; 65:25). The Lord will also cause war (symbolized by **bow and sword and battle;** cf. Hosea 1:7) to cease in **the land** of Israel. The nation will dwell safely, free from the threat of foreign invasion. This marks the reversal of an earlier judgment (cf. 1:5) and the return of covenant blessing (cf. Lev. 26:5-6, where the same expressions, **lie down** and **in safety,** are used).

2:19-20. The restoration of the Lord's marriage to Israel is described in terms of a betrothal. Kidner points out that the word **betroth** marks "a new beginning, with all the freshness of first love, rather than the weary patching up of differences" (*Love for the Loveless*, p. 34). It will be as though the Lord and Israel had returned to the days of courtship. Betrothal in ancient Israel was much more binding than engagement is in contemporary Western society. The Law treated a betrothed couple as though they were legally married (Deut. 20:7; 22:23-24). At the time of the betrothal the man would pay a price to seal the agreement (cf. 2 Sam. 3:14). The Lord's price will consist of **righteousness. . . justice . . . love. . . compassion,** and **faithfulness.** These qualities will characterize His relationship with Israel, which will never again be disrupted (cf. Hosea 2:19).

"Righteousness" (*ṣedeq*) and "justice" (*mišpāṭ*) refer here to the maintenance of Israel's just cause, which includes vindication through deliverance. "Love" (*ḥesed*) is an unswerving devotion which fulfills the responsibilities arising from a relationship. "Compassion" (*raḥămîm,* related to *rāḥam,* used in 1:6-7; 2:1, 4) is tender feeling which motivates

one to gracious action. "Faithfulness" (*'ĕmûnâh*) implies dependability and constant loyalty.

In response to the divine love showered on her, Israel **will acknowledge the Lord.** In contrast with her former tendency to forget (cf. v. 13) she will recognize His authority by demonstrating loyalty to Him. "Acknowledge" (*yāda'*, "to know") often occurs in covenantal contexts with the sense of "recognize." For example, the Lord recognized (lit., "knew") Israel's special relationship to Him (cf. Amos 3:2, KJV). Israel in return was to recognize (lit., "know") only the authority of her Lord (cf. Hosea 13:4). In Hebrew thought, such recognition was not a mere mental exercise; it implied action (cf. Jer. 22:16). In Israel's case it meant obedience to the Lord's commandments (cf. Hosea 8:1-2). In the future all Israel will "know" the Lord because, as Jeremiah wrote, He will put His "Law in their minds and write it on their hearts" (Jer. 31:33). This is the promise of the New Covenant (Jer. 31:31-34), which corresponds to the new marriage pictured in Hosea 2:19-20.

c. Renewed blessing (2:21-23)

2:21-22. The promise of restored agricultural blessing, mentioned briefly in verse 15, is expanded here. A series of cries and responses is envisioned as different elements of the natural world are pesonified. **Jezreel** (the nation of Israel here) will cry out **to the grain . . . wine, and oil. They** in turn **will respond** by calling **to the earth** from which they are produced. **The earth** in turn will look to the heavens, the source of the rain which makes the soil productive. The heavens will then call to the Lord, the One who ultimately controls the agricultural cycle. He will **respond** by providing the rain necessary for agricultural prosperity.

2:23. The Lord Himself is pictured as engaging in agricultural endeavors. He **will plant** Israel **in the land** (cf. comments on 1:2), where she will grow under His protective care. The nation called Lo-Ruhamah (**not . . . loved;** cf. 1:6) and Lo-Ammi (**not My people;** cf. 1:9) will experience God's compassion and will be addressed as His **people.** They will acknowledge that He, not Baal, is their **God.** This passage is parallel to 1:10–2:1, where the same reversal in the significance of the symbolic names is seen.

Hosea 2:23, along with 1:10, is quoted in Romans 9:25-26 and 1 Peter 2:10. Paul quoted those Hosea passages to say that both Jews and Gentiles will be converted during the Church Age (cf. Rom. 9:24). This does *not* mean, however, that he equated the Gentiles with Israel and regarded the conversion of Gentiles as a direct fulfillment of Hosea's prophecy. Paul clearly taught that national Israel would be saved as well (Rom. 11). Rather, Paul extracted from Hosea's prophecy a principle concerning God's gracious activity (cf. F.F. Bruce, *The Epistle of Paul to the Romans.* Grand Rapids: Wm. B. Eerdmans Publishing Co., 1963, p. 196).

According to Hosea, God will mercifully bring a previously rejected people into a relationship with Himself. Paul recognized this same pattern in God's dealings with the Gentiles. In Romans 9:25 Paul, then, was applying Hosea 2:23 to the Gentiles; he was not reinterpreting the verse (cf. comments on Rom. 9:24-26). Likewise Peter (1 Peter 2:10) saw the language of Hosea's prophecy as applicable to New Testament believers, who by divine mercy have been brought into a relationship with God (cf. 1 Peter 1:3).

C. The restoration of Hosea's marriage (chap. 3)

As Hosea's experience with his unfaithful wife portrayed Israel's rejection of the Lord, so the recovery of his wayward wife pictured the Lord's love for and restoration of Israel.

1. THE DIVINE COMMAND (3:1)

3:1. The Lord told Hosea to demonstrate his **love to** his adulterous **wife** once more. This gracious act would serve as an object lesson of God's great love (*'ahăḇâh*) for Israel despite her gross unfaithfulness. Rather than responding favorably to the Lord, she was turning to other gods and loving (*'āhaḇ*) instead the sacred raisin cakes, delicacies apparently employed in feasts associated with Baal worship. Perhaps they were similar to the cakes offered to the goddess Astarte (cf. Jer. 7:18; 44:19).

2. HOSEA'S OBEDIENT RESPONSE (3:2-3)

3:2. Hosea responded obediently to the Lord's command (cf. 1:3). He **bought** his wife back for a substantial price. **A homer and lethek of barley** were probably valued together at **15 shekels** (Wolff, *Hosea*, p. 61). So the payment with the 15 shekels of silver was equivalent to 30 shekels, the price of a slave (cf. Ex. 21:32).

The circumstances surrounding this purchase are uncertain. Whether Hosea had legally divorced Gomer is unknown. She may have become a temple prostitute or was perhaps the legal property of someone who employed her as a concubine or hired her out as a prostitute. The phrase "loved by another" (Hosea 3:1) seems to suggest she was owned by another. However, the word "another" (*rēaʿ*, "friend, fellow citizen") may refer to Hosea, not a paramour (cf. Jer. 3:20). The following statement concerning the Lord's love for Israel favors this. In this case one might translate, "Love a woman who is loved by her husband, yet [is] an adulteress" (Hosea 3:1, NASB).

3:3. After acquiring legal possession of Gomer, Hosea informed her that her adulterous lifestyle was over. She would remain at home *with* him, isolated from all potential lovers. The meaning of the final clause in verse 3 is unclear. The text literally reads, "and also I toward you." The NIV (**and I will live with you**) understands the expression to be analogous to the preceding **you are to live with me**, meaning that both parties would devote themselves entirely to each other. Others understand the clause to mean that Hosea would abstain from sexual relations with her for a prolonged period of time (NEB).

3. THE ILLUSTRATION EXPLAINED (3:4-5)

3:4. Gomer's lengthy period of isolation was designed to portray Israel's exile, when the nation would be separated from its illicit institutions and practices (cf. 2:6-7). The absence of **king** and **prince** implied loss of national sovereignty. The elimination of **sacrifice** and **sacred stones** meant the cessation of formal religious activity. Sacrifices, having been commanded by the Lord, were a legitimate aspect of worship when offered with an attitude of total devotion to God. However, in Israel sacrifices had become contaminated by their association with Baal worship (cf. 4:19) and by the people's failure to obey "the more important matters of the Law" (Matt. 23:23; cf. Hosea 6:6; 8:11-13). "Sacred stones" (*maṣṣēbâh*) had been a legitimate part of patriarchal worship (cf. Gen. 28:18, 22; 31:13). However, because of those stones' association with pagan religion, Israel was forbidden to use them after entering Canaan (Lev. 26:1; Deut. 16:22). In direct violation of this covenant stipulation Israel had erected such stones as part of its Baal worship (2 Kings 3:2; 10:26-27; 17:10; Hosea 10:1; Micah 5:13).

Ephod and **idol** refer to methods of divination. In this context the ephod was not the garment worn by a priest, but a cultic object (cf. Jud. 8:27 and Roland de Vaux, *Ancient Israel*. 2 vols. New York: McGraw-Hill, 1965, 2:350). Idols (*tᵉrāpîm*), sometimes found in homes (Gen. 31:19; 1 Sam. 19:13, 16) or in a king's collection of divination devices (Ezek. 21:21), were despised by the Lord (1 Sam. 15:23; 2 Kings 23:24). These two items (ephod and idol) are also mentioned together in Judges (17:5; 18:14, 17-18, 20) as part of the belongings of an Ephraimite's personal priest. These instruments of divination were confiscated by the Danites and used in their unauthorized worship system (Jud. 18:27-31).

3:5. After Israel's period of isolation she will repent **and seek the LORD**, rather than false gods (2:7; 5:15; cf. Deut. 4:29). Israel will also recognize the authority of the Davidic monarchy, which it rejected at the time of Jeroboam I (cf. 1 Kings 12). The nation will approach the Lord with a healthy sense of fear (**trembling**), even in the context of blessing. In the past the nation had taken the Lord's gifts for granted and proudly turned away from His commandments (cf. Hosea 13:6; Deut. 8:10-18). The **blessings** (lit., "goodness") in view here are wealth and agricultural bounty (cf. Deut. 6:11; Isa. 1:19; Jer. 2:7; 31:12, 14 where the same word, *ṭûb*, is employed). The concluding phrase, **in the last days**, was used by the eighth-century prophets as a technical expression for the time of Israel's restoration predicted by Moses (Isa. 2:2; Micah 4:1; cf. Deut. 4:30, "in later days").

III. Hosea's Message: God's Judgment and Restoration of Israel (chaps. 4–14)

The remainder of Hosea's prophecy expands the message of the first three chapters. Though emphasis is placed on Israel's guilt and impending doom, each of the three major sections (4:1–6:3; 6:4–11:11; 11:12–14:9) concludes on a positive note by referring to Israel's restoration (see "Purpose and Message" in the *Introduction*).

A. The Lord's case against Israel (4:1–6:3)

This first judgment-salvation cycle is comprised of three parts. Chapter 4 focuses on the sins of the Northern Kingdom, while 5:1-15a establishes the guilt of the entire nation (Judah included) and announces judgment. In 5:15b–6:3 Israel's repentance is envisioned.

1. ISRAEL'S GUILT EXPOSED (CHAP. 4)

The guilt of the Northern Kingdom is the main theme of this opening judgment speech. The people and their leaders (prophets, rulers, and esp. priests) were the objects of God's displeasure. While most of the verses are accusatory in tone, announcements of forthcoming judgment are also scattered throughout (cf. vv. 6-10).

a. Breach of covenant (4:1-3)

4:1-2. Hosea began this section with an indictment (**charge**, *rîb*; cf. "charge" in 12:2 and the verb *rîb*, "rebuke," in 2:2) of the nation for breach of covenant. The people were devoid of the qualities that were to characterize life within God's covenant. They failed to exhibit **faithfulness** and **love** (*ḥesed*; cf. 2:19) and did not acknowledge **God** as their covenant Lord. (**Acknowledgment** translates *dā'at*, related to *yāda'*, "to know"; cf. comments on 2:20.) Instead they blatantly disobeyed the Decalogue, which epitomized God's ideal for Israelite society. Violations of five of the Ten Commandments are specifically mentioned: **cursing, lying** (cf. 7:1; 12:1), **murder, stealing, and adultery** (commandments 3, 9, 6, 8, and 7, in that order). "Cursing" does not refer to improper speech as such, but to calling down a curse on another (cf. Job 31:30). Because such imprecations (for Israelites) entailed invoking God's name, they would be violating the third commandment when such an imprecation was unjustified (Ex. 20:7; Deut. 5:11; for an example of a justifiable curse invoking the Lord's name, see Num. 5:19-23).

4:3. **Because of** Israel's sin, severe drought would sweep over **the land** and people would die **(waste away)**. The three verbs in this verse should be translated in the future tense (cf. Hosea 2:9, 12). Drought was one of the curses threatened by the Law for breaking the covenant (cf. Lev. 26:19; Deut. 28:23-24).

b. The priests' guilt (4:4-11a)

The priests addressed in these verses shared the guilt of the people and therefore would not be exempt from punishment.

4:4. The guilt of the population as a whole is further established. The first two lines in this verse prohibit either lawsuits among the people (NIV) or formal opposition to God's charges (cf. Mays, *Hosea*, p. 67). In either case the reason for God's prohibition was that all the **people** were guilty of rebellion. They were **like those who** brazenly defy God's established human legal authorities (cf. Deut. 17:12).

4:5a-b. Here the accusation (v. 4) is extended to the religious leaders (NIV) or the demise of the religious leaders is announced (KJV, NASB). **Stumble** refers to their moral shortcomings (cf. 14:1, NASB; Isa. 3:8; Jer. 18:15; Mal. 2:8) or their coming downfall (cf. Hosea 5:5; Isa. 8:15; 28:13; 31:3; Jer. 6:21; 8:12; 20:11). These priests and **prophets** were attached to the official sanctuaries and royal court. Their allegiance was to their human king, not God (cf. 1 Kings 22:6-8; Amos 7:10-17), and they were characterized by self-gratification (cf. Isa. 28:7; Jer. 23:11) and greed (Jer. 6:13; Micah 3:11).

4:5c-6. The Lord held these leaders responsible for the people's **lack of knowledge** (cf. v. 1). The priests in particular had ignored their duty to communicate **the Law of . . . God** to the nation (cf. Deut. 31:9-13; 33:8-10; Mal. 2:7). So they would be severely but justly punished. Because of their part in the people's moral ruin mothers would be destroyed. This judgment, though unusual, appears elsewhere (cf. Jer. 22:26). In this way the source of the priestly line would be eliminated. As punishment for their rejection of knowledge, the **priests** themselves would be removed from their office by the Lord. Also because the priests ignored the Law, the Lord said He would ignore their **children,** apparently meaning they would not inherit their fathers' office (cf. 1 Sam. 2:27-35). In this way the future of the priestly line would be cut off.

The repetition of the verb in each cycle of the announcement of judgment (**destroy . . . destroyed. . . . rejected . . . reject . . . ignored . . . ignore**) emphasizes that each punishment fits each crime perfectly.

4:7. One would expect that an increase in the number of **priests** would have positive effects on the nation's moral climate. However, in Israel it only brought greater sin.

According to the NIV, verse 7b continues the accusation. This reading, which has some external support (cf. NIV marg.) suggests that the priests **exchanged their Glory,** the Lord, **for something disgraceful** (idols; cf. Ps. 106:20; Jer. 2:11). The Masoretic text, which reads, "I will change their glory into shame" (KJV, NASB, RSV), seems preferable. The Lord will take away the honor (*kābôd,* trans. here "glory," frequently carries this meaning) which they received because of their position.

4:8. In their greed the priests fed on **the sins of** the **people** by encouraging them to multiply the hypocritical sacrifices which the Lord hated (cf. 6:6; 8:11-13). The priests' underlying motive in doing this was greed, since they received portions of the offerings which were presented (cf. Lev. 7:7-10, 28-34; Num. 18:8-19; Deut. 18:1-5).

4:9-10a. Because the **priests** were no different from the other **people,** they also would experience the effects of the covenant curses. Despite their greedy schemes to accumulate food, their appetites would not be satisfied for drought would make food scarce (cf. 4:3; Lev. 26:26; Micah 6:14). Their efforts to promote fertility through cult **prostitution** would not succeed (cf. Hosea 2:13b; Deut. 28:18a).

4:10b-11a. The priests' sin is summarized here. They had **deserted the LORD** by breaking His covenant (cf. Deut. 28:20; 29:25; 31:16). The NIV puts the last three words of Hosea 4:10 with verse 11a, **to give themselves** (lit., "to keep or watch") **to prostitution** (RSV, "to cherish harlotry"). In this case prostitution was a sarcastic substitution for the Lord's commandments, which frequently appear as the object of the verb "to keep" (*šāmar*) in Deuteronomy (cf. Deut. 4:2; 5:10, 29; 6:2; etc.). The Hebrew reads literally, "for the Lord they have forsaken to obey" (KJV, NASB). In this case the clause must be understood as highly elliptical, the sense being, "they have forsaken the Lord, refusing to observe His commandments."

c. The people's guilt (4:11b-19)

4:11b-14. The scope of the accusation widened to include the **people** in general. Sensual pleasures had robbed them of their senses, leaving them without **understanding.** They engaged in pagan worship practices, including divination (seeking answers **by a stick of wood**), sacrificed to false gods, and engaged in cult **prostitution** (cf. 5:4). The Canaanite shrines, which Moses had commanded Israel to destroy (cf. Deut. 12:2-3), were located on **hills** and/or **under** shady trees (**oak, poplar, and terebinth**) throughout the Northern Kingdom (cf. 2 Kings 17:10-11). Here many young women (**daughters**) of Israel took part in sexual rites with male cult **prostitutes** (cf. Deut. 23:17-18; 1 Kings 14:24). The intent of such acts was to ensure human and agricultural fecundity by making the fertility deities Baal and Asherah favorably inclined to their offerings and prayers. However, these women would not be singled out for divine punishment because **the men** frequented the shrines as well (Hosea 4:14). In response to such an obvious failure to grasp and apply the most basic principles of covenant life, the Lord cried out, **A people without understanding** (cf. v. 11) **will come to ruin!**

4:15. **Judah** was now warned to avoid the sins of her sister **Israel.** This need not mean that the people of Judah were in the habit of visiting northern cultic sites, such as **Gilgal** (cf. 9:15) and **Beth Aven.** Mays explains, "The exhortation . . . is simply bitter condemnation of their cult . . . for the ears of those who did worship in them" (*Hosea*, p. 77). The threefold warning (**Do not go . . . do not go . . . do not swear**) is a rhetorical device designed to accentuate Israel's guilt. To associate oneself with Israel's false, hypocritical worship would be contaminating. Even Bethel (lit., "house of God"), the site of Jacob's dream (Gen. 28:10-19), had become "Beth Aven" (lit.,

"house of wickedness"; cf. Hosea 10:5; Amos 5:5) because of the religious practices conducted there (1 Kings 12:28-30; 2 Kings 10:29; 23:15; Amos 4:4). In the midst of this idolatrous, immoral worship the Israelites even had the audacity to employ the Lord's name in oaths. The Law commanded Israel to swear by the Lord's name (Deut. 6:13; 10:20). However, to make a semblance of devotion to **the LORD** while serving other gods was the grossest hypocrisy.

4:16. Through her refusal to repent Israel had separated herself from the Lord's protective guidance. As long as the nation responded like a young cow, stubbornly resisting His leading, God would treat her appropriately (cf. Jer. 31:18), not like a lamb which is allowed to graze leisurely in broad pastures. **Stubborn** refers to a rebellious attitude which **the LORD** finds deplorable (cf. Deut. 21:18-21).

4:17. Because of her strong attachment to idolatry (**joined to idols**) Israel was to be left to herself and allowed to go to her doom. **Ephraim,** a prominent tribe in the Northern Kingdom, mentioned 36 times in the Book of Hosea, stands for Israel as a whole (cf. the parallelism in 5:3, 5; also cf. Isa. 7:2, 5, 8-9, 17).

4:18. The accusation concludes as it began by referring to the carousing and immorality which characterized the people and their rulers (cf. v. 11). **Rulers** is literally "shields," a term which suggests the positive, protective role which a nation's leaders should play (cf. Pss. 84:9, 11; 89:18). Israel's rulers failed miserably in this regard, loving only **shameful** deeds.

4:19. The result of Israel's sin would be judgment. The first line of this verse reads literally, "the wind has enveloped her with its wings," suggesting that she soon would be swept **away.** At that time the idolatrous **sacrifices** (or, perhaps, "altars," following the LXX) would prove to be only a source of disappointment and **shame** (cf. 10:5-6).

2. ISRAEL'S JUDGMENT ANNOUNCED (5:1-14)

The Northern Kingdom remains the primary target group in this section. However, Judah, which had been warned to avoid Israel's example (4:15), was now brought within the scope of

God's judgment (cf. 5:5, 8, 10, 13-14). The chapter begins with an accusation of guilt (vv. 1-5) which merges into an announcement of judgment (vv. 6-15a).

5:1-2. Though the accusation encompassed the entire nation (**you Israelites**), the priesthood (**priests**) and monarchy (**royal house**) were singled out for special consideration (cf. 4:4-10, 18). The leaders had encouraged the people to engage in false worship at cult sites such as **Mizpah** and **Tabor.** In so doing they were like **a snare** or **net** used to trap a bird (cf. 7:12; Amos 3:5). Mount Tabor was in northern Israel, about 12 miles southwest of the Sea of Galilee. Mizpah in this context refers to a site either in Gilead or in Benjamite territory. If the former, then the places mentioned represent areas of the Northern Kingdom west and east of the Jordan River. If the reference is to Mizpah of Benjamin, the idea is that all cult sites from south to north were involved. In either case the selection of place names was designed to emphasize how the false worship led by the priests had permeated the land.

The rebellious priesthood (**rebels**) had gone to great depths (**are deep**) as it were, to **slaughter** their prey (continuing the hunting imagery of Hosea 5:1b), the people of Israel.

Verse 2b can be taken in one of two ways. It refers either to approaching discipline (**I will discipline**; cf. NASB and 10:10) or to past divine efforts to correct rebellion ("I have been a Rebuker of them all," KJV; cf. Amos 4:6-12). In either case "discipline" (*mûsār*) refers here to severe punishment designed to restore one to proper behavior. As such, it is an expression of love that arises out of a close relationship (cf. Prov. 3:11; 13:24; 15:5). The positive goal of the Lord's judgment is evident (cf. Hosea 2:6-7; 5:15b).

5:3-5. The guilt of the nation as a whole is declared. **Israel** could not hide its sin from the omniscient **God.** The nation had become **corrupt** (*ṭāmā'*, "to be unclean or defiled") through its spiritual adultery (cf. 6:10). This wording is probably drawn from Numbers 5:20, 27-28 where the same verb (*ṭāmā'*) describes the effects of adultery on the unfaithful party (cf. Lev. 18:20, 24). Sinful Israel had become so overpowered by **a spirit of prostitution** (Hosea 5:4; cf. 4:12) that any possibility of repentance and recognition of the Lord's authority was precluded for the time being. The nation's own **arrogance** served as a legal witness (**testifies**; cf. the same expression in 1 Sam. 12:3; 2 Sam. 1:16) to its guilt and, in accordance with the famous proverb (Prov. 16:18), had led to its fall (cf. **stumble** in Hosea 4:5). **Judah** had followed Israel's example and had come to mortal ruin as well.

5:6. The Lord's punishment of His people would be expressed in two ways: withdrawal of aid and blessing (vv. 6-7, 15a), and active warfare (vv. 8-14). In the days ahead Israel in desperation would **seek the** Lord through sacrifices of **flocks and herds.** However, this hypocritical ritualism, devoid of genuine covenant loyalty, would be ineffective (cf. 6:6; 8:11-13; Isa. 1:10-17).

5:7. God's people had been **unfaithful.** The Hebrew verb (*bāgad*) often refers to a failure to carry out the responsibilities of a natural (cf. Jer. 12:6) or contractual (cf. Jud. 9:6, 23; Mal. 2:14-16) relationship. Here marital infidelity provides the background (cf. Jer. 3:20). As in the preceding chapters, Hosea pictured Israel as the Lord's adulterous wife. Carrying on the figure, she had even given **birth to illegitimate children,** an inevitable result of her promiscuous activities. The reality behind the figure was perhaps those Israelite children whose birth was attributed to cultic sexual acts (cf. Hosea 4:13-15).

Such rituals only heightened the people's guilt. Participation in religious **festivals** (here represented by the **New Moon** celebrations; cf. 2:11) would actually hasten their destruction, not avert it. Rather than experiencing population growth, the people would ultimately be devoured by their own sins (cf. Lev. 26:21-22; Deut. 28:62-63). The **fields,** for which they sought fertility through Baal worship, would be destroyed by drought, blight, and insects, and would be overrun by invading armies (cf. Lev. 26:16, 19-20; Deut. 28:17, 22-24, 33, 38-42, 51).

5:8-9. The **sound** of **battle** trumpets was about to be heard in **Israel.** An invading force would sweep to the borders of the Southern Kingdom (cf. Kidner, *Love to the Loveless,* p. 61). **Gibeah** and **Ramah** were located a few miles north of Jerusalem in Benjamite territory in the

29

Southern Kingdom (cf. Josh. 18:25, 28). **Beth Aven** (probably Bethel; cf. Hosea 4:15), though originally a Benjamite town (Josh. 18:22), was then just inside Israel's southern border.

The significance of the last clause in Hosea 5:8, **lead on, O Benjamin** (lit., "behind you, O Benjamin") is not clear. The same expression appears in Deborah's song in reference to mustering Israel's troops (Jud. 5:14). At that time Benjamin went ahead of Ephraim into battle against the northern Canaanite forces (NASB). Perhaps this ancient song was given a sarcastic twist by Hosea. In the upcoming invasion **Ephraim** would be devastated. Rather than leading Ephraim into battle, Benjamin would be pursued by the same invader. The line might be paraphrased, "behind you, O Benjamin, Ephraim's conqueror advances."

The desolation of Ephraim was certain to take place because it had been announced by the Lord, whose word is inviolable (**I proclaim what is certain**). This coming judgment would fulfill the covenant curse in Leviticus 26:32-35.

5:10. Even Judah would not be spared ultimately (cf., however, 1:7). Its leaders were also guilty of breach of covenant. They were **like those who move boundary stones** for they showed no respect for God's commands. Moving boundary stones was clearly forbidden in the Law (Deut. 19:14) and carried a curse (Deut. 27:17). The act was tantamount to theft as it obscured the legal boundary between properties and was a way of taking some land that belonged to another. Perhaps this particular crime was cited in order to allude to the acts of social injustice being carried out by the Judean upper class (cf. Isa. 5:8; Micah 2:1-2). On **Judah's** sinful **leaders** the Lord would **pour out** His anger **like a flood of water** (lit., "like water"), possibly meaning like rainwater (cf. Amos 5:8; 9:6).

5:11. According to verses 11-14, judgment had already begun. **Ephraim** was **oppressed** and **trampled.** Again Hosea alluded to a covenant curse (cf. Deut. 28:33, NASB). This judgment may refer to the Assyrian invasion of 733 B.C. (cf. 2 Kings 15:29). However, Israel's troubles were ultimately attributable to her own sin, not to Assyrian imperialism. The word **idols** is a conjecture (cf. NIV marg.), for the Hebrew word ṣāw is obscure.

"Man's command" (NASB) is a highly unlikely translation. The word is possibly a corruption of "vanity" (šāw', RSV, following the LXX) or "filth" (ṣāw', i.e., "excrement"; cf. Andersen and Freedman, *Hosea*, pp. 409-10). The reference is probably to false gods (hence NIV's "idols"). The Hebrew literally reads, "for he persistently walked after vanity/filth (?)." The idiom "walk after," translated "follow(ed)(ing)," appears elsewhere with false gods as an object (cf. Deut. 4:3; 6:14; 8:19; 28:14; Jer. 2:5; etc.).

5:12. The Lord Himself was silently but effectively leading His people toward destruction. To Ephraim He was **like a moth,** which destroys clothing (cf. Job 13:28; Isa. 50:9; 51:8). To . . . **Judah** He was **like rot,** which progressively causes bones to decay (cf. Prov. 12:4; 14:30; Hab. 3:16). This unusual figurative language means that God was sovereignly in control of the international scene, which He was already manipulating to bring about Israel's demise.

5:13. The nation's response to its deteriorating condition (like a **sickness** with **sores**) was entirely misdirected. Following the path of political expediency, the Northern Kingdom **turned to** the invader himself, Tiglath-Pileser III of **Assyria,** in an effort to restore national stability. This probably refers to Hoshea's alliance with Assyria (2 Kings 17:3) at the time he usurped the throne of Israel (cf. 2 Kings 15:30). **Judah** had formed a similar alliance when threatened by Syria and Israel (2 Kings 16). Though Hosea 5:13b does not specifically mention Judah, the contextual references to her (vv. 13a, 14a) suggest that she was in Hosea's mind as well. These efforts to **heal** the nation's wounds would be futile. Assyria was a greedy overseer, not a physician. As soon as Hoshea withheld tribute, the Assyrians again invaded the land (2 Kings 17:3-6).

5:14. The moth (v. 12) is transformed into a raging **lion** which violently kills its prey. The use of six first-person forms (I) in the Hebrew emphasizes God's role in this judgment. In the final analysis the Lord Himself would be the attacker and destroyer, even though He would use foreign armies as His instruments.

For **Ephraim** this prophecy was fulfilled a few years later when Assyria conquered Samaria and carried the people into exile (2 Kings 17). **Judah** was overrun by the Assyrians in 701 B.C., but she experienced a miraculous deliverance after being severely ravaged (cf. comments on Hosea 1:7). The prophecy about Judah's fall and exile (5:14) was eventually fulfilled through Nebuchadnezzar (2 Kings 25).

3. ISRAEL'S RESTORATION ENVISIONED (5:15–6:3)

5:15. The ultimate purpose of the Lord's judgment on His people was to restore them (cf. 2:5-7). Having received the just punishment for their sins, God's people would turn to Him in repentance. The Hebrew word rendered **they admit their guilt** should be translated "they bear [their] punishment" (cf. its use in 10:2; 13:16). God would not hear their prayers. He would **go back** to His **place** like a lion returning to its lair (cf. 5:14) till the nation underwent its punishment. In contrast with their earlier hypocritical quest for the Lord through sacrificial ritual (cf. v. 6), the people will genuinely and earnestly **seek** Him.

6:1-3. These verses record the words the penitent generation of the future will declare as they seek **the LORD**. The message is constructed in two cycles, each containing an exhortation (vv. 1a, 3a) and a motivating promise (vv. 1b-2, 3b).

In contrast with her past folly (cf. 5:13), Israel will turn to **the LORD as** her source of healing and life (cf. Deut. 32:39). Assyria was not able to cure Israel (Hosea 5:13), but the Lord is able, even though like a lion (5:14) He had **torn** them **to pieces.** The people will confidently anticipate His forthcoming restoration of their national vitality. The equivalent expressions, **after two days** and **on the third day,** refer to a short period of time, indicating they expected the revival to occur soon. Israel will also resolve to **acknowledge** the Lord's authority (contrast 4:1, 6; 5:4). **Press on** is literally, "pursue or chase," which suggests the intensity of Israel's newfound devotion.

The Lord will surely respond favorably to such loyalty. His emergence from His hiding place (cf. 5:6, 15) will be as certain as the sunrise. He will pour out His blessings on His people, as the **winter** and **spring rains . . . water the**

earth and assure agricultural prosperity. The latter comparison was especially well chosen since the regularity of these rains was a sign of the Lord's favor (cf. Deut. 11:13-15).

B. The Lord's case against Israel expanded (6:4–11:11)

The Lord's case against Israel is greatly expanded in these chapters. Emphasis is placed on the nation's guilt, especially for her ingratitude. As in the preceding section (cf. 5:15–6:3), judgment changes to restoration by the end of the unit (cf. 11:8-11). Each of the subunits is marked out formally by an introductory direct address (cf. 6:4; 9:1; 11:8). Both of the judgment cycles (6:4–8:14; 9:1–11:7) refer to a return to Egypt (cf. 8:13; 11:5) in their conclusions, while the brief salvation passage (11:8-11) pictures God's people returning from that land (cf. 11:11).

1. ISRAEL'S GUILT AND PUNISHMENT (6:4–8:14)

This first judgment cycle contains two parts (6:4–7:16; 8). Both refer to a breach of covenant in their opening verses (6:7; 8:1) and mention Egypt near the end (7:16; 8:13).

a. Israel's ingratitude punished (6:4–7:16)

These verses are primarily accusatory, though judgment is announced formally in the closing passage (cf. 7:12-13, 16). The Lord's attempts to restore His people contrast with their rebellion. The references to the Lord's gracious disposition toward the nation introduce the subunits of the section (cf. 6:4-11a; 6:11b–7:12; 7:13-16).

(1) The first subunit (6:4-11a). **6:4.** The Lord's argument here begins with a rhetorical question addressed both to **Ephraim** and **Judah.** The mood is one of despair and frustration. God's people had rejected all His attempts to bring them to their senses. Their **love** (*ḥesed*; cf. 2:19; 4:1) for the Lord was at best transitory (6:4b). **Like the** early **morning** fog or **dew,** any expression of loyalty quickly evaporated.

6:5. God's measures to bring His disloyal people to repentance had been extreme (cf. Amos 4:6-11). His **words** of judgment, spoken through the **prophets,** had brought sudden death and destruction on many people (cf. Jer. 1:10; 5:14).

6:6. The reason for such severe discipline is reiterated: God's people had failed to understand His true **desire.** He longed for devotion (*ḥeseḏ*, **mercy**) and loyalty (**acknowledgment of God**; cf. 2:20; 4:1, 6) expressed through allegiance to the covenant demands. Unless offered in the context of obedience, sacrifices were meaningless and even offensive (cf. 1 Sam. 15:22; Isa. 1:11-20; Amos 5:21-24; Micah 6:6-8).

6:7. Rather than pleasing God, the people had **broken the covenant** and been **unfaithful** (*bāḡaḏ*; cf. comments on 5:7) to God. The Hebrew word for **like Adam** has been translated variously. "At Adam" (RSV) requires a slight change in the Hebrew and suggests a geographical place near the Jordan River. The presence of the word **there** in the next line, as well as references to other places in 6:8-9, might support this reading. "Like men" (KJV) takes the Hebrew *'āḏām* in its widely attested generic sense, rather than as a proper name. In this case a comparison is made with fallen mankind, whose propensity to be unfaithful is well established (cf. Isa. 40:6-8, man's *ḥeseḏ* ["glory," Isa. 40:6] is as transitory as grass and flowers that wither in the sun). On the other hand, the NIV and the NASB suggest a comparison with the first man, Adam, who blatantly violated God's requirement by eating from the forbidden tree.

6:8. Widespread physical violence was just one example of the people's unfaithfulness (vv. 8-9; cf. Ex. 20:13). Since **Gilead** was a district, not a city, the reference in Hosea 6:8a is probably to the **city** Ramoth Gilead, east of the Jordan. The town had become a center for **wicked men** (lit., "workers of iniquity"). In Psalm 5:5 this same expression is translated "who do wrong." It refers to the worst sort of men, who actively oppose righteousness and are the objects of God's hatred. In this case they were guilty of murder (Hosea 6:8b). The city streets are pictured as being tracked with **blood** from the murderers' sandals (cf. 1 Kings 2:5). The figurative language emphasizes both the extent and certainty of their guilt. Unfortunately the precise historical background for the crime cannot be determined. Perhaps oppression of the poor is in view. Elsewhere "workers

of iniquity" are said to be guilty of oppressing the poor which is only occasionally associated with murder (cf. Ps. 94:4-6; Isa. 1:21-23).

6:9. The background of this verse is equally obscure. Perhaps groups of **priests** were actually murdering travelers **to Shechem.** A more likely explanation is that the language is hyperbolic, perhaps pointing to the priests' false teaching and involvement in social exploitation. The references to (Ramoth) Gilead and Shechem are well chosen. Joshua had designated that both of these towns be cities of refuge, where manslayers could find asylum (Josh. 20:1-2, 7-8; see the map "The Six Cities of Refuge," near Num. 35). In this way the land would be spared outbreaks of bloodshed, and justice would be promoted. Ironically in Hosea's day these cities had become associated with bloodshed and injustice.

The priests' **crimes** were **shameful.** Elsewhere this word (*zimmâh*) is used of the vilest sexual sins, including incest (Lev. 18:17), cult prostitution (Lev. 19:29), rape (Jud. 20:5-6), and adultery (Job 31:9-11). This sexual connotation is probably applicable here because the priests' breach of covenant (Hosea 6:6-7) is likened to prostitution (v. 10).

6:10-11a. The nation's sin is described in powerful figurative language. The widespread breach of covenant (vv. 6-7) was a **horrible thing.** Jeremiah used a related term to describe rotten figs that are inedible (Jer. 29:17). **Israel** had become **defiled** by her prostitution, that is, her unfaithfulness to the Lord (cf. Hosea 5:3). The comparison of judgment to a **harvest** (cf. Jer. 51:33; Joel 3:13) emphasizes its certainty (**appointed**) and its thoroughness.

(2) The second subunit (6:11b-7:12).
6:11b-7:1. The reference to the Lord's desire to **heal** (cf. 6:1) His people comes near the beginning of this subunit. God longed to restore **Israel** to a place of blessing, but His efforts were met with new outbreaks of **sin** and **crimes.** The people's widespread **deceit** and robbery epitomized their lack of regard for the covenant (cf. Ex. 20:15).

7:2. To make matters worse, they disregarded God's moral character by failing to **realize that** He was taking careful notice of **their** sin (cf. Ps. 50:16-21). Therefore like a wall **their sins** had completely surrounded (did **engulf**) **them,** making repentance improbable. (The Heb. word for "their sins" is trans. "their deeds" in Hosea 5:4.)

7:3. The rulers were no different from their subjects. A godly ruler was to oppose all forms of **wickedness** within his kingdom (cf. Ps. 101), but these leaders delighted in it.

7:4. Israel was a nation of **adulterers.** It is not clear whether general breach of covenant (cf. 6:10) or literal adultery (cf. 4:2, 13-14) is described here. In either case Israel's passion for disobedience was like a fire **burning** low in **an oven** while **the baker** kneads **the dough** and waits for the leavening process to be completed. Like an oven **fire,** Israel's passion might subside for a short time, but it was ever present, ready to blaze forth when kindled (cf. 7:6).

7:5-6. Between 752 and 732 B.C. four of Israel's rulers were assassinated (cf. 2 Kings 15). This political intrigue provides the background for Hosea 7:5-7. Here a description is given of how the conspirators characteristically carried out their plots.

The day of the festival of our king probably refers to a special celebration in which the ruler was the center of attention. The king caroused with his **princes,** who are called **mockers** probably because they were completely under the influence of **wine** (cf. Prov. 20:1). While they partied with the naive king, they plotted his overthrow.

The NIV rendering, **Their passion smolders,** which has some external support, requires a slight emendation of the Hebrew. The Masoretic text reads, "their baker sleeps" (cf. KJV). The latter, while certainly more difficult, is not impossible since it is similar in thought to Hosea 7:4 and carries along the comparison of their hearts to **an oven.** One might paraphrase verse 6: "When **they approach** the king **their hearts,** like **an oven,** contain a **fire.** Just as the fire burns lowly while the baker is inactive, so their scheme remains a secret. But when their time for action comes, the destructive plot is realized, just as a fire in an oven **blazes** forth when the time for baking arrives."

7:7. Because the royal court of Israel was filled with such murderers, the kingship frequently changed hands. Throughout this period of palace revolt

and regicide no one bothered to look to the Lord, the true King of Israel and her only Source of national stability.

7:8. Instead **Ephraim** launched a futile foreign policy (vv. 8-12). The baking metaphor continues in verse 8 (cf. vv. 4, 6-7). Israel had formed alliances with foreign **nations** (cf. v. 11; 8:9). This is compared to the mixing of flour with oil to form cakes (*bālal,* **mixes,** is frequently used in this sense). This policy had proven self-destructive. Israel had become like an unturned **cake** on hot stones—burned and soon to be discarded.

7:9. The negative effects of Israel's foreign policy are described further in this verse. The nation is compared to an elderly man who has failed to **notice** the gradual effects of the aging process (loss of physical **strength,** graying **hair**). Death is much closer than he expects. The point was probably that Israel was experiencing loss of political autonomy. This loss was epitomized by the tribute payments that were an excessive drain on its wealth and economy (cf. 2 Kings 15:19-20; 17:3).

7:10. Despite her weakened condition, Israel did **not** repent. The nation's refusal (**arrogance**) to acknowledge the covenant God was self-incriminating (cf. **testifies against him;** also see comments on 5:5).

7:11. In her efforts to arrange foreign alliances, Israel could be compared to **a dove,** which exhibits little sense (cf. comments on 11:11). Under Menahem (ca. 743 or 738 B.C.) Israel submitted to Assyrian suzerainty (2 Kings 15:19-20). Pekah (ca. 734 B.C.) joined a coalition against **Assyria,** which Tiglath-Pileser III violently crushed (2 Kings 15:29). Hoshea (ca. 732-722 B.C.), after acknowledging Assyrian rulership for a time, stopped tribute payments and sought an alliance with **Egypt** (2 Kings 17:3-4a). This act of rebellion led to the destruction of the Northern Kingdom (2 Kings 17:4b-6), the inevitable result of a foreign policy which for 20 years had been characterized by vacillating and expedient measures.

7:12. Worst of all, Israel's policy had no place for the Lord (cf. vv. 7, 10). Consequently He Himself would intervene in judgment. While Israel sought out alliances with all the naiveté of a dove (v. 11), the Lord would come like a wise and well-equipped fowler and trap them.

(3) The third subunit (7:13-16). **7:13.**

This brief unit begins on an ominous note. Woe (*'ôy*) suggests impending doom (cf. Num. 21:29; Jer. 4:13, 31, "alas"; 48:46), as the next sentence (cf. **Destruction to them**) clearly shows. The basis for judgment was Israel's rebellion (cf. Hosea 8:1; 13:16) against the Lord (**because they have strayed from Me** and **because they have rebelled against Me**). Despite His desire to save them (God said, **I long to redeem them**), they had spoken **lies against** Him. The word for "redeem" (*pādāh*) is used frequently to describe the deliverance from Egypt (cf. Deut. 7:8; 9:26; 13:5; 15:15; 24:18; 2 Sam. 7:23; Ps. 78:42; Micah 6:4). Mays aptly comments, "The God of the Exodus is unchanged in His will, but because of Israel's lies there will be no 'exodus' from the Assyrian danger" (*Hosea*, p. 111). In this context "lies" probably refers to Israel's practical denial of God's redemptive ability, expressed through her attempts to find security through other nations.

7:14. Israel's rejection of the Lord is illustrated here. The nation desired a plentiful crop (**grain and new wine**) **but** refused to exhibit the wholehearted devotion to God without which agricultural prosperity was impossible. They wailed (*yālal*; lit., "howled"; cf. Joel 1:11) and cut their bodies as they mourned over the crop failure. In the second sentence, the reading in the NIV margin ("They slash themselves," following the LXX and some Heb. mss.) seems better than **They gather together.** Cutting oneself was a sign of mourning (cf. Jer. 16:6; 41:5; 47:5) forbidden by the Law (Deut. 14:1) because of its pagan associations. The prophets of Baal cut themselves in an effort to arouse Baal, the storm god, to action (cf. 1 Kings 18:28).

7:15. Israel's rebellion also revealed her ingratitude. The Lord had **trained . . . and strengthened them** (lit., "their arms," NASB). Elsewhere the expression "strengthen the arms" can refer to divine bestowal of military might (Ezek. 30:24-25). Perhaps Israel's past military successes (including those of Jeroboam II; cf. 2 Kings 14:25-28) are in view. Despite experiencing divine aid in battle, Israel treated God like an enemy. The phrase **plot evil against Me** suggests intense hostility and ill will. Similar language is used to describe Joseph's brothers' schemes to destroy him (Gen. 50:20).

7:16. Israel's hostility toward the Lord was an expression of her unfaithfulness. Israel was **like a faulty bow.** Such a weapon is unreliable because it fails to respond properly to the archer. In the same way Israel's hostile response to God's grace demonstrated her unreliable, disloyal character (cf. Ps. 78:57).

The nation's **leaders,** who had rejected their true source of strength (cf. Hosea 7:15), would be destroyed in battle **because of their** pride. **Insolent words** refers to a formal denunciation or curse. Israel's rejection of divine aid (cf. v. 13) in favor of foreign alliances is compared to a verbal reproach against God. Ironically Israel would become an object of derision among the Egyptians, whose aid they had foolishly sought (cf. v. 11).

b. Israel's rebellion punished (chap. 8)

This section includes several specific illustrations of the nation's rebellious attitude and announces God's coming judgment.

8:1. The chapter begins with a note of alarm. A **trumpet** must be blown to signal an impending battle (cf. 5:8). An enemy (the Assyrians) was ready to swoop down on Israel like a powerful **eagle.** The announcement of judgment recalls the **covenant** curse of Deuteronomy 28:49. **The house of the LORD** refers here to the land of Israel (as in Hosea 9:15; cf. "the LORD's land," 9:3). Again Israel was said to be rebellious (cf. 7:13).

8:2-3. **Israel** made a pretense of devotion to the Lord, addressing Him as her own **God** and claiming to **acknowledge** His authority over her. This profession, however, was mere lip service (cf. 4:1, 6; 5:4). Her sinful actions spoke louder than her words. In reality she had **rejected what** was **good** (the Lord's moral and ethical requirements; cf. Amos 5:14-15; Micah 6:8). Consequently **an enemy** would soon **pursue** her. The swift retreat pictured here fulfills another covenant curse (cf. Deut. 28:45).

8:4. Two examples of Israel's sin are given in verses 4-6. She had appointed **kings** and other leaders **without** consulting the Lord. This alludes to the series of palace revolts that plagued the Northern Kingdom after Jeroboam II's reign (cf. 7:5-7). Israel had also made **idols for themselves** in direct violation of the second commandment (cf. Ex. 20:4).

8:5. The **calf-idol** of **Samaria** (cf. v. 6) was singled out because it epitomized Israel's idolatrous ways. Since there is no record of such an idol being erected in Samaria, the city may stand here for the Northern Kingdom as a whole (cf. 7:1; 10:7). If so, the calf-idol was probably the image set up by Jeroboam I at Bethel (cf. 1 Kings 12:28-30; Hosea 10:5). By setting up golden calves (one in Dan and one in Bethel), Jeroboam repeated the sins of an earlier generation (cf. Ex. 32:1-4). Probably the people associated these calves with the storm and fertility god Baal (cf. Hosea 13:1-2).

The words **Throw out** follow the Septuagint. However, the Hebrew is literally, "He has rejected your calf, O Samaria" (NASB). This third person reference to God within a divine speech is unusual, but is attested elsewhere (cf. 1:7, "the LORD"; 2:22, "the LORD"; 4:6, "your God"; 4:10, "the LORD"; 4:12, "their God"; 8:13, "the LORD" and "He"). "Rejected" (in the Heb. in v. 5) makes a striking wordplay with the word "rejected" in verse 3. Israel had rejected (*zānah*) what is good and turned to idols. The Lord responded appropriately by rejecting (*zānah*) Israel's idols. As Moses and Joshua had warned (Deut. 11:17; Josh. 23:16), the Lord's **anger** burned **against** the idolaters. In despair the Lord asked, **How long will they be incapable of purity?**

8:6. The calf-idol (v. 5) was a product of a human craftsman's skill; how, then, could it be considered a god? (Cf. Isa. 40:18-20; 44:9-20.) The words, **it is not God,** were probably meant to refute Jeroboam, who said of the calves, "Here are your gods, O Israel" (1 Kings 12:28; cf. Ex. 32:4). The destruction of this image would demonstrate the futility of idolatry.

8:7. The phrase **they sow the wind** is transitional. It alludes to the futility of both her idolatrous worship (vv. 4-6) and her foreign policy (vv. 8-10). "Wind" here represents that which lacks substance and is therefore worthless and of no assistance (cf. Prov. 11:29). Israel would **reap** in extra measure what she had sown. The futility (wind) which she had planted like seed would yield a crop of destruction (represented by **the whirlwind**). All her efforts directed toward self-preservation would be self-destructive.

The agricultural metaphor continues. Israel's crop would be worthless, containing only stalks without **grain.** Even if she would produce grain, **foreigners would** take it away and the nation would not benefit from her labor.

8:8. Already **Israel** had been **swallowed up** by her foreign policy (cf. 7:8-12). Her involvement with foreigners was swiftly robbing the nation of its strength and identity as the Lord's people. Israel had become as worthless as a broken pot (cf. Jer. 22:28; 48:38). The words **worthless thing** are literally, "a pot in which no one delights" (NASB).

8:9. Israel's attempt to ally with **Assyria** could be compared to the **wandering** of **a wild donkey,** an animal well known for its desire to be independent of all restrictions (cf. Job 39:5-8). Israel's alliances were also compared to prostitution; like a harlot she had **sold herself to lovers** (i.e., foreign powers).

8:10. Despite Israel's desperate attempts to preserve herself, God's judgment was certain. The Lord is pictured as bringing her back from her wanderings to Assyria and Egypt so that He might oppress her (cf. 7:13). The instrument of judgment would be **the mighty King** (i.e., of Assyria; cf. 10:6) from whom, ironically, they had sought aid.

8:11-13. Another of Israel's sins was its hypocritical ritualism. The people had **built many altars for sin offerings.** But these altars had **become altars for sinning,** as the religious acts conducted there were hypocritical. Sacrifices are an offense to God when not combined with a wholehearted devotion to His commandments (cf. 6:6; Isa. 1:11). Israel had built many altars, but at the same time had treated **the many things of** God's **Law** (His covenant demands; cf. Hosea 8:1) **as something alien.** So the Lord would not accept the **sacrifices** she offered Him. Instead He would **punish** her for her **sins** by sending her into exile. **Egypt** stands here as a symbol for the place of future exile and bondage (cf. 9:3; 11:5; Deut. 28:68). This highlights the appropriateness of God's judgment. In the deliverance from Egyptian bondage Israel had experienced God's grace. Having spurned that grace, she would return to slavery.

8:14. A final illustration of the nation's unfaithfulness was her self-sufficiency. **Judah** is specifically included in the indictment at this point. Having **forgotten** (cf. 2:13) that her very existence depended on the Lord alone (cf. **his Maker**), God's people proudly sought prominence (**palaces**) and security (**fortified many towns. . . . fortresses**; cf. 10:14) through her own efforts. But the Lord was about to destroy (by **fire**) these sources of false security, fulfilling a covenant curse (cf. Deut. 28:52). God's judgment came through the Assyrians. Sennacherib "attacked all the fortified cities of Judah and captured them" (2 Kings 18:13).

2. ISRAEL'S GUILT AND PUNISHMENT
    REITERATED (9:1–11:7)

This judgment message contains four subunits. The first (9:1-9) begins with a direct address to Israel, which serves as a formal marker of a new section (cf. 6:4). Each of the other subunits begins with an allusion to Israel's early history (9:10; 10:1; 11:1).

a. *Israel's hostility punished (9:1-9)*

9:1-2. **Israel** was **not** to **rejoice** in expectation of a plentiful harvest (cf. v. 2) because her unfaithfulness had precluded any further divine blessing (v. 1; cf. 2:8-9). **At every threshing floor** Israel had erroneously attributed the prosperity of her harvests to Baal (cf. 2:5). She had become an adulteress, offering worship to Baal and receiving from Baal **the wages of a prostitute.** Those "wages" were wheat (at the threshing floor), vines and figs (2:12), and food, water, wool, linen, oil, and drink (2:5). That is, Israel believed that by prostituting herself in worship of Baal that Baal in turn blessed her crops and gave her other necessities of life.

The plentiful harvests were about to end (9:2; cf. 2:9-12). In fulfillment of several covenant curses (cf. Deut. 28:30, 38-42, 51) the Lord would take away her grain and **wine** (cf. Hosea 2:9; 7:14). **Winepresses** (*yeqeḇ*) were used for both grapes and olives (cf. Joel 2:24). Since wine is specifically mentioned (in the last line of Hosea 9:2), *yeqeḇ* may allude primarily to oil in this context (cf. grain, wine, and oil in 2:8, 22).

9:3. The judgment pictured in verse 2 would be accomplished ultimately through invasion and exile. The **land** belonged to the Lord (cf. Ex. 15:17; Lev. 25:23), who was responsible for its fertility (cf. Deut. 11:10-12). When the people attributed the produce of the land to Baal they forfeited the blessing of living on it in peace and prosperity (Deut. 11:8-21). **Egypt** is again mentioned as a symbol of the place of exile (cf. Hosea 7:16; 8:13; 11:5). **Assyria** would be the actual location (2 Kings 17:6). There in an unclean land (cf. Amos 7:17) Israel would be forced to **eat** ceremonially **unclean food** (cf. Ezek. 4:13), rather than the fruits of God's blessing. The punishment fit the crime. Israel had become defiled by her sin (cf. Hosea 5:3; 6:10). How appropriate, then, that she eat defiled food in a defiled land.

9:4. In exile, opportunity for legitimate worship **to the Lord** would end. Again the punishment was highly appropriate. Israel's Levitical worship had been corrupted by hypocrisy (cf. 6:6; 8:11-13). A nation that refused to conduct its formal worship in the proper spirit would be denied its privilege of worship. **Wine offerings,** which accompanied certain types of **sacrifices** (cf. Num. 15:1-12), would cease. **Sacrifices** offered in a foreign land would not be acceptable to the Lord. They would have the same effect on a worshiper as **bread** eaten by **mourners,** who made everything they touched ceremonially unclean because they had contacted a dead body (cf. Num. 19:14-15, 22). Such bread was not fit for use in worship.

Hosea 9:4b would be better translated, "**all who eat** it (i.e., the mourners' bread) become **unclean**; such bread can be used to satisfy one's appetite, but it may not enter the Lord's **temple**." In this way verse 4b is understood as a general statement about the nature of mourners' bread rather than an additional prediction about the exilic worshipers and their sacrifices.

9:5. The rhetorical question in this verse emphasizes the exiles' plight. Israel would be unable to celebrate the most important **festival** (**feasts** and **days** in Heb. are both sing.) on her religious calendar. Perhaps the Feast of Tabernacles is specifically in view (cf. Lev. 23:39).

9:6. **Destruction** would sweep over

the land (cf. 7:13; 10:14). Those who happened to **escape** the sword of the invading army would face exile. The reference to **Egypt** probably has the same meaning as in preceding verses (cf. comments on 8:13; 9:3). **Memphis,** about 20 miles south of modern Cairo, was famous as a burial place. Here it symbolizes the ultimate destination of the exiles—a foreign graveyard. Few would ever return to their homeland (cf. Jer. 44:1-14). Meanwhile back in Israel the exiles' possessions **(treasures of silver)** and homes **(tents)** would lie in ruins and would be overgrown by **briers and thorns** (cf. Hosea 10:8).

9:7. The people's hostility toward the true prophets of God was one of several reasons for judgment (vv. 7-9). **Maniac** refers to one who is insane (cf. 1 Sam. 21:13-15). The term is used elsewhere by godless men who ridiculed true prophets (cf. 2 Kings 9:11; Jer. 29:26-27). **Hostility** (also used in Hosea 9:8) refers to intense animosity, such as Esau felt toward Jacob after Esau had been cheated of the paternal blessing (Gen. 27:41, "held a grudge").

9:8. The irony of the situation is that Israel tried to ensnare the prophets God had placed as watchmen **over** the nation. A **watchman** was responsible for warning a city of an approaching enemy (cf. Ezek. 33:6). In the same way God's prophets were to warn the people of coming judgment on sin (cf. Jer. 6:17; Ezek. 3:17; 33:7-9). **The house of his God** refers to the land of Israel (cf. Hosea 8:1; 9:15).

9:9. The depth of the people's sin against God is emphasized by Hosea's reference to **the days of Gibeah** (cf. 10:9). The phrase recalls the events that involved the brutal rape and murder of the Levite's concubine by some bisexual men of Gibeah (Jud. 19). On that occasion it was said, "Such a thing has never been seen or done, not since the day the Israelites came up out of Egypt" (Jud. 19:30). But Hosea said that black mark on Israel's history was now rivaled by Israel's blatant **sins** against the Lord.

b. *Israel's idolatry punished (9:10-17)*

9:10. This section begins with a reference to Israel's origins, when the Lord **found** extreme delight in the nation (cf. 2:15). **Grapes in the desert** would be an unexpected source of surprise and delight. The delicious **early fruit on the fig tree** was irresistible (cf. Song 2:13; Isa. 28:4; Jer. 24:2; Micah 7:1).

However, the Lord's attitude toward His people soon changed. **When they** arrived at Peor they engaged in sexual immorality with Moabite and Midianite women as part of the fertility rites associated with the worship of **Baal Peor** (cf. Num. 25). This deity, which God called **that shameful idol,** may have been a local manifestation of the Canaanite fertility god Baal. This event in Moses' day was mentioned here because it set the pattern for Israel's subsequent history, characterized by unfaithfulness. In Hosea's day Israel had also defiled herself by making Baal her lover. Like the generation at Peor, they too had engaged in fertility rites (cf. Hosea 4:13-14).

9:11-14. As punishment for Israel's sin of involvement in the Baal fertility rites (v. 10), the Lord would bring the covenant curses of infertility (vv. 11, 14), death (vv. 12-13, 16), and exile (vv. 15, 17) on the nation. The name **Ephraim** is used in verses 11, 13, and 16 because it was associated with fertility and fruitfulness ("Ephraim" in Heb. sounds like "twice fruitful"; cf. Gen. 41:52).

Ephraim's glory, here associated with numerous offspring, would depart as swiftly as **a bird.** Appropriately many of those who had tried to secure fertility through Baal worship would become sterile and barren (cf. Hosea 4:10 and, in contrast, Deut. 7:14). Others would **miscarry** or watch their **children** die in the forthcoming invasion (Hosea 9:12-13; cf. v. 16b). The women's **breasts** would be **dry** for they would have no children to nurse (v. 14). The words **like Tyre, planted in a pleasant place** (v. 13) attempt to make sense of the difficult Hebrew text, which seems to contrast Ephraim's prosperous past (comparable to the Phoenician commercial center Tyre; cf. Ezek. 28) with its humiliating future. The RSV (following the LXX) translates Hosea 9:13a, "Ephraim's sons, as I have seen, are destined for a prey." This seems to provide better parallelism with verse 13b.

9:15. The **sinful** people were now the object of God's hatred, rather than His love. The language employed here should probably be seen against a domestic background. The Lord had become displeased with His wife, unfaithful Israel. Such displeasure is termed hatred (cf. Deut. 22:13; 24:3, where the same verb, *śānēʾ*, is used). God was prepared to drive her from the household (**drive them out of My house**), withdrawing His **love** (His devotion and protective care as her Husband; cf. Hosea 1:6; 2:4-5). The **rebellious** nation, whose opposition to the Lord's covenant was epitomized by the **Gilgal** fertility cult (cf. 4:15; 12:11), would be expelled from His "house" (i.e., the land; cf. 8:1; 9:8). "Drive . . . out" (*gāraš*) is used frequently of the conquest of Canaan, whereby the Lord gave Israel possession of His land (cf. Ex. 23:28, 31; Deut. 33:27). Now Israel was about to suffer the same fate as the Canaanites, whose practices it had assimilated. Hosea may also be alluding here to the sinful couple's initial expulsion from God's presence (cf. Gen. 3:24).

9:16-17. Ironically, because of widespread sterility and infant mortality (vv. 11-14), **Ephraim,** once a symbol of fruitfulness, would be compared to a **withered** plant incapable of bearing **fruit.** Because of her disobedience Israel would be rejected by **God** (cf. 4:6). In exile Israel's people would become **wanderers among the nations.** "Wanderers" translates the same Hebrew word (*nādad*) as "strayed" in 7:13. Again the punishment fit the crime. Those who willfully strayed from the path of covenant loyalty were condemned to wander aimlessly among those outside the covenant (foreign nations). As in 9:15, the language in verse 17 may also allude to the Genesis account. The same verb (*nādad*) is used with respect to Cain (Gen. 4:12).

c. Israel's "double sin" punished (chap. 10)

10:1. As in 9:10 this prophecy employs a botanical metaphor in referring to Israel's earlier history. The Lord planted **Israel** like a **vine** in the land of Canaan and blessed her with **fruit** (i.e., prosperity; cf. Ps. 80:8-11; Jer. 2:21; Ezek. 19:10-11). However, as the nation prospered she erroneously attributed her success to false gods rather than the Lord (cf. Hosea 2:8; Deut. 8:8-20). At the same time the people attempted to maintain a semblance of devotion to the God of Israel. The **altars** mentioned here probably refer

to this hypocritical formalism (cf. Hosea 6:6; 8:11-13), while **sacred stones** allude to idolatry (cf. 3:4; 10:2).

10:2. Israel's unfaithfulness established her **guilt** (cf. 12:14, 13:12, 16) and necessitated her punishment. **Is deceitful** (*ḥālaq*) literally means "is slippery, smooth." Often the term is used of deceitful, unreliable speech (cf. Pss. 5:9; 12:2; 55:21). With **their heart** (or mind) as subject *ḥālaq* refers to the hypocrisy which characterized her approach to the Lord. Appropriately **the LORD** would **destroy** the sites of her hypocritical and false worship (cf. **sacred stones** in 3:4; 10:1).

10:3. As a result of the approaching invasion, the nation's political structure would be shattered and her **king** removed (cf. vv. 7, 15). In the aftermath of the calamity the people would recognize their own unfaithfulness (i.e., failure to **revere the LORD**) as the basis for judgment. The situation would become so hopeless that most would realize that **even . . . a king** could bring no remedy (cf. 13:10).

10:4. The people's lack of respect for the Lord was illustrated by their lack of regard for legal **agreements** they made with each other. Their attitude toward fellow Israelites (including frequently taking each other to court) simply reflected their lack of loyalty to God.

10:5-6a. Some details of the approaching judgment and exile are described in verses 5-8. **The calf-idol** (cf. comments on 8:5) located in **Beth Aven** (i.e., Bethel; cf. comments on 4:15) would be **carried** away by the victorious Assyrian army, causing great consternation among its worshipers. **Idolatrous priests** translates a rare term (*kᵉmārîm*), used only of priests of Baal (2 Kings 23:5; Zeph. 1:4). The reference to the Assyrian army carrying off the idols of defeated foes is abundantly illustrated in neo-Assyrian literature and art. **The great king** refers to Assyria's king (cf. Hosea 8:10).

10:6b. The NIV takes verse 6b as a reference to Israel's shame over the fate of her gods, called **wooden idols.** The text is better translated, "Israel will be shamed of its own *counsel*" (cf. KJV, NASB, NIV marg.), the reference being to the nation's unwise political policy of courting Assyria's favor (cf. 5:13; 7:8-9, 11; 8:9-10; in Isa. 30:1 the same word ['ēṣâh] is used of a political alliance with Egypt).

10:7. Israel's **king** (cf. vv. 3, 15), as well as her calf-idol, would be removed in the coming invasion. **Float away** (*dāmâh*) is literally, "be destroyed" (cf. 4:5-6; 10:15 where NIV translates the same word as "destroy"). **Like a twig** floating **on the . . . waters** the nation would be swept away by the current and brought to ruin.

10:8. The sites of idolatrous worship would **be destroyed** as well, the ruins becoming overgrown with **thorns** (cf. 9:6) **and thistles.** The reference to the destruction of **the high places** (*bāmôt*) is ironic (cf. Lev. 26:30-31). When Israel entered the land the Lord commanded her to destroy these worship centers (Num. 33:52; Deut. 12:2-3). Because of Israel's dismal failure in carrying out this charge, the Lord chose to use a foreign army to accomplish His purpose. In utter desperation the people would beg **the mountains** to **fall on** them. A similar plea will be made by unbelievers in the Tribulation in response to the terror of God's wrath in the seal judgments (Rev. 6:16).

Wickedness translates *'āwen*, which occurs, spelled slightly differently, in "Beth Aven," the derogatory name for Bethel (cf. Hosea 4:15; 5:8; 10:5).

10:9. Hosea referred again to the shameful incident at **Gibeah** (cf. 9:9). Since that time **Israel** had persisted in sin. The question in 10:9b is better translated with the future tense, *Will* **not war overtake the evildoers in Gibeah?** (cf. NASB; 5:8) How appropriate that judgment should "overtake" the city that had served as a pattern for Israel's sinful history!

10:10. At the time of the Lord's choosing (**When I please**) He would **punish** (lit., "discipline"; cf. 5:2) Israel by gathering the **nations . . . against** her. The translation and meaning of the final line in 10:10 are uncertain. The NIV takes the **bonds** as a reference to captivity and approaching exile. Probably a better translation is, "when they are *harnessed* to **their double sin.**" The imagery is that of plowing (cf. v. 11). Israel is pictured as yoked to her sin like a heifer (cf. Isa. 5:18). As Wolff suggests (*Hosea*, p. 184), "double sin" probably refers to Israel's former sin (at Gibeah) and her present guilt.

10:11. The comparison of Israel to a cow is continued (cf. comments on v. 10). Israel (**Ephraim** stands for the Northern Kingdom; see comments on 4:17) was like **a trained heifer that loves to thresh.** A heifer would like to thresh because "threshing was a comparatively light task, made pleasant by the fact that the creature was unmuzzled and free to eat . . . as it pulled the threshing sledge over the gathered corn" (Kidner, *Love for the Loveless*, pp. 97-8). However, Israel had abandoned this relatively easy task and had insisted on being yoked, as it were, to sin (cf. 10:10b).

So the Lord would place a different **yoke** on Israel's **neck** and force her to engage in the extremely arduous work of plowing (**so** is better trans. "but"). Even **Judah** was included in this judgment. **Jacob** referred to the Northern Kingdom (cf. 12:2). In this figurative portrayal the nation's threshing corresponded to the service the Lord required within the covenant relationship, whereas the plowing referred to the hardship that would accompany the exile.

10:12. A brief call to covenant loyalty is included here. Even in the midst of a message of condemnation and judgment God held out the possibility of repentance and blessing (cf. Isa. 1:18-20). Using agricultural imagery, He urged Israel to **seek the LORD** by cultivating **righteousness** (or justice) and reaping His **unfailing love** (*ḥesed̲*, "loyalty"). The words **showers righteousness** compare God's future gift of righteousness (or just treatment in the form of **deliverance**; cf. Hosea 2:19) to abundant **rain** (cf. 6:3).

10:13. The exhortation in verse 12 actually summarizes the appeal made by Israel's prophets throughout her history. But the sinful nation had not responded properly, producing instead wickedness (cf. v. 15), **evil, and deception.** Rather than relying on the power of God, the nation had **depended on** her own military might. The contrast between God's desires and Israel's response heightens her guilt. So the call to repentance (v. 12) had a twofold function: it testified to the Lord's grace and contributed to the development of the prophet's accusation.

10:14-15. In response to Israel's pride the Lord said He would destroy a source of her false confidence (**fortresses**; cf. 8:14). The severity of the judgment is emphasized by a comparison with a historical incident that was apparently well known to Hosea's contemporaries. But the identity of **Shalman** and the location of **Beth Arbel** are uncertain. The most popular identifications of Shalman have been: (a) Shalmaneser III (an Assyrian ruler who campaigned against the West in the ninth century B.C.), (b) Shalmaneser V (the Assyrian ruler from 727 to 722 B.C.; but his invasion of Israel postdates Hosea's prophecy), and (c) Salamanu (a Moabite king mentioned in a tribute list of the Assyrian king Tiglath-Pileser III and a contemporary of Hosea). Beth Arbel has been identified by some (e.g., Eusebius) with modern Irbid (Arbela) in the northern Transjordan region about 18 miles southeast of the Sea of Galilee and by others with modern Arbel two miles west of the Sea of Galilee (Arbela in the apocryphal 1 Maccabees 9:2, JB). At any rate this particular **battle** was vividly remembered for its atrocities, especially the wholesale slaughter of women and **children**. **Bethel**, which here represents the nation as a whole, would experience a similar fate because of her great sin (cf. Hosea 4:15; Amos 7:10-17). The fall of Israel's **king** would signal the conquest of the nation by Babylon (cf. Hosea 10:3, 7; 2 Kings 17:4-6).

d. Israel's ingratitude punished (11:1-7)

11:1-2. Once again the Lord recalled Israel's early history to contrast the past with the present (cf. 9:10; 10:1). At the beginning the Lord's relationship with **Israel** had been like that of a father to a **son** (cf. Ex. 4:22-23). (On the quotation of this passage, see comments on Matt. 2:15.) The Lord displayed His love toward the nation by summoning her from **Egypt** (cf. Deut. 7:8; also cf. Hosea 12:9, 13; 13:4). However, when God subsequently called them (11:2) to covenant obedience through His prophets, the people rejected Him (cf. Jer. 7:25-26) and turned instead to false gods (cf. 2 Kings 17:13-17) including **the Baals** (cf. Hosea 2:13, 17). Hosea 11:2a is literally, "**The more** they [i.e., the prophets] **called** them, the more they [the Israelites] **went from** them" (NASB; cf. KJV, NIV marg.).

11:3-4. The Lord's goodness to Israel is further illustrated. Like a father patiently teaching a young child **to walk**, the Lord had established and sustained Israel (cf. Deut. 1:31; Isa. 1:2). He also

restored (**healed**) the nation's strength after times of judgment, though she failed to acknowledge His intervention.

In Hosea 11:4 Israel is compared to a work animal (cf. 10:11). The Lord is likened to a master who gently (in **kindness** and **love**; cf. 11:1) leads his animal and removes (or perhaps repositions) its **yoke** so that it might eat with greater ease the food he kindly provides. The Lord treated Israel with compassion and love.

11:5-7. Astonishingly Israel had responded to the Lord's kindness with ingratitude (cf. vv. 2, 3b). Even when the Lord called her to repentance through His prophets **they** refused **to repent** (cf. v. 7). Therefore inescapable judgment would fall in the form of military defeat and exile (vv. 5a, 6). Once again **Egypt** is named as a symbol of slavery and exile (cf. 8:13; 9:3, 6).

The wording **bars of their gates** (11:6) is supported by the parallel term **cities**. Another possible translation of the Hebrew for "bars of their gates" is "braggarts" (cf. Wolff, *Hosea*, p. 192). In favor of this is the following line (v. 6c) which literally reads, "on account of **their plans**." "Plans" refers to rebellious attitudes and practices (cf. **Micah** 6:16).

Put an end literally reads "eats, devours." The same **Hebrew** verb ('ākal) appears in Hosea 11:4 ("feed"). The repetition of this word **in verses 4** and 6 emphasizes the contrast between the Lord's past blessing and His future judgment. In the past He had given Israel food to eat. Now, ironically, He was about to send **swords** to eat Israel! For a similar wordplay involving the same Hebrew term, see Isaiah 1:19-20.

The Hebrew text of Hosea 11:7b is so obscure that any translation must remain tentative. The problem is evidenced by the variations in the English versions. According to the NIV rendering, God refused to hear the desperate prayer of His obstinate people. But the NASB translates the text, "Though they call them to the One on high, none at all exalts Him," with "they" referring not to Israel but to the prophets. In that view Israel rejected the prophets' calls to repentance.

3. THE LORD'S COMPASSION RENEWED (11:8-11)

As in earlier sections of this prophecy, Hosea's message of judgment concludes with an abrupt shift to a message of salvation (cf. 1:10–2:1; 2:14–3:5; 5:15–6:3). These verses should not be understood as a decision to withhold the judgment threatened uncompromisingly throughout the book. Instead, the words are a divine response to Israel's suffering and exile. The Lord would not totally abandon Israel. The effects of His wrath would be tempered by His compassion, and He would ultimately call His people back from exile.

a. The Lord's love for Israel (11:8-9)

11:8-9. One of the Bible's strongest expressions of divine emotion is in these verses. As God reflected on the severe judgment that His wrath would bring on **Israel,** He suddenly burst out with four rhetorical questions. They indicate that He would never completely desert His people. **Admah** and **Zeboiim,** which were annihilated along with Sodom and Gomorrah (Deut. 29:23; cf. Gen. 10:19; 14:2, 8), were symbols of complete divine destruction.

Changed (lit., "overturned") is the same word (*hāpak*) used to describe the overthrow of these cities (cf. Gen. 19:25; Deut. 29:23). Wolff comments on the wordplay, "Israel will not be completely 'overturned' as the cities mentioned here; rather, there will be an 'overturning,' that is, a change, in Yahweh's heart" (*Hosea,* p. 201).

Instead of carrying out His **fierce** (lit., "burning") **anger** to the fullest, God's **compassion** would be **aroused** (lit., "grow warm"; cf. "kindled" in KJV, NASB). The burning flame of God's anger would be replaced, as it were, by the fire of His compassion. **Ephraim** would never **again** experience the judgment of **God.** This promise is reliable because it was made by **the Holy One** (cf. Hosea 11:12) Himself, who condescends to dwell with His people (**among** them) and yet continues to transcend all that is human and fallible (He is **not man;** cf. 1 Sam. 15:29).

b. Israel's return to the Lord (11:10-11)

11:10-11. In the day of national restoration Israel will **follow the Lord,** who will lead the people back to **their homes.** His lion-like **roar,** often associated with judgment and destruction (cf. 5:14; 13:7; Amos 1:2; 3:8), will become a summons

to return from exile. The people will again demonstrate a healthy respect for **the Lord;** they **will come trembling** (cf. Hosea 3:5 for a similar idea), as an earlier generation did when God appeared in theophanic might at Mount Sinai (cf. Ex. 19:16, where the same Heb. word is used).

The comparison to **doves** is significant in light of Hosea 7:11, where Israel's naiveté in seeking foreign alliances is likened to that of a dove. Here the force of the simile is positive, the reference being to the swiftness with which the dove returns to its nest (cf. Ps. 55:6-8; Isa. 60:8). Again **Egypt** represents exile (see comments on Hosea 8:13). Restoration **from Assyria** is also mentioned in Zechariah 10:10-11.

C. The Lord's case against Israel concluded (11:12–14:9)

A hortatory and didactic tone characterizes the conclusion to Hosea's prophecy. As in earlier sections Hosea moves from judgment (11:12–13:16) to salvation (chap. 14).

1. A CONCLUDING INDICTMENT (11:12–13:16)

Once more Israel's guilt is established and her punishment predicted.

a. The nation's unfaithfulness (11:12–12:2)

These verses introduce the final section with a formal accusation (11:12–12:2a) and an announcement of judgment (12:2b).

11:12. The entire nation (**Judah** included) had broken her covenant with the Lord. **Lies** and **deceit** refer to hypocrisy and unfaithfulness. The latter (*mirmâh*; cf. comments on 12:7) is especially appropriate in light of the following comparison with the patriarch Jacob (cf. 12:3-4, 12). The same term was used to describe Jacob's deception in stealing Esau's blessing (cf. Gen. 27:35).

Ironically the nation was unfaithful to **the faithful Holy One,** who had always demonstrated fidelity to His covenant promises (cf. Hosea 12:9; 13:4-6). **Is unruly** (*rûd*) means to stray or roam restlessly, an apt picture of Israel's wandering off from God to Baal and to foreign nations for help. "Holy One" is plural here, emphasizing the magnitude of this divine characteristic. In this context

God's holiness refers primarily to His transcendence over fallible people (cf. 11:9).

12:1-2. Israel's unfaithfulness found expression in social injustice (she **multiplies lies and violence;** cf. 4:2; 7:1) and in foreign alliances with **Assyria** and **Egypt** (cf. 5:13; 7:8, 11; 8:8-9; 2 Kings 17:3-4). **Olive oil** was either used in the covenant-making ceremony or given as a token of allegiance. All this activity was futile and self-destructive, as the references to feeding on and pursuing **the wind** suggest (cf. Hosea 8:7; 13:15). **The LORD** had a **charge** (*rîḇ;* cf. 4:1; also see comments on 2:2) **against Judah** and was about to **punish** His people for their evil **ways.**

b. A lesson from history (12:3-6)

Before further developing the themes of guilt and judgment (cf. 12:9–13:16), Hosea reminded the nation of her need to repent (12:5-6). In doing so he drew a lesson from the life of Jacob (vv. 3-4).

12:3-4. Jacob's birth gave a hint of the kind of person he would be. His grasping Esau's **heel** (cf. Gen. 25:26) foreshadowed his deception of his brother in stealing his birthright and blessing (cf. Gen. 27:35-36). However, Jacob eventually came to a turning point. When he faced the prospect of death at Esau's hand on his return to the land of Canaan he wrestled **with God,** refusing to let go till he received a blessing (Gen. 32:22-32). Later **at Bethel,** the site of his dream years before (cf. Gen. 28:10-22), God appeared to Jacob again. God changed his name to Israel, blessed him, and renewed His covenant promise (cf. Gen. 35:1-14).

12:5-6. Like Jacob, the deceitful nation (cf. 11:12) needed to **return** (12:6) **to** her covenant Ruler, **the LORD God Almighty** with tears and prayers (cf. v. 4). Genuine repentance would involve a commitment to **love** (*ḥeseḏ*) **and justice,** as well as a dependence on the Lord (**wait for your God always;** cf. Ps. 27:14), rather than on herself.

c. The nation's pride (12:7-14)

12:7-8. Israel's repentance (v. 6) would necessitate a complete reversal in her dealings and attitudes. The nation was permeated by economic dishonesty

(*mirmâh;* cf. 11:12 for the same word), oppression (**defraud**), pride (**Ephraim boasts**), and insensitivity to her sin, thinking that her **wealth** would hide her **sin.** The Old Testament frequently spoke against using **scales** that were rigged to weigh out less merchandise than the buyer thought he was getting (cf. Lev. 19:36; Deut. 25:13-16; Prov. 11:1; 16:11; 20:10, 23; Amos 8:5; Micah 6:11).

12:9. The **LORD,** however, would not overlook such blatant disobedience and ingratitude. As their **God,** He had guided the nation since her days in **Egypt,** leading her through the wilderness to the Promised Land. As part of His coming judgment He would bring Israel into the wilderness **again,** making her **live in tents.** The wilderness experience, which the people commemorated in the Feast of Tabernacles (cf. Lev. 23:33-43), would be realized once more in the Exile.

12:10-11. Though the Lord had communicated His will to Israel through **the prophets,** the people had repudiated those messages (cf. 9:7 and comments on 11:2). The wickedness and hypocrisy manifested in **Gilead** (cf. 6:8) and **Gilgal** (cf. 4:15; 9:15) epitomized that of the nation. In the coming invasion the **altars** located there would be reduced to **piles of stones** (*gallîm;* cf. 10:8, "the high places . . . will be destroyed"). The use of this Hebrew word, which is a play on the name Gilgal facilitated by the repetition of the "g" and "l" sounds, is another example of Hosea's poetic techniques. Gilgal would become *gallîm.*

12:12-13. The Lord's past goodness is again recalled. Going back to Jacob's experience once more (cf. vv. 3-4), Hosea reminded the people of their humble beginnings. Their famous ancestor was once a refugee who had to tend **sheep in** order to acquire **a wife** (cf. Deut. 26:5). Later Jacob's descendants served **the** Egyptians till God delivered them **from Egypt** (cf. Hosea 11:1; 12:9; 13:4) and protected them through His **Prophet** Moses.

12:14. However, Israel had **provoked** the Lord **to anger** with her sin. Hosea probably was alluding here to idolatry because *kā'as,* the verb rendered "provoked to anger," is frequently used in reference to idols (cf., e.g., Deut. 4:25; 9:18; 31:29; 32:16, 21; Jud. 2:12; 1 Kings 14:9, 15). In response to this the **LORD**

would not extend forgiveness (He would **leave upon** the nation its **guilt**; cf. Hosea 10:2; 13:12, 16); He would **repay** her for her evil.

d. Impending doom (chap. 13)

13:1-3. Ephraim's prominent (**exalted**) place among the tribes of Israel was well known (cf. Gen. 48:13-20). Jeroboam I, who had led the Northern Kingdom's secession, was an Ephraimite (1 Kings 11:26; 12:25). However, this prominent tribe had also taken the lead in **Baal worship** and was as good as dead. As the Ephraimites (and the other Israelites they represent here) multiplied their **idols** and **images,** they added to their guilt. They debased themselves even further by kissing **the calf-idols** (cf. 1 Kings 19:18; also cf. "calf-idol" in Hosea 8:4-5; 10:5) in conjunction with their many sacrificial rites.

They offer human sacrifice literally reads, "sacrificers of men kiss calves." The Bible speaks of child sacrifice in conjunction with worship of the god Molech (cf. Lev. 18:21; 20:2-5; 2 Kings 23:10), which was apparently sometimes combined with Baal worship (cf. Jer. 32:35). However, the word used here, "men" ('ādām), does not suggest child sacrifice. A more likely interpretation is that "sacrificers of men" is idiomatic, meaning "sacrificers among men" or "men who sacrifice" (cf. KJV, NASB). One should compare this with the following expressions, "wild donkey of a man" (Gen. 16:12; i.e., a man who is like a wild donkey in character), "the poor of men" (Isa. 29:19, KJV; i.e., men who are poor), and "leaders (lit., princes) of men" (Micah 5:5; perhaps meaning men who are princes). In this case the prophet (Hosea 13:2) was emphasizing the absurdity of men kissing images of calves.

The judgment of God would make these idolaters quickly vanish (v. 3). Each of the four similes (**mist . . . dew**; cf. 6:4, **chaff . . smoke**) emphasizes the extremely transitory condition of the idolaters.

13:4-9. Once more the LORD reminded Israel of His gracious deeds at the beginning of their history (cf. 12:9a, 10, 12-13). He led them from **Egypt** (cf. 11:1; 12:9, 13), **cared for** (lit., "knew") them **in** the wilderness (13:5) and allowed them to feed in the Promised Land (v. 6).

When I fed them is literally, "when they pastured." It describes sheep or cattle grazing peacefully. In return for such blessings they should have acknowledged the Lord as their **God** and **Savior** (v. 4). Instead **they became proud** and **forgot** Him (v. 6; cf. comments on 2:13). **Like a** vicious and powerful wild beast (**lion . . . leopard,** or **bear**) the Lord would **attack** His people (still viewed here as a helpless flock or herd, 13:7-8; cf. 5:14). Ironically the **Helper** of **Israel** would become her Destroyer because she was **against** Him (13:9).

13:10-11. When the Lord would come to destroy (v. 9) no one would be able to **save** the people, not even the political leaders they had demanded from the Lord (v. 10; cf. 10:3, 7, 15). Hosea 13:11a (**in My anger I gave you a king**) probably refers to the Northern tribes' part in crowning Saul (1 Sam. 8:6-9; 12:12), as well as their secession under Jeroboam I (1 Kings 12:16). Hosea 13:11b refers to the cessation of Israel's kingship with Hoshea (2 Kings 17:1-6).

13:12. God had not overlooked Israel's **guilt** (cf. 10:2; 12:14; 13:16). Ephraim's sinful deeds were compared to a document which is bound up (NASB; cf. NIV's **stored up**) and a treasure which is stored up (NASB; cf. NIV's **kept on record**). Through both figures Israel's **sins** were pictured as something guarded carefully till the day of retribution when they would be brought forth as testimony against the nation.

13:13. Any basis for hope had all but disappeared. Israel had not responded to God's call for repentance during the period of grace He had extended. The procrastinating nation was compared to a baby which **does not come** out of its mother's **womb** despite her strenuous efforts in labor. Such a delay will result in death for both mother and child. Since the baby seemingly does not observe the proper time for his birth, he is referred to, figuratively, as **without wisdom** (cf. Ecc. 8:5).

13:14. Traditionally verse 14a has been interpreted as an expression of hope and a promise of salvation (NASB, NIV). However, this view is contextually problematic. Though Hosea's prophecy is characterized by abrupt changes in tone, such a shift appears to be premature here (the shift in this section appears to come in 14:1) and would leave 13:14a awkwardly connected with what follows (cf. v. 14b, **I will have no compassion**). The first two statements may be translated better as rhetorical questions implying a negative answer: "Shall I **ransom them from the power of** sheol? Shall I **redeem them from death?**" (RSV)

The next two questions (**Where, O death, are your plagues? Where, O grave, is your destruction?**) would then be appeals for death to unleash its "plagues" and "destruction" against Ephraim (cf. vv. 14b-16), not a triumphant cry of victory over death. Of course the Apostle Paul, writing under the inspiration of the Holy Spirit, applied the language of this text in the latter sense (cf. 1 Cor. 15:55-56). However, in that context Paul was drawing on the language of Scripture as traditionally understood (cf. the LXX); he was not offering a textual and exegetical analysis of Hosea 13:14.

13:15-16. With the Lord's compassion removed (v. 14; cf. 1:6), Israel's prosperity (**he thrives**) would come to an end. The LORD would **come** like a hot **east wind** which dries up everything in its path. The reality behind the figure is the Assyrian invasion, as the references to plundering and military atrocities make clear. Thus 13:15-16 correspond to the plagues and destruction of death mentioned in verse 14. The language is that of covenant curse (cf. Lev. 26:25; Deut. 28:21; 32:24-25; Amos 4:10). Again destruction would come, God said, because Israel had **rebelled against** Him (cf. Hosea 7:13; 8:1).

2. A CONCLUDING EXHORTATION (CHAP. 14)
a. *An appeal for repentance (14:1-3)*

14:1-3. Hosea's prophecy ends on a positive note with an exhortation to repentance (**Return . . . to the LORD**). Though this final appeal would surely be rejected by His arrogant and stubborn nation (cf. 10:12-15), it would instill hope in the hearts of a righteous remnant and provide the repentant generation of the future with a model to follow in returning to the Lord (cf. 3:5; 5:15b–6:3). True repentance would involve an acknowledgment of sin (**Say to Him, Forgive all our sins**) and a desire to praise the Lord (**that we may offer the fruit of our lips**), Israel's only Savior, God, and Helper

(contrast 5:13; 7:11; 8:4-5, 9; 13:2). No longer will **Israel** trust in **Assyria** or other nations, or will she call her hand-**made** idols **our gods.**

b. *A promise of restoration (14:4-8)*

14:4-6. In the day of Israel's repentance the Lord will turn from His **anger** and demonstrate His **love** by healing her (cf. 6:1). At that time the Lord's blessing will return **to Israel. Like . . . dew** it will cause the nation to **blossom like a lily** which was renowned for its beauty (cf. Song 2:2). This is a complete reversal of the imagery used in Hosea 13:15. Israel in her prosperity is also compared to **a cedar of Lebanon**, whose deep **roots,** luxuriant growth, and aromatic smell (cf. Song 4:11) were well known; and to **an olive tree,** widely recognized for its luxuriance (cf. Ps. 52:8; Jer. 11:16).

14:7. This verse is better translated: "Those who live in His shadow will again raise **grain,** and they **will blossom like** the **vine. His** renown **will be like the wine** of Lebanon" (NASB). **His shade** (or shadow) could refer to the Lord's protection (cf. v. 8, where He is compared to a "pine tree"; also cf. Isa. 4:6). However, as Keil notes, it is more likely that "Israel is itself the tree beneath whose shade the members of the nation flourish with freshness and vigor" (C.F. Keil, "Minor Prophets," in *Commentary on the Old Testament in Ten Volumes,* 10:166). This seems more consistent with the imagery in Hosea 14:5-6, which compares Israel to trees. The picture of Israelites again growing grain points to the return of covenantal blessing (cf. Deut. 28:4, 8, 11; 30:9; Hosea 2:21-23; Amos 9:13-15). Once again Israel will be "like a" fruitful "vine" (cf. Hosea 10:1) which produces the best "wine."

14:8. The first statement is best translated, "**Ephraim** shall say, **What have I to do** any more **with idols?**" (KJV) The contrast with Ephraim's earlier attitude is stark (cf. 2:8; 4:17; 8:4-6; 13:2). The Lord speaks in the latter half of 14:8 (**I will answer** and **I am like**), proclaiming His concern for Israel. The words **care for** translate the same Hebrew word (*šûr*) as "lurk" in 13:7. The same God who stealthily watched Israel like a leopard ready to pounce on its prey will become the One who carefully watches over His people to protect them! Comparing Himself to **a green pine tree,** the Lord also asserted that He is the nation's source of prosperity: **your fruitfulness comes from Me.**

c. A word of wisdom (14:9)

14:9. The book ends with a word on wisdom. One who **is wise** and **discerning** will learn a threefold lesson from Hosea's message. **The ways of the** LORD (i.e., His covenantal demands) **are right. The righteous walk in** (i.e., obey; cf. Deut. 8:6; 10:12; 11:22; 28:9; Jud. 2:17) **them** and experience the blessings of loyalty. **The rebellious** (cf. Hosea 7:13; 8:1; 13:16) **stumble** over (not **in**) **them** in the sense that destruction (stumbling) is the direct result of disobedience. The broken commandments become the ultimate reason for their downfall (cf. 5:5; 14:1). May all who read Hosea's words walk, not stumble!

BIBLIOGRAPHY

Andersen, Francis I., and Freedman, David Noel. *Hosea: A New Translation, Introduction and Commentary.* The Anchor Bible. Garden City, N.Y.: Doubleday & Co., 1980.

Brueggemann, Walter. *Tradition for Crisis: A Study in Hosea.* Richmond, Va.: John Knox Press, 1968.

Cohen, Gary G., and Vandermey, H.

Ronald. *Hosea/Amos.* Everyman's Bible Commentary. Chicago: Moody Press, 1981.

Feinberg, Charles L. *The Minor Prophets.* Chicago: Moody Press, 1976.

Harper, William Rainey. *A Critical and Exegetical Commentary on Amos and Hosea.* The International Critical Commentary. Edinburgh: T. & T. Clark, 1905.

Keil, C.F. "Minor Prophets." In *Commentary on the Old Testament in Ten Volumes.* Vol. 10. Reprint (25 vols. in 10). Grand Rapids: Wm. B. Eerdmans Publishing Co., 1982.

Kidner, Derek. *Love to the Loveless: The Message of Hosea.* The Bible Speaks Today. Downers Grove, Ill.: InterVarsity Press, 1981.

Mays, James Luther. *Hosea: A Commentary.* The Old Testament Library. Philadelphia: Westminster Press, 1969.

Pusey, E.B. *The Minor Prophets: A Commentary Explanatory and Practical.* 2 vols. Reprint. Grand Rapids: Baker Book House, 1950.

Riggs, Jack R. *Hosea's Heartbreak.* Neptune, N.J.: Loizeaux Brothers, 1983.

Tatford, Frederick A. *The Minor Prophets.* Vol. 1. Reprint (3 vols.). Minneapolis: Klock & Klock Christian Publishers, 1982.

Wolff, Hans Walter. *Hosea.* Translated by Gary Stansell. Philadelphia: Fortress Press, 1974.

JOEL

Robert B. Chisholm, Jr.

INTRODUCTION

Authorship and Date. This book is attributed to Joel son of Pethuel (1:1). Unlike most other prophetic books, no information is given in the opening verse that establishes the time limits of his prophetic ministry. Thus one is forced to rely on internal evidence in determining a date of authorship.

Scholars have proposed various dates, ranging from the ninth to the second centuries B.C. Three views are surveyed here.

1. An early preexilic date. Those who support an early date (ninth century B.C.) for Joel point to its position in the Hebrew Old Testament (between Hosea and Amos) and its references to Tyre, Sidon, Philistia, Egypt, and Edom as enemies (Joel 3:4, 19). Hobart Freeman writes, "The very naming of these particular nations is strong evidence for a preexilic date for the book, inasmuch as they were the early preexilic enemies of Judah, not the later nations of Assyria, Babylonia, and Persia" (*An Introduction to the Old Testament Prophets*. Chicago: Moody Press, 1968, p. 148; see also Gleason L. Archer, Jr., *A Survey of Old Testament Introduction*. Chicago: Moody Press, 1974, p. 305).

Both of these arguments lack weight. The canonical position of the book is inconclusive, especially when one notes that the Septuagint places it differently in the canon. Even the Old Testament prophets in the Babylonian period delivered oracles against the nations mentioned (cf. Jer. 46–47; 49:7-22; Ezek. 27–30; Zeph. 2:4-7). One who contends for a late preexilic date could argue that Joel 2 pictures the Babylonians vividly enough to make formal identification unnecessary to a contemporary audience well aware of their ominous presence on the horizon.

Some seek to support an early date for Joel by appealing to the type of government reflected in the prophecy (elders, 1:2; 2:16; and priests ruling, 1:9, 13; 2:17, in view of Joash's crowning at age seven) and to verbal parallels in other prophetic books (Archer, *A Survey of Old Testament Introduction*, pp. 304-5). The inconclusive nature of these arguments is apparent as they are also used by proponents of a late date.

Several details of the text (cf. esp. 3:2, 6) seem to militate against an early date (in Joash's reign) for the prophecy (cf. S.R. Driver, *The Books of Joel and Amos*, pp. 14-15).

2. A late preexilic date. The view that the book comes from the late preexilic period has much to commend it. If one dates the prophecy between 597 and 587 B.C. (with Wilhelm Rudolph, *Joel-Amos-Obadja-Jona.* Gütersloh: Gütersloher Verlagshaus Gerd Mohn, 1971, pp. 24-8), Joel 3:2b (with its reference to scattering God's people and dividing the land) would refer to the Babylonian invasion of 597 B.C. when 10,000 of Judah's finest men were deported (cf. 2 Kings 24:10-16). This would also account for Joel's references to the temple (Joel 1:9, 13; 2:17), for it was not destroyed until 586 B.C. (cf. 2 Kings 25:9). At that same time such a dating would mean that Joel 1:15 and 2:1-11 anticipated the final destruction of Jerusalem (which indeed came in 586 B.C.; cf. 2 Kings 25:1-21).

Joel's prophecy would then fit nicely with several other passages which relate the "day of the LORD" (or "day of the LORD's wrath" or "day of the LORD's anger") to that event (cf. Lam. 1:12; 2:1, 21-22; Ezek. 7:19; 13:5; Zeph. 2:2-3). Joel's description (Joel 2:1-11) would also coincide with Jeremiah's description of the Babylonians (cf. Jer. 5:17). The reference in Joel 3:6 to slave trade between the Phoenicians and Greeks (or Ionians) harmonizes well with the late preexilic period. Ezekiel also referred to this economic arrangement (Ezek. 27:13). Arvid S. Kapelrud shows that Ionian trade flourished in the seventh and early sixth centuries B.C. (*Joel Studies*, pp. 154-8).

Despite the attractiveness of this view, problems arise in relation to Joel 2:18-19. This passage seems to record God's mercy to Joel's generation, implying they truly repented (see comments on those verses). If so, such a sequence of events is difficult to harmonize with the historical record of Judah's final days. Second Kings 23:26-27 indicates that even Josiah's revival did not cause the Lord to relent.

3. A postexilic date. Four arguments are used to suggest a postexilic date:

(1) Joel 3:1-2, 17 refer, it is argued, to the destruction of Jerusalem and the Babylonian Exile. In this case the references to the temple in 1:9, 13; 2:17 apply to the second temple, completed by the returning exiles in 515 B.C.

(2) The "elders" (cf. 1:2; 2:16), rather than the king, appear as the leaders of the community. This is more consistent with the postexilic period (cf. Ezra 10:14).

(3) Joel quotes other prophets, including Ezekiel (cf. Joel 2:3 with Ezek. 36:35; Joel 2:10 with Ezek. 32:7; Joel 2:27-28 with Ezek. 39:28-29).

(4) The reference to Greek slave trade (Joel 3:6) reflects the postexilic period.

Against these arguments the following responses may be made:

(1) Joel 3:1-2, 17 could refer to the deportation of 597 B.C., not that of 586 B.C. (but as noted previously under "2. A late preexilic date," this view poses problems). Some attempt to explain the language of Joel 3:1-2, 17 in light of the events recorded in 2 Chronicles 21:16-17 (Archer, *A Survey of Old Testament Introduction*, p. 305). However, the captivity of the royal sons and wives recorded there hardly satisfies the language of Joel 3:2.

(2) Though the omission of any reference to the monarchy is curious, it can carry little weight for it is an argument from silence. Also elders were prominent in Judean society *before* the Exile (2 Kings 23:1; Jer. 26:17; Lam. 5:12, 14; cf. Kapelrud, *Joel Studies*, pp. 187-9).

(3) In the case of literary parallels with other prophetic passages, it is often difficult to determine in any given case who quoted from whom.

(4) Kapelrud has shown, as noted earlier, that Ionian slave trade flourished in the seventh century B.C.

In conclusion, it is impossible to be dogmatic about the date of the writing of Joel. The language of Joel 3:2b seems to favor a postexilic date. This verse suggests that nations in the future will be judged for having continued the policies of ancient Babylon in scattering the Israelites and dividing their land. Such a view is consistent with (but not proved by) several other observations (such as the reference to Phoenician-Ionian slave trade, the form of government implied in the book, and the literary parallels with other prophets). If one accepts a postexilic date, the references to the temple necessitate a date some time after 516 B.C. However, all this must remain tentative. Understandably, conservative scholars differ on the date of Joel.

Major Interpretive Problems

1. The nature of the army in 2:1-11. Some contend that the locust plague in Joel 1, or an even more severe wave of locusts, is described in 2:1-11. Several factors support this position:

(1) Literary parallels exist between chapters 1 and 2 (cf. 2:2, 11 with 1:6; and 2:3 with 1:19).

(2) Several details in 2:1-11 suggest that locusts are in view—the great numerical size of the invader (2:2, 5), the destruction of the land (2:3), the leaping and scaling ability of the invaders (2:5, 7), and the darkening of the sky (2:10).

(3) A literary association apparently exists between 2:11 ("His army") and 2:25 ("My great army," which is equated with the locusts).

(4) The "army" is compared to a literal army in 2:4-5, 7. The words "appearance of horses," "like cavalry," "like . . . chariots," "like a mighty army," "like warriors," and "like soldiers" seemingly imply that an actual army cannot be in view since an army is employed as the object of comparison (cf. Leslie C. Allen, *The Books of Joel, Obadiah, Jonah and Micah*, p. 29; and Driver, *The Books of Joel and Amos*, p. 28).

A more likely interpretation is that a literal foreign army is envisioned. The account is patterned after that of chapter 1, the army being described in locust-like terms in many respects (cf. Hans W. Wolff, *Joel and Amos*, p. 42). In this way the close relationship and continuity between the plague of chapter 1 and the army of chapter 2 is emphasized. Both were instruments of the Lord's judgment—one past, the other future. Locusts had come—more "locusts" were coming!

Several observations may be made in support of this position.

(1) The locust plague of chapter 1 was past; the invasion of 2:1-11 was still future from Joel's vantage point (cf. also 1:15). Thus the two accounts cannot deal with the same event (Wolff, *Joel and Amos*, pp. 6-7, 42). Joel 2:25, where the locusts are called the Lord's "great army," refers to the judgment in chapter 1. Its effects could be reversed but not averted. Joel 2:11 refers to a judgment which was yet future and thus *could* be averted (cf. 2:20). So 2:25 cannot be used to interpret 2:11, despite the aforementioned literary parallel. The literary association does not equate the two forces; it merely suggests their close relationship. The locusts were an "army" *sent* by the Lord (2:25); the "northern army" (2:20) would be *led* by Him (2:11).

(2) The army in 2:1-11 is called in 2:20 "the northern army" (lit., "the northerner"). Locusts usually attack Palestine from the south or southeast, not the north (though invasions from the north or northeast are not unknown; cf. Allen, *The Books of Joel, Obadiah, Jonah and Micah*, p. 88). The designation "northerner" more likely refers to a literal foreign army, since historical or eschatological armies are often described as invading Palestine from that direction (including Assyria, Isa. 14:25, 31; Babylon, Jer. 6:1, 22; 15:12; Ezek. 26:7; and Gog, Ezek. 38:15).

(3) The use of locust imagery in the description of the army in Joel 2 has parallels in the ancient Near East (cf. John A. Thompson, "Joel's Locusts in the Light of Near Eastern Parallels," *Journal of Near Eastern Studies* 14. 1955:52-5).

(4) The Deuteronomic curses closely associate locusts (Deut. 28:38-42) with invading armies (Deut. 28:25, 32-33, 36-37, 49-52). This association was natural since both devoured agricultural produce

(Deut. 28:33, 51; Isa. 1:7; Jer. 5:17). This accounts for the similarity between Joel 1:19 and 2:3. An Assyrian inscription from the time of Sargon II (722–705 B.C.) vividly illustrates the effects of an invading army on a land: "The city of Aniashtania . . . together with 17 cities of its neighborhood, I [Sargon] destroyed, I leveled to the ground; the large timbers of their roots I set on fire, their crops [and] their stubble I burned, their filled-up granaries I opened and let my army devour the unmeasured grain. Like swarming locusts I turned the beasts of my camps into its meadows, and they tore up the vegetation on which it [the city] depended; they devastated its plain" (D.D. Luckenbill, *Ancient Records of Assyria and Babylonia*. 2 vols. Chicago: University of Chicago Press, 1926–1927, 2:85).

The comparisons with an army (in 2:4-5, 7) do not necessarily mean that a literal army is precluded. Two explanations for the similes are possible. One is that an army, if portrayed under the figure of locusts, could be compared to an army, the simile in this case hinting at the reality behind the figure. In this regard Freeman states that "the prophet, with the recent plague of chapter 1 as the background, uses *that* calamity as the basis of his imagery" (*An Introduction to the Old Testament Prophets*, p. 152). E.W. Bullinger gives another explanation. He suggests that a simile sometimes implies "not merely a resemblance but the actual thing itself" (*Figures of Speech Used in the Bible*. Grand Rapids: Baker Book House, 1968, pp. 728-9). In such cases the Hebrew preposition k^e, "like, as," indicates that a specific object is in every respect like another object, meaning that the former partakes of the latter's nature. For example, Isaiah 1:7b states that Judah was "laid waste *as* when overthrown by strangers" (i.e., it was indeed overthrown by strangers). Similarly, Isaiah 1:8b notes that Jerusalem was "*like* a city under siege" (i.e., it *was* under siege, probably by Sennacherib). (However, k^e in Isa. 1:8-9 has its usual force: "like a shelter" and "like a hut," v. 8; and "like Sodom," v. 9.) Another example of the "identity" use of this preposition is in Joel 1:15, which states that "the day of the LORD . . . will come *like* a destruction from the Almighty" (i.e., it will indeed involve destruction brought about by God).

To summarize, the army in 2:1-11 is probably a literal northern army, described in locust-like terms to emphasize that it, like the locusts, was an instrument of the Lord which represented the culmination of the judgment initiated through the locust invasion.

2. *"The day of the LORD" in Joel.* Though the description of "the day of the LORD" was certainly influenced by traditions relating to the Lord's intervention in Israel's early wars (cf. Gerhard von Rad, "The Origin of the Concept of the Day of Yahweh," *Journal of Semitic Studies* 4. 1959:97-108), the expression itself is ultimately derived from the idea, prevalent in the ancient Near East, that a mighty warrior-king could consummate an entire military campaign in a single day (cf. Douglas Stuart, "The Sovereign's Day of Conquest," *Bulletin of the American Schools of Oriental Research* 220/21. December 1975, February 1976:159-64). So generally speaking, "the day of the LORD" is an idiom used to emphasize the swift and decisive nature of the Lord's victory over His enemies on any given occasion.

In the Old Testament "the day of the LORD" may refer to either a particular historical event or an eschatological battle which will culminate the present age. The following elements are associated with it:

(1) "The day of the LORD" sometimes involves the judgment of God's people, including the Northern Kingdom (at the hands of the Assyrians; cf. Amos 5:18, 20) and Judah (at the hands of the Babylonians; cf. Lam. 1:12; 2:1, 21-22; Ezek. 7:19; 13:5; Zeph. 2:2-3). Sometimes this judgment appears in the context of a more universal judgment on all nations (cf. Isa. 2:12; Zeph. 1:18).

(2) "The day of the LORD" often involves the judgment of foreign nations, including Babylon (at the hands of the Medes; cf. Isa. 13:6, 9), Egypt (at the hands of the Babylonians; cf. Jer. 46:10; Ezek. 30:3), Edom (cf. Isa. 34:8-9), and the eschatological northern coalition headed by Gog (Ezek. 39:8).

(3) "The day of the LORD" will bring purification and restoration for Israel (cf. Isa. 61:2; Mal. 4:5), but also intense suffering (Zech. 14:1-3).

"The day of the LORD," then, encompasses several specific past "days" or events (cf. A.J. Everson, "The Days of Yahweh," *Journal of Biblical Literature* 93. 1974:329-37). These include the destruction of the Northern Kingdom, the Babylonian Exile, Babylon's conquest of Egypt, and the fall of Babylon. These examples of the Lord's intervention in history prefigure that final time period when He will annihilate His enemies on a more universal scale and restore Israel (for a thorough development of this relationship between history and eschatology, see Isa. 13–27).

In Joel all three of the elements just listed appear in relationship to "the day of the LORD." Israel's judgment is threatened in Joel 1:15 and 2:1-11, Israel's deliverance is foreseen in 2:28-32, and universal judgment on the nations is depicted in chapter 3. Joel seemed to telescope events in his treatment of the Lord's "day." As he reported how his generation barely escaped "the day of the LORD," he envisioned Israel's ultimate deliverance from her enemies at the end of the age.

In discussing the day of the Lord in the end times, Joel focused on one major aspect of that "day," namely, the single event when the Lord will intervene in history to destroy His enemies and deliver His people Israel.

The day of the Lord, however, as other Scriptures show, will include other events:

(1) Before Israel's enemies will be destroyed they will plunder and devastate Israel (Zech. 14:1-2). This will be a time of anguish for Israel (Zeph. 1:7-18; cf. Dan. 12:1). Jesus called this time period (the Great Tribulation) a time of "great distress" (Matt. 24:21) for the nation.

(2) After the Lord will destroy His enemies (at Messiah's return) the day of the Lord will include a time of blessing for Israel (cf. Obad. 15 with Obad. 21), known as the Millennium.

(3) Then after the Millennium the day of the Lord will also include the destruction of the present heavens and earth and the making of new heavens and a new earth (2 Peter 3:10, 12-13).

Therefore, according to Scripture passages besides those in Joel, "the day of the LORD" will be a lengthy time period including both judgment and blessing. It will begin soon after the Rapture and will include the seven-year Tribulation, the return of the Messiah, the Millennium, and the making of the new heavens and new earth. Obviously this contradicts the view of some that at the end of the Great Tribulation the Rapture will occur and the day of the Lord will then begin (see comments on 1 Thes. 5:2; 2 Thes. 2:1-12 and the "Outline of End-Time Events Predicted in the Bible," between Ezek. and Dan.).

OUTLINE

COMMENTARY

I. Introduction (1:1)

1:1. As stated in the *Introduction*, the only fact given about **Joel** is that he was a **son of Pethuel.** The prophet indicated that his message was God's **Word,** but did not date his prophecy in 1:1 in the reign of any king of Judah or Israel (cf. comments under "Authorship and Date" in the *Introduction*).

II. The Locust Plague (1:2-20)

The opening chapter describes the effects of a severe locust plague which had swept over the land, destroying the agricultural produce on which both man and beast so heavily depended for survival. This disaster signaled an even worse calamity to come—the destructive day of the Lord.

A. An opening appeal (1:2-4)

1:2-3. The prophet opened his message with an appeal to **all who** were living **in the land,** headed by the **elders,** to consider the uniqueness and significance of the disaster which had come on them. The elders were civil leaders who played a prominent part in the governmental and judicial systems (cf. 1 Sam. 30:26-31; 2 Sam. 19:11-15; 2 Kings 23:1; Prov. 31:23; Jer. 26:17; Lam. 5:12, 14).

The rhetorical question in Joel 1:2b anticipates an emphatic negative response. Nothing in the experience of Joel's generation or that of their ancestors was able to match the magnitude of this recent locust plague. The unique event would be spoken of throughout coming generations (**your children . . . their children,** and **the next generation**).

1:4. The event in view was a massive invasion by **locusts** which completely destroyed the land's vegetation. Four terms are used for locusts here (**locust swarm,** *gāzām*; **great locusts,** *'arbeh*; **young locusts,** *yeleq*; and **other locusts,** *ḥāsîl*). Some have proposed that the four terms correspond to the locust's phases of development from the pupa to full-grown stages (e.g., Thompson, "Joel's Locusts in the Light of the Near Eastern Parallels," pp. 52-5). However, several problems attend this position (see Wolff, *Joel and Amos*, pp. 27-8). More likely, the terms are synonymous, used for variety's sake and to emphasize the successive "waves" of locusts in the invasion.

The threefold reference to the leftovers of one wave of locusts being devoured by the next emphasizes the thorough nature of the destruction. (For records of eyewitness accounts of locust plagues, see Driver, *The Books of Joel and Amos*, pp. 40, 89-93; George Adam Smith, *The Book of the Twelve Prophets*, 2:391-5, and John D. Whiting, "Jerusalem's Locust Plague," *National Geographic Magazine* 28. December 1915, pp. 511-50.)

B. A call to mourn (1:5-13)

Utilizing the form of a call to mourning, the prophet elaborated on the horrifying details and effects of the locust plague. This section contains four units (vv. 5-7, 8-10, 11-12, 13), each of which includes a call proper (vv. 5a, 8, 11a, 13a) followed by the reasons for sorrow (vv. 5b-7, 9-10, 11b-12, 13b). The personified land (or city?) as well as some of the groups most severely affected by the plague (drunkards, farmers, priests) were addressed.

1. DRUNKARDS SHOULD MOURN (1:5-7)

1:5-7. Drunkards were told to **weep** and **wail because** no **wine** would be available due to the destruction of the vineyards (v. 5; cf. vv. 7, 10, 12). Like a mighty **nation** an innumerable (**without number**) swarm of locusts had **invaded** the prophet's **land.** Their ability to devour was like that of **a lion,** which can rip and tear almost anything with its powerful **teeth** (likened to **fangs**). The locusts had destroyed the **vines** and **stripped** even the **bark** from the **fig trees. . . . leaving their branches white.** For photographs showing these effects of such an invasion, see *The Zondervan Pictorial Bible Dictionary*. Grand Rapids: Zondervan Publishing House, 1963, pp. 377, 435.

2. THE LAND SHOULD MOURN (1:8-10)

1:8. The grammatical form of **mourn** in verse 8 (fem. sing.) indicates that the addressee is neither the drunkards in verse 5 nor the farmers in verse 11 (both of which are addressed with masc. pl. forms). The land itself (cf. 2:18) or Jerusalem (called Zion in 2:1, 15, 23, 32) is probably addressed here, being personified as **a virgin** or young woman (cf. 2 Kings 19:21, "the virgin Daughter of Zion," and Lam. 1:15, "The virgin Daughter of Judah"). She was told to mourn bitterly, as a bride or bride-to-be would mourn over the unexpected death of the man to whom she was betrothed or married.

There is some debate over the meaning of the term translated "virgin" (*b'tûlâh*). If it refers to an actual virgin, then a betrothed woman, whose marriage had not been consummated, is in view. In this case the man could be called **the husband of her youth** because of the legally binding nature of betrothal. (Deut. 22:23-24 demonstrates that a betrothed woman could be referred to as both a "virgin" and a "wife.") However, possibly the word simply refers to a young woman (NIV marg.) regardless of her sexual status. If so, newlyweds are in view in Joel 1:8.

Sackcloth (cf. v. 13), a coarse, dark cloth, was worn in mourning rites as an outward expression of sorrow (cf. Gen. 37:34; 1 Kings 21:27; Neh. 9:1; Es. 4:1-4; Ps. 69:10-11; Isa. 22:12; 32:11; 37:1-2; Lam. 2:10; Dan. 9:3; Jonah 3:8).

1:9-10. The primary reason for mourning in this case was the plague's negative effect on the formal worship system (cf. v. 13). The destruction of the crops (**grain,** grapes, and olive **oil,** v. 10; cf. Hosea 2:22) had left **the priests** who served in **the house of the LORD** without the essentials for the daily **grain offerings** (*minhâh*), which included flour and oil (cf. Num. 28:5), **and drink offerings** (*nesek*), which included **wine** (cf. Ex. 29:40; Num. 28:7).

3. FARMERS SHOULD MOURN (1:11-12)

1:11-12. The **farmers** and **vine growers** also had reason to mourn since the fruit of their labor had been **destroyed.** These included grains (**wheat** and **barley**) and five kinds of fruits (grapes, figs, pomegranates, dates from **palm** trees, and apples). Because of the destruction of their crops they did not experience **the joy** of the harvest (cf. Ps. 4:7).

4. PRIESTS SHOULD MOURN (1:13)

1:13. The **priests** were told to take part (**wail**) in this lament because, as already noted (v. 9), the ingredients for certain daily **offerings** were no longer available. (On **sackcloth,** see comments on v. 8.)

C. A call to repentance (1:14)

1:14. The priests were told not only to mourn (v. 13) but also to **call a sacred assembly** at the temple for **all** the people. The nation was to **fast** and **cry out to the LORD.** Fasting was often associated with repentance (cf. 1 Sam. 7:6; Neh. 9:1-2; Jonah 3:5). The attitude that was to accompany this outward act is emphasized in Joel 2:12-17.

D. The significance of the plague (1:15-20)

1:15. This locust plague was meaningful because of its role as a harbinger of **the day of the LORD** (see comments under "Major Interpretive Problems" in the *Introduction*). The locusts had destroyed the crops in the fields (see esp. v. 10, where the Heb. verb *šādaḏ* is used twice and is trans. "ruined" and "destroyed" in the NIV). Similarly this coming **day** would be one of **destruction** (*šōḏ*, related to the verb *šāḏaḏ*) **from the Almighty** (*šadday*; cf. comments on Gen. 17:1; this divine name was probably used here because of its similarity in sound to the word *šōḏ*, "destruction").

It was natural for the prophet to see this plague as an ominous sign of an extraordinary event. In Egypt a locust plague (Ex. 10:1-20) had preceded the final plagues of darkness (Ex. 10:21-29; cf. Joel 2:2) and death (Ex. 11; 12:29-30). The Deuteronomic curses threatened locust plagues (Deut. 28:38, 42) in conjunction with exile and death (Deut. 28:41, 48-57, 64-68).

1:16-18. Verses 16-20 contain a detailed description of the aftermath of the locust plague. By again concentrating on the unique nature of this particular event, the prophet supported his contention that the destructive day of the Lord was around the corner (cf. "near" in v. 15).

The people were all too aware (**before their very eyes**) that their **food** supply, and with it all reason to rejoice, had disappeared (v. 16). Drought had appar-

ently set in as well, for the **seeds** had **shriveled. The clods** (v. 17) may be translated, "their (i.e., the farmers') shovels." When the farmers dug into the ground to investigate the absence of green life, the shovels uncovered seeds that had not germinated. With no harvest available, **the storehouses** and **granaries** had been left to deteriorate. The domesticated animals (**cattle. . . . herds . . . flocks of sheep**) were **suffering** from starvation.

1:19-20. The prophet, who clearly identified with his suffering nation (cf. "my" which occurs three times in vv. 6-7), cried out to the LORD in his anguish. He compared the locusts to a **fire** (in both vv. 19 and 20) which destroys everything in its path. Even **the streams** had **dried up,** causing the dehydrated **wild animals** to **pant** for **water.**

III. The Coming Day of the Lord (2:1-11)

In this section the theme in 1:15 is more fully developed as details about the approaching day of the Lord are given. Joel spoke of the Lord as a mighty Warrior-King leading His powerful army into battle. If one posits a preexilic date, the Assyrians or Babylonians may be in view (cf. comments under "Authorship and Date" in the *Introduction*). Both are pictured in the Old Testament as instruments of the Lord's judgment (cf. Isa. 10:5-15 on Assyria; and Jer. 27:4-11; 51:20-25; Hab. 1:5-12 on Babylon). Other Bible scholars, who hold a preexilic date, say the army in Joel 2:1-11 is eschatological, possibly equated with the army in verse 20; 3:9, 12; Daniel 11:40; and Zechariah 14:2.

If a postexilic date is taken, it is uncertain to which nation the section alludes. The army would then take on a more indefinite, apocalyptic character (cf. Wolff, *Joel and Amos,* pp. 7, 42), perhaps representing Israel's enemies in general.

As noted under "Major Interpretive Problems" in the *Introduction,* this invading force is described in locust-like terms to establish continuity with Joel 1. At the same time the comparisons to a literal army (2:4-5, 7) hint at the reality in view.

Within this section, four units are discernible (vv. 1-2, 3-5, 6-9, 10-11), the last three being introduced by "before them" (vv. 3, 10) or "at the sight of them" (v. 6). Verses 1-2 correspond to verses 10-11 thematically, forming a bracket around the section. These two units focus on the fearful response caused by the approaching army (vv. 1b, 10a), the darkness which accompanies it (vv. 2a, 10b), and its extraordinary size (vv. 2b, 11a). Two of these motifs appear (in reverse order) at the center of the section. Verse 5c refers to the army's great size and verse 6 to the response of fear by people from many nations. Two motifs appear in verses 3-5a: the army is like a destructive fire (v. 3), and it charges relentlessly ahead (vv. 4-5a). Both ideas are repeated in verses 5b and 7-9, respectively.

A. The nearness of the Lord's army (2:1-2)

2:1. The section begins with a call of **alarm,** emphasizing the nearness of the invader. **The trumpet** (*šôpār*) was a ram's horn, blown by a watchman to alert the people of great danger (cf. Jer. 4:5-6; Ezek. 33:2-6). The appropriate response was fear (**tremble;** cf. Amos 3:6), especially in this instance since **the day of the LORD** was **coming. Holy hill** (cf. Pss. 2:6; 3:4; 15:1; 24:3; 78:54; Dan. 9:16, 20; Obad. 16; Zeph. 3:11) refers to the temple mount.

2:2a. The day of the Lord is described as **a day of darkness and gloom . . . of clouds and blackness** (cf. Zeph. 1:15). The reference to intense darkness following the locust plague of Joel 1 recalls Exodus 10, where the same order of events appears. Darkness and clouds—often associated with the Lord in His role as the mighty victorious Warrior (cf. Deut. 4:11; 5:22-23; Pss. 18:9, 11; 97:2)—here symbolize both judgment and destruction (cf. Jer. 13:16; Ezek. 30:3, 18; 32:7-8; 34:12; Amos 5:18-20; Zeph. 1:15).

2:2b. The innumerable size of the invading force receives special attention. Like the rays of the morning sun (**dawn**) its hosts will cover the horizon. This **army** is said to be more awesome than any that had ever come or would come. The hyperbolic language may echo Exodus 10:14. If so, it emphasizes that the "locusts" of Joel 2:1-11 would be even more overwhelming than those that overran Egypt. Something even worse than the Egyptian plagues was about to engulf the land!

B. The destructive power of the Lord's army (2:3-5)

2:3. The invaders, like the locusts in Joel 1, are compared to a **fire** that consumes everything in its path (cf. 1:19). Fruitful lands, whose lush growth was comparable to **the Garden of Eden** (cf. Gen. 2:8-9), would become **a desert waste.** The reality behind this figure is the devastating effect of a huge, invading army on the land (cf. Deut. 28:49-51; Isa. 1:7; Jer. 5:17; also note the Assyrian text cited under "Major Interpretive Problems" in the *Introduction*). The words **nothing escapes them** may allude to Exodus 10:5, 15.

2:4-5. In the context of the overall comparison to locusts, the invading force is likened to an **army** (v. 5b) consisting of **horses . . . cavalry,** and **chariots** (vv. 4-5a). Such an association is facilitated by three facts: (1) The heads of locusts and horses are similar in appearance. The German and Italian words for "locust" literally mean "hay-horse" and "little horse," respectively (Wolff, *Joel and Amos*, p. 45, n. 46; cf. also Driver, *The Books of Joel and Amos*, p. 52). (2) Both locusts and human armies advance swiftly. (3) The locusts' buzzing wings resemble the sound of chariot wheels (for accounts of the sounds made by locusts, see Driver, *The Books of Joel and Amos*, p. 52).

Nothing can impede the invaders' swift approach. They seemingly **leap over the mountaintops.** The Hebrew verb for "leap over" (*rāqad*) suggests both flying locusts and speeding chariots (on the latter; cf. Nahum 3:2, where *rāqad* is trans. "jolting").

C. The relentless charge of the Lord's army (2:6-9)

2:6. The response to this awesome army was widespread terror, for it involved **nations. In anguish** (*ḥûl*) literally refers to writhing, as when a woman is overcome by labor pains (cf. *ḥûl* in Isa. 26:17; Jer. 4:31; Micah 4:10). This same response is seen elsewhere in contexts where the Lord comes to do battle (cf. Ex. 15:14; Deut. 2:25; Pss. 77:16; 97:4; Isa. 13:8; Hab. 3:10).

2:7-9. Once more the relentless advance of the army is emphasized (cf. vv. 4-5a). Again the language applies both to locusts (cf. Driver, *The Books of Joel and*

Amos, pp. 54-5; and Keil, "Joel," in *Commentary on the Old Testament in Ten Volumes,* 10:193, n. 1) and to a literal army. Both advance in orderly fashion (vv. 7-8a), **plunge through defenses** (v. 8b), and enter walled cities and homes. As elsewhere in this section (cf. v. 6), Joel seemingly alluded to Exodus 10.

D. The invincibility of the Lord's army (2:10-11)

2:10-11. The army's approach is accompanied by cosmic disorder. The entire world, from **earth** below to **sky** above, quivers (cf. **shakes** and **trembles**) before the thunderous battle cry of the divine Commander. This cosmic response is a typical poetic description of the Lord's theophany as Warrior (cf. Jud. 5:4; Pss. 18:7; 77:18; Isa. 13:13; Joel 3:16). The darkening of the heavenly bodies (cf. 2:2, 30; 3:15) is another characteristic of the Lord's day (cf. Isa. 13:10; Ezek. 32:7; Zech. 14:6-7; also note Isa. 34:4). The prophet concluded with a rhetorical question (**Who can endure it?**), to suggest that no one can endure this **great** and **dreadful** day (cf. Mal. 3:2; 4:5). If the army in Joel 2:1-11 was in Joel's **day,** it may foreshadow the army in chapter 3.

IV. Renewed Call to Repentance (2:12-17)

Before such an invincible army the nation's only hope was to turn immediately ("even now," v. 12) to the Lord in repentance. This section contains two formal appeals for repentance (vv. 12-14, 15-17). The first concludes with a motivational section (introduced by "for," vv. 13b-14).

A. An appeal for a sincere change of heart (2:12-14)

1. THE APPEAL (2:12-13A)

2:12-13a. The Lord Himself urged the people to repent with genuine sincerity (cf. **with all your heart** and **rend your heart and not your garments**) accompanied by **fasting and weeping and mourning.** Repentance is the desired outcome of the Lord's judgments (cf. Deut. 4:30; 30:1-2; Hosea 3:4-5; Amos 4:6-11).

2. THE MOTIVATION (2:13B-14)

2:13b. A recognition of the nation's relationship to **the LORD** her **God** and of His gracious nature should have motivated His people to repent. The expression "the LORD your God" was well known to Israel (this phrase occurs 263 times in Deut.) and testified to the covenantal relationship between God and the nation. The words **gracious and compassionate, slow to anger and abounding in love** (*ḥesed,* "loyal love") recall Exodus 34:6 (cf. Neh. 9:17; Pss. 103:8; 143:8; Jonah 4:2), where the same affirmation preceded the renewal of the covenant after the sin of the golden calf. Because God's character is merciful, **He often relents from sending calamity.** Again the golden calf episode is recalled. On that occasion Moses begged the Lord to "relent" and "not bring disaster" on His people (Ex. 32:12). The Lord responded favorably to his request (Ex. 32:14).

2:14. The words **who knows** testify to the Lord's sovereignty in the matter (cf. 2 Sam. 12:22; Jonah 3:9). Even if sinful Israel repented, she could not presume on God's mercy as if it were something under their control which He had to grant automatically. They could only hope that **He** would **turn and have pity** (cf. Mal. 3:7) by averting the disaster (cf. Joel 2:20) and restoring their crops (cf. v. 25). Agricultural **blessing** would mark a reversal of the curse that had come on them (in the form of the locusts; cf. Deut. 28:38-42) and would make it possible for **grain . . . and drink offerings** to be presented again (cf. Joel 1:9, 13).

B. An appeal for national involvement (2:15-17)

The second part of this call to repentance is an appeal to the nation to congregate for a formal ceremony of lamentation and prayer.

2:15. The opening words of verse 1, **Blow the trumpet in Zion,** are repeated. The fear elicited by the sound of the watchman's trumpet (v. 1) was to prompt another sound of the ram's horn, this time calling the people to **a holy fast** and **sacred assembly** (cf. 1:14). For the blowing of a ram's horn was also used to call religious convocations (cf. Lev. 25:9; Ps. 81:3).

2:16. The entire worshiping community (**assembly**) was to **gather,** from the oldest (**elders**) to the youngest (**those nursing at the breast**). Not even newlyweds were exempted (cf. Deut. 24:5).

2:17. The priests were to lead the

ceremony by weeping **before the** L ORD in the court of the temple (i.e., **between the temple porch and the** bronze **altar** of burnt offering; cf. Ezek. 8:16) and by offering a prayer for deliverance.

The prayer was to include a twofold petition: (a) **spare** (ḥûs, "pity or have compassion on"; cf. Jonah 4:11 for the same word, where the NIV renders it "be concerned about") and (b) **do not make,** a question aimed at motivating **God** to action. The concern of the latter was God's reputation. If Israel, God's own **inheritance** (cf. Deut. 4:20; 9:26, 29; Pss. 28:9; 33:12; 78:62, 71; 79:1; 94:14; Micah 7:14, 18), were to become **an object of scorn** (cf. Joel 2:19), the nations might erroneously conclude that He lacked the power and/or love to save those who belonged to Him (cf. Ex. 32:12; Deut. 9:26-29; Ps. 79:4, 10).

The rendering, **a byword among the nations,** though not the only way to translate the Hebrew here (cf. KJV, "that the heathen should rule over them"), is favored by the poetic structure (cf. the parallel phrase "object of scorn"; also see Jer. 24:9).

V. Forgiveness and Restoration (2:18-27)

This section marks a turning point in the argument of the book. It describes the divine response (v. 18) to the nation's repentance and records the Lord's comforting words to His people (vv. 19-27). The effects of the locust plague (chap. 1) are reversed (see esp. 2:25), and the threatened invasion (vv. 1-11) is averted (v. 20).

The divine message of verses 19-27 displays the following chiastic structure:
a. Verse 19
   b. Verse 20a
      c. Verses 20b-24
   *b.*¹ Verse 25
*a.*¹ Verses 26-27

Parts *a* and *a*¹ correspond as both parts promise a restoration of crops and a cessation of shame. Parts *b* and *b*¹ both refer to an elimination of enemies (or their effects). Part *c* contains two cycles (vv. 20b-21b; 21c-24), the second of which repeats and/or expands the three elements of the first (cf. v. 20b with v. 21c; v. 21a with v. 22; and v. 21b with vv. 23-24).

A. The Lord's gracious response described (2:18)

The relationship between verses 18-19a and the preceding context is problematic. The NIV translation (cf. also NASB, KJV), which employs the future tense ("will be jealous," etc.), interprets these verses as a promise conditional on the people's positive response to the call to repentance in verses 12-17. However, that interpretation of the Hebrew verbal forms in this context is unlikely (cf. S.R. Driver, *A Treatise on the Use of the Tenses in Hebrew.* 3rd ed. Oxford: Clarendon Press, 1892, p. 95; Keil, "Joel," in *Commentary on the Old Testament in Ten Volumes,* 10:200). The forms seem better translated with the past tense (cf. NIV marg., NASB marg., RSV) and the text understood as a description of the Lord's turning to His people in Joel's time. This would, of course, imply they had responded positively to the appeal of verses 12-17 (cf. Allen, *The Books of Joel, Obadiah, Jonah and Micah,* p. 86).

2:18. In response to this genuine repentance, **the** L ORD **was jealous for His land and** took **pity on His people.** The Lord's jealousy is His passionate loyalty toward what is His, a loyalty that prompts Him to lash out against anything that would destroy it (cf. Isa. 26:11; Ezek. 36:5-6; 38:19; Zech. 1:14; 8:2). The military protection described in Joel 2:20 is in view here.

B. The Lord's promise of restored agricultural blessing (2:19-27)

2:19-20a. The Lord's promise began with a proclamation that the agricultural produce (**grain, new wine, and oil**) destroyed by the locusts (cf. 1:10) would be restored. He then announced that His people would **never again** be **an object of scorn to the nations** (cf. 2:17). Similarly (vv. 26-27) He promised they would "never again . . . be shamed."

The seemingly unconditional tone of these statements is problematic if verses 18-19a describe a historical event in Joel's day. Whether one posits a preexilic or postexilic date for the writing of Joel, history shows that Israel, after Joel's day, often did become an object of scorn. Perhaps the best solution to this difficulty is to understand that at least this aspect of the promise is eschatological in its ultimate fulfillment. Joel's prophecy deals with Israel's future apart from the chronological gaps which one sees so readily in retrospect. Consequently prophecies pertaining to his own generation are merged here with those that await future realization. This is common in Old Testament prophecies (e.g., Isa. 9:6-7; 61:1-2; Zech. 9:9-10).

The Lord next announced that the threat described in Joel 2:1-11 would be averted (v. 20a). He would turn against the very army He had been bringing against His disobedient people (cf. v. 11), driving it into the desert (**a parched and barren land**) and the seas (**the eastern sea and the western sea,** probably the Dead Sea and the Mediterranean Sea; cf. Zech. 14:8).

The carcasses' **stench** would permeate the air. As in Joel 2:1-11, the language, though alluding to a literal army (cf. Isa. 34:3; Amos 4:10), applies to locusts as well. Eyewitness accounts tell how dead locusts, having been driven into the sea and then washed ashore, gave out a foul odor (cf. Driver, *The Books of Joel and Amos,* pp. 62-3; Smith, *The Book of the Twelve Prophets,* 2:411).

As noted in the *Introduction,* the designation **northern army** (lit., "northerner") suggests that a literal army is ultimately in view. If "the northerner" is yet future (eschatological), the army is possibly the army in Joel 3:9, 12; Daniel 11:40; and Zechariah 14:2. But if the reference is strictly historical, any precise identification of the army is precluded by the uncertainty surrounding the date of authorship. So in this case it would not be clear to what extent, if any, Joel 2:20 was historically fulfilled in Joel's day. If the invasion threatened in 2:1-11 had not actually begun, the language of verse 20 need not refer to a historical event. It would simply be a vivid and concrete way of saying that the destruction planned by the Lord had been averted at the last moment.

2:20b-21b. The NIV understands the last line of verse 20 as a statement about the Lord (cf. v. 21b; in this case *kî* in v. 20b is taken as an emphatic assertion: **Surely**). Other translations (KJV, NASB, RSV) join the words to the preceding context, making the army the subject (cf. NASB, "For it has done great things"). The insolent pride of the invader would then be in view (cf. Isa. 10:5-19 for a similar view). However, the NIV reading has much to commend it, especially the structural correspondence it produces (cf. note on Joel 2:18-27).

In the first two lines of verse 21 the personified **land,** which had been stripped of its produce (cf. 1:10), is encouraged to fear no longer but to **be glad and rejoice.**

2:21c-24. Each of the three elements in verses 20b-21b is repeated and/or expanded in these verses. The repeated affirmation that **the LORD has done great things** is followed by the expanded charges, **be not afraid** (v. 22) and **be glad and rejoice** (v. 23).

The first charge was directed to the **wild animals,** which had been affected so adversely by the locust invasion and accompanying drought (cf. 1:20). The effects of that judgment would be completely reversed. **The open pastures** (cf. 1:19) would again bring forth grass and vegetation. **The trees** and vines would again **yield their** fruit (cf. 1:7, 12, 19).

The second charge (2:23) was directed to the inhabitants **of Zion** (i.e., Jerusalem; cf. v. 1) who were earlier instructed to grieve over the destruction wrought by the locusts (cf. 1:5, 8, 11, 13). They could now "rejoice" because **the LORD** was prepared to restore fertility to their fields. As promised in Deuteronomy 11:14, the **autumn and spring rains** would come on schedule (in September-October and March-April), producing a bountiful harvest.

The phrase translated **a teacher for righteousness** (Joel 2:23) is better rendered, "in righteousness the autumn rains" (cf. NIV marg., NASB, KJV; see Allen, *The Books of Joel, Obadiah, Jonah and Micah,* pp. 92-3, n. 26; and Kapelrud, *Joel Studies,* p. 115). "Teacher" (*môreh*) is translated "autumn" later in the verse (cf. also Ps. 84:6). "For righteousness" would then probably mean, "according to justice" (i.e., in harmony with the covenantal principle that obedience is justly rewarded with agricultural blessing; see Kapelrud, *Joel Studies,* p. 116).

The abundance of the harvest will be evidenced by **the threshing floors** and **wine** and oil **vats** being filled to capacity (Joel 2:24).

2:25-27. Verse 25 nicely summarizes the overriding theme of verses 19-24. The effects of **the locusts** would be completely reversed. Speaking as though compelled by legal obligation, **the LORD** promised to **repay** (*šillēm*; cf. its use in Ex. 22:1; 2 Kings 4:7) the nation for the crops which His **great army** of locusts (cf. Joel 1:4) had devoured.

The agricultural abundance (2:26a) would prompt the people to **praise the name** (i.e., the revealed character) of their covenant **God,** who had **worked wonders for** them (v. 26b). This last expression placed the restoration of agricultural blessing in the mainstream of God's miraculous historical deeds on behalf of His people (cf. Ex. 3:15; 15:11; 34:10; Josh. 3:5; Jud. 6:13; Ps. 77:14).

The nation would also acknowledge (**know**) His active presence and His rightful place as their God (Joel 2:27). The words **I am in Israel** (lit., "I am in the midst of Israel") recall the Pentateuchal references to God being "among" (or, "in the midst of") His people (cf. Num. 11:20; 14:14; Deut. 7:21). The frequently used expression **you will know that . . . I am the LORD your God** also originated in the Pentateuch (cf. Ex. 6:7; 16:12). The association of that expression with the Lord's exclusive claim to be Israel's God (**there is no other**) reminds one of Deuteronomy 4:35, 39. Through these allusions to earlier traditions, the Lord affirmed that His relationship to His people was just as vital then as it had been in Moses' day.

VI. Promises of a Glorious Future (2:28–3:21)

This concluding section of the Book of Joel develops more fully the eschatological element of the Lord's promise (cf. comments on 2:19-20a; "afterward" in 2:28; "in those days" in 3:1; "in that day" in 3:18). The deliverance experienced by Joel's generation foreshadowed that of the end times. The day of the Lord, so narrowly averted by Joel's repentant contemporaries, will come in full force against the enemies of God's people (perhaps foreshadowed by the northern army of 2:20). The promises of 2:19-27 will find their ultimate and absolute fulfillment as the Lord intervenes on Israel's behalf (2:28-32), decisively judges the nation's enemies (3:1-16a, 19), and securely establishes His people in their land (3:1, 16b-18, 20-21).

A. Spiritual renewal and deliverance (2:28-32)

2:28-29. The Lord announced that His "day" (v. 31) would be accompanied by an outpouring of His **Spirit on all people** (lit., "all flesh"). The following context indicates that "all people" refers more specifically to all inhabitants of Judah (cf. the threefold use of **your** in v. 28, as well as the parallel passages in Ezek. 39:29; Zech. 12:10). This will be true regardless of age, gender, or social class (Joel 2:29 is better trans. "and even on the male and female servants"; cf. NASB).

At that time recipients of the divine **Spirit** will exercise prophetic gifts (**will prophesy . . . will dream dreams,** and **will see visions**) which in the past had been limited to a select few (cf. 1 Sam. 10:10-11; 19:20-24). This is probably an allusion to Numbers 11:29, where Moses, responding to Joshua's misguided zeal after an outpouring of the divine Spirit on the 72 elders (cf. Num. 11:24-28), declared, "I wish that all the LORD's people were prophets and that the LORD would put His Spirit on them!" This extensive outpouring of the Spirit will signal the advent of divine blessing (contrast 1 Sam. 3:1, where the absence of prophetic visions characterized a period of sin and judgment).

2:30-31. The great and dreadful day of the LORD will be preceded by ominous signs (**wonders**) of impending judgment (cf. v. 10; see also Ezek. 32:6-8 for literary parallels). **Blood and fire and billows of smoke** suggest the effects of warfare. The turning of **the moon to blood** refers in a poetic way to its being darkened (cf. the parallel line, **The sun will be turned to darkness,** and Joel 2:10; 3:15). Though such phenomena will signal doom for God's enemies, His people should interpret them as the precursors of their deliverance (cf. Matt. 24:29-31; Mark 13:24-27; Luke 21:25-28).

2:32. At this time of universal judgment, **everyone who calls on** (i.e., invokes) **the name of the LORD will be saved** (i.e., delivered from physical danger; cf. comments on Rom. 11:26). "Everyone" does not refer to all people, but the Spirit-empowered people of God mentioned in Joel 2:28-29. In Romans 10:13 Paul related this passage to Gentile (as well as Jewish) salvation, but he was suggesting a mere analogy, not a strict fulfillment of Joel 2:32, which pertains to Israel.

In the day of the Lord Jerusalem will be a place of refuge for **the survivors whom the LORD calls.** This remnant with whom the Lord initiates a special relationship (for the sense of "call" here, see Isa. 51:2) should probably be equated with the group described in Joel 2:28-29, 32a (cf. Wolff, *Joel and Amos,* pp. 68-9), though some (e.g., Driver, *The Books of Joel and Amos,* pp. 68-9) see this as referring to returning exiles.

On the day of Pentecost the Apostle Peter quoted Joel 2:28-32 in conjunction with the outpouring of the Holy Spirit (cf. Acts 2:17-21). His introductory words (cf. Acts 2:16, "this is what was spoken by the Prophet Joel") may seem to indicate that he considered Joel's prophecy as being completely fulfilled on that occasion. However, it is apparent that the events of that day, though extraordinary, did not fully correspond to those predicted by Joel.

In attempting to solve this problem one must recognize that in the early chapters of Acts the kingdom was being offered to Israel once more. Peter admonished the people to repent so that they might receive the promised Spirit (cf. Acts 2:38-39 where he alludes to Joel 2:32). Shortly thereafter Peter anticipated "times of refreshing" and the return of Christ in response to national repentance (cf. Acts 10:19-21). Not until later did Peter come to understand more fully God's program for the Gentiles in the present age (cf. Acts 10:44-48). When he observed the outpouring of the Spirit on the day of Pentecost he rightly viewed it as the first stage in the fulfillment of Joel's prophecy. Apparently he believed that the kingdom was then being offered to Israel and that the outpouring of the Holy Spirit signaled the coming of the Millennium. However, the complete fulfillment of the prophecy (with respect to both the extent of the Spirit's work and the other details) was delayed because of Jewish unbelief (for further discussion see comments on Acts 2:16-21; 3:19-21).

B. The judgment of the nations (3:1-16)

1. JUDGMENT IS ANNOUNCED (3:1-8)

Verses 1-8 are a judgment speech against the nations. They contain accusatory elements (vv. 2b-3, 5-6), as well as an announcement of judgment (vv. 1-2a, 4, 7-8).

3:1-3. In the future day of the Lord Judah and her enemies will be carefully distinguished. The Lord will **restore the fortunes of Judah and Jerusalem,** in fulfillment of Moses' promise (cf. Deut. 30:3). At the same time God will **gather** the **nations** for **judgment.**

The site of the judgment will be **the Valley of Jehoshaphat,** mentioned only in Joel 3:2, 12. Whether such a geographical site was known by this name in ancient Israel is not certain. Some scholars suggest it is a yet-future valley, to be formed by the splitting of the Mount of Olives at the Messiah's return (Zech. 14:4). At any rate, the importance of the name is not in its geographical location, but in its meaning, "the Lord judges."

The reason for God's judgment is the nations' treatment of His covenant people (**My inheritance**; cf. comments on Joel 2:17), **My people.** The nations had **scattered** the Lord's **people,** sold them as slaves to distant lands, and **divided up** His **land.** "Scattered" (from *pāzar,* "to disperse") seems to refer to the Babylonian Exile (cf. Jer. 50:17). Even though the Lord Himself assigned the land to Israel's enemies (cf. Lam. 5:2; Micah 2:4), He still held these nations guilty for their failure to recognize His sovereignty and for their cruel treatment of His **people.**

3:4-6. In verses 4-8 the Lord spoke directly to the Phoenicians (**Tyre and Sidon**) and the Philistines, two groups that profited economically from Judah's demise (cf. Ezek. 25:15; 28:20-24). The Lord identified Himself with His people (note **Me** in Joel 3:4) and denied that these nations had any justification for their actions (this is the force of the rhetorical questions in v. 4).

God then announced that He would repay them for their offenses (v. 4b). These are specified as robbery (v. 5) and slave trade (v. 6). Since neither the Phoenicians nor the Philistines are mentioned as robbing the temple treasuries during the destruction of **Jerusalem** (cf. 2 Kings 25), Joel 3:5 may refer to Israel's wealth in general, not to the temple (cf. Wolff, *Joel and Amos,* p. 78).

Phoenician and Philistine involvement in slave trade (v. 6) is mentioned elsewhere (cf. Amos 1:6, 9). According to Kapelrud, the Greeks mentioned here are actually Ionians ($y^e w \bar{a} n \hat{i} m$), who populated the coasts of Asia Minor (*Joel Studies*, p. 154). Ionian commerce was at its peak in the seventh and sixth centuries B.C. Ezekiel 27:13, 19 mentions Tyrian trading arrangements (including slaves) with the Ionians (or Greece). The trading recalled in Joel may have occurred in conjunction with Judah's fall to the Babylonians.

3:7-8. The divine judgment on these nations would be perfectly appropriate. The Lord would **rouse** His dispersed people and put them in the position of slave traders. *They* would sell the **sons and daughters** of the Phoenicians and Philistines as slaves **to the Sabeans** (cf. Job 1:13-15), an Arabian people noted for their commercial activities (cf. "Sheba" in Ezek. 27:22-23).

The judgment threatened here probably was fulfilled, at least in part, in the fourth century B.C. Allen explains, "The people of Sidon were sold into slavery by Antiochus III in 345 B.C., while the citizens of Tyre and Gaza were enslaved by Alexander in 332 B.C." (*The Books of Joel, Obadiah, Jonah and Micah*, p. 114). Perhaps Jews were involved in some of the transactions.

In the context (cf. Joel 3:1) the passage also carries an eschatological significance which any historical fulfillment merely prefigures. From the eschatological perspective Philistia and Phoenicia represent all of Israel's enemies (much as do Moab in Isa. 25:10-12 and Edom in the Book of Obad.). At that time God's people will gain ascendancy over their enemies (cf. Isa. 41:11-12; Amos 9:12; Obad. 15-21; Micah 7:16-17; Zeph. 2:6-7).

2. A CALL TO WAR: JUDGMENT IS DESCRIBED (3:9-16)

In this section the judgment of the nations is described. It contains three subunits: (a) a call to the participants (the nations and the Lord) to assemble their forces (vv. 9-11), (b) a statement by the Lord (vv. 12-13), and (c) a description of the battle site (vv. 14-16).

3:9-11. Unidentified messengers are instructed to issue a call of **war** to **the nations** (cf. "all nations" in Isa. 34:2; Obad. 15; Zech. 14:2). The nations are to **beat** their farming implements **into** weapons (Joel 3:10; contrast Isa. 2:4; Micah 4:3) and **assemble** for battle (Joel 3:11a; cf. Zech. 12:9). The LORD is urged

to **bring down** His **warriors.**

3:12-13. The Lord Himself now repeated the summons of the preceding verses, instructing **the nations** to enter **the Valley of Jehoshaphat** (cf. v. 2). Employing agricultural imagery, He then commanded His warriors to destroy His enemies. The first command (**Swing the sickle, for the harvest is ripe**) probably compares judgment to harvesting grain (cf. Isa. 17:5; Rev. 14:15). The second (**Come, trample the grapes**) compares the annihilation of the enemies to treading grapes in a **winepress** (cf. Isa. 63:1-6; Rev. 14:18-20). The underlying reason for the nations' demise is that **their wickedness is great.**

These verses (Joel 3:12-13) plainly indicate that the judgment mentioned in this chapter will actually take the form of divine warfare against Israel's enemies. So the event described here should be equated with Armageddon (cf. Rev. 14:14-20; 16:16; 19:11-21), rather than the judgment of the nations prophesied in Matthew 25:31-46.

3:14-16. An innumerable host will be assembled **in the valley of decision** (also called the Valley of Jehoshaphat, vv. 2, 12). Here the divine Judge's verdict will be executed on the nations. As in earlier passages (cf. 2:10, 31) the darkening of the heavenly bodies (3:15) serves as an ominous sign of the approaching **day of the LORD** (v. 14). **The LORD will** then emerge from His sanctuary in **Jerusalem** in theophanic splendor (v. 16; cf. Amos 1:2). His thunderous battle cry (cf. **will roar . . . and thunder**) will produce cosmic disorder (cf. Joel 2:10-11; Rev. 16:16, 18). He will then demonstrate that He is Israel's **Refuge** (cf. Pss. 46:1; 62:8; Isa. 25:4) and **Stronghold** (cf. Pss. 9:9; 18:2; 27:1; 37:39; 43:2; 144:2).

C. *Israel's ultimate restoration* (3:17-21)

3:17. After this awesome display of divine power, Israel will recognize (**know**) that **the LORD** truly dwells among them (cf. 2:27). **Jerusalem,** the site of the Lord's holy sanctuary (**My holy hill;** cf. comments on 2:1) **will be holy** in the sense that it will **never again** be defiled by foreign invaders (cf. Isa. 52:10-11; Nahum 1:15).

3:18a. At that time (**in that day,** when Messiah will reign over His people in the Millennium) the land will be a virtual paradise, enabling the Lord's people to enjoy His agricultural blessings to the fullest. The grape harvest will be so bountiful that **wine will** seemingly **drip** from **the mountains. Milk** will be just as plentiful. It too was a sign of prosperity; Canaan was described as a land "flowing with milk and honey" (see comments on Ex. 3:8; cf. Ex. 13:5; 33:3; Lev. 20:24; also note Isa. 55:1). The seasonal streams (**ravines,** or wadis) will no longer **run** dry. This abundance of wine, milk (implying the existence of extensive herds), and **water** represents a complete reversal of the effects of the locust plague (cf. Joel 1:5, 18, 20).

3:18b. A fountain will flow out of the LORD's house, the Jerusalem temple. Similar imagery is employed in Ezekiel 47:1-12 and Zechariah 14:8. This fountain (and the stream it produces) will be a tangible reminder that the Lord is the Source of the land's fertility (cf. Ezek. 47:8-10, 12). **The valley of acacias** is probably that portion of the Kidron Valley which runs through the arid wilderness to the Dead Sea (cf. Ezek. 47:8).

3:19-20. In contrast with the God-given abundance of Judah (v. 18), the lands of her enemies (represented by **Egypt** and **Edom**) will be infertile (**desolate** and **a desert waste**). The reason for this severe judgment is their mistreatment of **the people of Judah.** Israel's enemies are guilty of **violence** and of shedding **innocent blood.**

If the Book of Joel was written in the ninth century B.C., the reference to Egypt in Joel 3:19 may allude to her acts of violence committed during the invasion of the Egyptian Pharaoh Shishak (ca. 926 B.C.; cf. 1 Kings 14:25-26). But if the Book of Joel was written in the late preexilic or postexilic period, the invasion of Pharaoh Neco II may be in view (609 B.C.; cf. 2 Kings 23:29-35). Obadiah also referred to Edomite sins against the Lord's people (cf. Obad. 9-14).

The security and prosperity portrayed in Joel 3:17-18 will never again be interrupted. **Judah** and Jerusalem **will be inhabited forever** (cf. Ezek. 37:25; Amos 9:15; Zech. 14:11).

3:21. This verse has posed problems for interpreters. The NIV suggests that the first part of the verse is a declaration that Judah will be forgiven (**I will pardon**). Against this is the fact that the sin of **bloodguilt** on the part of Judah is not mentioned elsewhere in the Book of Joel. A better reading is that of the NASB (following the LXX), which relates the passage to the judgment on the nations (cf. v. 19) by portraying the Lord as the Avenger of Judah's blood ("I will avenge their blood"). Another option is to translate, "And shall I leave their bloodshed [the Judean blood shed by the nations] go unpunished? I will not" (cf. Allen, *The Books of Joel, Obadiah, Jonah and Micah,* p. 117; for a similar rhetorical question and response using the same Hebrew verb, *niqqâh;* cf. Jer. 25:29).

The book ends with an affirmation of the Lord's presence **in Zion** (cf. Joel 3:17). It is this fact, above all else, which will assure the nation's glorious future, portrayed in verses 17-21.

BIBLIOGRAPHY

Ahlström, G.W. *Joel and the Temple Cult of Jerusalem.* Supplements to *Vetus Testamentum.* Vol. 21. Leiden: E.J. Brill, 1971.

Allen, Leslie C. *The Books of Joel, Obadiah, Jonah and Micah.* The New International Commentary on the Old Testament. Grand Rapids: Wm. B. Eerdmans Publishing Co., 1976.

Driver, S.R. *The Books of Joel and Amos.* The Cambridge Bible for Schools and Colleges. Cambridge: University Press, 1915.

Feinberg, Charles L. *The Minor Prophets.* Chicago: Moody Press, 1976.

Kapelrud, Arvid S. *Joel Studies.* Uppsala: A.B. Lundequistska Bokhandeln, 1948.

Keil, C.F. "Joel." In *Commentary on the Old Testament in Ten Volumes.* Vol. 10. Reprint (25 vols. in 10). Grand Rapids: Wm. B. Eerdmans Publishing Co., 1982.

Price, Walter K. *The Prophet Joel and the Day of the Lord.* Chicago: Moody Press, 1976.

Smith, George Adam. *The Book of the Twelve Prophets.* 2 vols. Rev. ed. New York: Harper & Brothers, n.d.

Smith, John M.P.; Ward, William H.; and Bewer, Julius A. *A Critical and Exegetical Commentary on Micah, Zephaniah, Nahum, Habakkuk, Obadiah and Joel.* The International Critical Commentary. Edinburgh: T. & T. Clark, 1974.

Tatford, Frederick A. *The Minor Prophets.* Vol. 1. Reprint (3 vols.). Minneapolis: Klock & Klock Christian Publishers, 1982.

Thompson, John. A. "The Date of Joel." In *A Light unto My Path: Old Testament Studies in Honor of Jacob M. Myers.* Philadelphia: Temple University Press, 1974.

Watts, John D.W. *The Books of Joel, Obadiah, Jonah, Nahum, Habakkuk and Zephaniah.* The Cambridge Bible Commentary. Cambridge: Cambridge University Press, 1975.

Wolff, Hans Walter. *Joel and Amos.* Translated by Waldemar Janzen, S. Dean McBride, Jr., and Charles A. Muenchow. Philadelphia: Fortress Press, 1977.

AMOS

Donald R. Sunukjian

INTRODUCTION

The Prophet. Before Amos began prophesying, he had been one of the "shepherds" of Tekoa, a town in the hill country of Judah about 10 miles south of Jerusalem. The word used for "shepherds" in 1:1 is not the usual Hebrew word *rō'eh*, but the rare word *nōqēḏ*, suggesting instead "sheep breeders." The only other Old Testament occurrence of *nōqēḏ* is in 2 Kings 3:4 where Mesha, king of Moab, is said to have engaged in sheep-breeding on such a scale that he was able to supply the king of Israel with 100,000 lambs and the wool of 100,000 rams. Amos evidently managed or owned large herds of sheep and goats, and was in charge of other shepherds.

In Amos 7:14 the prophet further described himself as "a shepherd" and as one who "took care of sycamore-fig trees." This word for "shepherd," *bôqēr*, occurs only here in the Old Testament, and describes a "herdsman" or "cattleman."

Besides overseeing his livestock operations, Amos was also occupied in growing sycamore fruit, presumably as a sideline. The sycamore-fig tree was a broad heavy tree, 25 to 50 feet high, which produced a fig-like fruit three or four times a year. The sycamore did not grow in the heights of Tekoa, but only in the warmer lowlands, as the Jordan Valley and the fertile oases by the Dead Sea. Both of these places were near enough to Tekoa for Amos to supervise the taking care of the trees (7:14)—a technical term that describes the process of slitting or scratching the forming fruit so that some juice runs out, allowing the rest of the fig to ripen into a sweeter, more edible fruit.

The three terms together indicate that Amos, as a breeder, rancher, and farmer, was a substantial and respected man in his community.

The Times. Amos lived in times of material prosperity. The long reigns of Uzziah (790-739 B.C.) in Judah and of Jeroboam II (793-753 B.C.) in Israel (1:1) had brought stability, prosperity, and expansion to the two kingdoms.

The Southern Kingdom had subdued the Philistines to the west (see comments on 1:6; 6:2), the Ammonites to the east, and the Arab states to the south. Uzziah's political influence was felt as far as Egypt (cf. 2 Chron. 26:1-15).

The Northern Kingdom, to whom Amos' message was directed, was at the zenith of its power. Aram had not recovered from her defeat in 802 B.C. by Assyria under Adad-Nirāri III (811–783 B.C.). Assyria, however, had been unable to press her advantage further. A succession of inept rulers and the troublesome Urarteans to her north kept Assyria preoccupied until the accession of Tiglath-Pileser III in 745 B.C. Given a free hand, Jeroboam II was able to extend his borders northward into Aramean territory and to reclaim Israel's lands in Transjordan (cf. 2 Kings 14:23-29; Amos 6:13).

Because of the control this gave Israel over the trade routes, wealth began to accumulate in her cities. Commerce thrived (8:5), an upper class emerged (4:1-3), and expensive homes were built (3:15; 5:11; 6:4, 11). The rich enjoyed an indolent, indulgent lifestyle (6:1-6), while the poor became targets for legal and economic exploitation (2:6-7; 5:7, 10-13; 6:12; 8:4-6). Slavery for debt was easily accepted (2:6; 8:6). Standards of morality had sunk to a low ebb (2:7).

Meanwhile religion flourished. The people thronged to the shrines for the yearly festivals (4:4; 5:5; 8:3, 10), enthusiastically offering their sacrifices (4:5; 5:21-23). They steadfastly maintained that their God was with them, and considered themselves immune to disaster (5:14, 18-20; 6:1-3; 9:10).

The Date. For a period of probably no more than a year, Amos gave God's message to the Northern Kingdom. His ministry was two years before a notable earthquake (1:1; cf. Zech. 14:5). Josephus connects the quake with the events of 2 Chronicles 26:16-20 (*Antiquities of the Jews* 9. 10. 4). Archeological excavations at Hazor and Samaria have uncovered evidence of a violent earthquake in Israel about 760 B.C.

The Message. Amos, a man from Judah, was called to prophesy in Israel. This was possibly around 762 B.C. (see comments under "The Date"). The message God gave him was primarily one of judgment, though it ended with words of hope.

The Lord God Almighty, the sovereign Ruler of the universe, would come as a Warrior to judge the nations that had rebelled against His authority. Israel in particular would be punished for her covenant violations against Him.

Though the nation would be destroyed, God will preserve a repentant remnant from among the people. One day this remnant will be restored to political prominence and covenant blessing. And then, through them, God will draw all nations to His name.

OUTLINE

I. Prologue (1:1-2)
 A. The author and date (1:1)
 B. The theme (1:2)
II. The Roar of Judgment (1:3–2:16)
 A. Judgment against the nations (1:3–2:5)
  1. Judgment against Damascus (1:3-5)
  2. Judgment against Gaza (1:6-8)
  3. Judgment against Tyre (1:9-10)
  4. Judgment against Edom (1:11-12)
  5. Judgment against Ammon (1:13-15)
  6. Judgment against Moab (2:1-3)
  7. Judgment against Judah (2:4-5)
 B. Judgment against Israel (2:6-16)
  1. The broken covenant (2:6-8)
  2. The spurned grace (2:9-12)
  3. The resulting judgment (2:13-16)
III. The Reasons for Judgment (chaps. 3–6)

 A. The first message (chap. 3)
  1. The unique relationship (3:1-2)
  2. The inevitable judgment (3:3-8)
  3. The unparalleled oppression (3:9-10)
  4. The coming catastrophe (3:11-15)
 B. The second message (chap. 4)
  1. Economic exploitation (4:1-3)
  2. Religious hypocrisy (4:4-5)
  3. Refusal to repent (4:6-13)
 C. The third message (5:1-17)
  1. Description of certain judgment (5:1-3)
  2. Call for individual repentance (5:4-6)
  3. Accusation of legal injustice (5:7)
  4. Portrayal of a sovereign God (5:8-9)
  5. Accusation of legal injustice (5:10-13)
  6. Call for individual repentance (5:14-15)
  7. Description of certain judgment (5:16-17)
 D. The fourth message (5:18-27)
  1. Description of certain judgment (5:18-20)
  2. Accusation of religious hypocrisy (5:21-22)
  3. Call for individual repentance (5:23-24)
  4. Accusation of religious hypocrisy (5:25-26)
  5. Description of certain judgment (5:27)
 E. The fifth message (chap. 6)
  1. Their boastful complacency (6:1-3)
  2. Their luxurious indulgence (6:4-7)
  3. The complete devastation (6:8-14)
IV. The Results of Judgment (7:1–9:10)
 A. The swarming locusts (7:1-3)
 B. The devouring fire (7:4-6)
 C. The testing plumb line (7:7-17)
  1. The vision (7:7-9)
  2. The incident (7:10-17)
 D. The culminating fruit (chap. 8)
  1. The vision (8:1-3)
  2. The results (8:4-14)
 E. The avenging Lord (9:1-10)
  1. The inescapable sword (9:1-4)
  2. The universal Sovereign (9:5-6)
  3. The impartial shifting (9:7-10)

V. The Restoration after Judgment
(9:11-15)
A. Political renewal (9:11)
B. National purpose (9:12)
C. Prosperity, peace, and
permanence (9:13-15)

COMMENTARY

I. Prologue (1:1-2)

A. The author and date (1:1)

1:1. These are **the words of Amos, one of the shepherds of Tekoa,** a town directly south of Jerusalem. These sayings or messages resulted from **what he saw** (i.e., his visions; cf. comments at 7:12) **concerning Israel.** They were delivered to the Northern Kingdom **two years before the earthquake,** during the prosperous reigns of **Uzziah** in **Judah and Jeroboam** in **Israel.** (For a discussion of the prophet, the date, and Kings Uzziah and Jeroboam, see the *Introduction.*)

B. The theme (1:2)

1:2. Amos' theme is that Israel and the other nations were about to be violently judged for their sins. He pictured **the LORD** as a lion who had roared and begun His attack (cf. 3:4, 8; Jer. 25:30; Hosea 5:14; 11:10; 13:7). A lion's terrifying roar paralyzes its victim with fear, making it helpless before the lion's charge. Then the pounce, the tearing, and death are inevitable.

God's roar would have a similar paralyzing and withering effect. As the reverberating sound advanced **from Zion,** that is, **Jerusalem** (cf. Amos 6:1; see comments on Zech. 8:3) against the nations, it would shrivel and scorch the earth. To the south, **the pastures** near Bethlehem would **dry up** as the terrifying roar passed through Judah and continued toward Gaza (Amos 1:6-8), Edom (vv. 11-12), and Moab (2:1-3). Northward, the fertile south and west slopes of Mount **Carmel**—some of Israel's choicest farmland (Isa. 35:1-2; also note Isa. 33:9; Nahum 1:4)—would wither and die as the heat wave of God's wrath moved on to engulf Damascus (Amos 1:3-5), Tyre (vv. 9-10), and Ammon (vv. 13-15). Everywhere the sound passed, moisture would evaporate, the land would turn brown, and drought would crack the earth. With

pastures dried up, sheep would die and shepherds would suffer economic loss. And with crops withered farmers would face severe hardships.

The picture of drought suggests the reason for the Lord's angry roar—the nations had violated their covenants with God. The treaty or covenant between a suzerain lord and a vassal people was common in Near Eastern societies. In exchange for the suzerain's protection and provision, the vassal would pledge loyalty and obedience. The terms of the covenant, spelled out and mutually agreed on, were binding on both parties. Failure of the vassals to abide by the terms would cause the curses or punishments written in the treaty to descend on them. The curse of drought appears frequently as a punishment for covenant disobedience (cf. Deut. 28:20-24 in the Mosaic Covenant; for other ancient treaties see James B. Pritchard, ed., *Ancient Near Eastern Texts Relating to the Old Testament.* 3rd ed. Princeton: Princeton University Press, 1969, pp. 539, 660).

Those who heard Amos' words would understand that the sovereign Lord of the universe was about to judge them for their covenant violations. (On the question of the covenant relationship of the surrounding Gentile nations to God, see comments on Amos 1:3.) The Northern tribes of Israel in particular would perceive this charge of covenant rebellion as they heard that the Lord's roar was originating from Zion, that central holy abode from which they had revolted. (On the meaning of Zion, see comments on Lam. 1:4; Zech. 8:3.)

II. The Roar of Judgment (1:3–2:16)

The Lord's roar was first against seven nations surrounding Israel, then against Israel herself. A murmur of approval might have rippled among Amos' hearers as they heard the denunciation of Aram (1:3-5) and Philistia (vv. 6-8), Israel's historic and bitter enemies. But when the focus shifted to Tyre (vv. 9-10), a sometime ally (1 Kings 5), then in turn to Edom (Amos 1:11-12), Ammon (vv. 13-15), and Moab (2:1-3), blood relatives of Israel (cf. Gen. 19:36-38; 25:29-30), the encircling review might have seemed "a noose of judgment about to tighten round their throats" (J.A. Motyer, *The Day of the Lion,* p. 50). With the mention finally of Judah (2:4-5), Israel's own "brother," the conclusion was inescapable—God's judgment would be impartial. For the locations of these and other places in Amos see the map "Israel and Surrounding Nations in the Days of the Prophets," between Song of Songs and Isaiah.

For each nation the pronouncement of doom follows the same pattern: (a) a general declaration of irrevocable judgment, (b) a naming of the specific violation which caused the judgment, and (c) a description of God's direct and thorough punishment.

A. Judgment against the nations (1:3–2:5)

1. JUDGMENT AGAINST DAMASCUS (1:3-5)

1:3. The general declaration of irrevocable judgment occurs through the repeated phrase, **For three sins of . . . even for four, I will not turn back My wrath** (cf. vv. 6, 9, 11, 13; 2:1, 4, 6). The use of a number followed by the next higher number is frequent in the Old Testament (Job 5:19; Ps. 62:11-12; Prov. 30:15-16, 18-19, 21-23, 29-31). Usually the higher number is enumerated in detail, with special emphasis given the final item. Here Amos cited only the last of the crimes, the one which had finally gone beyond God's patience. Meir Weiss argues that the phrase should be translated, "For three sins of . . . *even* for four," as a poetic way of expressing the number seven, "a clearly typological number which symbolizes completeness" ("The Pattern of Numerical Sequence in Amos 1–2, A Re-examination," *Journal of Biblical Literature* 86. 1967:418). If this is correct, it means irrevocable judgment was pronounced on each nation for its full and complete sin. In the case of the surrounding nations, only the final and culminating sin was named. But for Israel, the complete list of seven was given (Amos 2:6-8, 12—one in v. 6, two in v. 7, two in v. 8, two in v. 12). Israel's panic would likewise be sevenfold in the day God judged them (2:14-16).

The cause of judgment for each nation was its "sins," its covenant violations. The word for "sin" (*peša'*) means "rebellion" or "revolt," and was used in secular treaties to describe a vassal's disobedience of the terms of a covenant

(1 Kings 12:19; 2 Kings 1:1; 3:5, 7; 8:22; Prov. 28:2). The Old Testament prophets also used the noun *peša'* or the verb *pāša'* in denouncing Israel's rebellion against God's covenant with her (Isa. 1:2, 28; 46:8; 66:24; Jer. 2:8; Hosea 7:13; 8:1; Micah 1:5, 13).

Amos specifically viewed the sins of Judah (Amos 2:4-5) and Israel (2:6-16; cf. 3:14; 4:4; 5:12) as violations of the Mosaic Covenant. She had failed to observe the terms of God's Law.

But not only Israel had sinned against a covenant with God. The Gentile nations also were guilty of *peša'*—rebellion against a divinely established and universally recognized agreement. Apparently Amos had in mind their rebellion against God's universal covenant with humanity made at the time of Noah (Gen. 9:5-17). In exchange for God's suzerain promise never again to destroy the earth with a flood (Gen. 9:11), the vassal peoples were to refrain from shedding blood because disregard for human life is an assault on God's own image in man (Gen. 9:5-6). Human life, rather than being destroyed or curtailed, was to multiply and increase on the earth (Gen. 9:7). This mutual agreement, whereby God would preserve the earth and people would honor and extend human life, was called an "everlasting covenant" (Gen. 9:16).

This is the covenant, Amos charged, that the Gentile nations had rebelled against. By their acts of barbarism (Amos 1:3), their wholesale deportations of slave populations (vv. 6, 9), their unnatural and stubborn hatreds (v. 11), their sickening atrocities (v. 13), and their desecrations of the dead (2:1), they had broken the covenant that forbade such inhuman acts. Because of these sins, the earth's sovereign Lord declared, "I will not turn back My wrath."

Similarly Isaiah (Isa. 24:4-6; 26:20-21) said that God would bring a "curse" of drought "to punish the people of the earth" because they had "broken the everlasting covenant" by shedding blood. As the New Testament confirms, though Gentiles may not have received the spoken or written Law, the requirements of human decency are nevertheless known to them, and their own accusing conscience tells them when they violate God's standard (Rom. 2:14-15).

The culminating sin of **Damascus,** the capital of Aram, is that **she threshed Gilead** (also mentioned in Amos 1:13) of Transjordanian Israel **with sledges having iron teeth.** Threshing (cutting and separating the grain from the husks) was done on a threshing floor by pulling a heavy sledge over the grain. The sledge was a pair of roughly shaped boards, bent upward at the front, studded with iron prongs or knives. The reference here could be quite literal, describing a method of torturing prisoners; it is also a figure for harsh and thorough conquest (cf. Isa. 41:15; Micah 4:13; Hab. 3:12). Aram's armies had raked across Gilead, slicing and crushing it as though it were grain on a threshing floor. This Israelite territory east of Jordan had suffered greatly during constant battles with the Arameans, particularly during the time of Hazael (841–801 B.C.) and his son and successor Ben-Hadad III (Amos 1:4; cf. 2 Kings 8:7-12; 10:32-33; 13:3-7; note the reference to "threshing" in 2 Kings 13:7).

1:4-5. In the judgment on each of the first seven nations God is pictured as a suzerain Lord who has brought his armies to punish a vassal city for its revolt. The attack begins in each case with a **fire** that would eventually **consume the** walls and/or **fortresses** of the city and leave it a smoldering ruin (vv. 4, 7, 10, 12, 14; 2:2, 5). In punishing Damascus God declared He would smash the bar of the city gate and **break down the gate,** stripping the city of its defenses. He would **destroy the** rebel **king who** reigned over the wicked and proud nations. **Valley of Aven** and **Beth Eden** may refer to other regions of Aram, Baalbek and Bit-Adini. More likely, they are derogatory references to the area and palace of **Damascus,** meaning "Valley of Wickedness" and "House of Pleasure." **The house** (dynasty) of **Hazael** would be terminated, and the Arameans would be exiled (cf. 1:15) back to their place of origin, a Mesopotamian site called **Kir.** In essence, this punishment would be a complete reversal of Aram's proud history. God, who had originally brought them out of Kir (9:7), would send them back, after obliterating all they had achieved. This judgment was carried out by the Assyrians under Tiglath-Pileser III in 732 B.C. (cf. 2 Kings 16:7-9).

2. JUDGMENT AGAINST GAZA (1:6-8)

1:6. In verses 6-8 four of the five cities comprising the Philistine pentapolis are mentioned—**Gaza,** Ashdod, Ashkelon, and Ekron. The omission of the fifth, Gath, may be due to its ruined condition at the time of Amos because of the batterings of Hazael in 815 B.C. and Uzziah in 760 B.C. (cf. 2 Kings 12:17; 2 Chron. 26:6; Amos 6:2). The Philistines' crime against humanity was that they captured **whole communities** in slave raids **and sold them** for commercial profit. Defenseless people were treated as mere objects and auctioned off in the slave markets of **Edom,** from which they were shipped to other parts of the world (cf. Joel 3:4-8).

1:7-8. For this sin, the Philistine cities would be completely annihilated—buildings, king, and people. God would **turn** His **hand against** them **till the last of the Philistines** was **dead.** This judgment was partially fulfilled in the subjugation of the Philistines to the Assyrians later in the eighth century B.C., and more completely during the Maccabean period (168–134 B.C.). **Sovereign Lord** (*'ăḏōnāy Yahweh*) occurs 19 times in Amos, but only 5 other times in all the Minor Prophets (Obad. 1; Micah 1:2; Hab. 3:19; Zeph. 1:7; Zech. 9:14). That title stresses both His lordship and His covenant relationship with His people.

3. JUDGMENT AGAINST TYRE (1:9-10)

1:9. The sin of **Tyre,** Phoenicia's leading city, was even more callous than Gaza's. Not only did **she** sell **whole communities of captives to Edom** (cf. v. 6), but she did so in violation of **a treaty of brotherhood,** a protective covenant between two partners. If Israel was the injured partner, the reference is probably to the pact between Solomon and Hiram (1 Kings 5) or perhaps to the later relations established through the marriage of Ahab and Jezebel (1 Kings 16:29-31).

1:10. Tyre's punishment is similar to that described in verse 7. Alexander the Great overran the city of **Tyre** in 332 B.C. after besieging it for seven months. Six thousand people were slain outright, 2,000 were crucified, and 30,000 were sold as slaves. Tyre had sold Israelites to Edom as captives; later many Tyrians became captives.

4. JUDGMENT AGAINST EDOM (1:11-12)

1:11. The sin **of Edom** was his persistent and unfeeling hostility against **his brother.** "Brother" could refer to some unknown treaty partner (cf. v. 9). But the frequent references in the Old Testament to Edom's brotherhood with Israel suggest that this refers to the physical kinship between the two nations that began with Esau and Jacob (Gen. 25:29-30; Num. 20:14; Deut. 2:4; 23:7). At some point in Israel's history Edom relentlessly **pursued his** defeated brother **with a sword** (cf. Obad. 10). Without any natural feelings of **compassion,** Edom let **his anger** rage **continually,** like a beast tearing its captured prey. He brooded over his **fury,** nourishing it so it **flamed unchecked.**

1:12. Because of this unnatural and vindictive hatred, God would **send fire upon Teman** and **Bozrah.** Teman was Edom's largest southern city; Bozrah was her fortress stronghold in the north. The two cities thus stand for the whole nation under God's wrath. Some scholars, however, say Teman was in the north near Bozrah. At any rate, both were major Edomite cities (cf. references to Teman in Jer. 49:7, 20; Ezek. 25:13; Obad. 9; Hab. 3:3). Edom was subjugated by the Assyrians in the eighth century B.C., turned into a desolate wasteland by the fifth century B.C. (Mal. 1:3), and overtaken by the Nabateans, an Arabian tribe, around 400–300 B.C.

5. JUDGMENT AGAINST AMMON (1:13-15)

1:13. The terrible cruelty of **Ammon** was that **he ripped open the pregnant women of Gilead** (cf. "Gilead" in v. 3). This atrocity, sometimes a feature of ancient warfare (cf. 2 Kings 8:12; 15:16; Hosea 13:16), was designed to terrorize and decimate an enemy. The Ammonites executed this crime against defenseless women and unborn children, not for self-preservation, but simply **in order to extend** their **borders.**

1:14-15. Because of this heartlessness God would **set fire to the walls** (cf. vv. 7, 10) **of Rabbah,** Ammon's capital city. **Amid** the engulfing flames the inhabitants would hear the **war cries** (cf. 2:2) of the attackers as they fell on their victims. **Violent winds,** symbolizing God's own awesome power (cf. Ps. 83:15; Jer. 23:19; 30:23), would lash at the city. And the enemy would take both **king** and **officials** (cf. Amos 2:3) **into exile** (cf. 1:5). This judgment was fulfilled through the Assyrian conquest under Tiglath-Pileser III in 734 B.C.

6. JUDGMENT AGAINST MOAB (2:1-3)

2:1. In ancient times much importance was placed on a dead man's body being peacefully placed in the family burial site, so that he could be "gathered to his fathers" and find rest in the grave. To rob, disturb, or desecrate a grave was an offense of the highest order. Many surviving tomb inscriptions utter violent curses against anyone who would commit such an outrage (G.A. Cooke, *A Textbook of North-Semitic Inscriptions.* Oxford: At the Clarendon Press, 1903, pp. 26-7, 30-2; Pritchard, *Ancient Near Eastern Texts Relating to the Old Testament,* p. 327). **Moab,** in a war against Edom (perhaps the incident referred to in 2 Kings 3:26-27), drove their opponents back to their own territory, opened the royal graves, and **burned, as if to lime, the bones of Edom's king.** This sacrilege was so thorough that bone ashes became as fine and white as powdered chalk.

2:2-3. Though this was not a crime against Israel, it was nevertheless a sin of rebellion (*pešaʾ;* see comments on 1:3) against the sovereign LORD of the universe, an assault against His own image in people. For such contempt and defilement, God would militarily annihilate **Moab.** A **fire** would **consume . . . Kerioth,** perhaps an alternate name for the capital Ar (cf. Num. 21:28; Isa. 15:1). In the **tumult** of battle, with **war cries** (cf. Amos 1:14) **and the blast of the trumpet** signaling her doom, **Moab** would **go down**—the people, **ruler,** and **all . . . officials** (cf. 1:15). Moab, like Ammon, fell to the Assyrians under Tiglath-Pileser III.

7. JUDGMENT AGAINST JUDAH (2:4-5)

2:4. The Gentile nations had rebelled against the "everlasting covenant" God made with them at the time of Noah (Gen. 9:5-17). But Judah's **sins** (*pešaʾ*) were against the Mosaic Covenant. They had **rejected the Law of the LORD.** They had not observed the **decrees,** or stipulations, of His unique agreement with them. Instead of holding to His objective truth, they let themselves be **led astray by** the same **false gods** which had deceived many of **their ancestors.** The word for false god is *kāzāḇ*, "a lie or something deceptive." The idols were deceptive for they were unable to help the people. In Deuteronomy God constantly warned the Israelites not to follow false gods (Deut. 6:14; 7:16; 8:19; 11:16, 28; etc.).

2:5. The punishment for this faithlessness would be the destruction of the nation, fulfilled in 586 B.C. when Nebuchadnezzar, after a lengthy siege, broke through Jerusalem's defenses, slaughtered the royal family, burned the temple, the palace, and all houses in the city, and deported almost the entire population to Babylon (2 Kings 25:1-12).

B. Judgment against Israel (2:6-16)

Having shown that the Lord is sovereign over the universe and holds all nations accountable for their rebellion against Him, Amos now addressed the Northern tribes of Israel. His message was that God would also judge them, because they had broken His covenant, despite His gracious acts on their behalf.

1. THE BROKEN COVENANT (2:6-8)

Israel had violated the Mosaic Covenant in several ways, including social injustice (v. 6b), legal perversion (v. 7a), sexual sin (v. 7b), abuse of collateral (v. 8a), and idolatry (v. 8b).

2:6. The first charge against the Israelites is that they callously sold into slavery the poor who could not pay their debts (cf. 2 Kings 4:1-7). Honest people **(the righteous)** who could be trusted to repay eventually, were sold **for the silver** they owed. The desperately poor **(the needy)** were enslaved because they could not pay back the insignificant sum they owed **for a pair of sandals** (cf. Amos 8:6). These sandals might refer to the custom of giving one's sandals as a kind of mortgage deed or title to confirm the legal transfer of land (cf. Ruth 4:7). The meaning would then be that the poor were being sold for either money or land. Such hardheartedness against Israel's *own* people, not against a foreign nation, was rebellion against God's covenant which called for generosity and openhandedness toward the poor (Deut. 15:7-11).

2:7a. Amos' second accusation against Israel was that legal procedures were being perverted to exploit **the poor.** Contrary to the covenant commands (Ex.

23:6; Deut. 16:19), the courts had gone into collusion with the creditors and were denying **justice to the oppressed.** This oppression was so terrible and painful it was like trampling **on** their **heads.**

2:7b. The third crime is that **father and son** were having sexual intercourse with **the same girl,** either a temple prostitute or a servant taken as a concubine (Ex. 21:7-9; Lev. 18:8, 15). By such promiscuity the men were showing their disregard for the Lord of the covenant and were profaning (i.e., treating as common) His **holy name.** God's "name" (see comments on Ex. 3:13-15) spoke of His character and His unique commitment to Israel. To flaunt His commandments openly was to mock His character and to disdain His special place in their lives.

2:8a. Fourth, God's Law placed restrictions on items which could be taken as collateral. Millstones were not to be taken since they were needed for grinding grain and thus were essential to sustaining life (Deut. 24:6). The cloak of a poor man was not to be kept as a pledge overnight (Ex. 22:26-27; Deut. 24:10-13; also note Job 22:6); a widow's garment could not be **taken in pledge** at all (Deut. 24:17). Yet the people openly and flagrantly were lying **down** with the forbidden **garments,** going so far in their contempt for the Law as to spread them at the sacrificial feasts by **every altar** (cf. 1 Sam. 9:12-13).

2:8b. Fifth, Israel had rebelled against the most basic covenant stipulation of all—they were worshiping other gods (as Judah was doing, v. 4). The **wine** they had unjustly extracted from the poor **as fines** was being raised in honor to a heathen **god.**

2. THE SPURNED GRACE (2:9-12)

2:9. Instead of announcing the punishment immediately after the accusation, as was done in the judgments against the seven other nations, God heightened Israel's guilt by setting her rebellion against the backdrop of His own gracious acts toward them. Israel's existence as a nation was only because of His intervention. By themselves they could never have conquered the Canaanites. **The Amorite** (cf. v. 10; note comments on Gen. 14:13-16), as the most formidable, stands for all the nations in Canaan at the time of the Conquest (cf.

Gen. 15:16-21; Josh. 24:8-15). The inhabitants of the land were the greatest of men, **tall as the cedars and strong as the oaks** (cf. Num. 13:28-33; Deut. 1:26-28). Yet God uprooted them, totally destroying them, both **fruit above** and **roots below.**

2:10. The Exodus from **Egypt** and God's preservation of Israel during **40 years in the desert** evidenced His kindness and good intentions toward her. (On **the Amorites** see comments on v. 9.)

2:11. God also **raised up** spiritual leaders for the nation. **Prophets from among** their own **sons** conveyed His words to them, and **Nazirites,** who consecrated themselves by vows for limited periods of time (cf. Num. 6:1-21), portrayed the depth of commitment that all Israel was supposed to share.

2:12. But despite these gracious acts Israel added two more sins to her account. She intimidated **the Nazirites** (cf. v. 11) to break their vows and **drink wine, and** she **commanded the prophets not to prophesy** (cf. 7:10-16). In so doing Israel revealed her own lack of commitment to God and her unwillingness to hear His Word.

3. THE RESULTING JUDGMENT (2:13-16)

2:13-16. Because of these sins God would not turn back His wrath (v. 6). He would **crush** rebellious Israel **as a cart crushes when loaded with grain.** There would be no hope in the devastating day of battle. Out of the entire army, none would be able to save his life—not (a) **the swift,** (b) **the strong,** (c) **the warrior,** (d) **the archer,** (e) **the fleet-footed soldier,** or (f) **the horseman.** So overpowering would be the onslaught that **even** (g) **the bravest warriors** would drop their weapons and cloaks in a futile attempt to **flee.** This wartime panic was sevenfold just as Israel's sins were seven (vv. 6b-8, 12).

The history of the Northern Kingdom came to an end only a few decades later with the Assyrian Captivity in 722 B.C. (2 Kings 17:1-23).

The roar of judgment ended. **The LORD,** the Sovereign of the earth, had spoken. He would come as a mighty Warrior to judge the surrounding nations for their rebellion against His authority. He would judge Israel too, because she also had broken His covenant despite His grace toward her.

III. The Reasons for Judgment (chaps. 3–6)

After announcing the judgment that would come against the Northern Kingdom, Amos gave a series of five messages to explain more fully the reasons for God's judgment. The first three messages are marked by the phrase "Hear this word" (3:1; 4:1; 5:1); the last two begin with "Woe to you" (5:18; 6:1). Each message describes in more detail the religious, legal, political, and social rebellion which had brought God's wrath against the nation. Within the messages are appeals for repentance and instructions as to how individuals could escape the awful calamity that was coming.

A. The first message (chap. 3)

In this message Amos declared that Israel would be punished because of her unique relationship with God. Her judgment was inevitable because of her unparalleled oppression of people. The message was addressed initially to both Israel and Judah (vv. 1-2), but then it was primarily directed to the Northern Kingdom (cf. vv. 9, 12).

1. THE UNIQUE RELATIONSHIP (3:1-2)

3:1-2. The reason God spoke **this word . . . against . . . Israel** and Judah —whom He **brought up out of Egypt**— was because they **only** had been **chosen of all the families of the earth.** "Chosen" (from *yāḏaʿ*, lit., "to know") was used in ancient treaties to describe a sovereign's commitment to a vassal in a special covenant relationship (Herbert B. Huffmon, "The Treaty Background of Hebrew *Yāḏaʿ*," *Bulletin of the American Schools of Oriental Research* 181. February 1966:31-7). They alone were God's people, the only nation He had ever really chosen to watch over and care for.

Therefore He would **punish** them **for** their **sins.** Because He had chosen them, intimately revealed Himself to them, and made available to them the greatest covenantal blessings a suzerain ever offered a vassal (Ex. 19:3-6; Deut. 28:1-14), they should have in return wanted to know Him and please Him. Because of His special commitment, their iniquities were even more terrible.

God's electing grace is always meant to influence one's conduct. His special commitments and blessings often contain special chastisements to discipline and to purge (Luke 12:47-48; 1 Cor. 11:27-32; Heb. 12:4-11; 1 Peter 1:7-9; 4:17). Because His love is so great, His people must be holy.

2. THE INEVITABLE JUDGMENT (3:3-8)

These verses show that Israel's punishment was inevitable. Much as there is often an inseparable link between two events in ordinary life, so there was an inseparable link between God's revelation to Amos and the inevitable appearance of judgment.

3:3. Through a series of seven rhetorical questions (in vv. 3-6) Amos reminded his listeners that certain events are inseparably connected (cf. Amos' other sevens in 2:6b-8, 11-12, 14-16). A second event does not happen unless it has been preceded by a necessary first event; once the first event has taken place the second is sure to follow.

First, **two** do not **walk together** along a road **unless they have** first met, chatted, and **agreed to** continue on together.

3:4. Second, **a lion,** does not **roar in the thicket** unless he has spotted his **prey** and begun his fearful charge (cf. Jud. 14:5). But once he has begun his savage rush, the paralyzing roar is inevitable (cf. comments on Amos 1:2). Third, in a similar way a lion's contented **growl in his den** is a sure sign that something has been **caught**; a successful hunt leads to his satisfied rumble.

3:5. Fourth, **a bird** does not **fall into a trap** unless a **snare** has first been baited and **set.** Nor, fifth, **does a trap spring up from the earth** unless something catchable has triggered it. A captured bird or wild animal usually means a trap was used.

3:6. Sixth, **people** do not **tremble** unless **a** war **trumpet** has been sounded **in a city**; but such an alarm always produces fear and apprehension. Nor does **disaster** finally come **to a city** unless **the LORD** has determined to cause **it** (cf. Isa. 45:7). But once His decision is made, the outcome is unavoidable. The "disaster" could be a plague, meager harvest, or hostile attack (cf. Amos 4:6-11), designed by God to lead the people to repent, acknowledge His sovereignty in their lives, and trust Him for deliverance (cf. Joel 1).

The seven examples of related events began innocuously, but become increasingly foreboding. The first example (Amos 3:3) had no element of force or disaster about it. The next two (v. 4), however, concerned the overpowering of one animal by another, and the two after that (v. 5) pictured man as the vanquisher of animal prey. In the final two examples (v. 6), people themselves were overwhelmed, first by other human instruments, then by God Himself. This ominous progression, to the point where God Himself is seen as the initiator of human calamity, brought Amos to a climactic statement (vv. 7-8).

3:7-8. Just as one event does not take place unless another necessary event has already happened, so **the sovereign LORD does nothing** regarding the history of Israel **without** first **revealing His plan to His servants the prophets.** But once this revelation has occurred—once **the lion has roared** and attacked (cf. 1:2; Hosea 5:14; 11:10; 13:7), once **the sovereign LORD has spoken**—Israel's judgment is sure to follow.

Major changes in Israel's history were preceded by revelations from God; He seldom acted without first giving warning through a prophet. Ahijah prophesied the schism in Solomon's empire (1 Kings 11:29-39; fulfilled in 1 Kings 12:15-20). An anonymous prophet forecast Josiah's reform (1 Kings 13:1-2; fulfilled in 2 Kings 23:15-20). Ahijah predicted the death of Abijah and the end of the dynasty of Jeroboam I (1 Kings 14:1-16; fulfilled in 1 Kings 14:17-18; 15:29). Elijah prophesied the deaths of Ahab and Jezebel, and the extermination of Ahab's descendants (1 Kings 21:17-24; fulfilled in 1 Kings 22:29-37; 2 Kings 9:30–10:11). Elijah also predicted the death of Ahaziah (2 Kings 1:2-4, 16; fulfilled in 2 Kings 1:17). Elisha forecast Moab's defeat by Jehoram and Jehoshaphat (2 Kings 3). Elisha repeated Elijah's prediction of the fall of Ahab's dynasty (2 Kings 9:7-10). Jeroboam II regained lost Israelite territory in fulfillment of an unrecorded prophecy by Jonah (2 Kings 14:25).

Isaiah predicted the collapse of the Assyrians in their invasion of Jerusalem (2 Kings 19:5-7, 20, 32-34; fulfilled in 2 Kings 19:35-37) and the extension of Hezekiah's life (2 Kings 20:1-11). Judah's exile to Babylon (fulfilled in 2 Kings 24-25) was repeatedly foretold—to Hezekiah by Isaiah (2 Kings 20:16-18), to Manasseh by anonymous prophets (2 Kings 21:10-15), and to Josiah by Huldah the prophetess (2 Kings 22:14-20). And Isaiah predicted that Cyrus would commission the rebuilding of the temple (Isa. 44:28; fulfilled in Ezra 1).

The Lord always revealed His major plans in advance to His servants the prophets. The prediction could precede the event by years or even centuries, but the fulfillment was always certain. Since the Lord had now roared His judgment like a lion, **who** could but **fear** the outcome? And since He had revealed His intentions to Amos, what could he do **but prophesy** God's message?

3. THE UNPARALLELED OPPRESSION (3:9-10)

3:9-10. Imaginary heralds were instructed to invite emissaries from **Ashdod** (in Philistia) and **Egypt** to **assemble . . . on the mountains** above **Samaria** and **see** what the city was like. These dignitaries, from countries where the art of injustice was well developed (cf. 1:6-8), would, ironically, be astonished at what they observed in Israel's capital. **Great unrest** was in the city. Instead of peace and order, panic and the terrifying disintegration of the rule of law prevailed. Instead of justice, violence and **oppression** were rampant. By means of threats and exploitation, the rich had amassed private fortunes, hoarding the results of **plunder and loot** in their homes. The words "plunder" and "loot" refer to acts of violence against persons and property, and stand essentially for "assault and robbery." Terrorizing had become so much a part of their lives that they no longer knew **how to do** what was **right** (i.e., what was straightforward, honest, and just).

The invitation was sent **to the fortresses** (3:9) of the neighboring states. A "fortress" was almost any building higher than an ordinary house. Containing several stories, it was constructed to be defensible, and often became part of a city's defense system. The king's palace usually included a fortress as part of its structure (cf. "citadel" in 1 Kings 16:18; 2 Kings 15:25); such buildings also served as residences of the rich and ruling class (Jer. 9:21). These residential strongholds were a national pride (Amos 6:8), a symbol of power and wealth, and therefore

the special focus of God's wrath (1:4, 7, 10, 14; 2:2, 5). Amos summoned leaders from the fortresses of Ashdod and Egypt to Samaria to see that the inhabitants of Israel's fortresses had outstripped even *them* in their ability to profit from oppression! Amos' accusation is similar to Paul's in 1 Corinthians 5:1—a level of sin was existing among God's people which did not even occur among pagans.

4. THE COMING CATASTROPHE (3:11-15)

In three progressive declarations Amos unfolded the catastrophe that would come on Israel because of her unparalleled oppression (cf. vv. 9-10).

3:11. An enemy, **the sovereign LORD** said, would invade and **overrun the land,** pulling **down** and plundering the nation's defenses. The **fortresses** (cf. v. 10) of the looters would themselves be looted.

3:12. Some of Amos' hearers might have objected to this announcement, insisting that somehow **the Israelites** would **be saved.** The word "saved" (usually trans. "rescued" or "delivered" in NIV) often described God's delivering or sparing of Israel (Ex. 3:8; 18:9-10; Pss. 54:7; 69:14; Jer. 15:21; Micah 4:10). This revealed the mistaken belief of Amos' hearers that God would surely rescue them from such a catastrophe. To dispel this false hope, Amos repeated **what the LORD** said: any "saving" of Israel would be like **a shepherd** saving a couple of **leg bones or** part **of an ear** from the jaws of a wild animal. These little bits of "rescued" evidence were to prove that a shepherd had not stolen or sold one of the sheep, but that it indeed had been torn by a beast of prey (Ex. 22:10-13; cf. Gen 31:39). The rescued shin bones and tip of an ear only proved that the rescue had come too late and that the animal was a total loss. **Those** Israelites in **Samaria** who dissolutely lounged on **their beds** and **couches** should not dismiss Amos' message with vague assurances of deliverance. Israel would be savagely and totally devoured.

3:13-15. God addressed the Northern Kingdom as **the house of Jacob,** using the patriarchal name (cf. 6:8; 7:2, 5; 8:7; 9:8) to remind them of His early commitment to their ancestors. In times past God had been a Warrior on their behalf. But now He would lead another army against them to **punish** them **for their**

sins (on "sins," *peša'*, as covenant violations, see comments on 1:3). **God Almighty** (lit., "God of hosts," i.e., "Head of armies") designates the most awesome Warrior. Throughout these chapters which describe Israel's violations (chaps. 3–6) **the LORD** is repeatedly presented (3:13; 4:13; 5:14-16, 27; 6:8, 14) as a mighty Suzerain who commands vast forces, whose power to punish rebels is both massive and irresistible.

In punishing them, God would **destroy the altars of Bethel** (cf. 9:1). Bethel was the royal sanctuary of Jeroboam II (7:10-13), the most popular religious center in Israel (cf. 4:4; 5:5). As the site of the golden calf erected by Jeroboam I (1 Kings 12:26-30; Hosea 10:5), its altars symbolized Israel's continued rebellion against God. **The horns** of these altars were projections on the altars' corners. Fugitives could grab these horns to claim asylum from their pursuers (1 Kings 1:50; 2:28; Ex. 21:12-13). Murderers, however, could not receive protection, but were torn by force from the altar (Ex. 21:14). Israel's sin was similarly so great that God Himself was going to **cut off** the means of claiming asylum. There would be no sanctuary from the enemy who was coming against them.

God would not only destroy their religious center; He would also **tear down** the luxurious **mansions** which resulted from their commercial exploitation. Once only kings could afford both a **winter house** and a **summer house**. For example, in the ninth century Ahab had a winter palace in the warmer plains of Jezreel (1 Kings 21:1) besides his Samaria residence. Luxury **houses adorned with ivory** inlay or furnishings (cf. Amos. 6:4) were likewise the province of royalty (1 Kings 22:39; Ps. 45:8). Yet the ill-gotten prosperity (cf. Prov. 10:2) of Israel's upper classes had enabled them to build such dwellings. All these, however, would **be demolished** on the day God would punish Israel.

B. The second message (chap. 4)

In the second message Amos declared that God would exile the upper-class women because of their economic exploitation, and judge the nation as a whole for its religious hypocrisy and obstinate refusal to repent, despite His repeated chastisements.

1. ECONOMIC EXPLOITATION (4:1-3)

4:1. The upper-class women were called **cows of Bashan.** Bashan, in Transjordan east of the Sea of Kinnereth (Galilee), was famous for its lush pastures (Jer. 50:19; Micah 7:14), and its well-fed cattle (Ezek. 39:18; Ps. 22:12). Amos accused the rich women of being equally pampered, insisting that their **husbands** continually supplied them with intoxicating **drinks.** The word for "husbands" is not one of the common Hebrew terms for husband, but a rare word meaning "master" or "lord" (cf. Gen. 18:12; Ps. 45:11). Amos scorned those husbands who were supposed to be "masters" but who in reality meekly obeyed like servants. The only way they could support their wives' expensive tastes was by ruthlessly exploiting **the poor** and **the needy** (cf. Amos 2:6-7; 5:11-12; 8:4-6). (Though the women are said in 4:1 to do the oppressing, apparently they did so by domineering their husbands.) The words **oppress** and **crush** describe threats and physical harassments used to squeeze money from the helpless.

4:2-3. In order to show the vehemence of His anger and the certainty of their punishment, **the sovereign LORD** had **sworn by His holiness** that every one of these society women would be dragged from the city either to captivity or to death. God had vowed the entire reality of His inmost being to this unchangeable sentence (cf. 6:8). An enemy would storm and capture the city. The destruction would be so thorough and the **breaks in the wall** so numerous that each woman, rather than going with others toward an exit gate, would simply be pushed **straight out** of the city. Once outside they would be fastened to ropes **with hooks** for a single-file march into Assyrian exile. Those who balked or refused to be led away would be forcibly snagged with large harpoons or **fishhooks,** much like fish pierced together and jerked over one's shoulder to be carried to market. Yanked in such manner, they eventually would be **cast out** as corpses as the march neared **Harmon.** (For the use of "cast out" to depict what is done with dead bodies; cf. 8:3; 1 Kings 13:24-25; Jer. 14:16.) "Harmon" may refer to Hermon, a mountain at the northern tip of the Bashan region on the way to Assyria. If so, an awful irony would at-

The Covenant Chastenings

Chastening	Amos	Leviticus	Deuteronomy	1 Kings
Hunger/famine	4:6	26:26, 29	28:17, 48	8:37
Drought	4:7-8	26:19	28:22-24, 48	8:35
Blight/mildew	4:9	26:20	28:18, 22, 30, 39-40	8:37
Locusts	4:9	—	28:38, 42	8:37
Plagues	4:10	26:16, 25	28:21-22, 27, 35, 59-61	8:37
Military defeat	4:10	26:17, 25, 33, 36-39	28:25-26, 49-52	8:33
Devastation	4:11	26:31-35	29:23-28	—

tach to their fate: the "cows of Bashan" (Amos 4:1) would end as carrion in Bashan!

2. RELIGIOUS HYPOCRISY (4:4-5)

4:4-5. Verse 4 is a parody of a priest's summons to pilgrims. The usual invitation was to "come into the sanctuary to worship" (Pss. 95:6; 96:8-9; 100:2-4). But with biting sarcasm Amos exhorted Israel to **go to Bethel** and **to Gilgal** in order to **sin** (i.e., to break their covenant with God; see Amos 1:3 for comments on "sin," *peša'*). Bethel was the chief sanctuary of the north, the place where the king worshiped (see comments on 3:14). Gilgal, with its memorial stones marking Israel's initial entrance into the land (Josh. 4), remained in the eighth century as a center for pilgrimage and sacrifice (Amos 5:5; Hosea 4:15; 9:15; 12:11).

Amos commanded the Israelites to bring the whole gamut of offerings to these shrines enthusiastically. **Sacrifices** were offerings in which an animal was slaughtered and consumed as part of a sacred meal (cf. 1 Sam. 1:3-5). **Tithes** of produce were set aside **every three years** in order to help the poor (Deut. 14:28-29). (A possible alternate trans. of Amos 4:4 refers to the custom of offering the regular tithes, Deut. 12:4-7; 14:22-27, on the third day after arriving at the sanctuary.) The purpose of the **thank** offerings was to express gratitude for blessings and answered prayers (Lev. 7:11-15). **Freewill offerings** were voluntary and spontaneous gifts, born of an inner devotion to God (Lev. 7:16; 22:17-19).

But all these offerings, Amos charged, had become a sham. The people's religious activities were carried out

to impress others, not to fellowship with God. The Israelites would brag **about** their devotion, but their day-to-day conduct violated the spirit of their offerings.

Some of the produce they tithed came from stolen land. Some animals they sacrificed had been fattened on unjustly seized fields. Their very worship was an offense to God as it hypocritically offered the fruits of their rebellion against His covenant (cf. Isa. 1:10-20; Micah 6:6-8).

3. REFUSAL TO REPENT (4:6-13)

The people had persisted in their economic exploitation and religious hypocrisy despite God's repeated attempts to bring them back to Him (vv. 6-11). Therefore because they would not return to Him He would come to them in final judgment. They must prepare to meet their God (v. 12), whose terrible greatness was inescapable (v. 13).

4:6. Ancient Near Eastern covenants spelled out the curses or punishments the suzerain would bring against his vassals for disloyalty or disobedience. Verses 6-11 record how God had brought the chastisements of the Mosaic Covenant against His people in order to bring them back to Himself. Leviticus 26 and Deuteronomy 28–29 had warned that God would use famine (Amos 4:6), drought (vv. 7-8), crop failure (v. 9), plagues (v. 10), military defeat (v. 10), and even burning devastation (v. 11) to punish His people for covenant violations. Solomon also foretold (1 Kings 8:33-37) that God would use these means to turn the people from their sin. The chart "The Covenant Chastenings" compares the covenant chastenings of Amos

4:6-11 with those predicted in Leviticus 26, Deuteronomy 28–29, and 1 Kings 8.

With each chastisement God anticipated repentance. But Israel refused. The fivefold refrain—**yet you have not returned to Me** (Amos 4:6, 8-11)—underscores her continued obstinacy. This persistent refusal had now become an accumulated guilt. Final judgment, therefore, was inevitable.

God had given them **empty stomachs** (lit., "cleanness of teeth," i.e., nothing to chew on). Hunger and famine had afflicted the whole land—**every city** and **every town.** But the people did not turn to God.

4:7-8. Such famines were often caused by a prior drought, as God would withhold the spring **rain** so essential to the summer **harvest.** This discipline was often selective, so that **one town** had **rain** while **another** did not, **one field** was rained on but **another** was not. As the wells and cisterns in some localities **dried up** and its **people staggered** exhausted **from town to town** in search of limited drinking **water,** the contrast between their judgment and another town's favor should have caused them to ponder God's action. But they did not consider.

4:9. God **struck** the vegetables and fruit trees of their **gardens** and the grape clusters of their **vineyards.** The hot blasting wind of the Arabian desert blew relentlessly, causing **blight,** a premature drying and scorching of the grain (cf. Gen. 41:6, 23, 27; 2 Kings 19:26). Parasitic worms brought **mildew,** a yellowing of the tips of green grain. **Locusts devoured** the leaves of **fig and olive trees** (cf. Joel 1:1-7). But all this did not cause repentance.

4:10. Wars brought **plagues** and death to the nation. As populations were crowded into walled cities or assembled in camps, contagious diseases broke out and spread. The mention of **Egypt** has caused some to think that the "plagues" are similar to those that struck Egypt's livestock at the time of the Exodus (cf. Ex. 9:1-7). But because of the military scenes mentioned in Amos 4:10, and because the word "plague" can denote an epidemic pestilence among humans (cf. Ex. 5:3; 9:15; Lev. 26:25; Jer. 14:12; 21:7, 9; Ezek. 5:17; 14:19), the most likely one is the bubonic plague which spreads from rats to people by fleas. The mention of Egypt is best interpreted as "like those that happen in Egypt," a reference to the notorious human plagues which periodically swept that country (cf. Deut. 7:15; 28:27, 60).

During the battles God **killed** (i.e., caused the enemy to kill) their strong **young men,** the elite of their fighting force. Their **horses,** the strength of their chariot corps, were **captured.** Because of the carnage, **the stench** of diseased and decaying corpses filled their **camps.** But still Israel did **not** return to the LORD.

4:11. Finally, God totally **overthrew some of** their cities with the same burning devastation He had wreaked on **Sodom and Gomorrah** (cf. Gen. 19:23-29; Deut. 29:22-23). So thorough had been the destruction from a military siege that certain cities had ceased to exist. The whole nation had come perilously close to obliteration, barely escaping **like a burning stick snatched from the fire.** But this too had proved futile.

4:12. Therefore, because **Israel** had resisted these chastenings and had continued her sinful rebellion, God would pronounce her sentence of doom. **This is what I will do to you** refers to God's devastating sweep through the land as predicted in 3:11-15. The nation was commanded to get ready for this terrifying moment—**prepare to meet your God, O Israel.**

Some understand the word "prepare" as an invitation to repent before this final catastrophe. Since the word, however, was often used of war preparations (cf. Prov. 21:31; Jer. 46:14; Ezek. 38:7; Nahum 2:3, 5), "prepare to meet your God" is most likely a military summons to an awful confrontation. Israel was to face God's final judgment.

4:13. Amos likened God's terrifying approach in judgment to the darkening of a storm. The One who formed **the mountains** and created **the wind** now covered those **high places** with churning clouds. The early **dawn** turned back to eerie **darkness** as black swells unfolded to shroud **the earth.** The flash of lightning and the reverberation of thunder marked God's ominous "tread" from one hilltop to another as He approached the Northern capital (cf. Micah 1:3-5). God had revealed **His thoughts to man;** His intent to judge had been made known (Amos 3:7). Now, as **the LORD God Al-**

mighty (see comments on 3:13), Commander of all forces in heaven and earth, He advanced against them. Their judgment was inescapable.

C. The third message (5:1-17)

Amos' third (vv. 1-17) and fourth (vv. 18-27) messages are structured and juxtaposed to highlight one overall truth: the nation would be judged by its mighty sovereign God, but individuals could yet repent and live.

Each message follows a chiastic structure in which the themes of the early paragraphs are repeated in reverse order in the later paragraphs:
a. Theme one
  b. Theme two
    c. Theme three
    c'. Theme three (repeated)
  b'. Theme two (repeated)
a'. Theme one (repeated)
Sometimes the middle theme is unrepeated.

In chiastic structures the second or middle theme, whether repeated or not, emerges as the central focus of the whole message. In Amos' third message this central focus is the might and sovereignty of God:
a. Description of certain judgment (vv. 1-3)
  b. Call for individual repentance (vv. 4-6)
    c. Accusation of legal injustice (v. 7)
      d. Portrayal of a sovereign God (vv. 8-9)
    c'. Accusation of legal injustice (vv. 10-13)
  b'. Call for individual repentance (vv. 14-15)
a'. Description of certain judgment (vv. 16-17)

The central focus of the fourth message is the call of individuals to repent:
a. Description of certain judgment (vv. 18-20)
  b. Accusation of religious hypocrisy (vv. 21-22)
    c. Call for individual repentance (vv. 23-24)
  b'. Accusation of religious hypocrisy (vv. 25-26)
a'. Description of certain judgment (v. 27)

Together these two messages present one overall truth: the mighty sovereign God would judge the nation as a whole for its legal injustice and religious hypocrisy, but He offered life to individuals within the nation who would yet repent and seek Him.

1. DESCRIPTION OF CERTAIN JUDGMENT (5:1-3)

5:1. Amos summoned the people to hear his lament over their death. A "lament" was ordinarily a poem of grief sung at the funeral of a relative, friend, or leader (cf. 2 Sam. 1:17-27; 3:33-34; 2 Chron. 35:25). Prophets, however, also used this poetic form to mourn the death of a city, people, or nation (cf. Jer. 7:29; 9:10-11, 17-22; Lam.; Ezek. 19; 26:17-18; 27:2, 32; 28:12; 32:2). Though Israel was at the height of prosperity under Jeroboam II, her judgment was so certain that Amos lamented her fall as though it had already happened. To his listeners, hearing this lament would be as jarring as reading one's own obituary in the newspaper.

5:2. Virgin Israel had fallen. This nation which had considered itself in the full bloom of youthful vigor had been cut off before her time in violent death. "Fallen" in funeral songs means "fallen by the sword" (cf. 2 Sam. 1:19, 25, 27; 3:34; Lam. 2:21). She had died in battle in her own land. Her corpse lay unattended, deserted by God Himself. The word "deserted" was often used of God's abandoning or forsaking His people (Jud. 6:13; 2 Kings 21:14; Isa. 2:6). There was no one to lift her up, no one to restore her to life. (Cf. 1 Sam. 2:6; Hosea 6:2; Amos 9:11 for the use of "to lift up," lit., "to raise up," to describe God's restoring to life.) Since the God who could help had Himself abandoned her, Israel had fallen, never to rise again.

5:3. Her armies had been decimated. The city or town that had detached a military unit of a thousand or a hundred (cf. 1 Sam. 17:18, NIV marg.; 18:13; 22:7; 2 Sam. 18:1, 4) saw only 10 percent return from war. An army could sustain a 50 percent loss and still fight (2 Sam. 18:3). But if 90 percent were slain, that nation had received its death sentence. Amos lamented an Israel that would cease to exist.

2. CALL FOR INDIVIDUAL REPENTANCE (5:4-6)

5:4-5. National judgment was certain, but individuals could yet seek God and live (cf. v. 6). They should **not**, however, **seek** Him at the sanctuaries, for these were doomed. See comments on **Bethel** and **Gilgal** in 3:14; 4:4. **Beersheba** was in the southern part of Judah's territory. Evidently northern Israelites crossed over the border to worship at a shrine associated with the patriarchs (cf. Gen. 21:31-33; 26:23-25; 46:1-4). **Gilgal,** the memorial of entrance *into* the land (Josh. 4), was to become the symbol of **exile** *from* the land. And **Bethel**, the "house of God," was to become "Beth Aven" (Heb.), a "house of **nothing**," a "house of spirits." In Hebrew, the last part of the city's name, "El," meaning "God," was changed by Amos to "Aven" (cf. NIV marg.; Hosea 4:15; 5:8; 10:5), meaning "nothing, empty, having no existence," a word often used to describe the powerless spirits of wickedness (cf. Isa. 41:22-24, 28-29). This sarcasm would have a stinging effect on the people.

5:6. The command to **seek** (cf. v. 4) **the LORD** meant to turn to Him, not in ritual worship, but by doing good and hating evil (cf. vv. 14-15). Those who did would **live**: when the unquenchable and devouring **fire** of the invader swept **through the house of Joseph** (the Northern Kingdom), the seekers would be the remnant spared in mercy (v. 15).

3. ACCUSATION OF LEGAL INJUSTICE (5:7)

5:7. Verse 7 connects in grammar and content with verses 10-13. Verses 8-9 are inserted to highlight God's awesome power to judge. See comments under "C. The third message (5:1-17)."

One reason for God's judgment was the corruption that permeated the courts. Court officials had turned **justice into bitterness and** had **cast righteousness to the ground.** "Justice" was the proper functioning of judicial procedures that enabled a court to declare who or what was right in a given case. "Righteousness" was the behavior of one who sought this end, who did "right" to those involved in the case. A righteous man was willing to speak in defense of an innocent person who had been wrongly accused. Righteousness was the action; justice was the end result.

To do what was "right" and "just" on behalf of the needy was a crowning gem of human behavior (Prov. 1:3; 2:9; 8:20; Isa. 1:21; 5:7; 28:17) and proved a special relationship with God (Gen. 18:19; Ps. 72; Jer. 22:15-17). Justice and righteousness were more than essential sacrifice and ceremony (Prov. 21:3; Amos 5:23-24). And nowhere were righteousness and justice more crucial than in the courts. Here the weaker members of society, those without money or influence, could receive protection from their oppressors and find fairness under the Law.

But Israel, through the alchemy of greed, had turned justice into "bitterness"—literally, "wormwood," a small plant known for its bitter pulp, usually associated with poison (cf. 6:12; Deut. 29:18, NASB; Jer. 9:15; 23:15). The judicial system, instead of being like a medicinal herb to heal wrongs and restore the oppressed, had itself become a fatal poison within the nation. The description of the poison's spread is continued in 5:10-13.

4. PORTRAYAL OF A SOVEREIGN GOD (5:8-9)

5:8-9. In the midst of this denunciation of human perversity, Amos identified the God who controlled the workings of the physical universe and who surely, therefore, would overturn the injustice of men.

He who **made** the constellations **Pleiades and Orion** (cf. Job 9:9; 38:31—the rising of Pleiades before daybreak signaled the return of spring while the rising of Orion after sunset heralded the onset of winter), He **who** controls the 24-hour cycle of day and night, turning **blackness into dawn** and **day into night,** He who controls the elements of nature, gathering by evaporation **the waters of the sea** and draining **them out over . . . the land**—this great Sovereign of the universe is also Israel's covenant God. **The LORD** (Yahweh) **is His name.** And He would judge their covenant faithfulness.

This God whose dominion was unchallenged in heaven was also irresistible on earth. Nothing could withstand His **destruction**—not the mightiest **stronghold** or the most **fortified city.**

5. ACCUSATION OF LEGAL INJUSTICE (5:10-13)

5:10-13. Verses 10-13 continue the denunciation begun in verse 7. Within the larger chiasmus of verses 1-17, verses 10-13 form their own internal chiasmus:

a. Intimidation of the righteous (v. 10)
b. Abuse of the poor (v. 11a)
   c. Judgment of covenant sin
     (vv. 11b-12a)
b'. Abuse of the poor (v. 12b)
a'. Intimidation of the righteous (v. 13)

Because of their zeal to profit illegally through the courts, they hated any righteous judge who reproved their injustice, and despised any righteous witness who told **the truth** in defense of the innocent (v. 10; see comments on v. 7). Their venom and intimidation were so severe that many felt the **prudent** thing to do was to keep **quiet in such times** (v. 13).

The abusers, thus freed of any rebuke or opposition, found corrupt judges to **take bribes** and **deprive the poor of justice** (v. 12b; in contrast with the covenant Law of Ex. 23:8; Deut. 16:18-20; cf. 1 Sam. 12:3). Rich landowners successfully manipulated legal proceedings to **trample on the poor,** gain ownership of his fields, and **force him to give** a large fee of **grain** to remain a tenant on the land (Amos 5:11a; in violation of the covenant Law of Ex. 23:2, 6; cf. Amos 2:6-7; 4:1; Isa. 10:1-2).

But God knew **how many** were their **offenses** (*peša'*, "covenant violations"; see comments on Amos 1:3). He knew **how great** were their **sins** (lit., their acts of "missing the mark" of His standard). **Therefore, though** they had **built stone mansions** fit for kings and had **planted lush vineyards** in the fields that once belonged to small farmers, they would neither **live in** the houses nor **drink** the **wine** (Amos 5:11b-12a). Their suzerain Lord would invoke the treaty punishments against covenant disobedience (Deut. 28:30, 38-40; cf. Micah 6:14; Zeph. 1:13; see comments on Amos 1:2; 4:6). Their greed would be met with poetic justice: as they had stripped the poor, so God would strip them.

6. CALL FOR INDIVIDUAL REPENTANCE
(5:14-15)

5:14-15. The possibility still existed, however, for individuals to separate themselves from their guilty nation (cf. vv. 4-6). If people would **seek good, not evil,** they might yet **live.** If they would go counter to the prevailing corruption—if they would **hate evil** instead of hating the righteous (v. 10), if they would **main-tain justice in the courts** instead of trampling it (vv. 11-12)—**then the LORD God Almighty,** the great suzerain Warrior (see comments on 3:13) would be their Defender instead of their Judge. He would indeed **be with** them, **just as** they were claiming **He** was.

"The LORD is with us" was Israel's ancient shout of assurance that their powerful God would fight for them in battle (Num. 23:21; Deut. 20:4; 31:8; Jud. 6:12; Isa. 8:10; Zeph. 3:15, 17) and defend them in adversity (Pss. 23:4; 46:7, 11). But in the time of Jeroboam II this shout had become an empty slogan. Their assurance, Amos insisted, was a delusion. God was no longer "with them." The guilty nation had been abandoned (cf. Amos 5:2). Their external prosperity was misleading; it had bred a false security (cf. 6:3; 9:10; Micah 3:11). In reality, there would be only a brief respite before their Sovereign would sweep them away in judgment.

If a handful, however, would turn and passionately seek the Lord, **perhaps** the great Suzerain would **have mercy on** that small repentant **remnant** of the Northern Kingdom, here called **Joseph** (see comments on Amos 9:8-15 for the fulfillment).

7. DESCRIPTION OF CERTAIN JUDGMENT
(5:16-17)

5:16-17. Amos concluded his third message by returning to his opening lament and its staggering death statistics (vv. 1-3). After **the LORD God Almighty** (see comments on 3:13) had decimated their forces, the land would be full of funerals. There would **be wailing . . . and cries of anguish** throughout the cities (5:16) and the fields (v. 17). So many would be dead that there would not be enough professional **mourners to wail;** **the farmers** would have to **be summoned** from their fields **to weep.** (The poor who had suffered the injustice would be called in to bury their oppressors!) **The vineyards,** often places of laughter and harvest merriment (Isa. 16:10), would be silent except for the sound of **wailing** (cf. Amos 5:16). The mourning among **all the** buildings of the city and **all the** vineyards of the fields would fulfill the verdict of God's judgment (cf. v. 11).

Wailing would fill the land because God would **pass through** their **midst.**

Their God, who once "passed over" Israel in order to "pass through" Egypt (Ex. 11:4-7; 12:12-13), would now "pass through" them on a similar errand of death.

D. The fourth message (5:18-27)

In this fourth message Amos declared that because of Israel's religious hypocrisy "the day of the LORD" would be a day of exile rather than exaltation. Repentant individuals, however, could escape this disaster. See the comments under "C. The third message (5:1-17)" on the chiastic structure of verses 18-27.

1. DESCRIPTION OF CERTAIN JUDGMENT (5:18-20)

5:18. **Woe** (hôy; cf. 6:1) was ordinarily the wail of grief over the dead (cf. 1 Kings 13:30 ["Oh"]; Jer. 22:18; 34:5 ["Alas"]). Pronounced over the living, "woe" was a prediction of death (cf. Amos 6:1; Isa. 5:8-24; 10:1-4; Micah 2:1-5; see comments on Amos 5:1) or an interjection of distress in the face of present or coming calamity (cf. comments on Isa. 3:9; 6:5).

The "woe" was addressed to those who were eagerly longing **for the day of the LORD.** Their earnest desire, Amos warned, was ill-founded, for **that day** would be a day of **darkness, not light** (cf. Amos 5:20).

In Israel's thinking, "the day of the LORD" was to be the time of God's culminating vengeance against her enemies, the day when their mighty Sovereign would fight on their behalf (Isa. 34:1-3, 8; Jer. 46:10). On that day, she thought, He would turn His wrath on the wicked nations, punishing with disaster and death those who had threatened His people (Zeph. 3:8; Zech. 14:1-3). On that day Israel would be permanently secured from danger, and exalted among all nations of the earth (Isa. 24:21-23; Joel 3).

Amos' hearers eagerly anticipated that day. They did not realize, however, that its horrors would fall, not only on the nations, but also on them. Israel mistakenly believed that their Sovereign was "with" her (see comments on Amos 5:14), and that on His day of conquest He would eradicate her enemies. The truth, Amos declared, was that Israel herself had become God's enemy. Her continual sins against His covenant had made her one of the adversaries. "The day of the

LORD," therefore, would not be the expected day of happiness. It would be instead the Suzerain's day of vengeance against the rebels within His kingdom (cf. 8:9-10; 9:1-10).

5:19. Their experience on that day would be like that of **a man** running **from a lion** who then meets **a bear.** Somehow eluding this second threat, he managed to flee to **his house** where he **rested his hand on the wall** in exhaustion and relief. But there, in the supposed safety of his home, a poisonous **snake** bit **him.** Similarly Israel would find no haven from God's judgment.

5:20. The day of the LORD, Amos repeated (cf. v. 18), would be a day of **darkness, not light** (Joel 2:1-2, 10-11; Zeph. 1:14-15), a day of **pitch-dark** gloom, **without a ray of brightness** or hint of hope.

The Old Testament prophets spoke of another brighter "day of the LORD," a day after the exile, when a chastened and impoverished remnant returned to the land, a day when God will restore His people's fortunes and turn their hearts toward Him (Jer. 30:8-11; Hosea 2:16-23; Amos 9:11-15; Micah 4:6-7; Zeph. 3:11-20).

2. ACCUSATION OF RELIGIOUS HYPOCRISY (5:21-22)

5:21-22. God's burning anger was directed mostly against Israel's religious hypocrisy. He hated, He despised (the repetition indicates vehemence and passion) their **religious feasts**—the three pilgrimage festivals of Unleavened Bread, Harvest (Weeks), and Ingathering (Tabernacles) which were celebrated annually at the sanctuary (Ex. 23:14-17; 34:18-24; Lev. 23; Deut. 16:1-17). He could not **stand** (lit., "smell") the offerings of their **assemblies. Though** they continually brought Him **burnt offerings** (Lev. 1) **and grain offerings** (Lev. 2), He would **not accept them** as legitimate sacrifices. **Though** they brought **choice fellowship offerings** (Lev. 3), He would **have no regard for** or awareness of **them.** He loathed every part of their religious worship (see comments on Amos 4:4-5).

3. CALL FOR INDIVIDUAL REPENTANCE (5:23-24)

In verses 23-24 the verbs "away" and "let . . . roll" are singular, whereas in verses 21-22 the pronouns "your" and "you" are plural. This indicates a shift from national accusation (vv. 21-22) to individual invitation (vv. 23-24).

5:23. God appealed to individuals to take **away** the burdensome **noise of** their praise **songs.** He would **not listen to the** accompanying **music of** their **harps.** Having shut His nostrils (as noted in v. 21b, "stand" means "smell"), He would also stop His ears.

5:24. Instead of ritual and performance, God wanted a relentless commitment to **justice** and **righteousness** (see comments on v. 7). He wanted a passionate concern for the rights of the poor, a concern that would **roll on like** an ever-flowing **river . . . like a never-failing stream** that did not run dry. God wanted a day-to-day life of surging integrity and goodness. Only this outer evidence of inner righteousness could offer the Israelites the possibility of survival in the day of the Lord (cf. vv. 6, 14-15).

4. ACCUSATION OF RELIGIOUS HYPOCRISY (5:25-26)

5:25. God returned to His denunciation of Israel's religious hypocrisy by reminding them that their sacrifices and rituals had been an affront to Him throughout their history. From the very beginning their worship had been falsely directed. It was often not to Him, but to a golden calf, to the sun, moon, and stars, and to Molech and other false gods that many of them brought **sacrifices and offerings** during their **40 years in the desert** (cf. Stephen's reference to Amos 5:25-27 in Acts 7:39-43).

5:26. Since then their worship had further degenerated as they began to honor "heavenly bodies" (Acts 7:42; 2 Kings 21:3-5; 23:4-5; Jer. 8:2; 19:13; Zeph. 1:5), in violation of their covenant Law (Deut. 4:19; 17:3). They **lifted up the shrine of** their false deity (their **king**), raised **the pedestal** on which their **idols** perched, and held high **the star** symbol of their **god.** The words "shrine" and "pedestal" could be translated as "Sakkuth" and "Kaiwan" (cf. NIV marg.), foreign deities associated with the starry heavens, especially the Planet Saturn.

5. DESCRIPTION OF CERTAIN JUDGMENT (5:27)

5:27. Because of this idolatry and hypocrisy in their worship, God said He would **send** Israel **into exile beyond Damascus,** toward the direction of Assyria (cf. 4:3). The horror of "exile" was more than the ruin of defeat and the shame of capture. For Israel, it meant being removed from the land of promise, the land of God's presence. Exile, in effect, was excommunication. Yet this was the judgment of their sovereign LORD, the mighty Suzerain whose covenant they had spurned (see 3:13 for comments on **God Almighty**).

E. The fifth message (chap. 6)

In his fifth message Amos pointed again to the reasons for Israel's judgment, declaring that God would completely devastate both the Southern and Northern Kingdoms (vv. 1, 14), partly because of their boastful complacency and luxurious indulgence.

1. THEIR BOASTFUL COMPLACENCY (6:1-3)

6:1. Woe was again uttered (see comments on 5:18), this time against those **who** were **complacent in Zion** and those **who** felt **secure on Mount Samaria.** Amos included Zion, capital of the South, in his opening lament, for they too were beginning to awaken God's wrath. The remainder of his message, however, was addressed to the careless pride of the Northern Kingdom.

The leaders of Samaria considered themselves the **notable men of the foremost nation.** Their nation was militarily and economically dominant, and they were its most distinguished citizens. All **the people of Israel** looked to them for guidance and for handling the nation's affairs.

6:2. But God directed these proud men to **go to** cities which once also considered themselves great, and to learn from their fall. **Calneh** (also called Calno, Isa. 10:9) and **Hamath** were city-states in northern Aram. They had been overrun by Assyria during Shalmaneser III's campaign in 854–846 B.C. **Gath in Philistia** had been devastated in 815 B.C. by Hazael, king of Aram, and again in 760 B.C. by Uzziah, king of Judah (2 Kings 12:17; 2 Chron. 26:6; cf. comments on Amos 1:6). Was Israel any **better** prepared to fend off an attack **than** were **those** powerful **kingdoms?** No. **Was their land larger than** Israel's? Yes. Those cities and their surrounding districts were greater in size than proud Samaria, yet they still were unable to stave off disaster.

6:3. Israel, arrogant and foolishly confident of its own prowess (cf. v. 13), **put off the evil day.** They scornfully dismissed any thought of coming calamity. But all the while, by their sinful actions, they were approaching **a reign of terror.** "A reign of terror" aptly describes the last years of Israel's history before her captivity by Assyria (2 Kings 15:8–17:6). In the 31 years after Jeroboam II, Israel had six kings, three of whom seized power by political coup and assassination. The fear and violence in this period is reflected in the atrocities of 2 Kings 15:16.

2. THEIR LUXURIOUS INDULGENCE (6:4-7)

6:4-6. Rather than heed the prophet's warnings of judgment, the leaders of Samaria instead gave themselves to a decadent hedonism. They reclined on expensive **beds** whose wood was **inlaid with ivory** (cf. 3:15). At their opulent feasts they "lounged" **on** their **couches.** The Hebrew word for **lounge** (*sāraḥ*) conveys a sprawled stupor of satiation and drunkenness, with arms and legs hanging over the side. They ate gourmet food—**choice lambs and fattened calves** —the tastiest and tenderest meat they could get. In their drunken revelry they imagined themselves strumming **like David** as they attempted to **improvise** music at their parties. Yet they were vastly different from David! Not content to **drink wine** from goblets, they consumed it **by the bowlful.** Only **the finest lotions** would do for their skin.

Their sole concern was for their own luxurious lifestyle. They did **not grieve over the** coming **ruin of Joseph,** the Northern Kingdom (cf. 5:6, 15). They had no concern for their nation's impending doom.

6:7. Therefore they, the first men of the first nation (v. 1), would **be among the first to go into exile.** Their festivities and drunken stupors would **end.** The sound of revelry would fade into bitter silence as they headed into captivity.

3. THE COMPLETE DEVASTATION (6:8-14)

6:8. Israel's **sovereign LORD** had **sworn by Himself,** binding the full force of His integrity to a solemn oath (cf. 4:2; 8:7), that He would utterly destroy the land. He abhorred their **pride** as they said their national fortunes resulted from their own strength (6:1, 13). **Jacob,** like Joseph, is a synonym for the Northern Kingdom (see comments on 3:13). God detested the **fortresses** which were filled with the results of their oppression against the poor (see comments on 3:9-10). Therefore, as a great suzerain Warrior (see 3:13 for comments on LORD **God Almighty**), He would storm their **city,** and **deliver up** everyone **and everything in it.**

6:9-10. So completely would God "deliver up" the city that even **if 10 men** should huddle **in one house** to escape the sword, **they** would **die** of pestilence. **A relative who** came **to take the bodies** to burn them would be so afraid of death that if he discovered a survivor **hiding** in the house he would quickly beg him **not** even to **mention the** Lord's **name** in any way (not in lament or in anger for the slaughter or in praise for having survived). For in such a situation, to "mention the name" of Him who had so terribly destroyed the city might draw His attention to those whom He had overlooked, and cause Him to slay them also.

6:11. After killing the inhabitants, the conquering Suzerain would then **command** His forces to **smash . . . great** and **small** houses **into bits.** The dwellings of both rich and poor would be totally demolished. All that would remain would be a field of debris.

6:12. Two preposterous images expose the utter perversity of Israel's leaders. That **horses** would **run on the rocky crags,** or that **one** would **plow** those perpendicular cliffs **with oxen** was unimaginable. Israel, however, had done the unimaginable! They had **turned justice into poison and the fruit of righteousness into bitterness** (see comments on 5:7). The judicial process, designed to preserve the nation's health, had become a lethal "poison" within its body. The "fruit" of fairness and integrity, intended to refresh and delight, had become instead a corrupt bitter pulp.

6:13. Israel's leaders considered themselves immune to disaster, as the evidence of their might was obvious to them (vv. 1-3). Under Jeroboam II they had won an unbroken string of military victories (2 Kings 14:25). They had even recovered all their lands east of the Jordan. But Amos subtly and intentionally mispronounced the name of one of the captured towns, **Lo Debar** (a town east of the Jordan River, mentioned in 2 Sam. 9:4; 17:27), so that it came out in Hebrew as "Lo Dabar," which means "nothing." And with biting sarcasm he stressed the name of another subdued city, **Karnaim,** whose literal meaning of "horns" symbolized the "strength" of a bull. Amos scoffed that they were rejoicing over what was really "nothing," and were falsely imagining that they had seized "strength" by means of their **own strength.**

6:14. Their air of invincibility would be shattered by their mighty Suzerain (see 3:13 for comments on **LORD God Almighty**). God too would do the unimaginable—He would **stir up a nation against** His own vassal. He would raise a scourge against His own people Israel, and they would be "oppressed." The word **oppress** deliberately evoked and promised again the bitter experiences of Egypt (Ex. 3:9) and the time of the Judges (Jud. 2:18; 4:3; 6:9; 10:11-12; 1 Sam. 10:17-18); Israel would again descend into slavery. All the territory they so boastfully held—**from** the northern frontier of **Lebo Hamath to** the southern border of **the Arabah,** the valley extending from the Sea of Kinnereth to the Dead Sea (2 Kings 14:25)—would be swallowed by the invading foe. Then Israel would know whose "strength" really determined the destiny of nations.

IV. The Results of Judgment (7:1–9:10)

In chapters 3–6 Amos had documented the reasons for God's judgment against Israel—legal injustice, economic exploitation, religious hypocrisy, luxurious indulgence, and boastful complacency. Because of these covenant violations "the LORD God Almighty," the great suzerain Warrior at the head of His armies, would crush His rebellious vassal. (Only in chaps. 3–6 does the title "the LORD God Almighty" occur in Amos.) Individuals who repented might yet be spared, but the nation as a whole was irrevocably doomed.

In chapter 7 Amos began to describe the results of this coming judgment. Through a series of five visions (7:1, 4, 7; 8:1; 9:1), he pictured God's total destruction of the land, its buildings, and its people.

Throughout this section of the book (7:1–9:10), two phrases stand out—"sovereign LORD" (7:1-2, 4 [twice], 5-6; 8:1, 3, 9, 11; 9:8) and "My people" (7:8, 15; 8:2; 9:10). As the sovereign Lord over all nations, God has absolute freedom of action in His universe. He was especially at liberty to implement His will against the people who had spurned His special grace (cf. 3:2).

A. The swarming locusts (7:1-3)

7:1. In the first of five visions Amos saw God actually **preparing swarms of locusts** at the nation's most vulnerable time of the year! (The Heb. expresses the prophet's amazement at such a thing; cf. "behold" in NASB.) The locusts were being loosed on the land **after the king's share had been harvested and just as the second crop was coming up.** The king had the right to claim the first cutting of the grain for his military animals (cf. 1 Kings 18:5). The "second crop"—either what grew after the first cutting or a separate late planting—was the final growth of the season before the summer's dryness. If it were lost the people would have nothing to eat until the next harvest.

A locust swarm was one of the most dreaded plagues of the ancient East. As a swarm made its ravenous way across the land, people despaired because it was an enemy against whom they were helpless. When the plague was past, suffering and death by famine followed. This misery was intensified in Israel, for locusts were recognized as God's instrument of punishment for covenant violations (Deut. 28:38, 42; cf. Amos 4:9; Joel 1:1-7).

7:2. In his vision Amos saw that the locusts **stripped the land clean** of all vegetation—both seeded crops and wild growth. Knowing that the nation would die if this vision became a reality, Amos begged the **sovereign LORD** to **forgive** the people of their sins. Though Israel was unrepentant, though her guilt was overwhelming, and though the punishment was just, Amos nevertheless pleaded with God not to bring this punishment on the nation. **Jacob** would never **survive** it. Jeroboam II's proud people might think themselves invulnerable (6:1-3, 8, 13; 9:10), but when viewed in the face of God's awesome might and wrath they were in reality **so small,** so helpless, so pitiable. By calling Israel "Jacob," Amos perhaps meant to remind God of His early commitment to the ancestor when he was at Bethel, a site still hallowed by his descendants (Gen. 28:10-22; Amos 3:14; 4:4; 5:5-6; 7:13). Jacob is mentioned in 3:13; 6:8; 7:2, 5; 8:7; 9:8.

7:3. Moved by the prophet's prayer, **the LORD relented** and promised that the swarm of locusts would **not happen.** (The word "relent" suggests a turning away and a relief from an earlier decision because one has been deeply stirred by the appeal of another; cf. comments on Ex. 32:11-14.)

The nation was not forgiven, but this particular punishment was withdrawn. Amos did not ask for forgiveness again (cf. Amos 7:2 with v. 5), for some judgment on Israel was inevitable. But by his prayers he was able to affect what form that judgment would take.

B. The devouring fire (7:4-6)

7:4. In a second vision **the sovereign LORD** showed Amos a second terror—a **judgment by fire.** God intensified the blazing summer heat till all grasslands and trees became tinder dry. Then fires broke out and spread in every direction with incredible speed (cf. Joel 1:19-20). Attempts to combat the sweeping inferno were futile, for **the great deep,** the subterranean waters that fed all springs (Gen. 7:11; 49:25; Deut. 33:13), had **dried up.** With the source of all waters consumed, the rivers and streams disappeared, and the flames raged unchecked until they had **devoured the land** (cf. Deut. 32:22).

7:5-6. Again, distraught by the vision, Amos begged God to **stop,** and **the LORD relented** a second time. Neither would fire be the means by which He would punish the nation (see comments on v. 3).

C. The testing plumb line (7:7-17)

1. THE VISION (7:7-9)

For the third time the prophet was shown a vision of judgment. This time the sentence was unalterable.

7:7-8. The LORD held **in His hand** a **plumb line. A plumb line** was a cord with a lead weight used by builders to make sure that walls were constructed straight up and down. A plumb line was also used to test existing walls to see whether they had settled and tilted, needing to be torn down.

God was **setting a plumb line** (possibly the covenant Law and its requirements; cf. Isa. 28:17) **among** His **people Israel.** The nation had been built "true to plumb," but now was out of line and needed to be torn down.

God quickly precluded any appeal from His prophet. The matter was settled; He would **spare them no longer.** This was the form His judgment would take (see comments on Amos 7:3, 5-6).

7:9. Having failed the test of the plumb line, the nation's chief "structures"—both religious and political—would be demolished. **The numerous high places** (hilltop shrines) **of Isaac** would **be destroyed.** Like "Jacob" (see comments on 3:13) and "Joseph" (cf. 5:6, 15; 6:6) "Isaac" was a name for the Northern Kingdom. The larger official **sanctuaries of** worship, such as Bethel and Gilgal, would **be ruined** (cf. 3:14; 4:4; 5:5-6; 7:13). **And the house** (political dynasty) **of Jeroboam** II would crumble under the stroke of God's **sword** (cf. 2 Kings 14:29; 15:10).

2. THE INCIDENT (7:10-17)

The incident recorded in verses 10-17 is integrally tied to Amos' third vision (vv. 7-9) in two ways. First, it reveals the immediate historical reaction to the vision's content. The fact that certain words appear in both the vision and the incident, but nowhere else in the book after 1:1 (viz., "Isaac" in 7:9, 16; "sanctuaries" and "sanctuary" in vv. 9-11), indicates that the episode was an immediate response to the revelation.

Second, the historical incident is linked to the vision because it represents a concrete example of the "plumb line" in operation, this time as a test of individuals. The vision had revealed that Israel's institutions, both religious and political, had failed the test and would have to come down. Now, in the incident with Amaziah, the sovereign Lord drew near to measure two men—one a prophet, the other a priest. One was accepted; the other was not. One heard and obeyed the voice of the Lord; the other refused to hear.

a. The challenge (7:10-13)

7:10-13. As **Amos** began publicly to recount his vision of ruined sanctuaries and dynastic demise, he was challenged by **Amaziah the priest of Bethel.**

Bethel was one of the two state sanctuaries established by Jeroboam I when in 931 B.C. he broke from Jerusalem and the kingdom there (1 Kings 12:26-33). In order to unite the 10 tribes around his rule, Jeroboam I created a new shrine and a duplicate religious system. The purpose of the calf, altar, priesthood, and festivals of Bethel was to give credence and stability to Jeroboam I's Northern Kingdom.

In Amos' day the shrine at Bethel was **the king's sanctuary and the temple** (lit., "house," but frequently used as a synonym for "temple"; cf. 1 Kings 6; 8:6-66; 2 Chron. 2:1) **of the kingdom** (Amos 7:13). Besides being the site where Jeroboam II worshiped, it was, more importantly, the religious symbol which rallied political commitment to the kingdom. As the temple in Jerusalem drew devotion to the lineage of David, so the existence of Bethel implied God's sanction and support of the Northern monarch. To denounce Bethel and its system of worship (cf. 3:14; 4:4-5; 5:5-6, 21-26; also note 7:9; 9:1) was to attack the very foundation of the kingdom.

Amaziah was evidently Bethel's chief priest, in charge of worship and personnel (cf. Jer. 20:1-2; 29:26). Hearing Amos' forboding words against the sanctuary and the monarch, Amaziah **sent a message to Jeroboam** charging Amos with **raising a conspiracy against** the king **in the very heart of** the Northern Kingdom. He warned Jeroboam that **the land** could not **bear** such repeated messages of catastrophe: the people would be demoralized or sooner or later some dissident rebel would be prompted to fulfill the predictions. On previous occasions a prophet's words against a king had been followed by internal revolt and by a change in dynasties (1 Kings 11:29–12:24; 16:1-13; 2 Kings 8:7-15; 9).

Amaziah refused to acknowledge in any way the divine source of Amos' prophecies, choosing instead to view him as a political agitator. In his report to Jeroboam he prefaced the threatening quote (Amos 7:11) with, **This is what Amos is saying,** rather than with, "This is what God has said." In quoting Amos, the priest deliberately omitted the prophet's words about God's claim of personal action, "with *My* sword *I* will rise against . . . Jeroboam" (v. 9). Amaziah substituted the simple fact, **Jeroboam will die.** He reported Amos' words in a form designed to incite the king, twisting the prediction of the dynasty's fall (v. 9) into a threat against Jeroboam himself (v. 11), and highlighting the announcements of national **exile** (v. 11; cf. 4:3; 5:5, 27; 6:7; cf. 7:17). Amaziah chose to see Amos as a menace to the status quo rather than as a messenger from the God of Israel.

Having dispatched his letter to the king, **Amaziah** then confronted **Amos** with the strong directive, **Get out, you seer!** Claiming authority over the activities **at Bethel,** the priest ordered Amos to **go back to** his home in **Judah** (cf. 1:1) and **do** his **prophesying there.**

A "seer" (7:12) was another name for a prophet (1 Sam. 9:9; 2 Sam. 24:11; Isa. 29:10). This title called attention to the prophet's activity of beholding or "seeing" visions (Isa. 1:1; 2:1; Obad. 1; Micah 1:1; Nahum 1:1; Amos 1:1). These visions were "seen" by the prophets mentally and spiritually. Amaziah, reacting to Amos' "visions" (7:1, 4, 7), used the word in a derogatory sense. His scornful advice to **earn your bread** in Judah implied that Amos was a professional predictor who made his living selling prophecies (Micah 3:5, 11; cf. the women of Ezek. 13:17-20 who prophesied "out of their own imagination. . . . for a few handfuls of barley and scraps of bread").

The stress in Amaziah's words fell on the location or geography of Amos' activity: "Go to *Judah,* earn your bread *there,* do your prophesying *there,* but don't prophesy anymore *at Bethel."* In his authority as the king's priest he commanded Amos, "Leave *Israel!"* Amos' response, however, was that a greater Authority had commanded him to prophesy *in Israel.*

b. The response (7:14-17)

7:14-15. Amos denied that his ministry was self-generated, insisting that it was solely the result of God's initiative. Amos had not chosen the calling of **a prophet nor** had he trained for it by becoming **a prophet's son** (i.e., a member of a prophetic school under the tutelage of a "father"; cf. 2 Kings 2:1-15; 4:1, 38; 5:22; 6:1-7; 9:1). On the contrary, he had been profitably and contentedly occupied as **a shepherd, and** as a grower **of syca-more-fig trees.** (For a discussion of Amos' occupation, see "The Prophet" section in the *Introduction*.) **But** one day **the LORD took** him—the same verb is used for God's calling the Levites (Num. 18:6) and David (2 Sam. 7:8; Ps. 78:70)— **from tending the flock, and** the Lord (the words "the LORD" are repeated in Heb.) commissioned him to **Go, prophesy to My people Israel.** In the NASB the contrast is heightened between Amos' threefold denial of self-seeking ("I" . . . "I" . . . "I," Amos 7:14) and his threefold assertion of "the LORD's" authority (vv. 15-16). God had commanded him not only what to say but also where to say it. The authority was not Amaziah's, but the Lord's. The place, therefore, would not be Judah, but Israel. The Lord had spoken, and Amos would prophesy as He directed (cf. 3:8; Acts 5:27-29).

7:16-17. Now this same **LORD** had a **word** for the priest who had dared to forbid what He had commanded (cf. 2:11-12). Because Amaziah had rejected God's word **against** the nation, he and his family would suffer the full fate of the nation. When the divine sentence of **exile** was carried out (cf. 5:5, 27; 6:7; 7:11; 9:4), he would be among those swept **away from their native land.** His **wife** would be forced to make a living as **a prostitute in the** very **city** where once she had been among the most distinguished women. His posterity and name would come to an end as **the sword** claimed the lives of his **sons and daughters.** His estate would **be measured and divided up** among foreigners (cf. 2 Kings 17:24; Jer. 6:12), and he himself would **die in a pagan** (lit., "an unclean") **country.** He would be stripped of his office, bereft of a shrine, and defiled by the unclean food of a heathen land (cf. Ezek. 4:13; Hosea 9:3-4).

Had Amaziah responded differently, had he repented at Amos' word, he might have been spared (Amos 5:4-6, 14-15). But instead he chose to align with an earthly monarch, to embrace the national mood of pride and security, and to assert his authority against God's messenger. So the Lord quietly withdrew the plumb line. He would spare Amaziah no longer.

D. The culminating fruit (chap. 8)

1. THE VISION (8:1-3)

8:1-2. The sovereign LORD appeared a fourth time to **Amos,** this time asking him to identify an object. When Amos **answered** that it was **a basket of ripe fruit . . . the** LORD then replied, **The time is ripe** (lit., "The end has come") **for My people Israel.**

The meaning of the Lord's reply lay in the similar sound and significance of the words "ripe fruit" (v. 1) and "time is ripe" (v. 2). "Ripe fruit" (*qāyiṣ*) was "summer fruit" or "end-of-the-year fruit"—the last fruit of the season, fully ripened, with a short edible life. "Ripe time" (*qēṣ*) was "end time" or "cutting time"—the "reaping time" of death.

Israel was ripe for a dreadful harvest; her end had come. There would be no stay of execution, no last-minute reprieve. The Lord would **spare them no longer.**

8:3. On the **day** (cf. vv. 9, 13; see 5:18-20 for comments on "the day of the LORD") when God would "end" Israel's life (cf. 5:2-3; 6:9-10), **the songs in the temple** would **turn to wailing** (cf. 8:10; 5:16-17). Hymns of joy and trust in the Lord would turn to howling chants of lamentation and disbelief at what His hand had done to them. The cause of their grief would be the **many, many dead bodies** lying **everywhere.** So great would be the **slaughter** that there would not be enough people or places to bury the dead. Innumerable corpses would lie on the ground, to be eaten by dogs and birds, or to become fertilizing dung for the fields (1 Kings 14:11; Jer. 8:2; 9:22; 16:4).

When the weary mourners would finally cease their weeping, when they would lift wet eyes and questioning faces to seek a reason for the sorrow that engulfed them, they would find only **silence.** No answer would come. God would have no more words to say.

2. THE RESULTS (8:4-14)

These two results of God's judgment—human grief and divine silence—are described more fully in verses 4-14.

a. Human grief (8:4-10)

Because of their greed and dishonest practices, God would cause an unprece-

AMOS

dented mourning in the land.

8:4-6. Israel's businessmen single-mindedly pursued a profit, and did not care that they were trampling **the needy and** doing **away with the poor of the land** (cf. 2:6-7; 5:11). Preoccupied with making money, the businessmen begrudged the interruptions caused by the monthly feast of **the New Moon** and the weekly observance of **the Sabbath.** They impatiently fidgeted till these days of rest and worship (Ex. 20:8-11; 23:12; 31:14-17; 34:21; Num. 28:11-15; 2 Kings 4:23; Isa. 1:13-14; Ezek. 46:1-6; Hosea 2:11) were **over** so that they could resume their aggressive dealings.

They cunningly found ways to add to their profits—**skimping the** standard **measure** so that customers got less than they paid for, **boosting the price** by substituting heavier shekel-weights so that customers were overcharged, **and cheating with dishonest scales** by tampering with the cross beam of the balances. Not content with these covenant violations (Lev. 19:35-36; Deut. 25:13-16; cf. Prov. 11:1; 16:11; 20:10, 23; Hosea 12:7; Micah 6:10-11), they compounded their sin by deceptively **selling** an inferior product— **the sweepings** of soiled and trampled grain mixed and packaged **with the** clean pure **wheat.** They cared nothing about human suffering or the inability of **the poor** to pay their prices. Instead, they forced **the needy** into slavery in exchange for insignificant sums (see Amos 2:6 for comments on **a pair of sandals**).

8:7-8. The LORD, however, had **sworn by** Himself (see comments on 4:2; 6:8; unlike its use in 6:8, **the Pride of Jacob** occurs here as a title for God; cf. 1 Sam. 15:29). God swore that He would **never forget** any of the evil things **they** had **done.** Because of their heartless greed and dishonesty, because of these covenant violations, their Warrior-God would advance against them and **the land** would **tremble** under His steps. The quaking tremors would be so violent that **the whole land** would **rise . . . and then sink like the** annual swelling and receding of **the Nile . . . the river of Egypt.** The shattered ruins of farms and buildings would cause all who lived in the wake of His path to weep and to **mourn.**

8:9-10. That day of punishment would be a day of darkness (cf. comments on 5:18-20), for **the sovereign**

LORD would bring about eclipses; **the sun** would **go down at noon and darken the earth in broad daylight.** Eclipses in 784 B.C. and 763 B.C. would have enabled Amos' hearers to imagine the eerie fear and panic of such a time. Then in the midst of earthquake (8:8) and darkness the avenging Lord would begin His decimation of the people (cf. 5:2-3; 6:9-10; 8:3). The sword of their God would bring unprecedented grief on the land as He turned their **feasts into** funerals, **and all** their glad **singing into weeping** laments (cf. v. 3). The loss of life would be so widespread that every family would grieve and every home would observe the rites of mourning. God would cause **all of** them to **wear sackcloth** (a coarsely woven material, generally made of goats' hair) against their bodies (Gen. 37:34; 2 Sam. 3:31; 2 Kings 6:30; Job 16:15-16; Dan. 9:3) and **shave** their **heads** as a sign of sorrow (Job 1:20; Isa. 3:24; 15:2-3; Jer. 47:5; 48:37; Ezek. 7:18; 27:30-31; Micah 1:16). The intensity of their grief would be like the most tragic mourning of all— the **mourning for an only son,** whose death ended every hope for a family's future (Jer. 6:26; Zech. 12:10).

The end of that day would not be the end of their grief. Instead, its culmination would usher in another **bitter day**—the mourners' own "bitter day" of death. (For the day of one's death as a "bitter day"; cf. 1 Sam. 15:32; Job 21:25; Ecc. 7:26.) After a day of mourning for others, the mourners themselves would die.

b. Divine silence (8:11-14)

This agony of human grief would be even more unbearable in the face of God's awful silence (v. 3).

8:11-12. Since Israel had rejected all His words (2:11-12; 7:10-13, 16), they would hear His words no more. **The sovereign** LORD would **send a famine,** but this would **not** be **a famine of food** as before (cf. 4:6), **but a famine of hearing the words of the** LORD. They would desperately inquire of Him, but He would not answer—not by dreams, not by Urim, not by prophet (1 Sam. 28:6; cf. 1 Sam. 3:1). **Men** would **stagger** to every corner of the land, wandering in a complete circuit of Israel's territory **(from the** Dead Sea in the south **to the Mediterranean Sea** in the west, and from the **north to the east), searching for the word of the**

Lord—a word of explanation, of forgiveness, of hope. **But they** would **not find it.** When their grief would finally drive them to "seek the Lord" (Amos 5:4-6), the Lord would not be found. It would be too late.

8:13-14. In that day (cf. vv. 3, 9) even **lovely young women and strong young men**—those capable of enduring and persisting in the search the longest—would **faint because of** an unrelieved **thirst** to hear God's Word. Those who had perverted the worship of God, who had seen in the idol-calves **of Samaria** (Hosea 8:5-6) and **Dan** (1 Kings 12:28-30; 2 Kings 10:29) and in the image **of Beersheba** (Amos 5:5) a symbol of His power, would flock to the capital or traverse to the farthest points in a bravado appeal. Samaria's idol is called its **shame** or more literally, its guilt, because the idol-worship resulted in the Samaritans being guilty before God. (The expression "from Dan to Beersheba" encompasses the full extent of the land; Jud. 20:1; 1 Sam. 3:20; 2 Sam. 3:10; 17:11; 24:2, 15; 1 Kings 4:25; 2 Chron. 30:5.) But their imploring would be futile. God would remain silent. And **they** would **fall, never to rise again** (cf. Amos 5:2).

E. The avenging Lord (9:1-10)

In a fifth and final vision, Amos witnessed the Sovereign of the universe wielding an inescapable sword against all the sinners among His people.

1. THE INESCAPABLE SWORD (9:1-4)

9:1. At the autumn festival, when a large congregation had assembled at the sanctuary at Bethel, and the Northern monarch had approached the altar with his sacrifice (1 Kings 12:31-33), Amos **saw the Lord standing by the altar.** The Lord was indeed "with them" (Amos 5:14), but to destroy and to kill, not to bless. The "end" had come for the altar, the sanctuary, and the people (3:14; 5:5-6; 8:1-3).

The Lord commanded, **Smash the tops of the pillars so that** the crashing roof would cause even **the** great stone **thresholds** to **shake.** The thresholds were massive foundation stones on which the doorposts were fixed (Isa. 6:4; Ezek. 40:6).

In his vision Amos apparently saw the entire structure collapse, killing most of the gathered worshipers (cf. Jud. 16:29-30), for a second command came quickly, **Cut off the heads of all the people** who yet remain alive. The Lord was determined that **not** one would **get away; none** would **escape** (cf. 1 Kings 18:40). **Those who** survived and fled the disaster He would pursue and **kill with the sword** (cf. Amos 9:4, 10).

9:2-4. Even if they could flee to the outer reaches of the universe, He would find them and **slay them.** Neither **the depths of the grave** nor the heights of **the heavens** could separate them from the wrath of God (cf. Ps. 139:7-8; and note the contrast in Rom. 8:38-39). **Though they** hid in the dense forests of Mount Carmel (cf. Amos 1:2) or in some of its many limestone caves, He would **hunt them down and seize them.** If **they** somehow could **hide from** Him **at the bottom of the sea,** they would discover that **there** too He ruled, for **the serpent** would obey His command. This serpent is a sea monster, sometimes called Leviathan or Rahab, the personification of the sea's defeated power (cf. Job 26:12-13; Pss. 74:13-14; 89:9-10; Isa. 27:1; 51:9-10). Even if **enemies** captured them and herded them like cattle **into exile,** to be under the protection of a foreign king and god, no foreign power could shield them from God's relentless **sword** (cf. Amos 9:1, 10). Escape was impossible, for wherever they went God would **fix** His **eyes** on **them for evil and not for good.** He was determined to destroy them.

2. THE UNIVERSAL SOVEREIGN (9:5-6)

9:5-6. The One Amos saw by the altar (v. 1) was **the Lord Almighty,** the great suzerain Warrior whose power was irresistible (cf. comments on 3:13). As the Sovereign, not only of Israel and the other nations (1:3–2:16; 3:9; 9:4, 7) but also of the vast universe, He could speak with certainty that there would be no escape for Israel anywhere in His universe. **He** whose finger merely **touches the earth,** causing the mountains to quake and "melt" (i.e., "flatten"; cf. Micah 1:3-4; Nahum 1:5), **the whole land** to undulate **like the Nile,** and the inhabitants to **mourn** (cf. Amos 8:8), would surely possess a powerful "hand" to "seize" (9:2-3) rebels from any spot on earth. **He who** built **His lofty palace in**

the heavens could not fail to reach any who sought refuge in "the heavens" (v. 2). He who controls the waters of the sea (cf. 5:8) would surely be obeyed by its denizens (9:3). The LORD is His name. His majesty and His power over creation means that they would not be able to escape Him. And as the Lord (Yahweh, the covenant-keeping God), He would keep His Word and judge those who had disobeyed Him. Interestingly the two verses in Amos that include the exclamation "The LORD is His name" speak of His sovereignty over the universe (5:8; 9:6).

3. THE IMPARTIAL SIFTING (9:7-10)

9:7. Israel's special position as His people would not save them from punishment (cf. 3:1-2). God would act toward them as toward any other nation within His universal domain. They would be **the same to** Him **as the Cushites,** who lived in what is today southern Egypt, all of Sudan, and northern Ethiopia. In Israel's thinking, the Cushites were a foreign and unimportant people living at the periphery of the known world.

God is the Sovereign of every nation. He had not only brought **Israel up from Egypt** (cf. 2:10; 3:1), but had also guided the historical migrations of their arch-enemies—**the Philistines from Caphtor** (cf. Jer. 47:4; Zeph. 2:5), probably another name for the island of Crete, **and the Arameans from Kir** (cf. Amos 1:5), a location in Mesopotamia. And as God had determined to reverse the destinies of those two nations (cf. 1:3-8), so He had determined to send Israel into exile (4:2-3; 5:5, 27; 6:7; 7:11, 17; 9:4). He would punish rebellion wherever it occurred.

9:8-10. Having declared that He would make no distinction between Israel and other nations, God then solemnly uttered His final edict of death. Verses 8-10 are the three final statements of judgment in the Book of Amos. They vow an impartial and certain death to all the sinners of the land.

Though these three statements seal the nation's doom, they also look forward to the final section of the book (vv. 11-15) where God speaks of a restoration after judgment. The first two statements (vv. 8-9) each conclude with a brief allusion to a spared remnant. The third statement (v. 10) is followed by God's full promise of renewal and covenant blessing.

The eyes (cf. v. 4) **of the sovereign** LORD were keeping close watch **on the sinful kingdom** (Israel) to make sure that the judgment came. His purpose was to **destroy it from the face of the earth.** Their Suzerain would fulfill the covenant curses until no trace of the nation remained (cf. comments on 1:2; 4:6; also note the use of "destroy" in the punishment sections of Israel's covenant; Deut. 28:20, 24 ["ruined"], 45, 48, 51, 61, 63). **Yet** God would **not totally destroy the house of Jacob** (i.e., the Northern Kingdom; cf. Amos 3:13-14; 6:8; 7:2, 5; 8:7). Some would be spared. The earlier possibility of a remnant (see "perhaps" in 5:15) was now made certain. God would indeed have mercy on those who repented (cf. 5:4-6, 14-15, 23-24).

Wherever His people were scattered **among all the nations,** God would impartially **shake** them **as grain is shaken in a sieve. But not a kernel** would **fall to the ground.** As a fine-meshed sieve lets the chaff and dust go through, but catches the good grain, so God would screen out and save any righteous among His people.

Others suggest that the sieve in view is the coarse-meshed sieve used at the beginning of the sifting process to screen out the stones and clods of earth, letting the smaller grains fall through (cf. the apocryphal Ecclesiasticus 27:5). If so, the "kernel" (lit., "pebble"; cf. the "piece" of a city wall in 2 Sam. 17:13) refers to a sinner who would not be allowed to escape through the screen of God's judgment.

In either interpretation the final point is the same: God's impartial sifting would separate the righteous from the sinners.

All the sinners among His **people** would then **die by** His inescapable **sword** (cf. Amos 9:1, 4). Their self-confident boasting would finally end (cf. 6:1-3, 13) for the promised **disaster** would destroy them.

V. The Restoration after Judgment (9:11-15)

After all God's judgments are past, when the nation has received full punishment for her sins, the Lord will move in mercy to renew and refresh His people. God will restore David's kingdom over both the North and the South, and through it He will bless all nations of the earth. He will reverse the covenant curses and bring unprecedented prosperity to the land. Dispersed Israel will be returned to her land, there to dwell securely and enjoy its goodness. Then He who has always claimed them as "My people" (7:8, 15; 8:2; 9:10, 14; cf. Hosea 2:23; Zech. 8:8; 13:9) will once again take the title "your God" (Amos 9:15).

A. Political renewal (9:11)

9:11. In that day (cf. Isa. 4:2; Micah 4:6; 5:10) God will **restore David's fallen tent.** Previous references in Amos to "that day" had spoken of it as a day of darkness and destruction (Amos 2:16; 3:14; 5:18-20; 8:3, 9, 11, 13). But when Israel's ordeal is finally over, "that day" will also become the day of her renewal.

God will reestablish David's "tent" over both the Northern and Southern Kingdoms. A "tent" (lit., "booth") or awning was made by setting up a simple frame and spreading branches over it. Its primary purpose was to shelter those under it, whether troops in the field (2 Sam. 11:11; 1 Kings 20:12-16), a watchman at post (Jonah 4:5), or pilgrims at the Feast of Booths (also called the Feast of Tabernacles, Lev. 23:33-42). David's dynasty, which had been a protective canopy over all the people of Israel, had "fallen" with the great schism of the 10 Northern tribes from the 2 Southern tribes (1 Kings 12). This booth had been broken in two. But God promised to unite the two kingdoms once again under Davidic rule (cf. Jer. 30:3-10; Ezek. 37:15-28; Hosea 3:4-5). He will restore the sheltering tent, **repair its broken places,** building it as it used to be. God will carry out His good promise to David that He would raise up a Descendant after him and establish His rule forever (2 Sam. 7:11-16, 25-29).

B. National purpose (9:12)

9:12. The united kingdom under its Davidic King will then become the source of blessing to all Gentiles. **Edom,** a nation perpetually hostile toward God's people (cf. Num. 20:14-21; Ps. 137:7; Obad. 1; see comments on Amos 1:11-12), and therefore representative of all Israel's enemies, will become a sharer in the promises to David: Israel will **possess the remnant of** Edom (cf. Obad. 19). In fact, **all . . . nations** will be brought under the dominion of the Davidic King, for they too **bear** God's **name.** To "bear someone's name" meant to be under the suzerainty and protection of that individual (cf. Deut. 28:9-10; 2 Sam. 12:26-28; 1 Kings 8:43; Isa. 4:1; 63:19; Jer. 15:16; Dan. 9:18-19). All nations belong to God (cf. Amos 1:3–2:16; 3:9; 9:4, 7) and therefore will be included in the blessings of the future kingdom.

From the beginning, God's plan has been to provide salvation for the Gentile nations. His promise to Abraham was that through his descendants "all peoples on earth" will be blessed (Gen. 12:3; cf. Gen. 18:18; 22:17-18; 26:3-4; 28:13-14). Through Isaiah God continually affirmed that a united Israel under its Davidic King, the Messiah, will bring light, justice, and full knowledge of **the LORD** to all nations on the earth (Isa. 9:1-7; 11:1-13; 42:1-7; 45:22-25; 49:5-7; 55:1-5). When God restores the kingdom (the Millennium) under David's Son, both Jews and Gentiles will bear the name of the Lord.

At the Jerusalem Council, James cited Amos 9:11-12 as proof that the Gentiles of his day need not be circumcised and live as Jews in order to be saved (Acts. 15:1-20). James was aware that Israel's judgments were not yet over (cf. the Lord's statements regarding the coming destruction of the temple and renewed persecution and death, Matt. 24:1-22; Luke 21:5-24, and that the restoration had not yet begun; cf. Acts 1:6-7). But James also knew from Amos' succinct statement and from extended passages in other prophets (cf. "prophets" in Acts 15:15; also note Isa. 42:6; 60:3; Mal. 1:11) that when the promised kingdom would come, the Gentiles will share in it as Gentiles and not as quasi-Jews. Since this was God's millennial purpose, James concluded that the church should not require Gentiles to relinquish their identity and live as Jews. James was not saying the church fulfills the promises to Israel in Amos 9:11-12. He was saying that since Gentiles will be saved in the yet-to-come Millennium, they need not become Jews in the Church Age (see extended comments on Acts 15:15-18).

C. *Prosperity, peace, and permanence (9:13-15)*

9:13. The days are coming when God will remove all curses (cf. the comments on 4:6 and the chart "The Covenant Chastenings") and restore covenant blessings to the land (cf. Lev. 26:3-10; Deut. 28:1-14).

Instead of drought and famine (Amos 1:2; 4:6-8), there will be unending prosperity (9:13; cf. Lev. 26:3-5, 10; Deut. 28:4-5, 8, 11-12).

Instead of the turmoil of war (Amos 2:13-16; 3:11, 15; 4:10-11; 5:2-3; 6:9-10; 7:17; 9:1, 10), there will be unbroken peace which will enable Israel to enjoy the fruit of her labor (v. 14; cf. Lev. 26:6; Deut. 28:6).

Instead of the fear of exile (Amos 4:2-3; 5:5, 27; 6:7; 7:11, 17; 9:4), Israel will confidently defend herself from every foe and remain in the land (v. 15; cf. Lev. 26:7-8; Deut. 28:7, 10).

In the days when God restores Israel, the land will be so productive (cf. Isa. 27:6) that **the plowman** who starts in October will have to wait for **the reaper** who should have finished in May. **The one** who treads **grapes** in July will find **the planter** still sowing new seed into the ground broken by the long-delayed plowman. The grapes will hang so heavy in the mountain vineyards that **the hills** will **drip** and **flow** (lit., "melt") with **new wine** (cf. Joel 3:18). So much juice will drip from the vines or overflow from the vats that **the mountains** will appear from a distance to be "dissolving" as softened mud will ooze down the slopes.

9:14. God's restored **people Israel** will live in peace and be able to enjoy lavish abundance. The frustration and insecurity of war will be a thing of the past (cf. Isa. 2:4; Micah 4:3). They will build houses (cf. Amos 5:11) and even whole **cities and live in them** (cf. Isa. 32:18). They will **drink** and **eat** and take pleasure in the labor of their hands.

9:15. God will **plant Israel in** her **own land, never again to be uprooted** and exiled **from the land** He has **given them** (cf. Gen. 13:14-15; 17:7-8; Deut. 30:1-5; 2 Sam. 7:10; Jer. 30:10-11; Joel 3:17-21; Micah 4:4-7). The land will be inhabited by Israel (cf. Ezek. 37:25; Joel 3:20; Zech. 14:11).

The LORD will certainly "do these things" (Amos 9:12), for He is the One who had been, was then, and always will be their **God.**

BIBLIOGRAPHY

Barton, John. *Amos's Oracles against the Nations: A Study of Amos 1:3–2:5.* Cambridge: Cambridge University Press, 1980.

Cohen, Gary G., and Vandermey, H. Ronald. *Hosea/Amos.* Everyman's Bible Commentary. Chicago: Moody Press, 1981.

Cripps, Richard S. *A Critical and Exegetical Commentary on the Book of Amos.* 2nd ed. London: S.P.C.K., 1955. Reprint. Minneapolis: Klock & Klock Christian Publishers, 1981.

De Waard, Jan, and Smalley, William A. *A Translator's Handbook on the Book of Amos.* Stuttgart: United Bible Societies, 1979.

Feinberg, Charles L. *The Minor Prophets.* Chicago: Moody Press, 1976.

Hammershaimb, Erling. *The Book of Amos: A Commentary.* Translated by John Sturdy. New York: Schocken Books, 1970.

Harper, William Rainey. *A Critical and Exegetical Commentary on the Books of Amos and Hosea.* The International Critical Commentary. Edinburgh: T. & T. Clark, 1905.

Mays, James Luther. *Amos: A Commentary.* Philadelphia: Westminster Press, 1969.

Motyer, J.A. *The Day of the Lion: The Message of Amos.* Downers Grove, Ill.: InterVarsity Press, 1974.

Tatford, Frederick A. *The Minor Prophets.* Vol. 1. Reprint (3 vols.). Minneapolis: Klock & Klock Christian Publishers, 1982.

Veldkamp, Herman. *The Farmer from Tekoa.* St. Catherines, Ontario: Paideia Press, 1977.

Wolf, Hans Walter. *Joel and Amos.* Translated by Waldemar Janzen; S. Dean McBride, Jr.; and Charles A. Muenchow. Philadelphia: Fortress Press, 1977.

OBADIAH

Walter L. Baker

INTRODUCTION

Obadiah, with its 21 verses, is the shortest Old Testament book. To many people this book has little appeal and is little known. Its message is primarily one of doom and judgment, and it is not quoted in the New Testament. Yet the Book of Obadiah merits careful study and reading for it contains a powerful message about the justice of God. His righteousness demanded vengeance on Edom, Israel's perennial enemy. Judgment against Edom is mentioned in more Old Testament books than it is against any other foreign nation (cf. Isa. 11:14; 34:5-17; 63:1-6; Jer. 9:25-26; 25:17-26; 49:7-22; Lam. 4:21-22; Ezek. 25:12-14; 35; Joel 3:19; Amos 1:11-12; 9:11-12; Obad.; Mal. 1:4).

In a sense Obadiah is a miniature profile of the message of all the writing prophets. In his thumbnail sketch, the Prophet Obadiah spoke of God's judgment on unbelieving Gentiles who oppressed the nation Israel. He also wrote of God's grace to believing Israel. This double thread is woven throughout the Major and Minor Prophets.

This small book speaks of the danger of the great sin of pride and arrogance, the feeling of superiority that often results from taking advantage of others. Obadiah graphically illustrates on a national scale the truth of Proverbs 16:18, "Pride goes before destruction, a haughty spirit before a fall."

Authorship. At least 12 Old Testament men were named Obadiah including an officer in David's army (1 Chron. 12:9), Ahab's servant (1 Kings 18:3), a Levite in the days of Josiah (2 Chron. 34:12), and a leader who returned from the Exile with Ezra (Ezra 8:9). Nothing is known of the author of this small prophetic profile except that his name means "Worshiper of Yahweh."

Date. Since the Bible gives no facts about the life or background of the man who wrote the Book of Obadiah, the date of its writing has been debated. Three suggestions for the date have been made: (a) in the reign of Jehoram (848–841 B.C.), son of Jehoshaphat, (b) in the reign of Ahaz (731–715 B.C.), and (c) in 585 B.C., soon after the destruction of Jerusalem by the Babylonians in 586.

Conservative scholars are about equally divided between the first and third views, and most liberal scholars hold the third view. A few hold the middle view because 2 Chronicles 28:17 speaks of the Edomites attacking Jerusalem and carrying off prisoners. Another argument used to suggest that the events in Obadiah (vv. 1-14) happened in Ahaz's reign (view b) is that the Edomites were able to move into Elath (at the southern tip of the Edomite territory) when Rezin drove out the Judahites in Ahaz's day (2 Kings 16:6). However, the Edomites' move into Elath does not correspond with the statements in Obadiah's book.

Arguments for the late date of the writing of Obadiah (after the fall of Jerusalem—view c) include the following:

1. The similarity of several verses in Obadiah to verses in Jeremiah 49 suggest that Obadiah quoted from Jeremiah.

Obadiah	Jeremiah
v. 1	49:14
v. 2	49:15
vv. 3-4	49:16
v. 5	49:9
v. 6	49:10
v. 8	49:7
v. 9	49:22b
v. 16	49:12

2. The word "destruction" in Obadiah 12 speaks of Judah's fall to Babylon.

3. The word "exiles" (gālûṯ), used twice in Obadiah 20, refers to the Jewish

captives exiled in Babylon.

4. Obadiah's description of the Edomites' opposition to Jerusalem is similar to the statement in Psalm 137:7 about the Edomites tearing down Jerusalem. Also Obadiah 16-18 is similar to Lamentations 4:21-22.

These arguments, however, are answerable:

1. Jeremiah often quoted from or alluded to earlier prophets. Also several verses in Joel are similar to those in Obadiah. The words "as the LORD has said" (Joel 2:32) clearly indicate that the contents of that verse refer to Obadiah 17. So Obadiah must have been written before Joel which may have been written about 830 B.C. Obadiah may also have been referred to by Amos who wrote in the eighth century. The references or allusions to Obadiah in Joel and Amos (not always word for word) are:

Obadiah	Joel	Obadiah	Amos
v. 10	3:19	vv. 9-10, 18	1:11-12
v. 11	3:3	v. 14	1:6
v. 15	1:15; 2:1; 3:3-4, 14	v. 19	9:12
v. 17	2:32; 3:17		

2. The word "destruction" in Obadiah 12 need not mean Judah's total devastation by the Babylonians.

3. The word gālûṯ in Obadiah 20 can refer to a small group of exiles, not necessarily to the entire populace of Jewish captives taken to Babylon.

4. True, the Edomites abetted the Babylonians in their destruction of Jerusalem in 586 B.C. (Ps. 137:7). But the Book of Obadiah does not refer to the total destruction of the city by Nebuchadnezzar, which included pillaging and burning of the temple, burning of houses, and the demolition of the walls. Also no extrabiblical record indicates that the Babylonians "cast lots for Jerusalem" (Obad. 11), though admittedly this is an argument from silence. Therefore the casting of lots possibly occurred earlier.

The early date, sometime in the reign of Jehoram (848–841 B.C.), seems preferable for the following reasons:

1. The form of the Hebrew verbs in

verses 12-14 ("you should not . . .") warned Edom against doing again what she had already done. Had Jerusalem already been destroyed, these commands would have had no meaning.

2. Verse 14 refers to "fugitives," people who escaped from Jerusalem, but when the Babylonians captured Jerusalem no Jerusalemites escaped (except King Zedekiah and a few with him, but they were soon captured).

3. Obadiah made no mention of the complete destruction of the city of Jerusalem, or the burning of its temple and houses or the destruction of its walls.

4. Edom's rebellion against Judah in the days of Jehoram (2 Kings 8:20-22) may have occurred at the same time the Philistines and Arabians attacked Jerusalem (2 Chron. 21:16-17). This best fits the statements in Obadiah 11-14. When the Philistines, Arabians, and Edomites entered the city, they cast lots to decide which portions of the city would be granted to each contingent for the purpose of plunder.

Historical Background. The animosity between the Edomites and the Israelites is one of the oldest examples of discord in human relationships. The conflict began with a struggle between Jacob and Esau in the womb of their mother Rebekah (Gen. 25:21-26). Years later, when Esau was hungry, he readily traded his birthright to Jacob for some red stew. For that reason Esau was also called Edom (Gen. 25:30), which means red. Also when Esau was born his skin appeared red (Gen. 25:25). Later Esau moved to the land of Seir (Gen. 36:8-9), the red sandstone area southeast of the Dead Sea. There his descendants, the Edomites, displaced the Horites (Deut. 2:12, 22). Interestingly the Hebrew word for Seir (śē'îr) is similar to the word for "hairy" (śē'ār), the meaning of "Esau" ('ēśāw). "Seir" and "Mount Seir" became synonyms for Edom (2 Chron. 20:10; 25:11; Ezek. 35:15).

Edom refused to let the Israelites pass through their land when Israel was on the way to the Promised Land (Num. 20:14-21). But God told Israel not to hate Edom since they were related (Deut. 23:7). However, hostility developed and continued for centuries (Ezek. 35:5). Saul (1 Sam. 14:47), David (2 Sam. 8:13-14),

Joab (1 Kings 11:16), and Solomon (1 Kings 11:17-22) all had problems with the sons of Edom. Jehoshaphat of Judah and Joram of Israel joined with Edom in an attack against Moab (2 Kings 3). Also in Jehoshaphat's reign Edom joined the Ammonites and the Moabites in an attack against Judah, but the attack ended with the Ammonites and Moabites defeating the Edomites (2 Chron. 20:1-2, 10-11, 22-26).

In the reign of Jehoram, Jehoshaphat's son, Edom revolted against Judah and crowned their own king (2 Kings 8:20-22; 2 Chron. 21:8). Later Amaziah, king of Judah, crushed Edom, and changed the name of the city Sela to Joktheel (2 Kings 14:7; 2 Chron. 25:11-12). Later Edom attacked Judah during Ahaz's reign (2 Chron. 28:17). In 586 B.C. Edom encouraged Babylon to destroy Jerusalem (Ps. 137:7).

In the late sixth or early fifth century B.C. the Nabateans, from northern Arabia, worshipers of gods and goddesses of fertility and the celestial bodies, drove out most of the Edomites (see comments on Obad. 7). Apparently some remained in Edom and were absorbed by the Nabatean Arabs. The Nabateans were the renowned stone-carvers of Petra. The expelled Edomites settled in Idumea, the Greek name for southern Judea. Later (ca. 120 B.C.) the Edomites there, then called Idumeans, were subdued by John Hyrcanus, a Maccabean, who forced them to be circumcised and to follow Judaism (Josephus *The Antiquities of the Jews* 13. 9. 1; 14. 7. 9). Herod the Great, king of Judea from 37 B.C. to 4 B.C., was an Idumean (Edomite).

The Idumeans joined the Jews in their rebellion against Rome in A.D. 70, but were almost obliterated by Titus, the Roman general. Only a few Idumean refugees escaped. The Edomites then faded from history.

OUTLINE

I. Edom's Destruction (vv. 1-9)
    A. The call to the nations to destroy Edom (v. 1)
    B. The prophecy of Edom's destruction (vv. 2-9)
        1. Edom's pride to be debased (vv. 2-4)
        2. Edom's wealth to be plundered (vv. 5-7)
        3. Edom's people to be slaughtered (vv. 8-9)
II. Edom's Crimes (vv. 10-14)
    A. Violations in attitudes (vv. 10-12)
    B. Violations in actions (vv. 13-14)
III. God's Judgment on Israel's Enemies (vv. 15-16)
IV. God's Blessings on Israel's People (vv. 17-21)
    A. The deliverance of Israel (vv. 17-18)
    B. The delineation of Israel's territories (vv. 19-20)
    C. The establishment of the Lord's kingdom (v. 21)

COMMENTARY

I. Edom's Destruction (vv. 1-9)

A. The call to the nations to destroy Edom (v. 1)

V. 1. The word **vision** is also used in Isaiah 1:1, Micah 1:1, and Nahum 1:1 to introduce those prophetic books (cf. Dan. 1:17; 8:1; 9:24; Hosea 12:10). It suggests that the prophet "saw" (mentally and spiritually) as well as heard what God communicated to him. Nothing is known of the background or life and ministry of **Obadiah**. His name was a common one, meaning "Worshiper of Yahweh." This prophet received a direct communication from **the Sovereign** (*'ǎdônāy*) **LORD** (*Yahweh*). The word "Sovereign" stresses His rule over all nations and "LORD" speaks of His covenant relationship with Israel.

Concerning **Edom . . . the LORD** gave **a message** (or a report). It came through a representative He **sent to the nations,** telling them to unite in humiliating Edom. The nations that had a part in destroying the Edomites included the Nabateans, the Jews (under John Hyrcanus), and the Romans. This points up a truth seen throughout much of the Bible: God sovereignly employs nations to accomplish His will on earth.

B. The prophecy of Edom's destruction (vv. 2-9)

1. EDOM'S PRIDE TO BE DEBASED (VV. 2-4)

V. 2. Edom prided herself in her great wealth (obtained by trading, looting, and by iron and copper mining in the region) and in her almost impregnable position geographically.

Yet God said He would cause her to be made **small** (emphatic in the Heb.) in contrast with her self-exaltation, and to **be . . . despised** (also emphatic in the Heb.).

Vv. 3-4. Her **pride** would be her undoing, for it would deceive her into thinking that no one could conquer her. "Pride" translates z*ͤdôn*, from z*îd*, "to boil up, to be presumptuous." This recalls Jacob's cooking (*zîd*) the stew (*nāzîd*) which Esau bought with his birthright (Gen. 25:29). The Edomites' arrogance was presumptuous, whelming over their bounds, portrayed by the stew their ancestor ate.

Contributing to this self-deception was the supposed security of Edom's geographical location in the mountains of Seir. She trusted in the natural protection provided by **the clefts of the rocks.** Living in caves high (**on the heights**) above the ground level she felt totally safe from enemy attacks. Some of the Edomites had settled in such high caves and other places up in the mountains that it was as if they, hyperbolically speaking, were soaring **like the eagle** and nesting **among the stars.**

In response to Edom's self-confident, arrogant question, **Who can bring me down to the ground? . . . the LORD** answered that *He* would **bring** them **down**! God, like an eagle, would swoop down (Jer. 49:22) on those who thought they were safe as eagles. Though Edom was almost impregnable to man, she was not inaccessible to God.

2. EDOM'S WEALTH TO BE PLUNDERED (VV. 5-7)

Edom prided herself in her wealth (v. 6), her alliances with her neighbors (v. 7), her wisdom (v. 8), and her soldiers (v. 9). Edom's fertile valleys had been developed through irrigation, and she had become a center in foreign trade routes.

Vv. 5-6. Obadiah now filled in details about Edom's coming judgment. First, he spoke of **thieves** stealing at **night . . . only as much as they** want. Second, he likened her humiliation to field workers gathering grapes, who **leave a few grapes** for the poor to glean.

By contrast, in Esau's **disaster** (cf. "disaster" for Jerusalem, v. 13) *nothing* would be left. Thieves and grape pickers normally do not take everything, **but** those who would plunder **Esau** would leave nothing. Esau is used here as a synonym for Edom, much as Jacob is often used as a synonym for Israel. The nation of Edom would **be ransacked,** and she would be stripped of her wealth. The invaders would find **treasures,** probably **hidden** in caves, and carry them all away, leaving her desolate.

V. 7. Edom prided herself in the alliances she had with her neighboring countries. Perhaps they became her allies to gain favorable trade relations with her. But those **allies,** in whom Edom trusted, would become her enemies. They would pursue her **to** her **border,** deceiving her and overpowering her. Ironically Edom, deceived by her own pride (v. 3), would then be deceived by her allies! What an alarming strategy—not an attack by a known enemy, but an ambush by an ally. **Those who eat your bread** refers to friends or allies (cf. Ps. 41:9).

Another point of irony in Obadiah 7 is that Edom, known for her wise men (cf. v. 8; Jer. 49:7), would be totally ignorant of her allies' deceptive scheme. The downfall referred to here probably occurred in the late sixth or early fifth century B.C. when the Nabateans (see "Historical Background" in the *Introduction*) went to the Edomites who took them in for a banquet. Once welcomed inside Edomite territory, the Nabateans turned against their ally and killed the guards.

3. EDOM'S PEOPLE TO BE SLAUGHTERED (VV. 8-9)

Vv. 8-9. God had said He would debase Edom (v. 2), bringing her down from her pride (v. 4), and destroy her. Now He said He would **destroy the wise men of Edom** and her **men of understanding.** Her wise leaders would be unable to rescue her. Even Edom's **warriors** would be in complete dismay, and all Edomites who sought safety **in Esau's mountains** (cf. vv. 19, 21) would be slaughtered.

Teman, Edom's capital named for Esau's grandson (Gen. 36:10-11), represented the entire nation (cf. Amos 1:12). (See the location of Teman on the map "Israel and Surrounding Nations in the

Days of the Prophets," between Song and Isa.)

Edom's arrogance led to her complete humiliation. Her security and wealth would be gone, and her wise leaders, soldiers, and others would all fall under God's mighty hand. Nothing could render her safe—not her geographical position or military power or wisdom. What a false hope pride gives unbelievers who try to find security in their own strength apart from God.

II. Edom's Crimes (vv. 10-14)

Obadiah, sensing the intensity of God's judgment on Esau's descendants, then stated the reasons for God's condemnation. The prophet spoke of the Edomites' sinful attitudes (vv. 10-12) and their actions against Judah (vv. 13-14).

A. Violations in attitudes (vv. 10-12)

V. 10. Edom, God predicted, would **be covered with shame,** contrasting starkly with her arrogance (cf. v. 3), and she would **be destroyed** (cf. vv. 7-8), because of her violent, hurtful, oppressive cruelty (cf. Joel 3:19) **against** her **brother Jacob,** that is, Jacob's descendants. Obadiah intentionally spoke of the Judahites as Edom's "brother" to suggest the awfulness of **violence** against one's own blood relatives. Strikingly the Hebrew words for "violence" and "brother" are together in this verse.

Vv. 11-12. In verses 11-14 the phrases **on the day** and **in the day** occur 8 times (10 times in Heb.). When foreign forces went against Judah, they **cast lots** to see who would plunder which parts of **Jerusalem.** Edom, because of her indifference (she **stood aloof**) was no different from the **strangers** who went against her own relatives. (**You** is emphatic in Heb.) Then in a downward spiral, the indifference was followed by (a) gloating (looking **down;** cf. v. 13) over the misfortune of her **brother** (cf. v. 10), (b) rejoicing **over** Judah's **destruction,** and even (c) boasting **of** her **trouble.** "Boast" is literally, "make your mouth large," talking big, another expression of arrogance.

B. Violations in actions (vv. 13-14)

Vv. 13-14. Edom's crimes against Judah went beyond being spectators who rejoiced over Judah's misfortune. Because of wrong attitudes, sinful actions

followed. Edom even entered Jerusalem's **gates,** looking **down** (cf. v. 12) in arrogance on God's people **in their calamity.** Edom looted **their wealth,** killed those who tried to escape, and handed **over** any **survivors** to the attacking armies. The threefold repetition of **in the day of their disaster** (v. 13) heightens the effect of the calamity Judah experienced. (The Heb. for "disaster"; cf. v. 5, is 'êḏ, similar to 'ĕḏôm, the Heb. for Edom.) Violence, harbored in the heart, gave birth to violent acts.

When did all this happen? This probably took place when the Philistines and Arabians attacked Jerusalem in the days of Jehoram, Jehoshaphat's son (2 Kings 8:20-22; 2 Chron. 21:16-17). Since Obadiah told Edom not to do such things (cf. "should not" in Obad. 12-14) again, he was probably writing about a time *before* Jerusalem's total destruction by Nebuchadnezzar (see additional comments in the *Introduction* under "Date" and "Historical Background").

III. God's Judgment on Israel's Enemies (vv. 15-16)

V. 15. Edom illustrates God's judgment to come on **all nations** (cf. Isa. 34:2) who rebel in arrogance against God. **The day of the Lord** may refer to any time God judges by entering into world affairs (e.g., Ezek. 30:3; see comments under "Major Interpretive Problems" in the *Introduction* to Joel). Most frequently, though, it refers to (a) God's judgments in the Great Tribulation and at the return of Jesus Christ in glory, and/or (b) God's establishing the Millennium. In other words the Lord's "day" is when He will bring all things under His rule.

Edom's humiliation foreshadows what the Lord will do to all nations who similarly mistreat Israel. Besides her past humiliation, Edom will be repopulated in the future (see comments on Obad. 16) and with other nations will again come under God's wrath in the forthcoming day of the Lord when Christ returns to establish His reign.

God's judgments on Edom corresponded to her crimes. What she (**you** is sing.) had **done** to Judah would then be **done to** her: (1) She looted Jerusalem (v. 13), so she was looted (v. 6; cf. Jer. 49:10). (2) Edom killed Judean fugitives (Obad. 14; cf. Amos 1:11), so she was slaughtered (Obad. 8; cf. Isa. 34:5-8; Ezek. 32:29; 35:8). (3) She handed over Judean survivors to the enemy (Obad. 14; cf. Ezek. 35:5), so Edom's allies expelled her (Obad. 7). (4) Edom rejoiced over Judah's losses (Obad. 12; cf. Ezek. 35:15), so she was covered with shame and destroyed (Obad. 10).

V. 16. Edom had been involved in a drunken celebration in Jerusalem (**My holy hill**; cf. Pss. 2:6; 3:4; 15:1; 24:3; 78:54; Dan. 9:16, 20; Zeph. 3:11) when she entered the city (Obad. 13). Other **nations** that oppose Israel will also reap God's judgment, often pictured as a cup to **drink** (cf. Isa. 51:17, 21-23; Jer. 25:15-33; Hab. 2:16; Rev. 14:9-10; 16:19; also see Isa. 63:6). Those nations will be so completely destroyed when Jesus Christ returns to the earth (Rev. 19:15, 17-18, 21) that it will be **as if they had never** existed. Edom will be included in that judgment. For though Edom ceased to exist as a nation when the Romans conquered Idumea, some of the Edomites' descendants will again populate their land in the future. Even today that land, now a part of Jordan, is not totally desolate. But the Edomites will then be completely wiped out (cf. Obad. 18) and their land in the Millennium will be occupied by Israelites (vv. 19, 21).

IV. God's Blessings on Israel's People (vv. 17-21)

A. The deliverance of Israel (vv. 17-18)

Vv. 17-18. Though Esau will be destroyed by God's wrath, Israel in God's grace will experience **deliverance.** Israel will be freed from her enemies. **Mount Zion** (cf. v. 21), a synonym for Jerusalem (cf. comments on 2 Sam. 5:7; Lam. 1:4; Zeph. 3:14), though desecrated by Edom (Obad. 13), **will be holy** (cf. Isa. 52:1; Zech. 14:20-21), and the land promised to Israel (Gen. 15:18-21) will be occupied by **the house** (descendants) **of Jacob** (cf. Obad. 19-20). God's covenant people who trust Him will finally be delivered; they will be set apart to God. **Jacob** (the Southern Kingdom) and **Joseph** (the Northern Kingdom) will be united (cf. Ezek. 37:15-23), and will destroy Edom **(the house of Esau;** cf. Obad. 6) like a **flame** easily setting **stubble . . . on fire** (cf. Zech. 12:6; Mal. 4:1). Then the Edomites, Israel's longtime enemies, will finally be wiped out. Edom will have **no sur-**

vivors, in reprisal for her treatment of Judah's survivors (Obad. 14). The certainty of this truth is affirmed by the words, **The LORD has spoken.** Since He has said it, none should question it.

B. The delineation of Israel's territories (vv. 19-20)

Vv. 19-20. Here Obadiah described some of the territories to be restored to God's people. (For locations of most of these places see the map "Israel and Surrounding Nations in the Days of the Prophets," between Song and Isa.) **People** in the southern desert portion of Israel **(the Negev) will** inherit Edom **(the mountains of Esau;** cf. Obad. 8, 21). This will fulfill the prophecies in Numbers 24:18, Isaiah 11:14, and Amos 9:11-12. Israelites in **the** western **foothills will** move south to **the land of the Philistines** with its coastal plains. Central Israel **(Ephraim and Samaria) will** be claimed, and small **Benjamin will** extend its borders to **Gilead,** east of the Jordan. **Exiles** sold into captivity will return and **possess the land as far** north **as Zarephath.** Others exiled **from Jerusalem** to **Sepharad, will possess . . . the Negev.** Suggestions on the location of Sepharad include two countries (Spain, Media) and two cities (Hesperides in Libya, and Sardis in Asia Minor). Sardis seems preferable. It may be the same as the Akkadian *Sapardu.* If Sepharad is to be identified with Sardis, then Jews there will be returning a distance of almost 400 miles to the Negev. At the beginning of the Millennium Israelites will return to their land from these and other lands, and their territory will be expanded.

C. The establishment of the Lord's kingdom (v. 21)

V. 21. From Jerusalem (**Mount Zion;** cf. v. 17) **deliverers** (judges) **will . . . govern** the people who will have occupied **the mountains of Esau** (cf. vv. 8, 19). In the Millennium, **the kingdom will** belong to the Lord (cf. Zech. 14:9). Israel will be restored as a nation (Obad. 17), she will occupy the land (vv. 18-20), and she will be ruled by her King, the Lord Himself (v. 21).

The short Book of Obadiah presents a powerful message. It shows what happens to those who reject God's Word and His grace, rebelling in foolish pride. During Edom's prosperity many in Israel could have asked, "Why do the wicked prosper?" (cf. Ps. 73:3) But the voice of Obadiah comes thundering through the pages of the Old Testament, and is echoed in the New: "Do not be deceived: God cannot be mocked. A man reaps what he sows" (Gal. 6:7). Obadiah's words underscore the fact of God's justice. "For we know Him who said, 'It is Mine to avenge; I will repay.' . . . It is a dreadful thing to fall into the hands of the living God" (Heb. 10:30-31).

One who responds in obedience to the grace of God has everything to gain, but a person who spurns His grace in pride has everything to lose.

BIBLIOGRAPHY

Allen, Leslie C. *The Books of Joel, Obadiah, Jonah and Micah.* The New International Commentary on the Old Testament. Grand Rapids: Wm. B. Eerdmans Publishing Co., 1976.

Feinberg, Charles L. *The Minor Prophets.* Chicago: Moody Press, 1976.

Gaebelein, Frank E. *Four Minor Prophets: Obadiah, Jonah, Habakkuk, and Haggai.* Chicago: Moody Press, 1977.

Keil, C.F. "Obadiah." In *Commentary on the Old Testament in Ten Volumes.* Vol. 10. Reprint (25 vols. in 10). Grand Rapids: Wm. B. Eerdmans Publishing Co., 1982.

Laetsch, Theo. *The Minor Prophets.* St. Louis: Concordia Publishing House, 1956.

Smith, J.M.P.; Ward, William H.; and Bewer, Julius A. *A Critical and Exegetical Commentary on Micah, Zephaniah, Nahum, Habakkuk, Obadiah and Joel.* The International Critical Commentary. Edinburgh: T. & T. Clark, 1974.

Tatford, Frederick A. *The Minor Prophets.* Vol. 2. Reprint (3 vols.). Minneapolis: Klock & Klock Christian Publishers, 1982.

Watts, John D.W. *Obadiah: A Critical Exegetical Commentary.* Winona Lake, Ind.: Alpha Publications, 1981.

JONAH

John D. Hannah

INTRODUCTION

Author. Jonah, whose name means "dove," was a servant of the Lord from Gath Hepher (2 Kings 14:25), a town in the tribe of Zebulun (Josh. 19:10, 13). Jonah lived when Jeroboam II of the Northern Kingdom was king (2 Kings 14:23-25). The Prophet Jonah's prediction that Israel's boundaries (2 Kings 14:25) would extend under Jeroboam came true. This prophet, a Hebrew (Jonah 1:9) and the son of Amittai (1:1; Amittai means "[my] true one"), was the only Old Testament prophet to attempt to run from God.

Jonah was one of four Old Testament prophets whose ministries were referred to by Christ (cf. Matt. 12:41; Luke 11:32). The others were Elijah (Matt. 17:11-12), Elisha (Luke 4:27), and Isaiah (Matt. 15:7).

Jonah's ministry had some parallels to his immediate predecessors, Elijah (1 Kings 17–19; 21; 2 Kings 1–2) and Elisha (2 Kings 2–9; 13), who ministered to Israel and also were called to Gentile missions in Phoenicia and Aram.

Some have suggested that Jonah was not the author of the book because he is referred to in the third person (cf. Jonah 1:3, 5, 9, 12; 2:1; 3:4; 4:1, 5, 8-9). This, however, is not a strong argument. Moses, author of the Pentateuch, often used the third person when describing his own actions. Also Isaiah and Daniel sometimes wrote of themselves in the third person (e.g., Isa. 37:21; 38:1; 39:3-5; Dan. 1:1–7:1). However, since *all* of the Book of Jonah is in the third person some scholars believe this book was written by a prophet other than Jonah soon after the events.

Date. Since 2 Kings 14:25 relates Jonah to the reign of Jeroboam II, the events in the Book of Jonah took place some time in Jeroboam's reign (793–753 B.C.). Jonah's prophecy about Israel's boundaries being extended may indicate that he made that prophecy early in Jeroboam's reign. This makes Jonah a contemporary of both Hosea and Amos (cf. Hosea 1:1; Amos 1:1). Jonah's reference to Nineveh in the past tense (Jonah 3:3) has led some to suggest that Jonah lived later, after the city's destruction in 612 B.C. However, the tense of the Hebrew verb can just as well point to the city's existence in Jonah's day.

Historical Setting. Jeroboam II, in whose reign Jonah prophesied, was the most powerful king in the Northern Kingdom (cf. 2 Kings 14:23-29). Earlier the Assyrians had established supremacy in the Near East and secured tribute from Jehu (841–814 B.C.). (On the atrocious nature of the Assyrians, see the comments on the Book of Nahum.) However, after crushing the Arameans, the Assyrians suffered temporary decline because of internal dissension. In the temporary setback of Assyrian imperialistic hopes, Israel's Jeroboam was able to expand his nation's territories to their greatest extent since the time of David and Solomon by occupying land that formerly belonged to Aram (northeast toward Damascus and north to Hamath).

However, the religious life of Israel was such that God sent both Hosea and Amos to warn of impending judgment. Because of Israel's stubbornness, the nation would fall under God's chosen instrument of wrath, a Gentile nation from the east. Amos warned that God would send Israel "into exile beyond Damascus" (Amos 5:27). Hosea specifically delineated the ravaging captor as Assyria: "Will not Assyria rule over them because they refuse to repent?" (Hosea 11:5) So Assyria, then in temporary decline, would awake like a sleeping giant and devour the Northern Kingdom of Israel as its prey. This prediction was fulfilled in 722 B.C. when Sargon II carried the Northern Kingdom into captivity

(2 Kings 17). The prophecies of Hosea and Amos may explain Jonah's reluctance to preach in Nineveh. He feared he would be used to help the enemy that would later destroy his own nation.

Nineveh was located on the east bank of the Tigris River, about 550 miles from Samaria, capital of the Northern Kingdom. Nineveh was large and, like Babylon, was protected by an outer wall and an inner wall. The inner wall was 50 feet wide and 100 feet high. Before Jonah arrived at this seemingly inpregnable fortress-city, two plagues had erupted there (in 765 and 759 B.C.) and a total eclipse of the sun occurred on June 15, 763. These were considered signs of divine anger and may help explain why the Ninevites responded so readily to Jonah's message, around 759.

Message. This record of Jonah's episode and mission to Nineveh was addressed to Israel. The book was written not simply to record a historical narrative; in addition it conveyed a message to the Northern Kingdom. Also in one sense Jonah is not the principal person in the book; God is. The Lord had the first word (Jonah 1:1-2) and the last (4:11). God commanded the prophet twice (1:2; 3:2); He sent a violent storm on the sea (1:4); He provided a great fish to rescue Jonah (1:17); He commanded the fish to vomit Jonah onto dry land (2:10); He threatened Nineveh with judgment and relented in compassion (3:10); He provided a vine to shade His prophet (4:6); He commissioned a worm to destroy the plant (4:7); and He sent a scorching wind to discomfort Jonah (4:8).

What then is the message God was seeking to deliver to Israel through His dealings with Jonah, the Ninevites, and natural phenomena? (i.e., the sea, animal life, plant life, and the wind)

First, one apparent message to Israel is God's concern for Gentile peoples. The Lord's love for the souls of all people was supposed to be mediated through Israel, God's elect and covenant nation. Through Israel the blessing of His compassion was to be preached to the nations (Isa. 49:3). The Book of Jonah was a reminder to Israel of her missionary purpose.

Second, the book demonstrates the sovereignty of God in accomplishing His purposes. Though Israel was unfaithful in its missionary task, God was faithful in causing His love to be proclaimed. In praise to God for miraculously delivering him, Jonah confessed, "Salvation [deliverance] comes from the LORD" (Jonah 2:9). Israel failed to proclaim God's mercies, but His work gets done in spite of human weakness and imperfection.

Third, the response of the Gentiles served as a message of rebuke to God's sinful nation Israel (cf. John H. Stek, "The Message of the Book of Jonah," *Calvin Theological Journal* 4. 1969:42-3). The spiritual insight of the mariners (1:14-16) and their concern for the Jewish prophet contrast starkly with Israel's lack of concern for the Gentile nations. Jonah's spiritual hardness illustrated and rebuked Israel's callousness. Nineveh's repentance contrasted sharply with Israel's rejection of the warnings of Jonah's contemporaries, Hosea and Amos.

Fourth, Jonah was a symbol to Israel of her disobedience to God and indifference to the religious plight of other nations. Hosea, Jonah's contemporary, graphically portrayed the unending love of God for His people by loving a prostitute (who was a symbol of Israel's religious waywardness). Similarly Jonah symbolized Israel by his disobedience and disaffection. God's punishment of Jonah shows His wrath on Israel. Yet the Lord's gentle, miraculous dealings with Jonah also picture His tender love and slowness of anger with the nation. As Jonah wrote the book from a repentant heart, God desired that the nation would heed the lesson Jonah learned and repent as Jonah and Nineveh had done.

Authenticity and Historicity. Critical scholars, with their antisupernatural bias, have denied the authenticity of the Book of Jonah for several reasons. First, critics scoff at the miracle of a great fish swallowing the prophet. But scholars have demonstrated the validity of such an event (e.g., A.J. Wilson, "Sign of the Prophet Jonah and Its Modern Confirmations," *Princeton Theological Review* 25. October 1927, pp. 630-42; George F. Howe, "Jonah and the Great Fish," *Biblical Research Monthly*. January 1973, pp. 6-8). The "great fish" was possibly a mammal, a sperm whale (*Catodon Macrocephalus*). Sperm whales are known to

Kings of Assyria in the Middle and New Assyrian Kingdoms

Ashur-uballiṭ I	1365–1330	Shamshi-Adad V	824–811
Enlil-nirāri	1329–1320	Adad-nirāri III	811–783
Arik-dēn-ili	1319–1308	Shalmaneser IV	783–772
Adad-nirāri I	1307–1275	Ashur-dan III	772–754
Shalmaneser I	1274–1245	*(Jonah preached to the*	
Tukulti-Ninurta I	1244–1208	*Ninevites in this king's*	
Ashur-nādin-apli	1207–1204	*reign.)*	
Ashur-nirāri III	1203–1198	Ashur-nirāri V	754–746
Enlil-kudurri-uṣur	1197–1193	Tiglath-Pileser III	745–727
Ninurta-apil-Ekur	1192–1180	(Pul)	
Ashur-dan I	1179–1134	*(This king attacked*	
Ashur-rēsha-ishi	1133–1116	*Israel and Aram.)*	
Tiglath-Pileser I	1115–1077	Shalmaneser V	727–722
Ashared-apil-Ekur	1076–1075	*(This king besieged Samaria for*	
Ashur-bēl-kala	1074–1057	*three years, 725–722 and*	
Eriba-Adad II	1056–1055	*destroyed it in 722.)*	
Shamshi-Adad IV	1054–1051	Sargon II	722–705
Ashurnaṣirpal I	1050–1032	*(This king engaged in*	
Shalmaneser II	1031–1020	*mopping-up operations*	
Ashur-nirāri IV	1019–1014	*in Samaria in 721*	
Ashur-rabi II	1013–973	*after Shalmaneser V*	
Ashur-rēsha-ishi II	972–968	*died in 722.)*	
Tiglath-Pileser II	967–935	Sennacherib	705–681
Ashur-dan II	935–912	Esarhaddon	681–669
Adad-nirāri II	912–889	Ashurbanipal	669–626
Tukulti-Ninurta II	889–884	*(Nahum wrote of the*	
Ashurnasirpal II	883–859	*fall of Nineveh in the*	
Shalmaneser III	859–824	*reign of this king.)*	
(This king attacked Israel		Ashur-etil-ilāni	626–623
and received tribute from		Sin-shar-ishkun	623–612
Jehu, king of Israel.)		Ashur-uballiṭ II	612–609

have swallowed unusually large objects including even a 15-foot shark (Frank T. Bullen, *Cruise of the Cachalot Round the World after Sperm Whales*. London: Smith, 1898). Others have written that whale sharks (the *Rhineodon Typicus*) have swallowed men who later were found alive in the sharks' stomachs.

Second, some scholars have questioned the size of Nineveh (3:3) and its population (4:11). True, the circumference of Nineveh's inner wall, according to archeologists, was less than eight miles. So the diameter of the city, less than two miles, was hardly a three-day journey. (One day's journey in open territory was usually about 15-20 miles.)

However, two answers may be given to this objection: (1) "The city" probably included the surrounding towns that depended on Nineveh. Three such cities related to Nineveh are mentioned in Genesis 10:11-12. (2) Taking three days to go through such a city and its suburbs is

reasonable since Jonah stopped and preached along the way (Jonah 3:3-4). (On the population of Nineveh see comments on 4:11.) A city of two miles diameter was a colossal size in the ancient Near East. So it is not surprising that it was called a great city (1:2; 3:2-4, 7; 4:11).

Third, the reference to the king of Assyria as "the king of Nineveh" (3:6), has puzzled some, but to substitute a capital city (e.g., Nineveh) for the particular country (e.g., Assyria) is fairly common in the Old Testament. Ahab is called "king of Samaria" (1 Kings 21:1), Ahaziah of Israel is also called "the king of Samaria" (2 Kings 1:3), and Ben-Hadad of Aram is referred to as the "king of Damascus" (2 Chron. 24:23).

Fourth, some reject the Book of Jonah because of the sudden repentance of the Ninevites. This, however, denies the supernatural work of the Holy Spirit. If Jonah had gone to the city during the reign of the Assyrian king Ashur-dan III

(772–754 B.C.; see the chart "Kings of Assyria in the Middle and New Assyrian Kingdoms"), the prophet may have found the city psychologically prepared for his message by two foreboding famines (in 765 and 759) and a total solar eclipse on June 15, 763. People in those days often took such events as indicators of divine wrath.

Fifth, some scholars reject the authenticity of the book because of the rapid growth of the vine (Jonah 4:6). This plant, however, was probably the castor bean known for its rapid growth, tall height, and large leaves (also see the comments on 4:6).

Several arguments support the historicity of the book: (1) Known cities are mentioned in the book, including Nineveh (1:2; 3:2-4, 6-7; 4:11), Tarshish (1:3; 4:2), and Joppa (1:3). (2) Jonah is viewed as a historical person, not a fictional character. He was said to be a prophet from Gath Hepher (2 Kings 14:25) who lived in the reign of a historical person, Jeroboam II. (3) Jesus recognized the historicity of Jonah (Matt. 12:41; Luke 11:29-30, 32) and called him a prophet (Matt. 12:39), assenting to the great miracle of Jonah's recovery from the fish (Matt. 12:40). Jesus based His call to repentance in His day on the validity of Jonah's message of repentance (Matt. 12:41; Luke 11:29-32). If the story of Jonah is nonliteral (i.e., fiction, allegory, or parable), such a literary form is highly unusual, different from all the other prophetic books.

OUTLINE

      1. The action of the people (3:5)
      2. The action of the king (3:6-9)
      3. The action of God (3:10)

COMMENTARY

I. The Disobedience of Jonah (chaps. 1–2)

A. *The commission of the prophet (1:1-2)*

1:1-2. The God of Israel commanded **Jonah** (see comments under "Author" in the *Introduction*), a prophet (2 Kings 14:25; Matt. 12:39), to travel **to the great city of Nineveh and preach against it.** ("Great" and "greatly" occur frequently in the book: "great city," Jonah 1:2; 3:2; 4:11; "great wind," 1:4; "great storm," v. 12; "greatly feared," v. 16; "great fish," v. 17; "greatly displeased," 4:1; and "very [lit., 'greatly'] happy," 4:6.) The message he was to preach is stated in 3:4. Jonah had divine authority for this message because **the word of the LORD came to** him. It was authoritative because of its origin. The city of Nineveh was located on the east side of the Tigris River about 550 miles northeast of Samaria. (See the map "The Assyrian Empire".) That distance required a journey of more than a month, if Jonah traveled the normal distance of 15-20 miles a day. The great city was second in size only to Babylon. (On Nineveh's size, see comments under "Authenticity and Historicity" in the *Introduction* and comments on 4:11.) It was in modern-day Iraq opposite the modern town of Mosul.

Nineveh was built by Nimrod (Gen. 10:11). After Jonah's day, it became the capital of the Assyrian Empire under Sennacherib (705–681 B.C.), the successor of Sargon II (722–705 B.C.) who destroyed the Northern Kingdom. The reason God sent Jonah to preach "against" Nineveh (i.e., to pronounce its doom under God's judgment) is that **its wickedness** had **come up before** Him, that is, the people were relentless and persistent in their sins. The Assyrian king acknowledged that his people's ways were "evil" and characterized by "violence" (Jonah 3:8). And they were "carefree" (Zeph. 2:15),

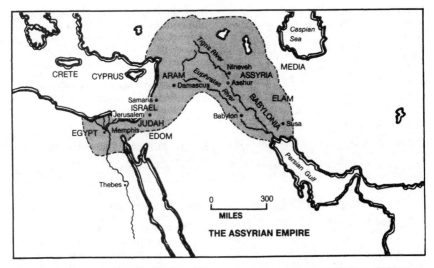

THE ASSYRIAN EMPIRE

thinking themselves invincible. The Prophet Nahum wrote about several of their crimes (Nahum 3:1, 4, 16). Nineveh was well known in the ancient Near East for the brutal atrocities it inflicted on its war captives. (For more on Nineveh's brutalities, see the *Introduction* to Nahum.) This city was also known for its idolatry; it had temples dedicated to the gods Nabu, Asshur, and Adad; the Ninevites also worshiped Ishtar, a goddess of love and war.

B. The disobedience of the prophet (1:3)

1:3. Though **Jonah** apparently understood and appreciated God's wrath against Assyria, he was not nearly so compassionate as God was. Motivated by patriotic duty that clouded religious obligation, and knowing God's forgiving mercy (cf. 4:2), Jonah shirked his responsibility. It is strange that a prophet of God would not follow God's command to preach condemnation.

Instead of traveling northeast he fled by sea in the opposite direction. He boarded **a ship** at **Joppa** (modern Jaffa), on Israel's coast about 35 miles from Samaria and about the same distance from Jerusalem. The ship was bound for **Tarshish,** probably Tartessus in southern Spain, about 2,500 miles west of Joppa. Since Tarshish was a Phoenician colony, the ship's sailors may have been Phoenicians. Phoenicians were known for their seagoing vessels and skill on the seas.

C. The consequences of the prophet's disobedience (1:4–2:10)

The structure of 1:4-16 is a chiasm, as seen in the following chart (adapted from Yehuda Radday, "Chiasmus in Hebrew Biblical Literature," in *Chiasmus in Antiquity: Structures, Analyses, Exegesis.* Hildesheim: Gerstenberg, 1981, p. 60).

a. The sailors' fright (vv. 4-5a)
b. The sailors' prayer to their gods (v. 5b)
c. The sailors' unloading the ship (v. 5c)
d. The captain's speech to Jonah (v. 6)
e. The sailors' word to each other (v. 7a)
f. The sailors' question to Jonah, "Who are you?" (vv. 7b-8)
g. Jonah's confession (v. 9)
f¹. The sailors' question to Jonah, "What have you done?" (v. 10a)
e¹. The sailors' question to Jonah, "What shall we do?" (vv. 10b-11)
d¹. Jonah's words to the sailors (v. 12)
c¹. The sailors' rowing of the ship (v. 13)
b¹. The sailor's prayer to the Lord (v. 14)
a¹. The sailors' fear of the Lord (vv. 15-16)

1. THE GREAT WIND (1:4-16)

The principal person in the narrative was God, not Jonah. To accomplish His purposes, God sovereignly controlled various events recorded in the book, overcame Jonah's rebellion, and opened the Ninevites' hearts. Here He miraculously altered the direction of His servant's itinerary.

103

a. The distress of the sailors (1:4-5a)

1:4-5a. God sent (*ṭûl*, "hurled") **a . . . wind on the** Mediterranean **Sea.** The wind was so **great** that it caused a **violent storm.** So terrible was the storm that **the sailors** thought **the ship** would **break up.** No wonder they were afraid! The fact that **each** sailor **cried out to his own god** suggests that many individual deities were worshiped by the Phoenicians. As seasoned seamen they also lightened **the ship** by tossing **the cargo** overboard (cf. Acts 27:17-18), hoping that the lighter ship would not sink.

b. The complacency of Jonah (1:5b-6)

1:5b-6. In contrast with the concern of the mariners Jonah's reaction is amazing. He went **below deck** and fell asleep, undisturbed by the storm's tossing the ship. Perhaps he felt secure there. Obviously he was insensitive to the danger. Ironically a pagan ship **captain** had to call a man of God to prayer. The captain was desperate; every known **god** should be appealed to so that one might grant relief from their peril (cf. **we will not perish,** v. 6). The need was so great that the men despaired for their lives; yet God's servant slept. What an object lesson to God's people then and now to awaken from apathy as crying people perish on the sea of life.

c. The reasons for the dilemma (1:7-9)

1:7. While the captain attempted to arouse Jonah (v. 6), **the sailors** concluded that the tragic storm was the result of divine wrath on the wrongdoing of some man on board. The casting of **lots** to determine a decision, in this case to find a culprit, was common in Israel and other countries in the ancient Near East (cf. Lev. 16:8; Josh. 18:6; 1 Sam. 14:42; Neh. 10:34; Es. 3:7; Prov. 16:33; Acts 1:26). Perhaps marked stones were put in a container, and one was taken out. God expressed His sovereignty over Jonah's affairs, causing **the lot** to "fall" on His disobedient prophet.

1:8-9. Though rebellious against God's command (cf. vv. 2-3) Jonah responded to the sailors' barrage of five questions by stating with no uncertainty his nationality (**I am a Hebrew**) and the worth and power of His God. Though disobedient to God, Jonah at least knew what He is like. Jonah said that God is **the Lord** (*Yahweh*), the covenant-making and covenant-keeping God of Israel. The prophet also said his God is **the God of heaven** (cf. Gen. 24:3, 7 and comments on Ezra 1:2), the one true Sovereign, in contrast with the sailors' many false gods (cf. Jonah 1:5). Jonah also affirmed that Yahweh is the Creator, the One **who made the sea and the land** (cf. Ex. 20:11; Ps. 95:5). As Creator of the world He can control nature, including storms on the sea (cf. Ps. 89:9). The sailors clearly acknowledged this fact in their question (Jonah 1:11). It may seem strange that Jonah claimed to worship this God when he did not obey Him, but this is often true of believers.

d. The calming of the sea (1:10-16)

1:10. Hearing that Jonah's God controls the sea, and knowing that Jonah was rebelling against his God, the sailors concluded that the upheaval of the sea evidenced God's displeasure with him. This brought fear to the sailors, for they felt helpless in appeasing someone else's god. Perhaps too they sensed, superstitiously, that Jonah's God was holding them responsible as accomplices in Jonah's "crime." By their question, **What have you done?** the seamen chided the prophet for his senseless action. This question affirmed emphatically that he was responsible for their predicament. It was more a statement of horror at Jonah's disobedience than a question of inquiry. The pagan sailors seemed to grasp the seriousness of his disobedience more than the prophet did!

1:11. The sailors' perceptiveness is again evident. Believing that Jonah's God controls **the sea,** as he had told them (v. 9), they appealed to Jonah for a resolution to their heightening dilemma. They sensed that since he was responsible for the storm, they needed to do something to him. Only then would the storm be abated.

1:12. Jonah's response was penitent. Recognizing the gravity of his disobedience that resulted in the **great storm,** he was willing to endure punishment, even death. So he told them to **throw** him **into the sea.** Only then, when he was overboard, would the sea be **calm.** Perhaps Jonah also thought this would be a way out of his assignment (cf. 4:3, 8). But God had another plan!

1:13-14. The sailors, however, were not anxious to take human life for fear they would be held accountable for murder. This contrasts sharply with Jonah's lack of compassion for the Ninevites (cf. 4:1-2). So **the men** on the ship (except for Jonah) tried again to get **back to land.** But against the sovereign God, the sailors' meager efforts brought no relief. In fact the storm intensified. Recognizing the futility of their efforts, and believing that Jonah's God controls the sea, they realized Jonah's instructions had to be carried out. Yet those Gentiles, not having the Law of God, instinctively recognized the worth of human life and pleaded for His mercy on them **for killing an innocent man.** By their words, **You, O Lord, have done as You pleased,** the sailors were acknowledging His divine sovereignty and providence in the storm (1:4) and in the casting of the lots (v. 7).

1:15-16. Following the prophet's instructions (v. 12), the sailors **threw** Jonah into **the raging sea** and it became **calm.** This showed them the reality and power of the God of Israel. They stood in awe of **(feared) the Lord.** He had done what their gods could not do. The sudden calm was an answer to the sailors' prayers (v. 5). The calm also revealed that the storm had resulted from Jonah's disobedience and that an innocent life had not been snuffed out in casting him overboard. Utterly amazed at the sudden calm, **they offered a sacrifice** in praise **to the Lord** (*Yahweh,* Israel's God) and promised (**made vows**) to continue their praise. Again the sailors are seen in contrast with their former passenger. Whereas **Jonah** was disobedient to God, they were praising Him!

2. THE GREAT FISH (1:17–2:10)

a. The swallowing of Jonah (1:17)

1:17. The prophet's expected death did not occur. The sovereignty and centrality of God as the major figure in this historical narrative are evidenced in His providing a fish to swallow Jonah. This is the first of four things in this book He **provided** (cf. 4:6-8). The **great fish** was possibly a mammal, a sperm whale, or perhaps a whale shark (see "Authenticity and Historicity" under *Introduction*). God controls not only the sea but all that is in it. By means of the large sea monster God preserved **Jonah** alive and later deposited

him unhurt on land. The phrase **three days and three nights** need not be understood as a 72-hour period, but as one 24-hour day and parts of two other days (cf. Es. 4:16 with 5:1 and comments on Matt. 12:40, where Jesus said His burial would be the same length of time as Jonah's interment in the fish's stomach).

b. The praise by Jonah (2:1-9)

This prayer by Jonah was not a plea for deliverance for there were no petitions in it. The prayer is a psalm of thanksgiving (v. 9) to God for using the fish to save him from drowning. The prayer was made while Jonah was in the fish's stomach (v. 1) but it was written of course after he was expelled from the fish's stomach. Sensing that the great fish was God's means of delivering him, Jonah worshiped God for His unfathomable mercies. Jonah praised God for delivering him from death (cf. Ps. 30:3) in a watery grave (cf. Bernhard W. Anderson, *Out of the Depths.* Philadelphia: Westminster Press, 1974, pp. 84-6). The contents of Jonah 2 correspond in several ways to the contents in chapter 1:

The Sailors	
1:4	Crisis on the sea
1:14	Prayer to Yahweh
1:15b	Deliverance from the storm
1:16	Sacrifice and vows offered to God
The Prophet	
2:3-6a	Crisis in the sea
2:2, 7	Prayer to Yahweh
2:6b	Deliverance from drowning
2:9	Sacrifice and vows offered to God

1. A summary of Jonah's experience. **2:1-2.** After noting the place (**inside the fish**) where he voiced this prayer, Jonah poetically recounted the story of his deliverance.

Though the sailors had sacrificed to **the Lord** (1:16), He was in a special sense Jonah's God. When the sailors cast him overboard, **in . . . distress** he prayed and **the Lord . . . answered** with a miraculous provision (the fish). The phrase **from the depths of the grave** refers to the fear of death that gripped the prophet. It does not mean he actually died. God **listened to** his **cry** for help and went to his rescue.

2. A description of Jonah's experience (2:3-7). Here the prophet recorded his watery horror and God's gracious deliverance.

2:3. Though the sailors had thrown him into the sea (1:15), actually God had **hurled** him **into the deep,** that is, He was behind their action. As **the currents of** the Mediterranean **swirled about** Jonah, he knew that God controls the **waves and breakers** (Jonah called them **Your;** cf. Ps. 88:7).

2:4. Banished by God because of his sin of disobedience, the prophet evidenced repentance and renewed faith, for he expressed confidence in approaching God (**I will look again toward Your holy temple**). The "holy temple" may be the Jerusalem temple or, perhaps more likely, God's heavenly abode (cf. Ps. 11:4), for the prophet said (Jonah 2:7) his prayer "rose" to God in His temple. Or verse 4 could refer to the Jerusalem temple and verse 7 to the heavenly temple.

2:5-6a. In his peril the **waters threatened** to take his life and the sea **surrounded** him. Ocean vegetation was bound about his **head** as if to imprison him. In the sea he **sank** to the bottoms **of the mountains,** and **the earth** was about to entrap him permanently. This is the prophet's description of his plunge into what appeared to be a watery grave.

2:6b-7. At the point of Jonah's hopelessness and utter despair, God used the fish to lift the prophet **up from the pit** ("pit" is a synonym for grave). Because God had saved his life, the repentant prophet confessed that the LORD was his **God** (cf. v. 1). Sensing that he was about to die by drowning and that his **life was ebbing away,** he turned to God, praying to Him (cf. v. 2) for deliverance (on the **holy temple;** cf. comments on v. 4). In the gravest of perils the prophet prayed and his petitions **rose** to heaven to be answered most uniquely.

3. An expression of Jonah's thankfulness. 2:8-9. The statement concerning the folly of trusting **worthless idols** provides a dark background against which God's brilliant grace is evident. No lifeless idol could effect so great a deliverance as the God of heaven, who made the sea and the land (cf. 1:9). In contrast with those who trusted weak idols for deliverance (cf. 1:5) Jonah offered a **sacrifice** (cf. 1:16) of praise to the true God who effected such a wondrous provision. Also he **vowed** to obey the Lord because **salvation** (i.e., deliverance) **comes from the LORD.** Deliverance from perilous situations is a provision from a gracious God.

c. The return of Jonah (2:10)

2:10. After the deliverance of **Jonah** from the watery grave, **the LORD commanded the fish** to deposit the prophet safely on **dry land,** presumably on the coast of Palestine after the three-day return journey (cf. 1:17). Seven miracles have taken place already in this short narrative: God caused a violent storm (1:4), had the lot fall on Jonah (1:7), calmed the sea when Jonah was thrown overboard (1:15), commanded the fish to swallow Jonah (1:17), had the fish transport him safely, had the fish throw Jonah up on dry land, and perhaps greatest of all, melted the disobedient prophet's heart (evidenced by his thanksgiving prayer in chap. 2).

II. The Obedience of Jonah (chaps. 3–4)

A. The recommissioning of the prophet (3:1-2)

3:1-2. After turning **Jonah** from willful disobedience **the LORD** again commanded the prophet to fulfill his appointed task (cf. 1:2). Three times Nineveh is described as a **great city** (1:2; 3:2; 4:11; cf. "very large city," 3:3). As noted in the *Introduction* the city was surrounded by an inner wall and an outer wall. The huge inner wall (50 feet wide and 100 feet high) was about eight miles in circumference while the outer wall encompassed fields and smaller towns (viz., Rehoboth Ir, Calah, and Resen; cf. Gen. 10:11-12). The words "great city" probably included the city of Nineveh proper and its administrative environs.

His instructions were simply to travel those 550 miles to **Nineveh** and preach **the message** the Lord would provide at the appropriate time (cf. Jonah 3:4). Interestingly in His recommissioning the prophet, God did not repeat the reason for the proclamation (cf. 1:2b).

B. The obedience of the prophet (3:3-4)

3:3. The prophet's response here differs from his response in chapter 1. Here he **obeyed the . . . LORD and** made his way northeast **to Nineveh.** Earlier (1:3) he disobeyed the Lord and went west.

Jonah again mentioned the great size of the **city,** commenting that **it took three days to go all through it,** that is, through Nineveh and its suburbs (see comments under "Authenticity and Historicity" in the *Introduction* and comments on 3:2).

3:4. Going a day's journey does not mean that Jonah traveled into the city for a whole day before preaching. Instead it means on the first day he entered the city he began preaching. The message God gave the prophet was the threat of complete destruction of **Nineveh** within **40 . . . days.** Perhaps this was a period of grace, giving the people an opportunity to repent before the judgment fell. Jonah continued this proclamation for three days before going "east of the city" (4:5).

C. The conversion of the Ninevites (3:5-10)

1. THE ACTION OF THE PEOPLE (3:5)

3:5. The words of Jonah spread rapidly through every quarter of greater Nineveh. **The Ninevites** accepted Jonah's message and **believed God.** As the prophet preached doom, the people—ironically—changed. Earlier Jonah had repented, and now these Gentiles repented. As outward symbols of inward contrition and humiliation they fasted (cf. 1 Sam. 7:6; 2 Sam. 1:12; Neh. 1:4; Zech. 7:5) and **put on sackcloth** (coarse cloth; cf. Gen. 37:34; 1 Kings 21:27; Neh. 9:1; Es. 4:1-4; Lam. 2:10; Dan. 9:3; Joel 1:8). People in every social strata, **from the greatest to the least,** hoped that God might turn from His anger and spare them.

As previously noted, some scholars find such an extensive turning to God incredible. True, Assyrian records make no mention of this city-wide penitence, but official historical records often delete events, especially those that might embarrass them (e.g., Egyptian records do not refer to the Israelites' crossing the Red Sea or did the Assyrians record the loss of 185,000 soldiers in Jerusalem, 2 Kings 19:35).

Another question about the Ninevites is whether their conversion was genuine. Was their religious response superficial as in the case of Ahab? (1 Kings 21:27-29) If the Ninevites' conversion was genuine, it may be difficult to explain why the Assyrians continued their violence and why they soon destroyed Israel (ca. 37 years later, in 722 B.C., the Assyrians destroyed the Northern Kingdom). Perhaps the next generation reverted to the Assyrians' typical violence.

Also Jonah's message concerned repentance from evil to avoid judgment; perhaps many believed Jonah's words without becoming genuinely converted. They could have believed the fact of God's threat of judgment without trusting in Yahweh as the *only* true God. C.F. Keil wrote, "But however deep the penitential mourning of Nineveh might be, and however sincere the repentance of the people . . . they .acted according to the king's command; the repentance was not a lasting one, or permanent in its effects" ("Jonah," in *Commentary on the Old Testament in Ten Volumes,* 10:409). Apparently the Ninevites responded from fear (cf. Jonah 3:8-9) under the power of Jonah's proclamation. Though the people were outwardly contrite (fasting and wearing sackcloth) there may have been no enduring spiritual change. At any rate, the preaching of Jonah occasioned extensive and intensive, if not durative, religious effects.

2. THE ACTION OF THE KING (3:6-9)

a. His repentance (3:6)

3:6. Word of the religious humiliation of the people **reached the king of Nineveh** (probably Ashur-dan III). Though Nineveh did not become capital of the Assyrian Empire until some time in the reign of Sennacherib (705–681 B.C.), some of her kings did reside there. Such news of pending, almost immediate doom caused the king to respond in the way his people did (cf. v. 5). Wearing **sackcloth,** a coarse garment, and sitting in **dust** (cf. Isa. 47:1) showed he was contrite and believed the prophet's message.

b. His proclamation (3:7-9)

3:7-8. The king's remorse led him **and his nobles** to issue a royal **decree.** The decree instructed the people to fast (this decree may have been the reason for the fast referred to in v. 5), to wear **sackcloth** (cf. comments on v. 5), to **call urgently on God,** and to relinquish **their** wickedness (**evil ways;** cf. v. 10). Even the animals were not allowed to **eat,** and were draped with sackcloth. This practice was not strange in the Near East; it was another sign of the people's remorse.

3:9. Who knows? (cf. 2 Sam. 12:22; Joel 2:14) hints at the possibility of God's withdrawing His threat. By their contrition the king hoped that Jonah's **God** would **relent** of His judgment and **turn from His . . . anger,** thereby sparing the city. (Cf. **we will not perish,** in Jonah 1:6.) This fear of judgment from God is startling because the Assyrians were a cruel, violent nation (cf. Nahum 3:1, 3-4) fearing no one (cf. 2 Kings 18:33-35).

3. THE ACTION OF GOD (3:10)

3:10. The prophet's message may have included conditions whereby the threats of God could be rescinded. As an evidence of His mercy to the Ninevites God sent Jonah to them, told him what to proclaim to them, and opened the hearts of a vast population. Also, seeing their repentant actions, **God** relented of His threat of **destruction.** He had spared Jonah (chap. 2); now He spared Nineveh. God's mercies are always unmerited; His grace is never earned. Repentance is never a work to be rewarded. But this is not to say that God does not act in response to such repentance. Nineveh's repentance delayed God's destruction of the city for about 150 years. The people evidently fell into sin again, so that later the city was destroyed, in 612 B.C. (see the Book of Nahum).

When God **threatened** punishment He provided a dark backdrop on which to etch most vividly His forgiving mercies. This emphasized His grace most forcefully to the sinners' hearts. God's readiness to have **compassion** on a wicked but repentant people and to withhold threatened destruction showed Israel that *her* coming judgment at God's hand was not because of His unwillingness to forgive but because of her impenitence.

D. *The sorrow of the prophet (chap. 4)*

1. THE DISPLEASURE OF JONAH (4:1-5)

a. *Jonah's anger (4:1)*

4:1. Jonah blatantly rejected and repudiated the goodness of God to the Ninevites. In that attitude he symbolized the nation Israel. Jonah's self-interests were a reminder to Israel of her lack of concern for the ways and mercies of God. The word **but** points up the contrast be-

tween God's compassion (3:10) and Jonah's displeasure, and between God's turning *from* His anger (3:9-10) and Jonah's turning *to* anger. Jonah's anger (**became angry** is lit., "became hot") at God for sparing Nineveh stemmed from his unbalanced patriotic fervor. Jonah probably knew from Amos and Hosea that Assyria would be Israel's destroyer. Jonah's fickle attitude toward God's dealings with him are remarkably abrupt and variegated (disobedience, chap. 1; thanksgiving, chap. 2; obedience, chap. 3; displeasure, chap. 4).

b. *Jonah's prayer (4:2-3)*

4:2. Out of anger and disgust the prophet rebuked his LORD, saying in essence, **"I know that You** are forgiving and now look what has happened!" Jonah admitted that he fled toward **Tarshish** because he did not want the Ninevites to be saved from judgment. (*He* wanted to be delivered from calamity, 2:2, 7, but he did not want the Ninevites to be kept from disaster.) The Ninevites were more ready to accept God's grace than Jonah was. Jonah, an object of God's compassion, had no compassion for Nineveh's people.

Jonah knew **God** is willing to forgive but he did not want his enemies to know it. Their threat of doom (3:4) could be diverted if his hearers turned to his forgiving God.

The prophet certainly had a clear grasp of God's character, as reflected in his near-quotation of Exodus 34:6. In fact Jonah's words about God are almost identical with Joel's description of Him (Joel 2:13; also cf. Neh. 9:17; Pss. 103:8; 145:8). **God** is **gracious** (i.e., He longs for and favors others) and **compassionate** (tender in His affection), **slow to anger** (He does not delight in punishing the wicked; cf. 2 Peter 3:9), **and abounding in love** (*ḥeseḏ,* "loyal love, or faithfulness to a covenant"). The psalmists often spoke of God being "gracious" and "compassionate," though sometimes in reverse order (Pss. 86:15; 103:8; 111:4; 112:4; 145:8). Jonah also said He knew God **relents from sending calamity.** The prophet feared that all these attributes of God would be extended toward the despicable, cruel Ninevites—and it happened!

4:3. Jonah's anguish over what God

did led him to request that he might **die** (cf. Jonah 4:8; 1 Kings 19:4). Earlier he had prayed to live (Jonah 2:2). Perhaps now he was embarrassed that his threat was not carried out. Because God relented of His wrath and did not destroy the city, Jonah was so emotionally disappointed that he lost all reason for living. God was concerned about the city (4:11) but Jonah was not.

c. Jonah's action (4:4-5)

4:4-5. Though Jonah knew that God is slow to anger (v. 2) he still wanted **the Lord** to execute His wrath swiftly. Yet God, hesitant to be angry with even His prophet, sought to reason with him. God asked the sulking messenger whether his anger was justified (cf. v. 9). This question implied a negative response: Jonah had no **right to be angry.** A person should never angrily question what God does, even when it differs from what he expects or wants.

Jonah was so distraught that he did not reply to God. Instead he left **the city** and built a crude **shelter,** perhaps from tree branches, and **sat** down (cf. the king's sitting in the dust, 3:6) **in its shade** (cf. Elijah under a broom tree, 1 Kings 19:4). Apparently Jonah had a clear view of the city. Why he **waited to see what would happen to the city** is difficult to understand. Perhaps he felt that God would answer his plea and judge the city anyway. Unable to imagine God not carrying out His justice on people who deserved it, Jonah was determined to wait till Nineveh was in fact judged. But he was wrong and his action was childish. Obviously he had forgotten that he, who also deserved death for disobedience, was delivered by God (chap. 2).

2. THE EXPLANATION OF THE LORD (4:6-11)

a. The illustration prepared (4:6-8)

God, being slow to anger (v. 2), again attempted to reason with Jonah (cf. v. 4). This time God gave him a visual lesson. God erected an object of Jonah's affection (creaturely comfort) and contrasted it with the object of His own concern (the souls of people). God rebuked Jonah, not through a storm in this instance, but by exposing the selfishness of his likes and dislikes.

4:6. God provided (cf. "provided" in 1:17; 4:7-8) **a vine** to give the prophet

shade that his crude shelter (v. 5) could not provide. The God of the sea, who could provide a fish to swallow **Jonah,** is also the God of the land (cf. 1:9) and its vegetation. Here is evidence that God is compassionate (4:2)—even when His servants are upset and depressed.

As this plant grew it covered the prophet's hut. The shade from the green plant, covering his booth with its dense foliage, protected him from the rays of the desert sun. The plant (*qîqāyôn*) may have been a castor-bean plant (*Ricinus communis*), which grows rapidly in hot climates to a height of 12 feet and has large leaves. It easily withers if its stalk is injured. The fact that the plant grew overnight (cf. "at dawn the next day," v. 7, and note v. 10) shows that more-than-usual rapid growth was as much a miracle as God's providing the fish for Jonah. Delighted with this relief, **Jonah,** though he had been angry and depressed, was now overjoyed. Ironically he was glad for his own comfort but not for the Ninevites' relief from judgment.

4:7-8. Early **the next day God provided** (cf. "provided" in 1:17; 4:6) **a worm** that destroyed the plant that had brought joy to the prophet. Then the following day **God provided a scorching east wind** that left Jonah comfortless and **faint.** The prophet's own shelter was not enough to protect him from the terribly hot wind from the east. Strikingly in chapter 1 God intervened by a storm and a huge fish; now He intervened with a lowly worm and a sultry wind. Again the prophet was so discomforted—first by Nineveh's repentance and now by the loss of the shade from the vine—that he wanted **to die** (cf. 4:3).

b. The explanation stated (4:9-11)

4:9. God asked **Jonah** the same question He posed earlier. **Do you have a right to be angry?** (cf. v. 4) But here He added the words **about the vine.** God was wanting Jonah to see the contrast between His sparing Nineveh and His destroying the vine—the contrast between Jonah's lack of concern for the *spiritual* welfare of the Ninevites and his concern for his own *physical* welfare. Both Jonah's unconcern (for Nineveh) and concern (for himself) were selfish. Jonah replied that his anger over the withered plant was justified, and that he was so

angry he wanted **to die.**

"Life for Jonah [is] a series of disconcerting surprises and frustrations. He tries to escape from God and is trapped. He then gives up, accepts the inevitability of perishing, and is saved. He obeys when given a second chance, and is frustratingly, embarrassingly successful. He blows up; his frustration is intensified" (Judson Mather, "The Comic Act of the Book of Jonah," *Soundings* 65. Fall 1982, p. 283).

4:10-11. God wanted Jonah to see that he had no right to be angry over Nineveh or the **vine** because Jonah did not give life to or sustain either of them. Nor was he sovereign over them. He had no control over the plant's growth or withering. The vine was quite temporal (**it sprang up overnight and died overnight**) and was of relatively little value. Yet Jonah grieved over it. Whereas Jonah had no part in making the plant **grow,** God had created the Ninevites. Jonah's affections were distorted; he cared more for a vine than for human lives. He cared more for his personal comfort than for the spiritual destiny of thousands of people. What a picture of Israel in Jonah's day.

God's words to the prophet indicate that Jonah had no right to be angry. Donald E. Baker paraphrases the Lord's response this way: "Let's analyze this anger of yours, Jonah. . . . It represents your concern over your beloved plant—but what did it really mean to you? Your attachment to it couldn't be very deep, for it was here one day and gone the next. Your concern was dictated by self-interest, not by genuine love. You never had the devotion of a gardener. If you feel as bad as you do, what would you expect a gardener to feel like, who tended a plant and watched it grow only to see it wither and die? This is how I feel about Nineveh, only much more so. All those people, all those animals—I made them; I have cherished them all these years. Nineveh has cost Me no end of effort, and it means the world to Me. Your pain is nothing compared to Mine when I contemplate their destruction" ("Jonah and the Worm," *His.* October 1983, p. 12).

Whereas Jonah had thought God was absurd in sparing the Assyrians, God exposed Jonah as the one whose thinking was absurd.

In contrast with an insignificant vine, greater **Nineveh** was significant; it had **more than 120,000 people.** The words, **who cannot tell their right hand from their left,** may refer to young children, in which case the population of Nineveh and its environs may have been, as some commentators state, about 600,000. But other commentators suggest that the 120,000 were adults, who were as undisciplined or undiscerning as children, thus picturing their spiritual and moral condition without God. (In that case the total population may have been about 300,000.) The figure of 120,000 for Nineveh *proper* accords with the adult population of Nimrod (Gen. 10:11-12; also known as Calah, a suburb of Nineveh). An inscription states that Ashurnaṣirpal II (883–859) invited 69,574 people of Nimrod to a feast (Leslie C. Allen, *The Books of Joel, Obadiah, Jonah and Micah,* p. 234, n. 27; Daniel David Luckenbill, *The Annals of Sennacherib.* Chicago: University of Chicago Press, 1924, p. 116). And according to Donald J. Wiseman, Nineveh's walls enclosed an area twice that of Calah ("Jonah's Nineveh," *Tyndale Bulletin* 30. 1979, p. 37).

Jonah is a remarkably tragic example of the plight of the nation Israel. Both Jonah and Israel were accused of religious disobedience and disaffection. What a tragedy when God's people care more for creaturely comforts than for the interests of God's will among men.

By contrast, God is unselfish. He has a right to **be concerned about** (*ḥûs,* "to spare"; cf. Joel 2:17) **that great city,** a city with many people who needed His grace.

The two Minor Prophets that deal almost exclusively with Nineveh—Jonah and Nahum—each end with a question (cf. Nahum 3:19). The question in Jonah 4:11 leaves the reader with a sense of uneasiness, for the curtain seems to drop abruptly. No response from Jonah is recorded. How is this silence to be understood? Most likely Jonah could not have written the book unless he had learned the point God was seeking to bring home to him. Apparently Jonah perceived his error and then wrote this historical-biographical narrative to urge Israel to flee from her disobedience and spiritual callousness.

As the book concludes, Jonah was angry, depressed, hot, and faint. And he was left to contemplate God's words about his own lack of compassion and God's depth of compassion. The Lord had made His points: (a) He is gracious toward all nations, toward Gentiles as well as Israelites; (b) He is sovereign; (c) He punishes rebellion; and (d) He wants His own people to obey Him, to be rid of religious sham, and to place no limits on His universal love and grace.

BIBLIOGRAPHY

Allen, Leslie C. *The Books of Joel, Obadiah, Jonah and Micah.* The New International Commentary on the Old Testament. Grand Rapids: Wm B. Eerdmans Publishing Co., 1976.

Banks, William L. *Jonah, the Reluctant Prophet.* Chicago: Moody Press, 1966.

Blair, J. Allen. *Living Obediently: A Devotional Study of the Book of Jonah.* Neptune, N.J.: Loizeaux Brothers, 1963.

Draper, James T., Jr. *Jonah: Living in Rebellion.* Wheaton, Ill.: Tyndale House Publishers, 1971.

Fausset, A.R. *A Commentary: Critical, Experimental and Practical on the Old Testament.* Vol. 4. Grand Rapids: Wm. B. Eerdmans Publishing Co., 1945.

Feinberg, Charles L. *The Minor Prophets.* Chicago: Moody Press, 1976.

Gaebelein, Frank E. *Four Minor Prophets: Obadiah, Jonah, Habakkuk, and Haggai.* Chicago: Moody Press, 1977.

Keil, C.F. "Jonah." In *Commentary on the Old Testament in Ten Volumes.* Vol. 10. Reprint (25 vols. in 10). Grand Rapids: Wm. B. Eerdmans Publishing Co., 1982.

Kleinert, Paul. "The Book of Jonah." In *Commentary on the Holy Scriptures.* Reprint (24 vols. in 12). Grand Rapids: Zondervan Publishing House, 1960.

Kohlenberger, John R. III. *Jonah-Nahum.* Everyman's Bible Commentary. Chicago: Moody Press, 1984.

Laetsch, Theo. *The Minor Prophets.* St. Louis: Concordia Publishing House, 1956.

Pusey, E.B. *The Minor Prophets: A Commentary.* Vol. 1. Grand Rapids: Baker Book House, 1970.

Tatford, Frederick A. *The Minor Prophets.* Vol. 2. Reprint (3 vols.). Minneapolis: Klock & Klock Christian Publishers, 1982.

MICAH

John A. Martin

INTRODUCTION

Author and Date. Little is known about the author of this book. His name Micah, a shortened form of the name Micaiah, means "Who is like Yahweh?" In Jeremiah's day the elders referred to Micah and quoted Micah 3:12 in defense of Jeremiah's message of judgment on the nation (Jer. 26:18).

Micah was from Moresheth (Micah 1:1; cf. 1:14), a Judean town about 25 miles southwest of Jerusalem near the Philistine city of Gath (see the map "Israel and the Surrounding Nations in the Days of the Prophets," between Song and Isa.). Moresheth, in Judah's fertile foothills, was also near Lachish, an important international trading point.

Like his contemporary Isaiah, Micah prophesied about the Assyrian destruction of the Northern Kingdom and the later defeat of the Southern Kingdom by the Babylonians. Micah prophesied in the eighth century B.C. during the reigns of Jotham, Ahaz, and Hezekiah (Micah 1:1; cf. the chart "Kings of Judah and Israel and the Preexilic Prophets," near 1 Kings 12).

Message and Style. The book has three messages (Micah 1:2–2:13; chaps. 3–5; chaps. 6–7), each beginning with the exhortation to "hear" or "listen" to what the Lord has to say to the nation. Though Micah mentioned the destruction coming on the Northern Kingdom of Israel, his main audience was the people of the Southern Kingdom of Judah. Micah's three messages showed that Judah was just as guilty as Israel. They too would be disciplined by God.

God's standard of measurement in the Book of Micah (as in all the prophetic writings) was the Mosaic Covenant God made with His people when the nation was redeemed from Egypt. The people were expected to live according to the covenant stipulations. If they did they would be blessed by God (Deut. 28:1-14). If they did not, they would be judged by God and eventually He would cast them out of the land of promise (Deut. 28:15-68). Micah pointed up how the people had failed to live up to the covenant stipulations. He announced that God was just in disciplining them. Actually God's discipline on the nation showed that He cared for them and would restore them.

Though the theme of judgment is prominent in each of Micah's three messages, the prophet also stressed restoration. Micah mentioned the "remnant" in each of his three messages (Micah 2:12; 4:7; 5:7-8; 7:18). He was confident that someday the Lord would restore the people of Israel to a place of prominence in the world under the Messiah. This emphasis would have greatly encouraged the righteous remnant in Micah's day.

Like many portions of the prophetic books, the Book of Micah is in poetry, not prose. Most of his statements therefore were in parallelism (see comments on parallelism under "Nature of the Psalms" in the *Introduction* to the Book of Pss.). His book includes several puns (see comments on Micah 1:10-15) and several probing questions. Micah is quoted twice in the New Testament (5:2 is quoted in Matt. 2:5-6, and Micah 7:6 is quoted in Matt. 10:35-36). Micah wrote about the Messiah's birthplace, lineage, and origin (Micah 5:4), and reign (4:1-7), and referred to Him as Israel's King (2:13) and Ruler (5:2).

OUTLINE

I. First Message: Judgment Will Come (chaps. 1–2)

113

COMMENTARY

I. First Message: Judgment Will Come (chaps. 1–2)

Here Micah foretold God's judgment on Israel and Judah. He also wrote that the nation will ultimately be restored to prominence and prosperity. The prophet was sure because of the promises God had given other writers. God had promised Abraham that he would have many descendants and they would dwell in Palestine (Gen. 12:2; 15:18-21; 17:1-8, 16, 19-20). Through Moses God promised the people they would enjoy great blessing in the land (Deut. 30:1-10). He told David that his offspring and throne would continue forever (2 Sam. 7:11b-16). The Major and Minor Prophets also wrote messages of consolation that God will ultimately bless the nation because of His promises. Isaiah, Micah's contemporary, also prophesied that God will restore the nation (see, e.g., Isa. 65–66).

The theme of judgment, voiced repeatedly in the prophetic books, can be traced back to Deuteronomy 27–28 when Moses warned the people about to enter the Promised Land about the dangers that awaited them there. The previous adult generation (except Caleb and Joshua) had died in the wilderness because of their refusal to follow God's command to possess the land. So Moses told the new generation that they had a choice. They could either follow the covenant given them by God and live in the land with prosperity (Deut. 28:1-14), or they could refuse and be cursed in the land with a lack of fertility and productivity (of people, animals, and crops) and ultimately be exiled from the land of promise. From that point on, much of the narrative and prophetic portions of the Old Testament focus on Israel's failure to live according to God's covenantal stipulations. Micah, along with Amos, especially pointed up the social failures of the nation in not keeping the covenant (see, e.g., Micah 2:1, 8-9; 3:11; 6:11).

A. Introduction (1:1)

1:1. A number of important introductory points are made in this opening verse. **Micah** said the message of his book was **the word of the LORD.** This phrase, common to many of the prophets, is important in light of this revelation or "word" from the Lord to His people. God wanted Israel to react rationally to His word and to make proper decisions based on it. Her religious system contrasted directly with the contemporary pagan fertility religions in which sensory experience was the highest form of religious expression.

The prophet said he was from **Moresheth** (called Moresheth Gath in v. 14; perhaps modern Tell Judaiyideh). The town was about 25 miles southwest of Jerusalem, though its exact location has been disputed.

Micah prophesied **during the reigns of Jotham, Ahaz, and Hezekiah.** Micah prophesied about both the Northern and the Southern Kingdoms, but he mentioned only these three kings of Judah because the kings in the north were not in the Davidic line. The dates of these three kings means that Micah's ministry fell between 750 and 686, though scholars normally assume that Micah's ministry ended in the early part of Hezekiah's reign (perhaps before 700 B.C.).

Micah's book relays **the vision** (cf. Isa. 1:1; Obad. 1; Nahum 1:1) **he saw concerning Samaria,** capital of the Northern Kingdom (Israel), **and Jerusalem,** capital of the Southern Kingdom (Judah). The Hebrew word for "vision" suggests that God gave these passages to Micah who "saw" them mentally and spiritually. These cities obviously represented all 12 tribes of the nation. The prophet denounced evil which was rampant throughout the nation. The Northern Kingdom had long before strayed from the covenant given through Moses. And the people in the Southern Kingdom were acting like their brothers and sisters to the north, failing to live according to the covenant.

B. Prediction of coming judgment (1:2-7)

1:2. Verses 2-7 form the backdrop for the rest of the book. After calling on the earth to **hear** God's lawsuit against His covenant people (v. 2), the prophet spoke of the results of God's punishment (vv. 3-4), the reason for the judgment (v. 5), and the certainty of judgment (vv. 6-7). In a kind of cosmic law court Micah asked **all** the **peoples** of the **earth,** like a jury, to "hear" what God as a **witness** would say about the nation's sins. Micah

implied that everyone, given the opportunity, would agree that God's judgment **against** His people was just.

Micah called God **the Sovereign** (*'ǎdōnāy*) **LORD** (*Yahweh*), and in the last line of verse 2 he used *'ǎdōnāy* (**Lord**) again. In 4:13 Micah used the shortened form *'ǎdôn.* On the title "Sovereign LORD" see comments on Ezekiel 2:4. Micah noted that the Lord would come **from His holy temple.** Of course the temple did not contain God; even all creation could not contain Him (1 Kings 8:27). His dwelling place (Micah 1:3) is in heaven (2 Chron. 6:21, 30, 33, 39). However, God had chosen to localize His presence in the tabernacle and later the temple above the atonement cover, the lid of the ark of the Testimony. Inside the ark were the two tablets on which were written the Ten Commandments, a portion of God's Word. As stated earlier, the Israelites were responsible to live according to the Mosaic Covenant. The sacrificial system and the temple were at the core of the covenantal system. Therefore to speak of the Lord going "from His holy temple" to witness against the nation meant He would judge them on the basis of the Mosaic Covenant which gave Him every right to do so.

1:3-4. Micah called on the people to look for God **coming** in judgment **from** heaven, **His dwelling place** (cf. comments on v. 2). The prophet pictured God treading or walking on **the high places** (the mountains; cf. v. 4) **of the earth.** In His majesty He was like a gigantic person stepping from one mountain peak to another. Thus God is capable of doing whatever He wants to do without being stopped by anyone. As God trod **the mountains** they melted **like wax before** a **fire** or **like water rushing down a slope** which cannot be stopped. Even **the valleys split,** disturbed by God's awesome power. These "high places" (v. 3) may have also subtly implied (by double entendre) the pagan altars on hilltops (cf. comments on v. 5).

1:5. The reason for this judgment was **Jacob's transgression** and **the sins of the house of Israel.** "Jacob" or "Jacob's" occurs 11 times in Micah. Nine times it refers to the entire nation of Israel (in the first question in v. 5 Jacob means the Northern Kingdom, and in 7:20 Jacob is the patriarch). "Jacob" and "Israel" are used together as synonyms in 1:5a; 2:12; 3:1, 8-9. **Transgression** and "sin(s)" occur together four times in Micah (1:5; 3:8; 6:7; 7:18).

The sins of the residents in **Samaria**, capital of Israel, and **Jerusalem**, capital of Judah, typified the sins of people throughout both nations. The capital cities apparently "set the pace" for the rest of Israel and Judah, with the worst sins being committed in the largest urban areas.

A **high place** was a place on a mountain or hill where people worshiped God (see, e.g., 2 Chron. 33:17) or idols. Pagan people in the land of Israel often worshiped on hilltops (perhaps to symbolize a closer relationship to their gods). Before David placed the central sanctuary in Jerusalem, the people worshiped the Lord at altars throughout the land. After the central sanctuary was set up the Israelites were then supposed to go to Jerusalem to worship God. But many of them, attracted to the nearby pagan high places, abandoned the worship of the Lord for pagan worship. This even took place in Jerusalem. No wonder that Micah sarcastically called Jerusalem the high place of Judah. The Jerusalemites were disobeying God outwardly as well as inwardly.

1:6. God's judgment was to come first on the Northern Kingdom (vv. 6-7) and then on the Southern Kingdom (vv. 9-16). The capital city of the North would be completely destroyed, even to its **foundations.** Samaria's ruins can still be seen today. Rather than a populated city, **Samaria** is only **a heap of rubble** (cf. 3:12), a field for **vineyards.** This prophecy was fulfilled in 722 B.C. when the Assyrian army captured the city after a three-year siege (2 Kings 17:1-5). The time leading up to the fall had been filled with political intrigue and assassinations (cf. comments on 2 Kings 15:8-31). Most of the people of Samaria and the Northern Kingdom were taken away and others were brought in to intermarry with the remaining people (cf. 2 Kings 17:6, 22-24).

1:7. Because much idolatrous worship had been going on in Samaria (**idols** and **images** were numerous) the Lord said He would bring it all to an end by a great destruction of the city. Samaria's idols would be smashed, the **temple gifts . . . burned,** and the images destroyed. In Baalism, a pagan fertility religion, "sacred" **prostitutes** were set apart for the "worship" of pagan fertility deities. **Wages** paid to temple **prostitutes** were in turn given by them to the temple as "temple gifts." Apparently this practice had permeated Samaria. This illicit sexuality graphically pictured the illicit departure of the Northern Kingdom from their solemn covenant arrangement with the Lord. In effect, they were bound to God in a "marriage agreement" and to depart to other gods was tantamount to committing spiritual adultery (cf. comments on Hosea 4:10-15).

Since Israel had committed adultery with temple prostitutes, the temple gifts would be smashed by the Assyrians and used **again** by them in *their* prostitution. Becoming captives of Assyria the Israelites would be forced to continue in a prostituted relationship. They had sought out other gods so now God would send them away to lands where foreign gods were worshiped, giving them what they evidently wanted.

C. Lament over the people (1:8-16)

Micah said he would lament because of Samaria's destruction (vv. 8-9); then through a clever use of several wordplays he called on certain towns of Judah to mourn for Samaria and for themselves because they too would feel the brunt of an Assyrian invasion (vv. 10-16).

1. MICAH'S LAMENT (1:8-9)

1:8-9. Because of the punishment to come on the Northern Kingdom, Micah was in a state of agitation. To **weep and wail** and to **go . . . barefoot and naked** were signs of extreme mourning (cf. 2 Sam. 15:30; Isa. 20:2; 22:12; Jer. 25:34). Identifying with the people, Micah felt as desolate as **a jackal** (a nighttime scavenger) and **an owl** (a nocturnal bird) who live in desolate places. Micah viewed the punishment as already having happened. It was as inevitable and **incurable** as a **wound.** In fact the sins of the Northern Kingdom had so influenced **Judah** that the "wound" (from God's judgment) would **come** on her too (cf. Isa. 1:5-6). Judgment would reach **the very gate of Jerusalem.** This happened in 701 B.C. when Sennacherib's Assyrian army destroyed 46 towns in Judah and then surrounded Jerusalem (2 Kings 18–19).

2. MICAH'S CALL FOR OTHERS TO MOURN (1:10-16)

Micah used several clever wordplays to describe the desolation the Assyrian invasion would bring to Judah's cities. (See the map "Israel and the Surrounding Nations in the Days of the Prophets," between Song and Isa.) Interestingly Sennacherib too used wordplays when recording *his* conquests.

1:10. Tell it not in Gath recalls 2 Samuel 1:20 where David made the same statement. In that case David did not want the Philistines to be glad about the demise of Saul, Israel's former ruler. In Micah's case he did not want the inhabitants of Gath to hear about the Assyrian attack on Judah. Nor should Gath **weep,** for then others would know about the desolation. "Gath" (*gaṯ*) and "tell" (*taggîḏû*) sounded something alike in Hebrew because of the letters "g" and "t."

However, Micah told the people of **Beth Ophrah** ("house of dust") to **roll in the dust,** in an expression of their grief (cf. Jer. 25:34; also note "roll in ashes," Jer. 6:26; Ezek. 27:20).

1:11-12. When attacked by Assyria, **Shaphir** ("beautiful or pleasant") would become the opposite of its name—a town of **nakedness and shame.** In Hebrew **Zaanan** (*ṣa'ănān*) and **come out** (*yaṣ'âh*) are related words; in contrast with their city's name, the Zaananites would not dare go outside their city walls because of the warfare. Nor would anyone go to **Beth Ezel** ("house of nearness or proximity") for **protection,** for that town would itself be **in mourning** and in need of help. In **Maroth** (which sounds in Heb. like the word for "bitterness") people would **writhe in pain** while **waiting for relief** from Jerusalem. But no relief would come because the destruction would go all the way **to the gate of Jerusalem** (cf. v. 9).

1:13. Sarcastically Micah urged the citizens of **Lachish** (*lāḵîš*), which sounds something like the word for a **team** (*reḵeš*) of horses, to get a **chariot** ready for escaping from the Assyrians. (Lachish was known for its horses.) But their escape attempt would be in vain. Lachish was **the beginning of sin** to Jerusalem's inhabitants (**the Daughter of Zion**; cf. comments on 3:10; 4:8; Lam. 1:6). Perhaps this means that Lachish influenced Jerusalem toward idolatry. "Zion" occurs

nine times in Micah (cf. comments on Zech. 8:3).

1:14. Moresheth Gath would be given **parting gifts,** perhaps by Jerusalem, if it is the city intended by the word **you.** "Parting gifts" means betrothal gifts, as a father gives his daughter when she marries. Similarly Jerusalem would "give" Moresheth Gath to the Assyrian king.

The town of Aczib (*'aḵzîḇ,* "deception") when conquered by the Assyrians, would become **deceptive** (*'aḵzāḇ*), unable to offer help **to** Israel's **kings.**

1:15. A conqueror, a reference to Sennacherib, would go **against . . . Mareshah,** another Judean town. The two words in Hebrew are similar ("conqueror" is *hayyōrēš,* and "Mareshah" is *mārēšâh*). Ironically Mareshah, which means possessor, would become the possession of Sennacherib. As David had escaped **to Adullam** (cf. 1 Sam. 22:1), so **the glory of Israel,** probably her leaders, would be shamed by becoming fugitives in Adullam.

1:16. Even **the children** in those Judean towns would be exiled by the Assyrians. This would cause the people of the area to mourn, one sign of which was to **shave** their **heads** (cf. Job 1:20; Isa. 15:2; Jer. 47:5; Ezek. 27:31; Amos 8:10). With heads shaved the mourners would look like **bald** vultures.

D. Sins of Judah (2:1-11)

All the sins of Judah mentioned in these verses violate stipulations in the Mosaic Covenant. Therefore the destruction coming on them (cf. 1:9-16) was justified.

1. SINS OF THE PEOPLE (2:1-5)

2:1. Micah first noted that many of the people lay awake at night thinking up **evil** things to do the next day. On such people Micah pronounced **woe,** a term used by several prophets to announce guilt and coming judgment on the sinful people (cf., e.g., Isa. 3:9, 11; 5:8, 11, 18, 20-22; Jer. 13:27; Ezek. 13:3, 18; Hosea 7:13; 9:12; Amos 5:18; 6:1; Hab. 2:6, 9, 12, 15, 19; Zeph. 2:5; 3:1).

2:2-3. In their crass materialism, the people coveted others' **fields** and **houses** and took **them** simply because they wanted them. **They** would **defraud** another by stealing **his home** or **inheritance** (i.e., land). Micah was probably speaking against the influential people who had the power to do such things. Their sin, besides materialistic greed and theft, was wanton disregard for the rights of their **fellowman.**

The ancestors of the people Micah addressed had all been slaves in Egypt. In taking them out of Egypt, the Lord had freed them from slavery. Therefore the Israelites were not to enslave each other. Since God had given each tribe and each family its share of the land, the people were not to take away others' land. To take their financial holdings was to disregard the Law of God. As a result, God was **planning disaster** (cf. 1:12) **against** the **people.** They would be unable to **save** themselves from God's judgment because the **calamity,** when started, would not be stopped (cf. 1:3-4). Pride would be replaced with a debased condition.

2:4-5. Along with being unable to save themselves (v. 3) the people also would be derided by those around them. The people's enemies would mockingly sing to them what those in grief would normally have said about the loss of their **fields.** Ironically those Judahites who took away the land of others (v. 2) would have their own land taken **from** them. No longer would anyone be present to pass judgment about the division of **the land,** for their whole system would be destroyed. **The assembly of the LORD** referred to the covenant nation as a whole (cf. Deut. 23:1, 8).

2. SINS OF THE FALSE PROPHETS (2:6-11)

In much of her history, Israel in the Old Testament had both good (true) and bad (false) prophets. The true prophets spoke for God to the people, after urging them to return to the moral and ethical values of the covenantal Law. The false prophets often said that God would not harm the people so long as they were involved in the outward ceremonial aspects of the Law. True prophets urged the nation to follow the covenant, as outlined in Deuteronomy 27–28. A strong ethical dimension was in their messages. In fact their messages were often more ethical than eschatological. The yet-future peace and prosperity for the nation (promised in the Abrahamic Covenant; cf. Gen. 17:3-8; 22:17-18) will come only when the nation turns to the Lord and follows His Word.

In contrast with the true prophets the false prophets spoke only what the people wanted to hear. Those messengers said God was for their nation and would not destroy it. This was of course partly true and partly false. God was for the nation of Israel, but He had said He would punish them if they did not obey Him.

2:6-7a. Apparently these false **prophets** were indignant that Micah mentioned coming disaster (vv. 3-5), so they enjoined him **not** to **prophesy** that the **disgrace** of judgment would come. They naively questioned whether **the Spirit of** God would ever be **angry** with His people, or that God would ever **do such things.** They were forgetting that a father often shows his love for his children by disciplining them. Had God not followed through on the discipline He would have been untrue to His own word.

2:7b-9. Micah answered the false prophets' objections by describing the situation in the nation at that time. He first reminded them that God's **words do good to him whose ways are upright.** God accurately judges human behavior. He blesses those whose ways are righteous.

In prophesying peace and not destruction, the false prophets were actually treating God's people as if they were the prophets' **enemy.** The false messengers robbed personal possessions (e.g., a **rich robe**) from people who were walking along oblivious to any danger. The victims were happy, carefree, and rich like soldiers **returning** with spoils **from** a victorious **battle.** Also the false prophets separated families by driving away mothers **from their . . . homes.**

By not telling the people to repent and return to the Lord, the prophets were neglecting the only thing that could save the people from the invading Assyrians. In effect, the prophets were opening the way for the Captivity by not warning the people to turn back to the Lord.

2:10-11. Partly because of the false prophets' perverted teaching, the land became irretrievably **defiled.** So the people would be exiled. Sarcastically Micah told the people to **go away,** that is, into exile (cf. Amos' sarcasm in Amos 4:4-5). The people's values were so degraded that they would readily respond to a false **prophet** who would deceptively predict not exile but continued prosperity, including **plenty of wine and beer.**

E. Prediction of future regathering (2:12-13)

2:12-13a. Though the outlook was grim for Judah, the Prophet Micah voiced a ray of hope, based on God's covenant promises to Abraham. Each of the three sections of Micah's prophecy includes a promise of regathering and blessing on the nation (2:12-13; 4:1-8; 7:8-20). Here in chapter 2 the promise of blessing is brief. Two truths are stated in verses 12-13 which are expanded greatly in chapters 4-5. The first is that the Lord will regather and renew His people as their Shepherd (2:12-13a), and the second is that the Lord will lead His people as their King (v. 13b). **Jacob** and **Israel** are synonyms for the entire nation (cf. comments on 1:5). When God restores the believing remnant of Israel to their land, He will be like a shepherd leading his **flock** (cf. 5:4; 7:14). So great will be the regathering of the sheep that **the place** (i.e., the land) **will throng with people.** The Old Testament frequently spoke of God as a Shepherd and His people as sheep (cf. Pss. 23:1; 77:20; 78:52; 80:1; 100:3; Isa. 40:11; also note Jer. 23:3; 31:10). The people would be **like sheep** brought together **in a pen** for safekeeping.

That long-awaited time of blessing will come about for the nation of Israel in the Millennium. Some interpreters claim that this promise of blessing is being fulfilled now in the church, rather than in the future for Israel. However, if Micah 2:12 refers to spiritual blessings for the church, then Israel has been misled all these centuries since Abraham to think that she will inherit the land forever.

Much as a shepherd **breaks open** or clears the way for his sheep, going **before them** and leading them out **the gate** to pastures, so the Lord will remove all obstacles to blessing for His people Israel.

2:13b. A second fact about the forthcoming blessing is that **the LORD** will lead His people as **their King** (cf. Isa. 33:22; Zeph. 3:15; Zech. 14:9). He has not abandoned them. He will lead them, passing **through before them** as **their Head.** The

false prophets were partially correct when they stated that the Lord is for the covenant nation. He will fulfill His promises to Israel for, like a good king, He loves His people.

II. Second Message: Blessing Will Follow Judgment (chaps. 3–5)

In Micah's first message (chaps. 1–2) he emphasized the people's sins and their failure to take seriously God's righteous demands on their lives. In only two verses (2:12-13) did Micah discuss God's future blessings on His nation. In this second message the emphasis is different. Two of the three chapters (chaps. 4–5) discuss God's blessing on Israel and Judah. (Chap. 3 details the sins of the *leaders* of Israel and Judah.) As is true throughout Scripture, God's plans for the future are given not simply to inform people of what will occur, but also—and more so—to motivate people to change their lives on the basis of God's plans for them. Certainly the promise of Israel's future blessings (chaps. 4–5) should have caused the nation—and first its leaders (chap. 3)—to turn to God in repentance and gratitude.

A. Judgment on the nation's leaders (chap. 3)

1. JUDGMENT ON THE RULERS (3:1-4)

3:1-2a. In perverting justice the **leaders** and **rulers** (cf. v. 9) of the nation were acting like wild beasts. (On **Jacob** and **Israel** as synonyms for the 12-tribe nation, see comments on 1:5.) They were the ones who **should . . . know** and carry out **justice.** But instead of practicing justice they hated **good and** loved **evil.** Of course this is the opposite of the way leaders should act (cf. Amos 5:15). Their perverse standards (cf. Micah 3:9) showed that they did not love the Lord (cf. Ps. 97:10) or fear Him ("To fear the Lord is to hate evil," Prov. 8:13).

3:2b-3. Micah likened the unjust leaders to hunters who killed and ate (i.e., took undue advantage of) God's **people,** who were supposed to be under their care. The leaders were so harsh that they were not satisfied with tearing off **the skin** and eating **the flesh.** They even chopped up **their bones** as if they were preparing a stew. By unfair legal actions, by bribery (cf. v. 11; 7:3), by theft (cf. 2:8), by oppression (cf. 3:9), and even by bloodshed (cf. v. 10; 7:2), they left the people helpless.

By contrast faithful leaders protected their charges and looked out for their welfare. David, the epitome of a good leader for God, was taken from shepherding sheep (1 Sam. 17:15) to become a shepherd of the people (2 Sam. 5:2; 7:7). The people in Micah's day were being betrayed by their leaders, for if they really cared about the people, they would have turned them back to the Lord.

3:4. Because of Israel's sins a time would come when **they** would **cry out to the LORD but He** would **not answer them** (cf. v. 7). Micah was speaking of the **time** when Israel would be taken into captivity. The false prophets and leaders had refused to believe that the Lord would actually follow through and punish them for their behavior. However, when the Captivity came they would realize that God was actually punishing them. Then it would be too late for Him to deliver them. They would have to live with the consequences of their actions, enduring the punishment for their evil. Of course God listens to the prayers of His people, but sometimes He refuses to relieve them immediately from the consequences of their actions.

2. JUDGMENT ON THE FALSE PROPHETS
(3:5-8)

3:5. Rather than serving as shepherds of the nation, caring for them, and leading them properly, the false **prophets** were leading the **people astray.** These leaders were giving the people false hope by telling them they would not be punished by God, that there would be no calamity. If someone paid the false shepherds well (**if one feeds them**) they would pronounce **peace** on him. In other words they told a person what he wanted to hear for a price (cf. v. 11). On the other hand if one did **not** feed them (i.e., pay the prophets their price) they were ready to oppose him (**to wage war against him**). The prophets were concerned with their own welfare rather than the nation's welfare. Materialism was their master (cf. v. 11).

3:6-7. Because the false prophets were not leading the people correctly and were taking advantage of them materially, these leaders would be shamed and humiliated. **Night** would **come over** them, **the sun** would **set for** those **prophets,** and **darkness** would come even in the daytime. Nightfall pictures impending doom. When that devastation would come, the prophets would have no **visions** or **divination.** They had been counseling the people to go on living as they had been, thinking that God surely would not judge His own nation. But suddenly judgment would come. And when it did, the people would ask the prophets why it came, and they would be unable to explain it. **The seers** (which corresponds in Heb. to "visions" in v. 6) would **be** totally **ashamed** (cf. Zech. 13:4). And **the diviners** (which corresponds in Heb. to "divination" in Micah 3:6; on the Heb. word *qāsam,* "to divine," see comments on Deut. 18:10) would be **disgraced** (cf. Micah 2:6). The prophets would **cover their faces** in humiliation, realizing they had **no answer from God** (cf. 3:4). The people would then see that the prophets were not true prophets after all. Because God would hide His face (v. 4) the false shepherds would "cover their faces"!

Micah warned the people and leaders about impending judgment so that they would see the folly of their ways and turn back to God. This true prophet warned them of the coming doom in hope that they would change their ways.

3:8. In contrast with the leaders (vv. 1-4) and false prophets (vv. 5-7), who had not been speaking God's message, Micah, **filled with** God's **power,** spoke **with** the authority of **the Spirit of the LORD** in denouncing the people's sins and predicting judgment. Micah's words, he said, were **with justice** because God is just in carrying out His judgment against the covenant people. And Micah's words had **might** because God is totally capable of carrying out His sentence against His people. The leaders, however, dealt unjustly (cf. vv. 9-10) and their prophets had no spiritual strength.

Micah declared the **transgression** and the **sin** (cf. 1:5; 6:7; 7:18) of the nation (on **Jacob** and **Israel** as synonyms; cf. 3:1, 9, for the entire nation, see comments on 1:5). Micah could see from God's perspective what was going on in the nation. Because she was not living according to God's covenant standards, He had to punish her.

3. JUDGMENT ON ALL THE NAIVE LEADERS (3:9-12)

3:9-11. Because Micah was filled with the Spirit of the Lord (v. 8), he boldly confronted the leaders about their sins and the eventual outcome. He first called on the **leaders** and **rulers** (cf. v. 1) to listen to him (**hear this**). Micah did not say if the leaders listened or responded to him, but apparently they did not, for no major change is recorded about them.

Micah then described what their leadership was like (vv. 9b-11). They despised (*tā'aḇ,* a strong word meaning "to abhor or regard as an abomination") **justice** (cf. vv. 1-3) and distorted (*'āqaš,* "twisted") **all that is right** (lit., "all that is straight"). Of course a ruler over God's people was supposed to be just and equitable, like God Himself. A leader was to desire righteous behavior in his own life and in the lives of his people. Instead of this, these rulers deliberately perverted uprightness. They even encouraged and took part in **bloodshed** and **wickedness** in the city of **Jerusalem,** where justice and righteousness should have reigned. **Zion** (cf. comments on 1:13) and Jerusalem are used together in Micah as synonyms four times (3:10, 12; 4:2, 8).

Micah noted that the **leaders . . . priests,** and **prophets** were always out **for money** (cf. 7:3) and yet had the audacity to say that God was still with them and that therefore the nation would not face destruction (cf. 2:6). (Tell **fortunes** translates, *qāsam,* "to divine"; cf. 3:6-7 and comments on Deut. 18:10.) To be influenced by bribery violated God's command in Deuteronomy 16:19.

3:12. Destruction would come on the nation **because of you,** that is, the leaders. This does not suggest that the *people* were guiltless, and that only the leaders were sinning. Probably the leaders were leading the people into wicked behavior and therefore the whole nation was guilty before God. **Zion (Jerusalem;** cf. 3:10; 4:2, 8) would **be plowed like a field,** turned over, and overthrown. It would be in ruins (**a heap of rubble;** cf. 1:6). Even **the temple hill** would be **overgrown with thickets** (weeds).

B. Kingdom blessings for the nation (chaps. 4–5)

In these chapters Micah foretold the coming kingdom, which was announced by almost all the writing prophets. He spoke of the characteristics of the coming kingdom (4:1-8), events that will precede it (4:9–5:1), and the King who will establish it (5:2-15).

1. CHARACTERISTICS OF THE KINGDOM (4:1-8)

Micah 4:1-3 is similar to Isaiah 2:2-4. In Micah 4:1-8 Micah mentioned 11 characteristics of the kingdom.

a. The millennial temple will be prominent in the world (4:1a)

4:1a. The words **in the last days** denote the time when God will bring to consummation all the events in history (cf., e.g., Deut. 4:30, "in later days"; Ezek. 38:16, "in days to come"; Hosea 3:5). Usually "the last days" refers to the Tribulation and the Millennium (in the OT the word "kingdom" often referred to the Millennium). Micah did not state when "the last days" will occur, for Israel was supposed to be looking all the time for the consummation of the ages.

The **mountain of the LORD's temple**—Mount Zion where the millennial temple will be built (cf. Ezek. 40–43)—will become **chief among the mountains** (cf. Zech. 8:3). That is, the temple site will be the center of the millennial government, the place where Christ will rule. This fact contrasts sharply with the desolate condition of Jerusalem stated in Micah 3:12.

The religious and political systems will be closely related. From Moses' day, Israel's government was totally intertwined with her religious system. The king was anointed by God to govern the nation, and the priest was anointed to carry out the functions of worship.

Also in the Millennium, Israel's political-religious system, directed by the Messiah-King, will be predominant in the world. **It will be raised above the hills.** God's plan to bless the world through Israel (Gen. 12:3) was not nullified by her sin. Eventually Israel will be prominent above all other nations.

b. Peoples of the world will be attracted to Jerusalem (4:1b)

4:1b. In the Millennium people everywhere will realize the unique place Israel occupies in God's plans. No longer thinking of her as a small, insignificant nation, they will be attracted to her. In fact many **peoples will** travel **to** Jerusalem (cf. v. 2; 7:12) and her temple. "The verb **stream** may be a conscious play on the streams said to issue from the holy mount to water the earth (Ps. 46:4; see also Ps. 65:9; Isa. 33:21; Joel 3:18; Ezek. 47); a reverse flow of people begins toward the center" (James Luther Mays, *Micah: A Commentary,* pp. 96-7).

c. Jerusalem will be the place of instruction for the entire world (4:2a)

4:2a. The mountain of the LORD (cf. "the mountain of the LORD's temple," v. 1) and **the house of . . . God** both refer to the temple complex. People from **many nations will** go to Jerusalem (cf. v. 1; 7:12) to be taught **His ways so that** they **may walk in His paths.** In the kingdom saved Gentiles will want to learn the ways of the Lord, whereas ironically Israel was *not* interested in obeying the Lord. What a rebuke this was to Micah's contemporaries.

d. Revelation will go forth from Jerusalem (4:2b)

4:2b. This fact is closely related to the former one. **Law** (*tôrâh,* "instruction," not the Mosaic Law) will be given in **Zion** (i.e., **Jerusalem**; cf. 3:10, 12; 4:8), and God's **Word** (i.e., revelation about Him and His standards) will be communicated. Since God will be the Ruler (v. 3), it is natural that His Word should come from His place of rule.

e. The Lord will be the Judge at Jerusalem (4:3a)

4:3a. Many peoples and even **strong nations** will bring their disputes to the Lord. They will submit to God's judgment, realizing that He will decide what and who is right. Micah's readers were chafing under the Word of God, not wanting to be told by Him or by His prophet that they were wrong. By contrast eventually the whole world will submit willingly to God's Word and His decisions.

f. Peace will be universal (4:3b)

4:3b. Implements of warfare (**swords** and **spears**) will be changed into tools of agriculture (**plowshares** and **pruning hooks**). Neither will there be a need to **train** people for warfare because the na-

tions will be at peace. The Millennium is the kind of world people long for, a time when the earth's resources can be used for good instead of destruction. Justice and righteousness will be rewarded rather than scorned.

g. Israel will dwell in security and peace (4:4)

4:4. Each person sitting **under his own vine** and **his own fig tree** depicts security (cf. 1 Kings 4:25; Zech 3:10). **No one** will fear losing his security, for **the LORD Almighty has** declared (cf. Obad. 18) that they will be secure. In Micah's day Israel's leaders were forecasting peace for those who could pay the price (Micah 3:5) but the only way to peace and security is to submit to God in trust.

h. Israel will be spiritually sensitive to God (4:5)

4:5. The nations who were following **their gods** refer to pagan nations in Micah's day. They could not be the nations in the future Millennium because Micah had just written (vv. 2-3) that they will go to Jerusalem to learn of the Lord. Though pagan nations worshiped idols, Israel (**we**) in the Millennium **will walk** (cf. "walk" in v. 2) **in the name of the LORD,** that is, she will follow and obey His standards.

i. Israel will be regathered (4:6)

4:6. In that day (i.e., at the beginning of the Millennium; cf. v. 1, "in the last days"; v. 7, "that day"; 5:10, "in that day") **the LORD . . . will** restore **the exiles,** those who had been removed from the land. Micah did not know when this regathering would be. In fact he might have supposed that when the coming Babylonian Exile was over the kingdom would begin. From books of the Bible written later it became clear that God's millennial kingdom did not come with the return from the Babylonian Exile (see the Books of Ezra, Neh., Es., Hag., Zech., and Mal.). Micah was certain, however, that in the kingdom Jewish exiles who had experienced **grief** will be restored. In the Tribulation, Jews will be persecuted (Dan. 7:25) and scattered (cf. Zech. 14:5); then when Christ returns they will be regathered (Matt. 24:31).

j. Israel will be made strong (4:7)

4:7. In contrast with Israel's spiritual and moral weakness in Micah's day (spiritually they were **lame**; cf. Zeph. 3:19) and in contrast with Israel's being **driven away** into exile, the returned **remnant** (cf. Isa. 37:32; Micah 2:12; 5:7-8; 7:18; Rom. 9:27; 11:5) of believing Jews will become a **strong nation** (cf. "strong nations" in Micah 4:3). And **the LORD will rule over them** (cf. 5:2; Zeph. 3:15) **in Mount Zion** (Jerusalem) throughout the Millennium **and forever** (cf. Ps. 146:10; Luke 1:33; Rev. 11:15).

k. Jerusalem will have dominion (4:8)

4:8. In this 11th characteristic of the millennial kingdom Micah returned to his thought in verse 1, namely, that Jerusalem and God's government centered there will be preeminent. Jerusalem's people are addressed as the **watchtower of the flock.** Much as a shepherd watches his sheep or a farmer views his crops from a tower, so Jerusalem will watch over the nation. ("Flock" refers to Israel in Isa. 40:11; Jer. 13:17, 20; Micah 5:4; Zech. 10:3.) **Daughter of Zion** (cf. Micah 4:10, 13) and **Daughter of Jerusalem** refer to the city's inhabitants (cf. Isa. 1:8; Jer. 4:31; Lam. 1:6; 2:13; Micah 1:13; Zech. 9:9). Jerusalem's **dominion will be restored** to her since the Messiah Himself will reign from Zion. The nation will no longer be under the domination of others, for "the times of the Gentiles" (Luke 21:24) will be ended.

2. EVENTS PRECEDING THE KINGDOM (4:9–5:1)

Here Micah spoke of four events that would occur before the millennial kingdom will be established.

a. Israel would be exiled to Babylon (4:9-10a)

4:9-10a. Much as **a woman** in childbirth has tremendous **labor** pains, so the nation, carried away into exile, would **cry aloud** (*rûa'*, "cry out in distress"; cf. Isa. 15:4) in panic and **pain** (cf. Jer. 4:31; 6:24; 13:21; 22:23; 30:6; 49:24; 50:43). Then the nation would have **no king** or **counselor.** A king, making decisions in leading the nation, was like a counselor.

The Jews, being taken captive from their homeland, would **writhe in agony.**

(On **Daughter of Zion** see comments on Micah 1:13; 4:8.) But like a woman in labor pains they could do nothing to stop the agony; they had to go through the experience.

On the trek from their homeland the exiles were forced by their captors **to camp in the open field.** The prediction that they would be taken **to Babylon** was an amazing prophecy because in Micah's time Babylon was not the most powerful empire. It was still under Assyria.

b. Israel would be rescued from Babylon (4:10b)

4:10b. Israel, Micah wrote, would **be rescued** and redeemed by the covenant God, who cares for her. The Exile, besides punishing the nation, was used to purge her and to encourage the people to more godly living. Captivity also was necessary because God had said that He would cast them out of the land if they did not obey Him. In a sense the Exile was a test of God's integrity.

c. Nations will gather against the nation Israel (4:11-13)

4:11-13. Many nations (vv. 11a, 13) will unite **against** Jerusalem to try to conquer it. They will long to defile it by destroying it. But they will be ignorant of God's plans (**thoughts**) to defeat them. They will be devastated **like sheaves** of grain being broken up when threshed on a **threshing floor** (cf. Isa. 21:10; Jer. 51:33; Hosea 13:3).

Micah did not say when this would occur. Perhaps it was in Micah's day, for Israel certainly has had many enemies. If Micah 4:11 refers to Micah's time, then verses 12-13 seem to point ahead to a future time when other nations, gathered against Jerusalem, will be defeated. The **Daughter of Zion,** that is, the people of Jerusalem (cf. comments on v. 8) will **thresh** those **nations** (cf. Zech. 14:12-15), and **the LORD** will fight on Israel's behalf against them (Zech. 14:3). This battle—the Battle of Armageddon (Rev. 16:16; cf. Rev. 19:19)—will take place when the Messiah-King returns to establish the kingdom. The things Israel will capture in battle will be devoted (cf. comments on Josh. 6:17) **to the LORD,** whom Micah rightly calls **the LORD of all the earth** (cf. Ps. 97:5; Zech. 4:14; 6:5).

d. The ruler of Israel will be humiliated (5:1)

5:1. Jerusalem, besieged by the Babylonians (2 Kings 25:1), was called a **city of troops** (lit., "daughter of troops"), that is, a city surrounded by marauding soldiers. Micah challenged the people to **marshal** their **troops,** though of course her defense efforts were in vain because of Nebuchadnezzar's **siege.** (This Heb. word for "siege" is used in the OT only of his siege of Jerusalem, 2 Kings 24:10; 25:2; Jer. 52:5; Ezek. 4:3, 7; 5:2.)

Micah did not identify the **ruler** of Israel except to say that he would be struck **on the cheek with a rod.** (To strike someone on the cheek was to humiliate him; cf. 1 Kings 22:24; Job 16:10; Lam. 3:30.) Some suggest this ruler was Christ, because (a) Christ was struck on the head (Matt. 27:30; Mark 15:19) and face (John 19:3) and (b) He is referred to in Micah 5:2. However, several factors show that the ruler is probably Judah's king Zedekiah: (1) The first part of verse 1 refers to the Babylonian attack on Jerusalem. (2) The word "ruler" translates šōpēṭ ("judge"), whereas the word for ruler in verse 2, which does clearly refer to Christ, is mōšēl. (Šōpēṭ forms an interesting wordplay on the similar-sounding word for "rod," šēbeṭ.) (3) Christ was not smitten by troops of an enemy nation while Jerusalem was besieged. However, Nebuchadnezzar did capture Zedekiah and torture him (2 Kings 25:1-7). (4) A soon-coming event, not a distant-future one, seems to be suggested by the Hebrew word for "but now" in Micah 5:1 (not trans. in the NIV). This is followed by the distant future in verses 2-6. This pattern of present crisis followed by future deliverance is also seen in 4:11-13 in which the present (4:11) is introduced by "but now" and the distant future is discussed in 4:12-13.

3. THE RULER OF THE KINGDOM (5:2-15)

Micah described the birth of the Ruler (v. 2) and His work on behalf of the nation (vv. 3-15).

a. The birth of Israel's Ruler (5:2)

5:2. The pattern of this verse is similar in some ways to that in 4:8. In each verse, a city is personified and addressed as **you;** the words **will come** are in both verses; and deliverance is suggested by

similar Hebrew words (trans. "dominion" in 4:8 and **Ruler** in 5:2). The "Ruler," Christ, will be from **Bethlehem Ephrathah,** about five miles from Jerusalem. Ephrathah, also called Ephrath (Gen. 35:16-19; 48:7), was an older name for Bethlehem or the name of the area around Bethlehem. David was born in Bethlehem (1 Sam. 16:1, 18-19; 17:12) as was His greatest Descendant, Jesus Christ (Matt. 2:1). The chief priests and teachers of the Law understood this verse in Micah to refer to the Messiah (Matt. 2:3-6). That confused some of the people in Jesus' day (John 7:42) for though He was born in Bethlehem He was raised in Nazareth, in Galilee.

The Messiah-Ruler, who will deliver His people, was born in an insignificant, **small** town (not even mentioned in the list of towns in Josh. 15 or Neh. 11) where **the clans of Judah** lived. And God said this One, who will minister on Yahweh's behalf (**for Me**), will be Israel's "Ruler" (cf. "rule" in Micah 4:7). Christ accomplished and will accomplish the Father's will (cf. John 17:4; Heb. 10:7).

This Ruler's **origins** (lit., "goings out," i.e., His victories in Creation, theophanies, and providential dealings) **are from of old, from ancient times.** The KJV renders "ancient times" as "everlasting," but the NIV translation is preferable for the Hebrew is literally, "days of immeasurable time." Other verses such as John 1:1; Philippians 2:6; Colossians 1:17; Revelation 1:8 point up the eternality of Jesus Christ.

b. The work of Israel's Ruler (5:3-15)

Christ, Israel's Ruler, will accomplish several things for the nation during the Millennium:

1. He will reunite and restore the nation. **5:3.** As Micah had written earlier (4:9), Israel's spiritual pain in being dispersed (**abandoned**) was like a woman's physical pain **in labor.** But the time will come when the labor will end and **birth** will come. This refers not to Mary's giving birth to Jesus, but to Israel's national regathering (cf. 2:12; 4:6-7), likened here to a childbirth when **His brothers** (fellow Israelites; cf. Deut. 17:15) will **return** and **join** other **Israelites.** Christ will be one of them.

Micah 5:2-3 puts together the two

Advents of Christ, much as is done in Isaiah 9:6-7; 61:1-2.

2. He will care for His people and give them security. **5:4.** The Messiah **will . . . shepherd His flock** (cf. 2:12; 7:14; Zech. 10:3), something the nation's leaders in Micah's day were refusing to do (cf. comments on Micah 3:1-11). Christ's caring, guiding, and protecting role will be accomplished by the Lord's **strength** and for His sake. As He shepherds the nation they will have peace and security (cf. Zech. 14:11) because **His greatness will reach to the ends of the earth** (cf. Mal. 1:11a). Since He will rule over the entire world (Ps. 72:8; Zech. 14:9), all will know of His sovereign power, which will guarantee Israel's safety.

3. The Ruler will destroy Israel's enemies (5:5-9). **5:5-6.** This is one of Messiah's several accomplishments in bringing peace to Israel (vv. 5-15). **He will be** Israel's **peace** because He will subdue the hostile powers around that nation. Though **Assyria** will not exist as a nation in the future, it represents nations who, like Assyria in Micah's time, will threaten and attack Jerusalem (cf. Zech. 12:9; 14:2-3). **The land of Nimrod** (cf. Gen. 10:8-9; 1 Chron. 1:10) was a synonym for Assyria (cf. Assyria as a name for Persia in Ezra 6:22). Christ will enable Israel to defeat her foes, giving the nation a more-than-adequate number of **shepherds** or **leaders** (on the formula **seven . . . even eight**; cf. comments on "three . . . even four" in Amos 1:3). Whereas many nations have ruled Israel **with the sword,** in the Millennium the tables will be turned and Israel will rule over her foes because **He,** Messiah, **will deliver** her (cf. Zech. 14:3).

5:7. After Christ will destroy Israel's enemies **the remnant** (cf. 2:12; 4:7; 5:8; 7:18) of believing Israelites will be refreshing and influential (**like dew** and **showers**) among **many peoples.** Because the rainy season in Palestine was from October through March, nighttime dew in the other six months helped nourish the crops. As the dew and rain come from God in His timing (they **do not wait for man**), so God will refresh the nations in His own timing, apart from man's doings.

5:8-9. The remnant (cf. v. 7) of Israel will also be **like a lion.** Like a ferocious lion, domineering over other animals, Israel will be dominant and powerful over other nations of the world (cf. Deut. 28:13). God said He will lift **up** Israel's **hand . . . over** her **enemies,** and that **all** her **foes will be destroyed.**

4. The Ruler will also purge Israel of her reliance on military power. **5:10-11. In that day** (cf. 4:6 and comments on "in the last days" in 4:1), **the LORD . . . will destroy** the **horses** (cf. Zech. 9:10) and **chariots** in which she trusted (cf. God's prohibition in Deut. 17:16 against relying on horses). **Cities** in which Israel will build **strongholds** for protection will be demolished (cf. Micah 5:14).

5. The Ruler will destroy false worship from within Israel (5:12-14). **5:12.** Besides destroying enemies from outside Israel, the Messiah will purge the nation of every trace of occultic and idolatrous practices, which were "enemies" within. **Witchcraft** ($k^e\check{s}\bar{a}p\hat{i}m$, lit., "sorceries") is used in the Old Testament only here and in 2 Kings 9:22; Isaiah 47:9, 12; Nahum 3:4. In the last three of these verses the NIV renders the word "sorceries." The Hebrew word suggests seeking information from demonic sources. The casting of **spells** (from the verb '$\bar{a}nan$) may refer to using demonic powers to exercise manipulative influences over others (in Lev. 19:26 and Deut. 18:10 the NIV translates this word "sorcery"; in Jer. 27:9 it is rendered "sorcerers"). Though prohibited in the Law, these and similar practices—common in the ancient Near East —were attractive to many Israelites throughout much of Israel's history. Occultism will be practiced in the Tribulation (cf. "magic arts" in Rev. 9:21), but it will be wiped out by the Lord.

5:13-14. Carved images ($p^e s\hat{i}l\hat{i}m$) were idols of foreign gods (cf. *pesel,* "idol," in Ex. 20:4). **Sacred stones** (or pillars) and **Asherah poles** (cf. 1 Kings 14:23; 2 Kings 17:10; 18:4; 23:14) were objects used in worshiping male and female Canaanite idols. God forbade their use by Israel (Deut. 16:21-22; cf. Ex. 34:13). Asherah was the Canaanite goddess of the sea and the consort of Baal. When the Ruler comes and banishes every evidence of idolatry from His people (cf. Zech. 13:2), they will no longer worship **the work of** their **hands** (cf. Hosea 14:3). Instead they will worship Yahweh, the true and living Creator. All the **cities** (cf. Micah 5:11) where Israel practiced idolatry or relied on her military strength will be demolished.

6. The Lord will judge the nations who oppose Him. **5:15. Nations** who refuse to obey the Lord will suffer God's **anger and wrath.** He will rule with an iron scepter (Ps. 2:9; Rev. 12:5; 19:15), that is, with firmness, strength, and justice.

III. Third Message: An Indictment of Sin and a Promise of Blessing (chaps. 6–7)

This third main section of the book summarizes what has gone before and adds a plea from God's prophet on behalf of His people. The section focuses on the blessings that will come to the people because of God's goodness.

A. An indictment by the Lord (6:1-5)

6:1. Again (cf. 1:2) **the Lord** called on witnesses to **listen to** His **case** (*rîḇ,* "lawsuit or litigation"; trans. "accusation" in 6:2a and "case" in v. 2b) against His covenant people. He then challenged Israel to **stand up . . . before the mountains** and give her side of the dispute with God. He was calling for outside witnesses to confirm that He had been just and righteous with His people and that Israel had been wrong in its attitudes and actions before God. The witnesses He appealed to were people everywhere, represented by "the mountains" (cf. v. 2) and **the hills.**

6:2. The **Lord** then began to set forth His **case against His people.** He repeated His call to the **mountains** (cf. v. 1) to listen to His **accusation** (*rîḇ;* cf. comments on v. 1) and "case" (*rîḇ*) against His people **Israel.**

6:3-4. In setting forth His case the Lord addressed the nation as **My people** (cf. v. 5). By a question (**What have I done to you?**) the Lord affirmed His innocence (cf. "What have I done?" in 1 Sam. 17:29; 20:1; 26:18; 29:8). He also asked the people to **answer** Him by naming some way in which He had **burdened** (lit., "wearied") them. Though the Israelites had often complained against God, they had no grounds for such complaints. For that reason they could not answer God's accusation.

God reminded the people of His goodness in leading them **out of Egypt** into the Promised Land. The prophets often reminded the people of their deliverance from Egyptian **slavery.** The Exodus was a great focal event in the life of Israel because by it God had delivered them from foreign domination and also because it was followed by the Lord's giving the Law to them through **Moses.** The word **redeemed** (*pāḏâh,* "to ransom"; cf. Deut. 7:8; 9:26; 13:5; 15:15; 24:18) would remind them of the slaying of the Passover lambs so that the oldest son of each Israelite family would not be killed (Ex. 12:3, 7, 12-13). God's mention of Moses would remind the people of the Law, and the name of **Aaron** would bring to mind the priesthood. Perhaps **Miriam** is mentioned because her name would bring to mind her song to the Lord (Ex. 15:21) and her role as a prophetess (Ex. 15:20). Because Moses represented God to man and Aaron represented man to God, the people had a unique relationship with the Lord.

6:5. Micah next reminded God's **people** (cf. "My people" in v. 3) of their forefathers' experience in the wilderness when **Balak . . . of Moab** tried to get **Balaam** to prophesy against the covenant people (Num. 22–24). Rather than cursing the people, Balaam blessed them. This was another evidence of God's goodness to them. Another great event in the nation's life was the **journey from Shittim,** the Israelites' last campsite east of the Jordan River (cf. Josh. 3:1), **to Gilgal,** the first encampment after the miraculous crossing of the Jordan River (cf. Josh. 4:18-19). In all these things God had not burdened His people. Rather He was their Protector and Defender, giving them grace over and over.

B. The response of Micah for the nation (6:6-8)

In these well-known verses the prophet responded to the Lord's indictment. Micah spoke as a righteous person who understood his people's guilt. He was not like the many leaders who had refused to shepherd the people properly.

6:6. Speaking for the nation, Micah asked what he must take **before the Lord** in worship to regain His good favor. Micah asked if he should approach the Lord with **burnt offerings.** Should he go **with calves** ready to be sacrificed? By these questions the prophet was not downplaying the importance of the sacrificial system. The Lord had set up the Levitical system to provide, among other things, atonement for the people's sin. Micah, as a righteous member of the covenant community, was no doubt involved in the sacrificial system. He knew, however, that the sacrifices were meant to be outward expressions of inner trust and dependence on God for His grace and mercy.

6:7. Micah then asked in hyperbole if **the LORD** would want **thousands of rams,** or **10,000 rivers of oil,** or even his own **firstborn** child (**the fruit** of his **body**) to atone **for** his **transgression** and **sin** (cf. 1:5; 3:8; 7:18). He of course knew these would not appease God's wrath on the nation. Nor was Micah condoning the evil practice of child sacrifice, forbidden in the Law (cf. Lev. 18:21; 20:2-5; Deut. 12:31; 18:10). He asked those rhetorical questions to suggest to Israel that nothing—not even the most extreme sacrifice—could atone for what she had done. Also this emphasized that God did not want them to "pay" Him. Instead God wanted them to change their actions and attitudes.

6:8. Micah then told the nation (**O man** means any person in Israel) exactly what God did desire from them. God did not want them to be related to Him in only a ritualistic way. God wanted them to be related inwardly—to obey Him because they desired to, not because it was a burden on them. That relationship, which **is good** (beneficial), involves three things: that individuals (a) **act justly** (be fair in their dealings with others), (b) **love mercy** (ḥeseḏ, "loyal love"; i.e., carry through on their commitments to meet others needs), and (c) **walk humbly with . . . God** (fellowship with Him in modesty, without arrogance). "Humbly" translates the verb ṣānaʻ (which occurs only here in the OT); it means to be modest. (The adjective ṣānûaʻ occurs only once, in Prov. 11:2.) The Lord had already told them of these demands (Deut. 10:12, 18). Doing justice "is a way of loving mercy, which in turn is a manifestation of walking humbly with God" (James Luther Mays, *Micah: A Commentary*, p. 142). Many people in Micah's day were *not* being just (Micah 2:1-2; 3:1-3; 6:11), or showing loyal love to those to whom they were supposed to be committed (2:8-9; 3:10-11; 6:12), or walking in

humble fellowship with God (2:3).

C. The Lord's judgment because of sin (6:9-16)

Because of Israel's failure to meet God's requirements (v. 8), the Lord said He would have to punish the nation.

1. THE SINS (6:9-12)

These verses give a sampling of the sins in which Israel was involved. They are part of the reason for God's lawsuit (vv. 1-2). This list, though not complete, is sufficient to emphasize that the nation was guilty.

6:9. Again Micah told the people to **listen** (cf. 3:1; 6:1). In response to the Lord's **calling,** they should **heed the rod,** God's instrument of punishment. The second line, translated differently in various Bible versions, seems to mean (as the NIV has rendered it) that when the Lord speaks, it is wise to respond to Him in **fear** (reverence and obedience; cf. Prov. 1:7).

6:10-12. Not acting justly (cf. v. 8), the people were amassing wealth by devious means (**ill-gotten treasures;** cf. Prov. 10:2). They were being dishonest in their business practices by using a **short** (i.e., small) **ephah,** a dry-measure standard of about six gallons. In other words they were cheating their customers. Likewise, sellers used **dishonest scales** and **false weights** to give less merchandise than the buyers thought they were getting. God said He hates such unfair practices, that take advantage of others (cf. Lev. 19:35-36; Deut. 25:13-16; Prov. 11:1; 16:11; 20:23; Hosea 12:7; Amos 8:5). Obviously the people were not acting justly or loving mercy (Micah 6:8). Violence by **rich** people and lying by almost everyone were common (v. 12).

2. THE PUNISHMENT (6:13-16)

6:13-15. Because of the sins cited in verses 10-12 (and probably others as well), God's punishment had already **begun** to bring them **ruin** (cf. v. 16; Deut. 28:20). Their food would not satisfy them (the first line in Micah 6:14 quotes Lev. 26:26). What they would **store up** would be taken by their enemies (cf. Lev. 26:16-17; Deut. 28:33). Their planting would bring no **harvest** for them (cf. Deut. 28:30). Taken into captivity, they would not be allowed to enjoy the fruit of their labor (Micah 6:15; cf. Deut. 28:39-40). As God had stated (Deut. 28) these punishments resulted from the people's failure to obey Him.

6:16. Instead of following the Lord, the people **observed the statutes of Omri and all the practices of Ahab's house** (dynasty). Omri and Ahab were considered two of the worst kings in the Northern Kingdom for in their rule great apostasy flourished, including Baal worship (1 Kings 16:21–22:40). In Ahab's reign true prophets of the Lord were murdered (1 Kings 18:4). Judah (**you**) had **followed** those sinful **traditions.** As a result of such idolatry and violence, God said He would **give** Judah **over to ruin** (cf. Micah 6:13). Being taken captive, she would be ridiculed by **the nations** (cf. Lam. 2:15-16).

D. Micah's pleading with the Lord (chap. 7)

1. MICAH'S BEMOANING OF THE NATION'S SINS (7:1-6)

7:1-2. Micah bemoaned his position in the midst of a people who were totally godless. He lamented the evil times in which he lived. He felt like a person who goes into the fields to pick **fruit** but finds it all gone. **No . . . grapes** or **early figs** were left for him to gather and eat (cf. 6:14). In like manner the nation was devoid of **godly** (*ḥāsîd*, "loyal or faithful," from *ḥesed*, "loyal love") and **upright** people. It was as if each person were hunting **his brother,** trying to kill him (cf. 3:10; 6:12). This violence and lack of loyalty is described in 7:3-6.

7:3-4a. The only thing the people could do well was to sin! In their government **the ruler** ruled only in favor of those who gave him **gifts** even if justice were cast aside; in the courtroom **the judge** accepted **bribes** (cf. 3:11), and **the powerful** (rich and influential people) got whatever they wanted. The leaders even conspired **together** in taking advantage of others. Even **the best** of the leaders were **like a brier** and **worse than a thorn hedge,** entangling and injuring all who came in contact with them.

7:4b. What God's true prophets (the nation's **watchmen** warning of impending danger) had predicted would someday **come** true. **God** would "visit" the people in judgment and they would be confused, not knowing what to do.

7:5-6. The situation was so bad that even familiar relationships were distorted. Neighbors, friends, spouses, and children turned against each other. Treachery was so rampant that a person's own family members were his **enemies.**

2. MICAH'S CONFIDENCE IN THE LORD (7:7-13)

7:7. Speaking for himself and the godly remnant mentioned throughout the book, Micah said that even though the nation was in terrible shape he would continue to **watch** (cf. "watchmen," v. 4) and **wait in hope** for the LORD. Yes, judgment would come, but he knew also that salvation would follow. **God** would be Israel's **Savior** (cf. Isa. 59:20).

7:8-10. The prophet, still speaking as a representative of the nation (**me . . . my,** and **I** occur 15 times in vv. 8-10), expressed confidence in the fact that eventually God would reverse Israel's sad situation. Though the nation was in a depressed condition and would go into captivity, the **enemy** should **not gloat.** Though the situation was dark, the LORD would **be** her **light** (cf. v. 9), and would bring her out of her desperate circumstances. In the words **I have sinned** Micah identified himself with the people's sins (cf. Daniel's similar identification in his prayer, Dan. 9:5, 8, 11, 15). Because of their sins God's **wrath** would be tolerated for it would be His means of bringing them **into the light** (cf. Micah 7:8) and establishing **justice** (lit., "righteousness"). When God once again establishes Israel in her own land, the tables will be turned and her **enemy . . . will be ashamed** (cf. v. 16; Obad. 10). The enemy (pagan nations) taunted Israel with the question, **Where is the LORD your God?** (cf. Pss. 42:3, 10; 79:10; Joel 2:17) But God will vindicate His own, for Israel's enemies will fall and **be trampled** (be humiliated; cf. Micah 7:17).

7:11-13. When Israel will be restored to her land in the Millennium (when she will "rise," v. 8), she will rebuild her **walls** and expand her **boundaries.** *Gāḏēr* means a wall around a vineyard (cf. Num. 22:24; Isa. 5:5), not around a city. Jerusalem, established in peace by the Messiah, will need no protective wall (Zech. 2:4-5). (For specifics on Israel's boundary extensions see comments on Ezek. 47:13-23 and Obad. 19-20.) **Assyria**

and **Egypt,** enemies of Israel, will be inhabited by people who will travel to Jerusalem (cf. Isa. 19:23-25). In fact people from around the globe (**from sea to sea**; cf. Ps. 72:8; Zech. 9:10, **and from mountain to mountain**) will go to Jerusalem to learn of and worship the Lord (cf. Micah 4:2). Immediately before that glorious time, however, the nations, **because of** their sinful **deeds,** will be judged (Matt. 25:32-33, 46) and therefore **the earth will be desolate** (cf. Isa. 24:1).

3. MICAH'S PRAYER THAT GOD WOULD AGAIN SHEPHERD HIS FLOCK (7:14)

7:14. Is the speaker in this verse God or Micah? Probably the prophet is addressing God. Because of God's promise in 2:12 and 5:4, Micah asked the Lord to restore and provide for His people as a shepherd cares for his **flock.** The **staff** would be a rod (*šēḇeṭ*) of blessing, not of judgment as in 6:9. Micah prayed that God's people (His **inheritance**; cf. 7:18 and comments on Deut. 4:20), then isolated like sheep **in a forest,** would enjoy prosperity and peace as they had in **Bashan and Gilead** (cf. Jer. 50:19) in former times (**in days long ago**; cf. Micah 7:20). Those two areas east of the Jordan River (see the map "Israel and Surrounding Nations in the Days of the Prophets," between Song and Isa.) were fertile grazing grounds for sheep and cattle. In 734 B.C. these areas were overrun by Tiglath-Pileser III, king of Assyria (745–727).

4. THE LORD'S PROMISE TO SHOW MIRACULOUS THINGS TO HIS PEOPLE (7:15-17)

7:15. In response to the prophet's request (v. 14) the Lord told the nation through Micah that a time would come when He would again be known as a miraculous God. **When** Israel **came out of Egypt,** God did **wonders** (cf. Ex. 3:20; 15:11; Jud. 6:13; Ps. 78:12-16) on her behalf, releasing her from Egypt, enabling her to cross the Red Sea on dry ground, and providing for her in the desert. Once again the nation will have a great "exodus" from its places of habitation and God will miraculously move the Israelites into their land. This will occur when the Messiah returns and sets up His millennial rule.

7:16-17. When God miraculously regathers Israel the **nations will see** it **and**

be ashamed (cf. 3:7; 7:10) for His **power** will be greater than theirs. Overwhelmed, they will be speechless and will refuse to hear about Israel's victories. In humiliation they will **lick** the **dust** like snakes (cf. Ps. 72:9; Isa. 49:23), and like animals coming **out of their** hiding places (**dens**) **they will** surrender **to the LORD** and will be fearful of Israel. These facts must have greatly encouraged the righteous remnant in Micah's day.

5. MICAH'S AFFIRMATION THAT GOD IS UNIQUE (7:18-20)

7:18-20. The author concluded his book by reminding himself and his readers about the goodness and uniqueness of their God (cf. Ex. 34:6-7a). Micah's final words of praise show that he had great faith in God's eventual out-working of His plans for His covenant people. Today orthodox Jews read these verses in their synagogues on the Day of Atonement, after they read the Book of Jonah.

The rhetorical question, **Who is a God like You?** (cf. Ex. 15:11; Pss. 35:10; 71:19; 77:13; 89:6; 113:5) may be a wordplay on Micah's name which means, "Who is like Yahweh?" The obvious answer is that no one is like the Lord. The remainder of Micah 7:18-20 describes what He is like. God's acts on behalf of His people prove that He is completely trustworthy and merciful.

Micah affirmed six things about God: (1) He **pardons** the **sin** and **transgression** (cf. 1:5; 3:8; 6:7) **of the remnant** (cf. 2:12; 4:7; 5:7-8) **of His inheritance** (cf. 7:14).

(2) He does **not stay angry forever** (cf. Ps. 103:9) and (3) He likes **to show mercy** (*ḥesed*; cf. Micah 7:20). What encouragement these truths would have been for the godly remnant living in Israel's corrupt society. Confident that (4) the Lord **will again have compassion** (*reḥem*, "tender, heartfelt concern"; cf. Pss. 102:13; 103:4, 13; 116:5; 119:156; Hosea 14:3; Zech. 10:6) **on** Israel, Micah knew that (5) God would deal with her **sins** by, figuratively speaking, treading them **underfoot** (subduing them as if they were enemies) and hurling them **into . . . the sea** (thus completely forgiving them). Three Old Testament words for sin are used in Micah 7:18-19: sin(s), transgression, and iniquities.

Micah knew God would do these things because (6) He is **true** (faithful) **to**

Jacob and shows **mercy** (*ḥeseḏ*; cf. v. 18) **to Abraham.** God cannot lie; He is true to His Word and loyal to His commitments and His **oath.** Therefore Micah was trusting in God's promises to Abraham (Gen. 12:2-3; 15:18-21), which were confirmed to Jacob (Gen. 28:13-14), that He will bless their descendants.

Israel's peace and prosperity will be realized when the Messiah-King reigns. Christ will exercise justice over His and Israel's opponents and He will extend grace to His own. This promise gave Micah confidence in his dark days and is also a source of comfort to believers today.

BIBLIOGRAPHY

Allen, Leslie C. *The Books of Joel, Obadiah, Jonah and Micah.* The New International Commentary on the Old Testament. Grand Rapids: Wm. B. Eerdmans Publishing Co., 1976.

Bennett, T. Miles. *The Book of Micah: A Study Manual.* Grand Rapids: Baker Book House, 1968.

Cohen, A. *The Twelve Prophets.* London: Soncino Press, 1948.

Feinberg, Charles L. *The Minor Prophets.* Chicago: Moody Press, 1976.

Hillers, Delbert R. *Micah.* Philadelphia. Fortress Press, 1984.

Keil, C.F. "Micah." In *Commentary on the Old Testament in Ten Volumes.* Vol 10. Reprint (25 vols. in 10). Grand Rapids: Wm. B. Eerdmans Publishing Co., 1982.

Laetsch, Theo. *The Minor Prophets.* St. Louis: Concordia Publishing House, 1956.

Mays, James Luther. *Micah: A Commentary.* Philadelphia: Westminster Press, 1976.

Pusey, E.B. *The Minor Prophets: A Commentary.* Vol. 2. Grand Rapids: Baker Book House, 1970.

Smith, John M.P., Ward, William H., and Bewer, Julius A. *A Critical and Exegetical Commentary on Micah, Zephaniah, Nahum, Habakkuk, Obadiah and Joel.* The International Critical Commentary. Edinburgh: T. & T. Clark, 1974.

Snaith, Norman H. *Amos, Hosea, and Micah.* London: Epworth Press, 1954.

Tatford, Frederick A. *The Minor Prophets.* Vol. 2. Reprint (3 vols.). Minneapolis: Klock & Klock Christian Publishers, 1982.

Wolff, Hans Walter. *Micah the Prophet.* Translated by Ralph D. Gehrke. Philadelphia: Fortress Press, 1981.

NAHUM

Elliott E. Johnson

INTRODUCTION

The Prophet Nahum. Nothing is known of the human author of this brief prophecy except that he is Nahum the Elkoshite (Nahum 1:1). His name means "consolation" or "comfort," which is appropriate for his ministry to Judah. His message about the destruction of Nineveh, the enemy dreaded by many nations in that day, would have been a great comfort to Judah. "Elkoshite" suggests that Nahum's hometown was Elkosh, but the site of such a city is unknown. Jerome said it was in Galilee; others said it was on the Tigris River north of modern-day Mosul near Nineveh; some place Elkosh east of the Jordan River; others have suggested it was Capernaum. While no conclusive evidence exists, it seems best to locate Elkosh in southern Judah. This would help explain Nahum's concern for Judah (Nahum 1:12, 15) to whom his message was written.

The City of Nineveh. The subject of this prophecy is Nineveh (Nahum 1:1). A heavy weight of doom, a burden ("an oracle") rested on the Assyrian capital. Several other Old Testament passages refer to Assyria's fall (Isa. 10:12-19; 14:24-25; 30:31-33; 31:8-9; Ezek. 32:22-23; Zeph. 2:13-15; Zech. 10:11).

Nineveh is first mentioned in the Bible in Genesis 10:11-12. Nimrod built several cities in southern Mesopotamia (Gen. 10:8-10) and then "went to Assyria where he built Nineveh, Rehoboth Ir, Calah, and Resen." Inscriptions refer to Gudea restoring the temple of the goddess Ishtar in Nineveh, which he said was founded around 2300 B.C. Hammurabi, king of Babylon (ca. 1792–1750 B.C.), referred to Nineveh. The town was expanded by the Assyrian king Tiglath-Pileser I (1115–1071), who referred to himself as "king of the world." Ashurnasirpal II (883–859) and Sargon II (722–705) had their palace in Nineveh. In the ninth, eighth, and seventh centuries B.C. the Assyrian Empire became strong and repeatedly attacked nations to the east, north, and west, including Israel. (See the chart "The Kings of Assyria in the Middle and New Assyrian Kingdoms," in the *Introduction* to Jonah.)

Shalmaneser III (859–824 B.C.) made the city of Nineveh a base for military operations. During his reign Israel came into contact with Nineveh. He wrote that he fought a coalition of kings of Aram and others including "Ahab the Israelite" (in 853 B.C.). Later he wrote that he received tribute from "Jehu, son of Omri," who is pictured in the Black Obelisk of Shalmaneser. Neither of these events is mentioned in the Bible. Azariah, king of Judah (790–739), paid tribute to Tiglath-Pileser III (745–727). Menahem, king of Israel (752–742), did the same (2 Kings 15:14-23). In the reign of Ashur-dan III (772–754) Jonah preached to the Ninevites (see the *Introduction* to Jonah).

In 731 B.C. Ahaz, king of Judah (732–715), became a vassal of Tiglath-Pileser III, and Assyria invaded Damascus in the Syro-Ephraimite war. Shalmaneser V (727–722) besieged Samaria and defeated it in 722 B.C., thus defeating the Northern Kingdom (2 Kings 17:3-6; 18:9-10). Twenty-one years later (in 701), Sennacherib (705–681) invaded Judah and destroyed 46 Judean towns and cities. After encircling Jerusalem, 185,000 of Sennacherib's soldiers were killed overnight and Sennacherib returned to Nineveh (2 Kings 18:17-18; 19:32-36; Isa. 37:36). Esarhaddon (681–669) regarded Judah as a vassal kingdom, for he wrote in a building inscription, "I summoned the kings of the Hittite land [Aram] and [those] across the sea, Ba'lu, king of Tyre, Manasseh, king of Judah . . . " (Daniel David Luckenbill, *Ancient Records of Assyria and Babylonia.* 2 vols. Chicago: University of Chicago Press, 1926-7, 2:265).

In 669 B.C. Ashurbanipal succeeded · his father Esarhaddon as king of Assyria. He may have been the king who released Manasseh king of Judah (2 Chron. 33:10-13). Ashurbanipal defeated Thebes in Egypt in 663 and brought treasures to Nineveh from Thebes, Babylon, and Susa. He established an extensive library at Nineveh.

The city of Nineveh fell to the Babylonians, Medes, and Scythians in August 612 B.C.

Nineveh was situated on the east bank of the Tigris River (see the map "The Assyrian Empire," near Jonah 1:1). Sennacherib fortified the city's defensive wall whose glory, he said, "overthrows the enemy." On the population of Nineveh, see "Authenticity and Historicity" in the *Introduction* to Jonah and comments on Jonah 4:11. Jonah called Nineveh "a great city" (Jonah 1:2; 3:2-4; 4:11).

The city's ruins are still evident today. The city was easily overtaken when the Khosr River, which flowed through it, overflowed its banks (see Nahum 1:8; 2:6, 8).

Nineveh was the capital of one of the cruelest, vilest, most powerful, and most idolatrous empires in the world. For example, writing of one of his conquests, Ashurnaṣirpal II (883–859) boasted, "I stormed the mountain peaks and took them. In the midst of the mighty mountain I slaughtered them; with their blood I dyed the mountain red like wool. . . . The heads of their warriors I cut off, and I formed them into a pillar over against their city; their young men and their maidens I burned in the fire" (Luckenbill, *Ancient Records of Assyria and Babylonia,* 1:148). Regarding one captured leader, he wrote, "I flayed [him], his skin I spread upon the wall of the city . . . " (ibid., 1:146). He also wrote of mutilating the bodies of live captives and stacking their corpses in piles.

Shalmaneser II (859–824) boasted of his cruelties after one of his campaigns: "A pyramid of heads I reared in front of his city. Their youths and their maidens I burnt up in the flames" (ibid., 1:213). Sennacherib (705–681) wrote of his enemies, "I cut their throats like lambs. I cut off their precious lives [as one cuts] a string. Like the many waters of a storm I made [the contents of] their gullets and entrails run down upon the wide earth.

. . . Their hands I cut off" (ibid., 2:127).

Ashurbanipal (669–626) described his treatment of a captured leader in these words: "I pierced his chin with my keen hand dagger. Through his jaw . . . I passed a rope, put a dog chain upon him and made him occupy . . . a kennel" (ibid., 2:319). In his campaign against Egypt, Ashurbanipal also boasted that his officials hung Egyptian corpses "on stakes [and] stripped off their skins and covered the city wall(s) with them" (ibid., 2:295).

No wonder Nahum called Nineveh "the city of blood" (3:1), a city noted for its "cruelty"! (3:19)

Ashurbanipal was egotistic: "I [am] Ashurbanipal, the great [king], the mighty king, king of the universe, king of Assyria. . . . The great gods . . . magnified my name; they made my rule powerful" (ibid., 2:323-4). Esarhaddon was even more boastful. "I am powerful, I am all powerful, I am a hero, I am gigantic, I am colossal, I am honored, I am magnified, I am without equal among all kings, the chosen one of Asshur, Nabu, and Marduk" (ibid., 2:226).

Gross idolatry was practiced in Nineveh and throughout the Assyrian Empire. The religion of Assyria was Babylonian in origin but in Assyria the national god was Assur, whose high priest and representative was the king.

Date of the Book. The fall of Thebes (to Ashurbanipal) is mentioned in Nahum 3:8. Since that event occurred in 663 B.C. the book was written after that date. Then the fall of Nineveh, predicted in Nahum, occurred in 612 B.C. So the book was written between 663 and 612. Walter A. Maier suggests that Nahum gave his prophecy soon after Thebes fell, between 663 and 654 B.C. (*The Book of Nahum*, pp. 30, 34-7). His arguments include these:

1. The description of Nineveh (1:12; 3:1, 4, 16) does not match the decline of the Assyrian nation under Ashurbanipal's sons, Ashur-etil-ilāni (626–623 B.C.) and Sin-shar-ishkun (623–612 B.C.).

2. When Nahum prophesied, Judah was under the Assyrian yoke (1:13, 15; 2:1, 3). This fits with the reign of Manasseh over Judah (697–642) more than with the reign of Josiah (640–609).

3. The Medes rose in power around 645 B.C. as an independent nation, and

Fulfillments of Nahum's Prophecies

Nahum's Prophecies	Historical Fulfillments
1. The Assyrian fortresses surrounding the city would be easily captured (3:12).	1. According to the Babylonian Chronicle the fortified towns in Nineveh's environs began to fall in 614 b.c. including Tabris, present-day Sharif-Khan, a few miles northwest of Nineveh.
2. The besieged Ninevites would prepare bricks and mortar for emergency defense walls (3:14).	2. A.T. Olmstead reported: "To the south of the gate, the moat is still filled with fragments of stone and of mud bricks from the walls, heaped up when they were breached" (*History of Assyria.* Chicago: University of Chicago Press, 1951, p. 637).
3. The city gates would be destroyed (3:13).	3. Olmstead noted: "The main attack was directed from the northwest and the brunt fell upon the Hatamti gate at this corner. . . . Within the gate are traces of the counterwall raised by the inhabitants in their last extremity" (*History of Assyria,* p. 637).
4. In the final hours of the attack the Ninevites would be drunk (1:10; 3:11).	4. Diodorus Siculus (ca. 20 b.c.) wrote, "The Assyrian king . . . distributed to his soldiers meats and liberal supplies of wine and provisions. . . . While the whole army was thus carousing, the friends of Arbakes learned from some deserters of the slackness and drunkenness which prevailed in the enemy's camp and made an unexpected attack by night" (*Bibliotheca Historica* 2. 26. 4).
5. Nineveh would be destroyed by a flood (1:8; 2:6, 8).	5. Diodorus wrote that in the third year of the siege heavy rains caused a nearby river to flood part of the city and break part of the walls (*Bibliotheca Historica* 2. 26. 9; 2. 27. 13). Xenophon referred to terrifying thunder (presumably with a storm) associated with the city's capture (*Anabasis,* 3. 4. 12). Also the Khosr River, entering the city from the northwest at the Ninlil Gate and running through the city in a southwesterly direction, may have flooded because of heavy rains, or the enemy may have destroyed its sluice gate.
6. Nineveh would be destroyed by fire (1:10; 2:13; 3:15).	6. Archeological excavations at Nineveh have revealed charred wood, charcoal, and ashes. "There was no question about the clear traces of the burning of the temple (as also in the palace of Sennacherib), for a layer of ash about two inches thick lay clearly defined in places on the southeast side about the level of the Sargon pavement" (R. Campbell Thompson and R.W. Hutchinson, *A Century of Exploration at Nineveh.* London: Luzac, 1929, pp. 45, 77).
7. The city's capture would be attended by a great massacre of people (3:3).	7. "In two battles fought on the plain before the city the rebels defeated the Assyrians. . . . So great was the multitude of the slain that the flowing stream, mingled with their blood, changed its color for a considerable distance" (Diodorus, *Bibliotheca Historica* 2. 26. 6-7).
8. Plundering and pillaging would accompany the overthrow of the city (2:9-10).	8. According to the Babylonian Chronicle, "Great quantities of spoil from the city, beyond counting, they carried off. The city [they turned] into a mound and ruin heap" (Luckenbill, *Ancient Records of Assyria and Babylonia,* 2:420).
9. When Nineveh would be captured its people would try to escape (2:8).	9. "Sardanapalus [another name for King Sin-shar-ishkun] sent away his three sons and two daughters with much treasure into Paphlagonia, to the governor of Kattos, the most loyal of his subjects" (Diodorus, *Bibliotheca Historica,* 2. 26. 8).
10. The Ninevite officers would weaken and flee (3:17).	10. The Babylonian Chronicle states that "[The army] of Assyria deserted [lit., ran away before] the king" (Luckenbill, *Ancient Records of Assyria and Babylonia,* 2:420).
11. Nineveh's images and idols would be destroyed (1:14).	11. R. Campbell Thompson and R.W. Hutchinson reported that the statue of the goddess Ishtar lay headless in the debris of Nineveh's ruins ("The British Museum Excavations on the Temple of Ishtar at Nineveh, 1930–1," *Annals of Archaeology and Anthropology.* 19, pp. 55-6).
12. Nineveh's destruction would be final (1:9, 14).	12. Many cities of the ancient Near East were rebuilt after being destroyed (e.g., Samaria, Jerusalem, Babylon) but not Nineveh.

the Neo-Babylonian Empire began in 626. If Nahum had written shortly before Nineveh's fall to those nations in 612, mention of them would be expected. But since Nahum does not mention the Medes or the Babylonians, he probably wrote his prophecy before 645.

4. Most important, however, is the fact that nine years after Thebes was destroyed, it was restored (in 654). Nahum's rhetorical question in 3:8 would have had little or no force if it had been written after 654.

Unity of the Text. Some scholars have suggested that Nahum wrote most of 2:4–3:19 with some phrases having been inserted later by some other writer(s), and that 1:1–2:3 was written by someone other than Nahum. Some have even questioned the authenticity of 1:1 because, they say, it is a double title: "An oracle concerning Nineveh. The book of the vision of Nahum the Elkoshite." But these phrases supplement each other; the first indicates the subject and the second the author. This is similar in form to Isaiah 13:1; Amos 1:1; Micah 1:1 (in Isa. 13:1 and Amos 1:1 "saw" means "saw in a vision"). Other scholars have sought to establish the notion that Nahum 1:2-10 is not original but was an acrostic psalm added years after Nahum. It is questionable that these verses constitute an acrostic, but even if they do this does not prove that someone other than Nahum wrote them.

Literary Form of the Text. Some writers have tried to prove that the Book of Nahum was not a prophecy but was a liturgy for the annual "enthronement festival" of the Lord held in Jerusalem after the fall of Nineveh in 612 B.C. According to this analysis the book consists of fragments of various literary categories and features, questions and responses, passages given by soloists and choruses antiphonally—all of which form a liturgy commemorating Nineveh's destruction. But this theory contradicts the title which identifies the contents as "an oracle" and a "vision." The liturgy view destroys the prophetic nature of the book.

Though the book is a literary unit written by one author, it does use several literary forms. These include an introduction extolling God's attributes (1:2-8), a series of announcement oracles addressed to both Nineveh and Judah (1:9-15), a vivid prophetic description of Nineveh's fall (chap. 2), and a denunciation of Nineveh for her guilt (chap. 3). These parts are laced together with a series of rhetorical questions (1:6; 3:7-8, 19). In metaphors and similes Nineveh is likened to dry stubble (1:10), lions (2:12), and a harlot and a sorcerer (3:4). The city's fortresses are said to be like ripe figs (3:12), and its guards and officials like locusts (3:17). Nahum wrote tersely as he described the battle leading to the city's conquest (2:8-10; 3:2-3, 14).

Purpose of the Book. The initial clue to the book's purpose is in the title "oracle" (or burden; see comments on 1:1 and those prior to Zech. 9:1). Nahum placed a burden on Nineveh; he wrote a prophetic word of a threatening nature. Though the prophet primarily addressed Nineveh (Nahum 1:8, 11, 14; 2:1, 8; 3:7), he also addressed Judah (1:12, 15; 2:2) in comfort. The coming judgment on Nineveh (in return for her terrible atrocities on various nations including Israel, the Northern Kingdom, in 722 B.C.) would bring great comfort to the afflicted Judah (1:12). Judah had felt the threat of the Assyrian Empire breathing down her neck. In fact Assyria had defeated much of Judah and had even surrounded Jerusalem in 701 B.C. And during much of Manasseh's reign Judah had to pay tribute to Assyria. So the purpose of Nahum's book is to announce the fall of Nineveh and thereby comfort Judah with the assurance that God is in control.

OUTLINE

B. The defeat and the plundering (2:7-13)

IV. The Reasons for God's Judgment on Nineveh (chap. 3)
  A. Her violence and deceit to result in shame (3:1-7)
  B. Her treatment of Thebes to result in her own defeat (3:8-11)
  C. Her defense efforts to be useless (3:12-19)

COMMENTARY

I. The Title (1:1)

1:1. The book was **an oracle** against **Nineveh.** As an oracle it was a burden (*maśśāʾ*; see comments on Isa. 13:1 and those prior to Zech. 9:1), a threatening message about Nineveh's doom. It was a **vision** (*ḥāzôn*), that is, a message which the prophet "saw" mentally and spiritually (cf. Isa. 1:1; Obad. 1; Micah 1:1; Zech. 1:8). On **Nahum the Elkoshite** see "The Prophet Nahum" in the *Introduction.*

II. The Certainty of God's Judgment on Nineveh (1:2-15)

Nahum wrote that Nineveh's end would certainly come. Because Nineveh had plotted against the Lord (vv. 9-11) she would receive His wrath (vv. 2-6, 8). Yet God remains a refuge for those who trust Him (v. 7). Nineveh's destruction would comfort Judah who had been afflicted by the Assyrian threat (vv. 12-15).

A. God's wrath to be extended to Nineveh and His goodness to His own (1:2-8)

1:2. The LORD is righteous in relation to His covenant people and in relation to her wicked oppressors. As a righteous God, He is **jealous,** that is, zealous to protect what belongs to Him (see comments on Deut. 6:15; cf. Deut. 4:24; 5:9; 32:16, 21), namely, Judah. He will allow no rivals. He is also an **avenging God.** This fact is strongly emphasized, for the word *nōqēm* ("avenging") occurs three times in this verse (twice trans. **takes vengeance**). God said, "It is Mine to avenge" and "I will take vengeance on My adversaries and repay those who hate Me" (Deut. 32:35, 41). God avenges His people in the sense that He champions their cause against their enemies. He

does so because He is jealous or protective of His people. While God is avenging *for* or on behalf of His people, He is avenging **against** His adversaries. Judah's enemies were **His enemies.** He is **filled with wrath** (lit., "He is baal [i.e., master] of fury"). *Ḥēmâh,* related to the verb meaning "to be hot," speaks of God's burning rage or intense fury against sin.

1:3a. Though God takes vengeance on His enemies, He **is slow to anger** (lit., "long of anger"), that is, He withholds His judgment for a long time (cf. Ex. 34:6; Num. 14:18; Neh. 9:17; Pss. 86:15; 103:8; 145:8; Joel 2:13; Jonah 4:2). Such "length of anger" accounts for the apparent delay, from Judah's perspective, which allowed Assyria to act in such lustful freedom. But this does not suggest that God is weak. He is long-suffering and patient (2 Peter 3:9) because of His desire that people repent. This was exhibited in His sending Jonah to Nineveh, about 100 years before Nahum prophesied.

Also **the LORD** is **great in power.** Though He may prolong His mercy, His omnipotence remains. The word for power is *kōaḥ,* which suggests the ability to endure or the capacity to produce, and from there comes the idea of the ability to cope with situations (e.g., Deut. 8:17-18). That ability is seen in God's acts of judgment. For, the prophet added, **He will not leave the guilty unpunished** (cf. Num. 14:18). He would serve as the Ninevites' Judge because of their guilt. He would not treat them as if they were innocent. Though the Ninevites had repented under Jonah's preaching, the city had gone into iniquity again, and therefore would not escape His wrath.

1:3b-5. The greatness of God's power (v. 3a) is evident in His control over nature. Because He is powerful over inanimate nature, He certainly would be able to cope with and judge Nineveh. He causes **the whirlwind and the** threatening **storm** (cf. Job 9:17a), two awesome and often destructive forces of nature. In His dealings with Nineveh, He would be as destructive as a devastating whirlwind and storm. He is so great that the **clouds are** like **dust** under **His feet** (cf. 2 Sam. 22:10; Ps. 18:9). "His strides cover the vast areas of extenuated clouds. His movements are marked by the darkening of the heavens as the whirlwind sweeps and the tempest howls" (Maier, *The Book of Nahum: A Commentary*, pp. 158-9).

In His power He merely speaks (**rebukes**) **the sea**, and **the rivers . . . dry** up. This refers to His delivering Israel from Egyptian bondage (cf. Ex. 14:21; Pss. 66:6; 106:9; Isa. 50:2; 51:10; also note Ps. 18:15). Since He could defeat Egypt in that way, certainly He is powerful enough to destroy Nineveh. **Bashan,** a region east of the Sea of Kinnereth (Galilee), **Carmel,** a mountain range near present-day Haifa, and **Lebanon,** north of Israel, were fertile areas (cf. Isa. 33:9; also note Carmel in Amos 1:2 and Bashan in Micah 7:14). God's ability to dry up verdant areas shows He could judge Nineveh. Even **the mountains,** symbolic of stability, shake under His power, as did Mount Sinai (Ex. 19:18) and **the hills melt** (cf. Micah 1:4). Even the entire **earth** and its people, including the Ninevites, will tremble before His awesome power.

1:6. The two rhetorical questions (**Who can withstand. . . ? Who can endure. . . ?**) forcefully affirm that no one can stand before the Lord, angered by man's wickedness. Sennacherib's field commander (2 Kings 18:17) had challenged Hezekiah with the questions, "Who of all the gods of these countries has been able to save his land from me? How then can the Lord deliver Jerusalem from my hand?" (2 Kings 18:35) Assyria was soon to learn that *God*, not Assyria, has the last word! **Indignation** translates *za'am*, which means to be enraged like foam on water. Two synonyms of indignation were already used (**anger** in Nahum 1:3 and **wrath,** *ḥēmâh,* in v. 2). God's wrath is destructive and devastating **like fire.** When He comes in judgment even **the rocks** shatter **before Him** (cf. 1 Kings 19:11).

1:7-8. Though **the Lord** is wrathful and powerful against those who oppose Him, He **is good** (cf. Ex. 34:6; Pss. 106:1; 107:1; 136:1; Jer. 33:11) to **those who trust in Him.** He is good in the sense that He is faithful and merciful, protecting (**a refuge in times of trouble**), helpful, and caring. The Hebrew word for "refuge" is *mā'ôz.* Translated "stronghold" in Psalms 27:1; 37:39; 43:2; 52:7, it means a strong, fortified place. The people of Nineveh thought they were safe in their fortifications, but their security was short-lived

compared with the comfort and safety God provides for His people.

On the other hand God's enemies will experience His judgment. By **an overwhelming flood** God would **make an end** (cf. Nahum 1:9) **of Nineveh.** "Nineveh" is literally, "its site" (cf. "the place," kjv), but Nineveh is clearly intended. ("Nineveh" is also supplied in vv. 11, 14; 2:1.) This reference to a flood could suggest figuratively an unrestrained army invasion (cf. Isa. 8:7-8; Jer. 47:2; Dan. 9:26; 11:40). Or it may refer to a literal destruction by water, the Tigris and Khosr rivers overflowing and destroying part of the city walls (cf. Nahum 2:6, 8; see the chart "Fulfillments of Nahum's Prophecies," in the *Introduction*).

Nahum added that God **will pursue His foes into darkness.** Darkness symbolizes the spiritual condition of persons without God, their defeat, and ultimately eternal judgment (Job 17:13; Pss. 82:5; 88:12; Prov. 4:19; 20:20; Isa. 8:22; 42:7; Jer. 23:12; Matt. 4:16; 8:12; John 3:19; Col. 1:13; 1 Peter 2:9; Jude 6; Rev. 16:10).

B. Nineveh's plotting against the Lord to come to an end (1:9-11)

In affirming Nineveh's end, Nahum made a forthright prediction about Nineveh (vv. 9-10), a promise to Judah (vv. 12-13), a command and prediction to Nineveh (v. 14), and a call to Judah (v. 15).

1:9. Though Sennacherib, king of Assyria, had failed in his attempt to destroy Jerusalem, the Ninevites continued to **plot** ways to overcome the city. In plotting evil or calamity against His people they were actually plotting **against the Lord** (cf. v. 11). But their schemes would fail for God would keep those plans from being carried out (cf. **end** in v. 8). Assyria in fact never got a second chance to attack Jerusalem; just as God said, **trouble** to the holy city did **not come** from Assyria **a second time.** Any challenge to the Lord's declaration about Nineveh's end (cf. v. 8) would be thwarted.

1:10-11. Nineveh's being **entangled among thorns** has been interpreted in various ways: (a) the thorns symbolize wicked enemies, as in Ezekiel 2:6, but this does not fit; (b) the thorns (i.e., thornbushes) refer to the habitat of lions, but nothing in the text suggests this; (c) the entanglement of thorns refers to the confusion of the Ninevites when they were attacked in 612 B.C. This third view is preferable. This confusion, because of their drunkenness, resulted in complete disaster: the people were **consumed** quickly and fully **like** the burning of **dry stubble** (cf. Isa. 10:12, 17). A wordplay is suggested by the similarity in sound between the Hebrew words for "entangled" (sᵉḇûḵîm) and "drunk" (sᵉḇûʾîm). **The one** who was plotting evil (i.e., calamity) **against the LORD** (Nahum 1:11; cf. v. 9) was an Assyrian king (Sennacherib or someone after him). **Wickedness** translates bᵉliyyaʿal, "worthlessness" (trans. "wicked" in v. 15). His plans were both worthless and wicked (cf. Job 34:18). In 2 Samuel 16:7 and Proverbs 16:27 the word is rendered "scoundrel."

C. Judah's affliction to end because of Nineveh's destruction (1:12-15)

1:12-13. The promise to Judah in these two verses is introduced by the statement **This is what the LORD says.** This clause, occurring in Nahum only here, guarantees that what He predicted would indeed be fulfilled. For centuries Nineveh had gone **unscathed**; no enemy had penetrated her walls. And her inhabitants were many, presumably well able to defend the city. Yet God promised that Nineveh would be **cut down** (defeated) **and** would **pass away** (vanish). God had used Assyria to afflict **Judah** in several ways: by Sennacherib's attack in 701 B.C., by Judah's having to pay tribute to Assyria during much of Manasseh's reign, and by Judah's King Manasseh being taken captive (2 Chron. 33:11). But that Assyrian oppression, like a **yoke** on an animal's **neck,** would be broken when Nineveh fell.

1:14-15. Whereas Nineveh would have no heirs or places of worship (v. 14), Judah was called on to worship **the LORD** in view of her coming deliverance (v. 15). The Lord's **command** (ṣāwâh) to **Nineveh** indicates that she was subject to God's decrees. The Lord's judgment on the city would touch her prosperity and her false worship. **No** one would be left to worship and no idols would be left to be worshiped. Many times Nineveh had desecrated the altars and temples of her defeated foes and carried off their **images** and **idols.** Assyria thought this meant

her gods were superior. But now Nineveh would experience the same fate it had placed on others. **The temple of** her **gods** was either the temple of Ishtar or of Nabu.

God would see that Nineveh was buried (**I will prepare your grave**; cf. Ezek. 32:22-23) because she was **vile** (qālal, "to be of no account, to be unworthy"; cf. Job 40:4).

In contrast with Nineveh's fall (Nahum 1:14), **Judah** would experience freedom (v. 15). The prophet spoke as if the fall of Nineveh had already occurred and as if a messenger were arriving **on the mountains** around Jerusalem to bring the **good news.** And the fall of the capital of Assyria, the ruthless nation, would indeed be a message of **peace.** Therefore Judah could resume her worship, keeping her festivals (the Feast of Unleavened Bread, the Feast of Harvest or Pentecost, and the Feast of Ingathering or Tabernacles, Ex. 23:14-17) to express her gratitude to God and to keep her vows (cf. Lev. 22:21; 27:2, 8). **The wicked** one (bᵉliyyaʿal; see comments on Nahum 1:11) would **no** longer **invade** Judah (cf. v. 9) because he would be **completely destroyed** (cf. v. 10). Nineveh was never rebuilt. So complete was its destruction that when Xenophon passed by the site about 200 years later, he thought the mounds were the ruins of some other city. And Alexander the Great, fighting in a battle nearby, did not realize that he was near the ruins of Nineveh.

III. The Description of God's Judgment on Nineveh (chap. 2)

Chapter 1 includes more or less general statements about the Lord's judgment on His enemy, but now the book moves to more specific descriptions of the attack and plundering of the city. Nineveh would be attacked (2:1, 3-6), defeated (vv. 7-8), and plundered (vv. 9-13), but Judah's glory will be restored (v. 2). Associated with this change in emphasis is a shift in tone—from calmness and dignity to increasing emotion and vivid descriptions. Concerning some of these tense, graphic descriptions of action in battle Raymond Calkins wrote, "Nahum portrays [the] siege, reproduces its horrors and its savagery, its cruelties and mercilessness, in language so realistic that one is able to see it and feel it. First comes the fighting in the suburbs. Then the assault upon the walls. Then the capture of the city and its destruction" (*The Modern Message of the Minor Prophets*. New York: Harper & Brothers, 1947, p. 82).

A. The attack (2:1-6)

2:1. Under attack, Nineveh was called on to defend itself. In an alternating pattern Nahum had addressed Nineveh in 1:11, 14 and now in 2:1; he had addressed Judah in 1:12-13, 15. The advance of **an** unnamed **attacker** (*mēpîs*, "scatterer or disperser"; cf. 2:8b; 3:18) **against . . . Nineveh** was so certain that Nahum spoke of it in the present tense. The verb **advances** is literally "goes up" (*ālâh*), a word used of hostile military operations (e.g., Jud. 1:1, "go up"; 1 Sam. 7:7, "came up"; 1 Kings 20:22, "attack"; Isa. 7:1, "marched up"; Isa. 7:6, "invade"; Isa. 21:2, "attack"). The attacker was Nabopolassar, the Babylonian who, with Cyaxeres the Mede, conquered Nineveh.

Then a series of four terse commands follows. They reflect the Ninevites' scurry of activity to defend their great city. In bitter irony, a subtle form of ridicule, Nahum urged the city to prepare for the approaching siege by guarding **the fortress,** watching **the road** for invaders, bracing themselves (lit., **brace** "the loins," i.e., exert strength physically and mentally), and marshaling **all** their **strength** (*kōaḥ*; see comments on Nahum 1:3). The prophet knew that such precautions could not hold back the siege or change its outcome. All Nineveh's efforts to defend itself would be futile because, as God said (1:15), the city would be destroyed.

2:2. The description of the attack is interrupted by a word about Jacob and Israel. Perhaps **Jacob** and **Israel** are synonyms for the entire nation, though possibly Jacob refers to the Southern Kingdom and Israel the Northern Kingdom. The destruction of Nineveh makes it possible for God's people to be taken out of their humbled, debased condition and to have their **splendor** (*gā'ôn*, "excellence or majesty") restored. This will not be fully realized till Israel is in the land in the millennial kingdom which the Messiah will establish. This will contrast with her

having been **laid . . . waste** by Assyria (the defeat of the Northern Kingdom in 722 B.C.), which included the ruining of her grape **vines.**

2:3-4. Nahum spoke of the equipment and speed of the "attacker" (v. 1) and his soldiers and chariots. **His** in the first line of verse 3 probably refers not to the defending Assyrian king but to the unidentified "attacker." **The shields of** the Medes and Babylonians were **red** either from blood, or from red-dyed leather over the wooden shields, or by being covered with copper. The warriors' **scarlet**-colored attire (cf. "red" in Ezek. 23:14) would make them awesome in appearance. (Xenophon wrote about the Persians in Cyrus' army being dressed in scarlet, *Cyropaedia* 6. 4. 1.) **The metal on the chariots** glistened in the sun, as the soldiers' wooden **spears** were **brandished** (swung) in their wild attack.

The charging **chariots** of the besieging enemy seemed to bolt furiously in wild frenzy (cf. Jer. 46:9). They moved so quickly that they looked **like lightning. The streets** "may include the avenues and suburban highways about Nineveh and leading to the city, for the context describes an attack that gradually leads to the city's walls" (Maier, *The Book of Nahum: A Commentary,* p. 243). **The squares** were the wider open spaces within a city (cf. streets and squares in Prov. 5:16; 7:12; Jer. 5:1; 9:21).

2:5-6. He in verse 5 probably refers to the Assyrian king because he summoned **his . . . troops** to defend **the city wall** and set up **the protective shield.** The exact nature of this protective covering is unknown but somehow it protected the defenders against the attackers' stones, spears, and arrows.

Several possible interpretations of **the river gates** have been suggested: (a) fortified bridges, (b) city gates near the banks of the Tigris River, (c) sluice gates in dams in the city moats (but no archeological evidence supports this), (d) breaches made in the wall by the torrential rush of water, (e) floodgates to control the flow of the Khosr River that passed through the city.

The fifth view is supported by the most natural sense of the language and by archeological remains. "Sennacherib . . . dammed the . . . Khosr [River], outside the city, and thus made a reservoir.

Thompson and Hutchinson report that the water was restrained by a magnificent double dam with two massive river walls at some distance from Nineveh itself. In the ruins they found traces of the original dam gates, or sluices, by which the water flow to the city could be increased or reduced" (Maier, *The Book of Nahum: A Commentary*, p. 253). So perhaps at the beginning of the siege the enemy closed the floodgates. When the reservoirs were completely full, they threw **open** the gates **and the palace** collapsed. The waters may have also been increased by heavy rains as Diodorus Siculus wrote (see point 5 in the chart "Fulfillments of Nahum's Prophecies," in the *Introduction*). The palace may have been Ashurbanipal's palace in the north part of the city. The nation that had ruined many enemy palaces now found its own palace devastated.

B. The defeat and the plundering (2:7-13)

2:7. Nineveh's destiny was **decreed** by God: she would be taken into exile. The word translated "decreed" is *ḥūṣṣaḇ*. The KJV renders this "Huzzab" and translates the first part of the verse, "And Huzzab shall be led away captive." This is supposedly the capture of the queen by that name. However, no queen by this name is known in extrabiblical records. The NIV rendering "It is decreed" is preferred. Though this seemingly interrupts the flow of thought, it does so to affirm that such an event as Nineveh's exile was established by God. Such words of divine purpose occur repeatedly (1:13-14; 2:2, 13; 3:5-6). The **slave girls** wailed **like doves,** whose cooing resembled lamenting (cf. Isa. 38:14; 59:11), and in sorrow **beat . . . their breasts,** knowing they were to **be exiled.**

2:8-10. With their city flooded, the Ninevites would flee, leaving their possessions behind. The word **pool,** perhaps meaning a reservoir, aptly describes Nineveh as an inundated area (cf. comments on v. 6). The people, like **water** flowing out of a tank, would flee rapidly from the city. As they would leave in panic, some would shout for them to **stop . . . but no one** would turn back. Who shouted **stop** is not stated. Perhaps they were the city leaders, or army officers, or perhaps even the attacking enemy.

Nahum now encouraged the victorious invaders to gather the spoils. For many years Nineveh had exacted huge booties from her foes, so that her **supply** of **silver** and **gold** was almost limitless. She also acquired **wealth** by tribute and by trading. In his annals Ashurbanipal mentioned silver and gold together 27 times in his inventories of booty taken from other nations. Luckenbill records the reports of vast amounts of wealth acquired by several Assyrian kings, including Ashurnaṣirpal, Shalmaneser III, Adad-nirari, Tiglath-Pileser III, Sargon II, Sennacherib, and Esarhaddon (*Ancient Records of Assyria and Babylonia*, 1:181, 211, 263, 276; 2:20, 133, 205). The words **pillaged, plundered,** and **stripped** render three similar-sounding Hebrew words: *bûqâh,* *meḇûqâh,* and *meḇullāqâh.* Because their wealth was being plundered and their lives were being endangered, the Ninevites were frightened and terror-stricken.

2:11-12. Nahum responded to the envisioned destruction of the city with a taunt, **Where now is the lions' den?** His rhetorical question implied that the capital no longer existed. The symbolism of the lions' den (and the **lion . . . lioness,** and **cubs;** cf. "young lions," v. 13) is uniquely appropriate. Like a **lion** hunting for his lioness and **cubs,** Assyria had plundered other nations. Assyrian kings prided themselves in their ability to kill lions in lion hunts. And the kings likened their own ferocity and fearlessness to that of lions. For example, Sennacherib boasted of his military fury by saying, "Like a lion I raged." Lions were frequently pictured in Assyrian reliefs and decorations. No wonder Nahum likened Nineveh to a lions' den! But now the **lairs** would be empty. No longer would there be lions, cubs, and ripped carcasses.

2:13. God's hostility against Nineveh is stated in forceful words: **I am against you** (cf. 3:5; Jer. 21:13; 50:31; 51:25; Ezek. 5:8; 13:8; 26:3; 28:22; 39:1). Fire would destroy her **chariots;** the **sword** would cut down her soldiers (**young lions**); and Nineveh would **no longer** be permitted to pounce on defenseless nations (**prey**) and helpless vassals. Nor would the haughty city be able to send any more **messengers** or heralds (as Sennacherib's field commander, 2 Kings 18:17-25) to demand submission, or to exact tribute (or to blaspheme the Lord; cf. 2 Kings 19:22; Isa. 37:4, 6).

IV. The Reasons for God's Judgment on Nineveh (chap. 3)

This final section of the book continues the vigorous emotion and intensified tones of the second chapter. But the focus turns from the fact of judgment to the reasons for it. The prophet showed the spiritually depraved condition of the once-haughty and prosperous city.

A. Her violence and deceit to result in shame (3:1-7)

3:1. **Woe** is an interjection pronouncing either grief or, as here, impending death (cf. comments on Isa. 3:9). Nineveh was truly a **city of blood**—blood spilled by her uncontrolled lust and murder. She earned this title by her "atrocious practice of cutting off hands and feet, ears and noses, gouging out eyes, lopping off heads, and then binding them to vines or heaping them up before city gates [and] the utter fiendishness by which captives could be impaled or flayed alive through a process in which their skin was gradually and completely removed" (Maier, *The Book of Nahum: A Commentary*, p. 292). It was also a city of deception (**lies**). The tactics Assyria followed when surrounding Jerusalem clearly display this characteristic (2 Kings 18:31). On Nineveh's plundering see comments on Nahum 2:9.

3:2-4. Nahum's accusation of Nineveh's guilt (v. 1) is followed by several terse descriptions of the final assault on the city. These statements are a progression from **whips,** to **wheels** and **horses** of **chariots,** to **cavalry** with **swords** and **spears,** to widespread slaughter and carnage (**bodies without number**). These describe the attack on Nineveh (cf. 2:3-4), which was surprisingly like Nineveh's own war tactics. She had piled up many dead bodies, but now the *Ninevites'* **corpses** would be piled up.

The reason for this terror is that she had lusted for power like the lusting **of a harlot.** Nineveh sold her military aid and power in order to lure **nations** under her control. By this statement Nahum may have also subtly alluded to Ishtar, the Assyrian-Babylonian goddess of sex and war, who was called a harlot and some of

whose exploits were acts of savagery. Nineveh's control over others was exercised by **sorceries** and **witchcraft.** The Assyrians used hundreds of incantations in order to seek to foretell the future and influence others' lives; they also read omens in the movements of birds, animals, clouds, and in dreams.

3:5-7. Her shameless actions against others would be matched by shameless exposure. God was **against** her (cf. comments on 2:13) and is against every nation, no matter how wealthy, powerful, or self-sufficient it may be, that disregards divine authority and tramples on human life. God said He would uncover what the privacy of her **skirts** had once covered (cf. the similar fate of Babylon, Isa. 47:1-3; and Jerusalem, Ezek. 16:37). She had caused others disgrace and **shame** by her prostitution, but now *she* would be shamed. Added to this indignity would be the disgrace of being pelted **with filth** (human excrement) and **contempt.** The Hebrew word for filth (*šiqqûṣ*) is used of anything that is detestable. It often refers to idols (e.g., Deut. 29:17; Jer. 4:1; Ezek 20:7-8). Nineveh's glory would turn into filth.

Nineveh's shame would reach a climax when she would be **in ruins,** and have no one **to comfort** her. Her cruelties had irreconcilably estranged her victims. The once-attractive harlot would be exposed in shame and would no longer be attractive to anyone.

B. Her treatment of Thebes to result in her own defeat (3:8-11)

3:8. Nineveh's strength, God said, would be no greater than that of the Egyptian city of **Thebes,** which Assyria had conquered in 663 B.C. Before that date Jeremiah (Jer. 46:25) and Ezekiel (Ezek. 30:14, 16) had predicted Thebes' fall. The Hebrews called the city No-Amon (city of the god Amun). Thebes was at the site of modern-day Karnak and Luxor, 400 miles south of Cairo. The city was built on the eastern bank of **the Nile** River but its suburbs were on both shores. One strength of Thebes was her strategic location. **Water** was all **around her,** that is, moats, canals, and water channels flowed throughout much of the city. These helped defend the city as enemy soldiers would find it difficult to cross numerous canals to get to the heart of the city. The **waters** were thus like a **wall.** In this way Nineveh and Thebes were similar (cf. Nahum 2:8).

3:9. Another strength of Thebes was her support by notable alliances and their almost limitless resources. Nineveh, by contrast, had no allies. Thebes was the most prominent city in **Cush,** the region of the upper Nile River, which corresponds to present-day southern Egypt, Sudan, and northern Ethiopia. The lower Nile region was known as **Egypt,** and at that time this territory was subjugated by Cush. While **Put** is sometimes identified as **Libya,** the mention of both here favors a location for Put on the coast of the Red Sea as far south as present-day Somaliland. The Libyans inhabited the territory west of Egypt. So Thebes' **allies** were south, north, east, and west of her. Yet their combined help was unable to defend her against Nineveh.

3:10. In spite of her strength, Thebes endured an ignominious end. Assyrian records describe in detail the conquest of Thebes. Most of the people of Thebes were **taken . . . into exile.** (Similarly many Ninevites would be exiled, 2:7.) Rather than taking Thebian **infants** into captivity, the Assyrians ruthlessly massacred them (cf. Hosea 13:16; other nations did the same: Ps. 137:9; Isa. 13:16, 18; Hosea 10:14). The Assyrians did this in full view of many Thebians **at the** intersection (**head) of every street.** This created maximum fear and agony among the people and also helped wipe out a future generation of Thebians. Such terrible atrocities added to Nineveh's deep guilt. While many of the people of the great city of Thebes were herded into captivity, the nobility were bid for by casting **lots,** perhaps to become the Ninevites' slaves, a humbling experience.

3:11. Nineveh's treatment of Thebes would be turned back on Nineveh. Like **drunk** persons, the Ninevites would be bereft of sense and direction under attack, frantically seeking to hide. Also the people of Nineveh literally became drunk (cf. 1:10) with intoxicants, which contributed to their aimless tottering and inability to defend themselves.

C. Her defense efforts to be useless (3:12-19)

3:12. Under attack by the Medes, Scythians, and Babylonians, Nineveh would find that its **fortresses** were weak. The initial yield on **fig trees** (cf. Num. 13:20) in the spring (which is followed by a later crop; see comments on Song 2:13) falls easily to the ground when the tree is **shaken.** The figs **fall,** as it were, **into the mouth of the eater** with the slightest effort. Similarly Nineveh's defenses would easily and quickly succumb to the attackers. This was actually the case in 612 B.C.

3:13. Seeing the attackers, the men trying to defend the city would lose their courage and become like **women,** afraid and defenseless (cf. Isa. 19:16; Jer. 50:37; 51:30). The dreaded Assyrians, ferocious as lions, would become weak.

Because of the destructive effect of the floodwaters on the city (see comments on 2:6), enemy soldiers were able to enter it. Then they set **fire** to the city **gates** and their **bars** (cf. Isa. 10:16-17) and rushed headlong into the city.

3:14. Nineveh's efforts at defense would be no match for the Lord's judgment. The scene of the destruction moves from the fortresses and gates (vv. 12-13) to within the city itself (vv. 14-17).

In ridiculing irony (cf. 2:1; also see 3:15) Nahum again ordered the Ninevites to defend themselves. When a city is under **siege,** one of its most urgent needs is an adequate supply of clean drinking **water.** And when the enemy would tear off some of the bricks of the city's wall (as the Assyrians often did), the city under attack would need to **repair** those weakened places in the walls with new bricks and **mortar.** In Nehemiah 3:19 the past tense of the Hebrew word here translated **strengthen** is rendered "repaired." Nineveh's ruins include traces of a counterwall built by the inhabitants to defend the city near places where the enemy had broken down some of the city's **defenses.**

3:15-17. When those defense efforts would prove futile, then disaster would strike with fire and **sword.** On destruction by **fire** see point 6 on the chart "Fulfillments of Nahum's Prophecies," in the *Introduction.* The attacking soldiers entered the city, killing many of the people with swords. The soldiers were **like grasshoppers,** consuming and destroying entire crops for miles (on devastation caused by grasshoppers and locusts, see comments on Joel 1:2-13). Nahum's command to **multiply like grasshoppers** and like **locusts** may be directed to the Ninevites to increase their numbers (as if they could!) to defend themselves more adequately. Or it may be addressed to the enemy to increase themselves (to be successful) in their conquest of Nineveh.

Again the prophet spoke of **locusts** (Nahum 3:16). The city had **increased** its wealth by commercial trading with numberless **merchants,** but they would become like countless locusts stripping **the land** of its vegetation. Nineveh had acquired vast amounts of wealth by trading (probably often done deceptively; see comments on v. 4), but now those merchants by looting would take back much merchandise. Neither military power (v. 15) nor wealth (v. 16) could deliver the Ninevites.

The **locusts** provided still another point of comparison (v. 17). When Nineveh would be attacked her military **guards** and national **officials** would be so afraid (cf. v. 13a) that they would escape overnight. In the cool of the evening, locusts settle on walls but when the warmth of the sun comes in the morning, **they fly away.** Similarly, in panic the guards on the walls would also suddenly vanish.

3:18. The final dirge-like words in verses 18-19 may be addressed to Sin-shar-ishkun, the **king** who was ruling Nineveh when it was destroyed in 612 B.C. or, perhaps more likely, to King Ashur-uballiṭ (612–609 B.C.) who tried to hold together the Assyrian Empire in the city of Haran, until it finally crumbled completely in 609, three years after Nineveh's fall. In surveying his devastated empire, he would realize that his leaders (**shepherds** and **nobles**) were dead (spoken of as if they were sheep; cf. Pss. 13:3; 76:6; Dan. 12:2) and that **people** who were not taken as captives were **scattered,** never again to be gathered. This empire that for centuries had been invincible would be totally disintegrated.

3:19. The devastation of the burned and looted city of Nineveh would look like a **wound** (cf. Isa. 1:6-7). So **fatal** and final was her fall that she would never be rebuilt. Archeology has confirmed this fact. Peoples who had been oppressed by the brutally atrocious Ninevites would now rejoice in her demise. Judah especially would be greatly comforted by the fact that Nineveh's fall would mean the end (cf. Nahum 1:8-9) of the seemingly **endless cruelty** that had lasted for centuries. In this way the Lord would pour out His wrath (cf. 1:2-3, 6) on Nineveh and demonstrate His care for those who trust in Him (1:7). Readers today know from the Book of Nahum that God's wrath will eventually fall on inveterate sinners, and can be comforted by knowing that those who turn to Him are safe.

BIBLIOGRAPHY

Bennett, T. Miles. *The Books of Nahum and Zephaniah.* Grand Rapids: Baker Book House, 1968.

Feinberg, Charles L. *The Minor Prophets.* Chicago: Moody Press, 1976.

Freeman, Hobart E. *Nahum, Zephaniah, Habakkuk: Minor Prophets of the Seventh Century B.C.* Chicago: Moody Press, 1973.

Keil, C.F. "Nahum." In *Commentary on the Old Testament in Ten Volumes.* Vol. 10. Reprint (25 vols. in 10). Grand Rapids: Wm. B. Eerdmans Publishing Co., 1982.

Kohlenberger, John R., III. *Jonah-Nahum.* Everyman's Bible Commentary. Chicago: Moody Press, 1984.

Laetsch, Theo. *The Minor Prophets.* St. Louis: Concordia Publishing House, 1956.

Maier, Walter A. *The Book of Nahum: A Commentary.* St. Louis: Concordia Publishing House, 1959. Reprint. Grand Rapids: Baker Book House, 1980.

Tatford, Frederick A. *The Minor Prophets.* Vol. 2. Reprint (3 vols.). Minneapolis: Klock & Klock Christian Publishers, 1982.

Watts, John D.W. *The Books of Joel, Obadiah, Jonah, Nahum, Habakkuk, and Zephaniah.* New York: Cambridge University Press, 1975.

HABAKKUK

J. Ronald Blue

INTRODUCTION

Planet Earth may look marvelous from a satellite, but for those who live on the dusty globe things tend to look rather grim. Increased turmoil, rising terrorism, mounting tragedies, unprecedented trauma, increasing pollution, deepening trials, and unparalleled tensions cast dark shadows over earthlings. The world looks more and more like some ominous black sphere with a very short fuse, a time bomb sizzling to explode.

It is little wonder thinking people begin to ask questions. Why is there so much oppression? Why all the injustice? Why do evil men prosper? Why do the righteous suffer? Why doesn't God do something? Why doesn't God clean up this mess? Why? Why? Why?

These penetrating questions are hardly new. Centuries before Christ visited this planet, an ancient prophet looked around at the violence and wickedness of the world and cried out to God, "Why do You make me look at injustice? Why do You tolerate wrong? . . . Why are You silent while the wicked swallow up those more righteous than themselves?" (Hab. 1:3, 13) The prophet not only asked the mysterious whys that plague mankind; he also received answers to his questions. The answers given by the Creator of the universe are carefully recorded in the little book called Habakkuk.

Habakkuk is a unique book. Unlike other prophets who declared God's message to people this prophet dialogued with God about people. Most Old Testament prophets proclaimed divine judgment. Habakkuk pleaded for divine judgment. In contrast with the typical indictment, this little book records an intriguing interchange between a perplexed prophet and his Maker.

This is not merely a little on-the-street interview with God, however. Habakkuk went beyond that. The *dialogue*

developed in chapter 1. The prophet's complaints were then met with the Lord's command, "Write down the revelation," in chapter 2. God's declaration included a lengthy *dirge*, or taunt-song, of five woes on the evil Babylonians. Chapter 3 climaxes with a magnificent *doxology* of praise. The ever-present "Why?" is best answered by the everlasting "Who!" Though the outlook may elicit terror, the uplook elicits trust. The prophet's complaints and fears were resolved in confidence and faith. This is the heart of the message of Habakkuk: "The righteous will live by his faith" (2:4).

The Author. Little is known of Habakkuk the prophet. The book simply records his name and his profession. His name has meaning, and conjecture about its meaning runs free. Most scholars trace the name "Habakkuk" to the Hebrew verb *ḥābaq,* "to fold one's hands or to embrace." But is it to be considered active or passive? Is he an "embracer" or the "embraced"? Luther took it in the active sense and saw Habakkuk as one who embraced his people to comfort and uphold them. Jerome saw Habakkuk as one who embraced the problem of divine justice in a wicked world. Others prefer the passive sense and picture Habakkuk as one embraced by God as His child and messenger. More recently the word *ḥambaququ* has been found in Akkadian literature in texts from Mesopotamia which indicate it was the name of a garden plant. So some scholars contend that the prophet's name shows the influence of Assyria and Babylonia on the Israelites, or that Habakkuk was of a mixed Israelite and Assyrian marriage.

Whatever the meaning of his name, Habakkuk was a prophet. In the title of other prophetic books various items of information are given: the name of the prophet's father (Isa. 1:1), the names of the kings contemporary with the prophet

(Hosea 1:1), the prophet's hometown (Amos 1:1). But only three times is the writer designated as a "prophet" in the title of his book: Habakkuk, Haggai, and Zechariah. Habakkuk, therefore, is the only *preexilic* prophet to be so designated.

Though Habakkuk is specifically called a prophet, his book resembles the literary style of the Psalms and the Wisdom books. The concluding note in his book, "For the director of music. On my stringed instruments" (Hab. 3:19), suggests that Habakkuk may have been a musician of the Levitical office. In the apocryphal book, Bel and the Dragon, Habakkuk is described as the son of Jeshua, of the tribe of Levi, in a legend of fantasy in which the prophet supposedly was commanded by an angel to take a meal to Daniel, who had been cast a second time into a lions' den. When Habakkuk complained that he did not know the location of the lions' den, the angel allegedly transported the prophet by a lock of his hair on the appointed journey.

It has been suggested by Rabbinic tradition that Habakkuk was the son of the Shunammite woman mentioned in 2 Kings 4, whom Elisha restored to life. This is apparently based solely on the meaning of Habakkuk's name, "embrace," and Elisha's words to the Shunammite, "You shall embrace a son" (2 Kings 4:16, NASB).

All conjecture and speculation aside it is safe, and perhaps sufficient, to say that Habakkuk was an officially ordained prophet who took part in temple liturgical singing. He was well educated, deeply sensitive, and in his literary style was as much a poet as he was a prophet. Above all, he was God's choice servant who penned one of the most penetrating books of the Old Testament.

The Date. It is generally accepted that the reference to the Babylonians (Hab. 1:6) places the book within the seventh century B.C. More precise dating of the prophecy has provoked controversy. The dates proposed fall into three time periods: the reign of Manasseh (697–642), the reign of Josiah (640–609), and the reign of Jehoiakim (609–598).

Those who date Habakkuk's prophecy in the reign of Manasseh say that the statement of 1:5, "I am going to do something in your days that you would not

believe, even if you were told," indicates a time before Babylon's rise as a world power. The date, then, would have to be before the battle of Carchemish in 605 B.C., when Nebuchadnezzar defeated Pharaoh Neco II of Egypt and Babylon rose to become a formidable nation making its bid for world power, and most likely before 612 B.C., when Babylon overthrew Nineveh. However, if the fulfillment of Habakkuk's prophecy (v. 5) is the fall of Jerusalem at the hands of the Babylonians in 586 B.C., the book definitely was not written early in the reign of Manasseh. The prophecy is said to be fulfilled "in your days" (v. 5) and those who heard the prophecy in Manasseh's early days would probably have died before its fulfillment.

A date in the latter years of Manasseh's reign or during the reign of Josiah might fit, but Habakkuk's complaint (vv. 2-4) points to a period in the history of Judah when lawlessness and violence were rampant. The reforms in the latter part of Manasseh's reign (2 Chron. 33:15-16) and the extensive reforms of Josiah (2 Chron. 34) do not fit Habakkuk's dire description.

It seems far better to understand the disbelief referred to in Habakkuk 1:5 as a reaction to God's use of such a sinful nation to judge Israel rather than the surprise that a nation as yet unrecognized would emerge in power. That the Babylonians had already attained renown for their power seems evident from the description recorded by Habakkuk in verses 7-11. Thus the most likely date falls between 606 and 604 B.C., sometime around Babylon's victory at the battle of Carchemish (605).

The Setting. Habakkuk wrote in a time of international crisis and national corruption. Babylonia had just emerged as a world power. When the Babylonians rebelled against Assyria, Judah found a brief period of relief reflected in the reforms initiated by Josiah. The Assyrians were forced to devote their energies to stop the Babylonian rebellion. The Babylonians finally crushed the Assyrian Empire and quickly proceeded to defeat the once-powerful Egyptians. A new world empire was stretching across the world. Soon the Babylonians would overtake Judah and carry its inhabitants away into captivity. On the eve of pending destruction, a period of uncertainty and fear, Habakkuk wrote his message.

The crisis internationally was serious. But of even greater concern was the national corruption. Great unrest stirred within Judah. Josiah had been a good king. When he died, Josiah's son Jehoahaz rose to the throne. In only three months, the king of Egypt invaded Judah, deposed Jehoahaz, and placed his brother Jehoiakim on the throne. Jehoiakim was evil, ungodly, and rebellious (2 Kings 23:36–24:7; 2 Chron. 36:5-8). Shortly after Jehoiakim ascended to power, Habakkuk wrote his lament over the decay, violence, greed, fighting, and perverted justice that surrounded him.

No wonder Habakkuk looked at all the corruption and asked, "Why doesn't God do something?" Godly men and women continue to ask similar "whys" in a world of increasing international crises and internal corruption. Nation rises up against nation around the world and sin abounds at home. World powers aim an ever-increasing array of complex nuclear weapons at each other while they talk of peace. World War III seems incredibly imminent.

While the stage is set for a global holocaust, an unsuspecting home audience fiddles a happy tune. The nation's moral fiber is being eaten away by a playboy philosophy that makes personal pleasure the supreme rule of life. Hedonism catches fire while homes crumble. Crime soars while the church sours. Drugs, divorce, and debauchery prevail and decency dies. Frivolity dances in the streets. Faith is buried. "In God We Trust" has become a meaningless slogan stamped on corroding coins.

In such a world of crisis and chaos, Habakkuk speaks with clarity. This little book is as contemporary as the morning newspaper.

The Message. In the dark days of Jehoiakim's reign just before the Babylonian Captivity, the Prophet Habakkuk penned an unusual message of hope and encouragement for God's people. Though doubts and confusion reign when sin runs rampant, an encounter with God can turn those doubts into devotion and all confusion into confidence. Habakkuk's book begins with an in-

terrogation of God but ends as an intercession to God. Worry is transformed into worship. Fear turns to faith. Terror becomes trust. Hang-ups are resolved with hope. Anguish melts into adoration.

What begins with a question mark ends in an exclamation point. The answer to Habakkuk's "Why?" is "Who!" His confusion, "Why all the conflict?" is resolved with his comprehension of who is in control: God!

OUTLINE

B. God's presence of majesty (3:3-15)
1. God's arrival (3:3a)
2. God's appearance (3:3b-7)
3. God's actions (3:8-15)
C. Habakkuk's peace in ministry (3:16-19)

COMMENTARY

I. A Dialogue with God: Habakkuk Previewed God's Discipline of Judah (chap. 1)

The prophet was perplexed. Wickedness and violence seemed to go unchecked. Would there be no end to the rising tide of sin? Habakkuk took his complaint to God. "Why don't You do something?" God answered, "I am doing something. Judah will be punished by Babylon." Then the prophet was *more* perplexed. Habakkuk's distress deepened to a profound dilemma. So he continued his conversation with God. "Why would You use those wretched Babylonian barbarians to judge Judah?"

A. Habakkuk's distress (1:1-4)

1. WHY IS GOD INDIFFERENT TO SUPPLICATION? (1:1-2)

1:1. Little wonder the book was titled **The oracle that Habakkuk the prophet received.** The prophet called his writing a *maśśā'*, a "burden." This Hebrew noun is derived from a verb meaning "to lift up," and consequently signifies "what is lifted up," and thus "a burden." The message Habakkuk presented is indeed a weighty one. However, *maśśā'* was not always used to preface a burdensome message. It was used, for example, as a title for the rather non-threatening sayings recorded in Proverbs 30 and 31 (where the NIV renders *maśśā'* "oracle" in 30:1; 31:1). Nonetheless, if there ever was a heavy message, Habakkuk had one.

The title here might be more literally translated, "The burden that Habakkuk the prophet saw." The same two Hebrew words, "burden" and "saw," are used in Isaiah 13:1. The word "saw" (*ḥāzâh*), when used of the prophets, often means to see in a vision (cf. Isa. 1:1; 2:1; Ezek. 12:27; Amos 1:1; Micah 1:1). Receiving glimpses from God into the future (i.e., "visions," *ḥāzôn*) the prophets were

sometimes called God's "seers" (*ḥōzeh*).

1:2. The prophet's long-standing concern which finally erupted into a volcanic complaint was twofold. First, he wanted to know why God seemed so indifferent: Why doesn't God hear? Second, he wanted to know why God seemed so insensitive: Why doesn't God **help?**

Habakkuk's words **How long** show his agony over God's seeming delay in responding to the prophet's concerns. Many Christians today sense the same problem. They wonder why God seems silent when they pray. Like several psalmists (David, Pss. 13:1-4; 22:1, 11, 19-20; Asaph, Ps. 74:1-2, 10-11; the sons of Korah, Ps. 88), Habakkuk went to God to complain about his troubles and the troubles of his people. He described the injustice that was rampant around him and then asked "How long?" (Hab. 1:2) and "Why?" (v. 3) Later he used these same words again: "Why?" (twice in v. 13) and "How long?" (2:6)

This prophet sounded more like a singer than a seer. Part of Israel's worship involved making impassioned pleas to God for help in times of desperate trouble. Israel did not normally complain about its troubles in "letters to the editor." They took their pleas directly to God in worship.

Habakkuk's concern was not only that his cries went unheeded but that the corruption continued unchecked. He cried out to God, **Violence!** but God seemed to do nothing. The stark word "violence" sums up all the chaos Habakkuk witnessed around him. The word is sprinkled throughout the book (1:2-3, 9; 2:17) like inkblots on a crumpled page in history.

2. WHY IS GOD INSENSITIVE TO SIN AND SUFFERING? (1:3-4)

1:3. Sin was abounding and God seemed both indifferent and idle. Habakkuk put the blame on God with his penetrating question, **Why do You make me look at injustice?** Then he asked an even greater question: **Why do You tolerate wrong?** God caused Habakkuk to witness injustice (lit., "iniquity"), but He Himself also tolerated (lit., "beholds"), the very same wrong. It is bad enough that a weak *sinner* should have to behold wickedness. But to have a righteous *God* see the evil and do nothing about it seemed beyond comprehension (cf. v. 13).

The picture was bleak indeed. **Destruction and violence** were coupled with **strife and conflict** (cf. "violence" in vv. 2, 9; 2:17). "Destruction" (šōḏ, "violent treatment causing desolation") and "violence" (ḥāmās, "malicious conduct intended to injure another") frequently appear together (e.g., Jer. 6:7; 20:8; Ezek. 45:9, "violence and oppression"; Amos 3:10, "plunder and loot"; in each case here the two words in Heb. are in the reverse order from their order in Hab. 1:3). Habakkuk described the scene well.

1:4. The greatest tragedy, however, was the people's neglect of God's Law. Habakkuk described the consequence: **Therefore the Law is paralyzed** (lit., "becomes cool, numbed"). The divine Law appeared to have suffered a knockout; also civic **justice**, Habakkuk said, **never prevails**, or never came forth to fight (cf. "injustice," v. 3). It appears that wickedness was the uncontested victor. **The wicked hem in the righteous.** The righteous were locked up and the wicked vigilantes had thrown away the key. Therefore **justice** was **perverted** (from 'āqal, "to bend or twist out of shape," a word used only here in the OT). With wicked men in power, justice was twisted and turned till it came out injustice! The situation in Habakkuk's day was perilous.

B. God's disclosure (1:5-11)

Though the prophet was engaged in a typical Jewish lament and was asking essentially rhetorical questions, God answered his complaint. The Lord was neither indifferent nor insensitive. God was not idle; He was already at work on specific plans to discipline erring Judah. He revealed those plans to the distressed prophet.

1. GOD'S INTENTION OF DISCIPLINE (1:5)

1:5. Look at the nations and watch was God's reply. The change in speakers is apparent from the verbs "look" and "watch," which in Hebrew include the plural "you." God addressed both the prophet and the people. Habakkuk had complained about being made to look at injustice. But the prophet and people suffered from myopia. They were too nearsighted. God instructed them to get their eyes off the immediate havoc and look

out on the international horizons. They needed to develop a world view that included "the nations." As they did so, they would **be utterly amazed.** The political developments about to be revealed to Habakkuk and the people would stun them (the verb tāmâh means "to be astounded, bewildered, or dumbfounded"). In fact Habakkuk *was* dumbfounded (vv. 12, 17). What God was about to perform would be hard for them to **believe, even** though God would reveal it to them.

2. GOD'S INSTRUMENT OF DISCIPLINE (1:6-11)

Judah's sin would not go unchecked. Justice was not dead, nor did it sleep. Discipline was forthcoming; correction was on the way. But the surprise was not the anticipated discipline but the dispenser of that discipline. It was not coming correction that was unbelievable but the channel of correction that seemed so incredible.

a. Destruction by the Babylonians (1:6)

1:6. God dropped a bombshell: **I am raising up the Babylonians.** Granted, sin had abounded all too long in Judah. But the sinners of Judah were but soiled saints next to the barbaric Babylonians. Babylon was a nation known for its violent impulses. Its people readily committed atrocities without forethought or remorse. The historical records present the Babylonians as a fierce and pitilessly cruel people. And God affirmed it to Habakkuk by calling them **that ruthless** (mar, "bitter," i.e., bitter in temper, or fierce) **and impetuous** (lit., "swift") **people.** Ezekiel too called Babylon a ruthless nation (though he used the Heb. word 'ārîṣ, meaning "terror-striking," Ezek. 28:7; 30:11; 31:12; 32:12). Furthermore, their conduct matched their character. They swept **across the whole earth** to plunder and possess. No doubt "the whole earth" meant much of the then-known world, for Babylon did conquer many of the nations including Assyria, Judah, Egypt, and Edom. Judah was just a speck of loose dust before this gigantic vacuum cleaner.

b. Description of the Babylonians (1:7-11)

The Babylonians, also known as Chaldeans, lived in southern Mesopotamia and were called "an ancient . . . nation" (Jer. 5:15), a primeval people. Abram, of course, migrated from Ur of the Chaldees to Canaan. God had called a people out of this increasingly savage populace. Now this nation had burst out of the Tigris-Euphrates Valley and like some awesome lava flow it spilled across the world. Its quiet little cousin, Judah, would soon lie in its wake.

(1) Their status. 1:7. Babylon apparently was without rival. This terrible and dreadful people were a law to themselves. They promoted their own honor, that is, they lifted themselves up. They recognized no law or judge but themselves and their superiority and authority was gained by their own ruthless conquests.

(2) Their speed. 1:8. In vivid and awesome imagery, the Lord further described the foe as a people with horses . . . swifter than leopards, fiercer than wolves at dusk. Both leopards and wolves are fierce, fast, and excellent hunters. At dusk, wolves are hungry and ready to pounce on prey. The Babylonians' voracious speed in conquest was also likened to a vulture swooping to devour. This "vulture" (nešer) may have been the great griffon vulture, a majestic bird often seen in Palestine circling higher and higher and then rapidly swooping down on its prey. Jeremiah wrote about the Babylonians devouring everything in their path, including fields, people, animals, trees, and cities (Jer. 5:17; also cf. Lam. 4:19). Certainly the Babylonians, likened to ferocious beasts and birds, were a terrible enemy.

(3) Their success. 1:9. There was no hope of stopping the Babylonians. Collectively they all came bent on violence. The nation's entire military force would be engaged in the invasion and would be irresistibly victorious. The second line in this verse, their hordes advance like a desert wind, consists of three words in Hebrew and is variously interpreted. The first word in the clause occurs nowhere else and is variously rendered "resisting," "striving," "eagerness," "assembling," and a "gathering host," "troops," or "horde." The last Hebrew word "desert wind" is also the word for the East. Here it means a wind that comes from the East. Such fierce scorching winds moving across the desert from the East often devastated vegetation (cf. Jer.

18:17; Ezek. 17:10; 19:12; Jonah 4:8). The enemy was coming like a whirlwind and would gather prisoners like sand, a figure expressing numbers too vast to calculate.

(4) Their scoffing. 1:10. Confident in their strength, the Babylonians scoffed at kings and ridiculed rulers. It was their custom to exhibit captive rulers as public spectacles. Their brutality is seen in the way they treated Zedekiah after Jerusalem fell. They killed his sons before his eyes and then, with that awesome sight burned into his memory, they put out his eyes, bound him in shackles, and took him prisoner to Babylon (2 Kings 25:7).

But not only did the Babylonians scoff at their foes; they also laughed at all fortified cities (lit., "every fortress"). They poured derision on the strongholds which their victims considered impregnable. They simply built earthen ramps (lit., "heaped up earth") against the walls of cities built on mounds, and raced up those ramps, attacked the cities easily, and seized the fortified strongholds. This practice was fairly common in ancient warfare, but the "siege ramp" (2 Kings 19:32; cf. Ezek. 4:2) was more developed by the Babylonians.

(5) Their sacrilege. 1:11. The first part of this verse is difficult to translate. The KJV has, "Then shall his mind (rûaḥ, 'spirit' or 'wind') change, and he shall pass over." That is, the Babylonians changed their minds and went beyond all restraint to their own destruction. However, it is unlikely that rûaḥ is the subject; the verb "change" can better be translated in its normal sense "to pass through." The NIV has a more likely rendering, Then they sweep past like the wind (cf. "desert wind," v. 9). Their major offense was clearly recorded. They considered their own strength as their god. They treated their might as their master. For them, "might was right" became "might was divine." It is little wonder that God declared them guilty for such sacrilege.

C. Habakkuk's dilemma (1:12-17)

God's amazing disclosure left the prophet even more perplexed and bewildered. Habakkuk's complaint about the sin and lawlessness in Judah (vv. 2-4) was met by God's response that He was not ignorant of His people's conduct. Judgment was on its way. The Babylonians would soon take these erring people captive. The prophet was astonished, just as God said he would be (v. 5). He was appalled that Yahweh would employ so evil an instrument to punish Judah. Habakkuk expressed his deep concern; he questioned God's plan.

1. WHY WOULD GOD EMPLOY A PEOPLE OF INIQUITY? (1:12-13)

However devastating the divine judgment may sound, the prophet drew consolation and hope from God's holiness and faithfulness. In a sea of confusion, Habakkuk clung to the life buoy of God's holy character. In a chaotic storm, the prophet grasped the rock of his steadfast Lord.

1:12. In Hebrew, the form of the question—**O Lord, are You not from everlasting?**—requires an affirmative reply. It is as much a declaration as an interrogation. The prophet's confidence in the living, eternal God, Yahweh, contrasts starkly with the previous verse in which the Babylonians considered their own strength to be their god.

Humanly speaking, of course, Babylon could very easily extinguish the people of Judah. But the prophet found utterly unthinkable the extinction of God's people and thereby the destruction of their covenant relationship with Yahweh. Habakkuk based his conclusion on two truths: (a) the immutable and everlasting Lord (cf. 3:6) who will not break His covenant with Israel, and (b) the holy (cf. 3:3) and righteous God who will not allow sin to go unpunished in Israel or in her foes. The prophet rightly concluded, **My God, my Holy One, we will not die.**

Habakkuk reminded himself that the Lord had **appointed** the Babylonians **to execute judgment** (i.e., discipline), not total destruction on Judah. The enemy was God's instrument **to punish,** not to demolish. The prophet referred to his Lord as the **Rock** (ṣûr), a term first applied to Yahweh in Deuteronomy 32:4 to indicate the Almighty's stability and security (cf. Deut. 32:15, 18, 30-31).

1:13. A burning question remained in Habakkuk's heart. Why would the everlastingly preeminent Yahweh, the absolutely Holy One, the immutably permanent Rock, utilize so wicked a people to administer discipline on Judah? **Your eyes are too pure to look on evil,** complained the prophet. **You cannot tolerate wrong.** In his first address Habakkuk questioned why he was forced to look on injustice and why God seemed to be less contentious and more comprehensive than the thought he expressed in verses 2-4. His focus seemed to be shifting from the sin problems to the sovereign Person in control.

In light of Yahweh's character, however, it seemed fair to Habakkuk to ask, **Why** (cf. v. 3) **do You tolerate the treacherous? Why** would God allow such a **wicked** nation to devour **those** who were **more righteous?** That seemed like a perversion of justice. Sinful though Judah had been, her wickedness was dwarfed by the atrocities committed by the Babylonians. Habakkuk was in a dilemma. Certainly his concern over God's seeming silence has concerned many of God's people (cf. Job 19:7).

2. WHY WOULD GOD ENDORSE A PEOPLE OF INJUSTICE? (1:14-15)

1:14. Habakkuk said that God **made men like fish in the sea, like sea creatures that have no ruler.** Helpless as fish, Judah's people were easy prey for powerful invaders. So helpless were they that they lacked the ability to organize themselves for self-protection. They were like sea creatures that are on their own, with no leader to guide them.

1:15. The wicked (cf. v. 13) Babylonians were pictured catching unsuspecting men, like fish, **with hooks,** sweeping them into a **net,** and gathering them in a large seine or **dragnet** (cf. v. 16). The imagery is vivid. Jeremiah used a similar analogy of fishermen, coupling it with that of hunters (Jer. 16:16). The evil Babylonians had as little regard for the welfare of humanity as fishermen have for unprotesting fish. The victorious Babylon foe rejoiced and was **glad**. It was hard to understand why God would permit such blatant injustice. Habakkuk was in a dilemma.

3. WHY WOULD GOD EXCUSE A PEOPLE OF IDOLATRY? (1:16-17)

1:16. The hooks and nets brought **food** and plenty to the Babylonians. Their conquests provided not only a livelihood but also **luxury.** So these barbaric people paid homage to the instruments that contributed to their prosperity. The enemy sacrificed to their nets and burned **incense to** their dragnets. (This word for **dragnet** occurs in the OT only here and in v. 15). The metaphor is potent. The Babylonians worshiped the means that brought them military success. Already God had declared that the Babylonians saw their might as their god (v. 11). Now Habakkuk added that their military power brought monetary profit.

Idolatry is not limited to those who bring sacrifices or burn incense to inanimate objects. People of position, power, or prosperity often pay homage to the business or agency that provided them their coveted status. It becomes their constant obsession, even their "god."

1:17. The prophet asked the fat fisherman Babylon if **he** was **to keep on emptying his net, destroying nations** (cf. 2:8, 17) **without mercy?** The action depicted signified a seemingly perpetual operation. They emptied their net so they could fill it again, again, and again. When would God put a stop to the Babylonians' greed for conquest? How could He let a people continue in power when they so openly worshiped that very power as their god? Habakkuk was confused.

II. A Dirge from God: Habakkuk Pronounced God's Destruction of Babylon (chap. 2)

The prophet's dilemma deepened. Why should God use an ungodly nation such as Babylon as the instrument of judgment on His own people Judah? Habakkuk had boldly lodged his contentions and now he waited for God's reply. Surely some logical explanation would be given.

A. Habakkuk's anticipation: "Watch" (2:1)

2:1. Like a sentinel standing in a watchtower to detect the first signs of an approaching enemy, Habakkuk stationed himself **on the ramparts . . . to see what** God would **say to** him. He had made his complaint and now he resolved to position himself so he might obtain the earliest and clearest information and then, like a watchman, inform his waiting brethren. It is likely that the **watch** (*mišmeret*, "observation station") and the ramparts (*māṣôr*, "watchtower or fortress") refer to the prophet's attitude of expectation rather than his physical loca-

tion. This vivid imagery was common in Habakkuk's society (2 Sam. 18:24; Isa. 21:6). The prophet or seer, like a lookout, waited to *see* more than *hear* what God would say.

The prophet was also concerned about what He would reply **to this complaint.** Probably Habakkuk referred to his own complaint lodged in his dialogue with God (Hab. 1:2-4, 12-17). Some translators, however, say that the "complaint" (*tôkaḥat*, "correction, rebuke, or argument") was *against* the prophet rather than *by* the prophet. Thus they render the phrase, "what to answer when I am rebuked" (NIV marg.). Whether or not Habakkuk anticipated reproof in God's response one thing is certain: the prophet anxiously anticipated God's answer.

B. God's admonition: "Write" (2:2-5)

True to his profession, Habakkuk was a spokesman for God's revelation. He waited for God's message, not simply for his own satisfaction. He was ready to carry God's message to his people. Habakkuk waited; God spoke.

1. GOD'S CLEAR REVELATION (2:2)

2:2. God does not mumble. He speaks with clarity and forthrightness. He told Habakkuk, **Write down the revelation and make it plain on tablets.** The revelation (lit., "vision") was to be recorded on tablets of baked clay so God's Word would be preserved and, even more important, publicized—**so that a herald** could **run with it.** This phrase has been mistaken by some to signify that the messenger should be able to read the tablet on the run. On the contrary, the point is that the messenger would read it and then run to spread the news to others.

2. GOD'S CERTAIN REVELATION (2:3)

2:3. Every prophetic revelation demands a certain degree of patience. One must **wait for** its fulfillment. God's words to Habakkuk were reassuring: **the revelation awaits an appointed time.** The prophecy pointed toward a future goal (lit., "it pants toward the end," like a runner toward the finish line). Reference to **the end** seems to signify not only the coming destruction of evil Babylonia but the broader fulfillment of the messianic judgment in the fall of "Babylon the Great" at the close of the Tribulation (Rev. 17–18).

One thing is certain: God's revelation **will not prove false. Though** the fulfillment seems delayed, **it will . . . come** to pass in accord with His perfect plan. For those in Judah about to experience the awesome Babylonian invasion and Captivity, this assurance of fulfillment should have been a great comfort. Their barbaric captors would themselves in God's due time suffer divine judgment!

The writer of Hebrews referred to this verse in his appeal for persecuted believers to persevere (Heb. 10:37). In his quote, he stressed the messianic significance of this passage in Habakkuk. The day is coming when the King of kings will reign on earth with perfect justice.

3. GOD'S CONDEMNATORY REVELATION (2:4-5)

2:4. As an introduction to the woeful taunt-songs Habakkuk was instructed to record, God gave His summary condemnation of the conceited character of the Babylonian: **He is puffed up.** Like a bloated toad, these arrogant people hopped along toward destruction. They were swollen (the Heb. verb '*āpal* is used only here in the OT) with evil passions. Their **desires** were **not upright.**

Yahweh then declared that a **righteous** person, by stark contrast, **will live by his faith** (*ĕmûnâh*, "steadfastness or faithfulness"). A righteous Israelite who remained loyal to God's moral precepts and was humble before the Lord enjoyed God's abundant life. To "live" meant to experience God's blessing by enjoying a life of security, protection, and fullness. Conversely, an apparently victorious but proud and perverse Babylonian would die. Faithfulness (NIV marg.) and faith are related. One who trusts in the Lord is one who relies on Him and is faithful to Him.

The key clause "the righteous will live by his faith" sparkles like a diamond in a pile of soot. In the midst of God's unrelenting condemnations of Babylon stands a bright revelation of God's favor that is quoted three times in the New Testament (Rom. 1:17; Gal. 3:11; Heb. 10:38). In those passages the words "will

live" have a broader meaning than in Habakkuk. In the New Testament they mean to enjoy salvation and eternal life. In contrast with the self-reliant, boastful ways of the unrighteous, the righteous are found to be reliant on God and faithful to Him.

2:5. The general description of the Babylonians' wickedness is made more specific. They were betrayed by **wine.** (They also used wine to betray others, v. 15.) The Babylonians were said to be very addicted to wine. For example, Babylon was conquered while Belshazzar and his leaders were feasting at a riotous banquet (Dan. 5). The treachery of wine is described in Proverbs 23:31-32. It looks so inviting in the glass but "in the end it bites like a snake and poisons like a viper."

As God continued His condemnation, He said the typical Babylonian **is arrogant** (*yāhîr*, "haughty," occurs only here and in Prov. 21:24) **and never at rest.** These proud, restless people were **as greedy as the grave.** Just as **death** and the grave are not **satisfied** till all come into their grasp, so the Babylonians sought to take **captive all the peoples** (cf. Hab. 1:17). Like some hideous monster, the grave devours the nations. Likewise, Babylon opened wide her insatiable jaws to devour all peoples. But this evil nation would not continue unpunished. God's judgment would fall!

C. Habakkuk's annotation: "Woe" (2:6-20)

The destruction of Babylon intimated in God's comments to Habakkuk was announced in fuller detail in a song of woe in five stanzas of three verses each ("woe" occurs in vv. 6, 9, 12, 15, 19). All those nations conquered and plundered by the Babylonians would in due time witness the fall of their conqueror and join in a song of derision and denunciation. Habakkuk recorded a satirical outburst or taunt-song. The NIV's rendering, "Will not all of them taunt him?" (v. 6a) is literally, "Will not all of them take up against him a taunt-song?" The song (*māšāl*) is any form of poetical composition in which parallelism is the principle of construction. It may denote a parable, proverb, ode, or a dirge such as the doleful lamentation recorded here. Five woes follow.

1. WOE FOR INTIMIDATION (2:6-8)

2:6. **Woe** is an interjection of distress pronounced in the face of disaster or in view of coming judgment (e.g., Isa. 3:11; 5:11; 10:5) because of certain sins. "Woe" was used frequently by the prophets (22 times by Isaiah, 10 times in Jer. and Lam., 7 times by Ezekiel, and 14 times in the Minor Prophets). The first woe compares the Babylonians to an unscrupulous pawnbroker who lends on extortionate terms. As spoil for their own gain they had been merciless in heaping up the wealth of the nations. It was, of course, sheer theft. The valuables taken were not the property of the invaders. **How long must this go on?** How long would these evil aggressors be permitted to retain their ill-gained plunder? (Cf. Habakkuk's "How long?" about Judah's violence, Hab. 1:2.)

2:7. The question in verse 6 was answered by two other questions. **Will not your debtors suddenly arise?** The victimized nations would suddenly arise in revolt. The debtors (lit., "biters") would unexpectedly strike back. They would not only get their bite of the stolen goods but also give their aggressors a good shakedown. **Will they not wake up and make you tremble?** That shake would not be a handshake. With hurricane force the evil creditor would be shaken as a violent wind shakes the leaves and branches off a tree. Babylon would **become their victim,** the victim of the very nations she had victimized. Babylon who had attacked (cf. 1:6, 8-10) and extorted (1:6, 16) would now herself be attacked and extorted.

2:8. The spoiler would be spoiled, for the **plundered** would suddenly rise to **plunder.** The **nations** subdued by Babylon but not destroyed, **the peoples who are left,** would lead the encounter. The boomerang would spin back. Babylon's intimidation and inhumanity would recoil on their own heads. They would reap what they had sown (Prov. 22:8; Gal. 6:7). They had ruthlessly **shed man's blood** and had recklessly ravaged (cf. Hab. 1:17; 2:17) both **lands and cities** (lit., "land and city," in the collective sense). "Blood" is literally "bloods." "Bloodshed" in verse 12 and "blood" in verse 17 are also "bloods" (pl.). Now Babylon would suffer the penalty for her crimes (cf. 1:12).

2. WOE FOR INTEMPERANCE (2:9-11)

2:9. Not only were the Babylonians guilty of **unjust gain** (vv. 6-8), but they also used that plunder for self-aggrandizement. They sought their own exaltation. Like an eagle setting **his nest** inaccessible to all predators by building it **high** on a mountainside, the Babylonians sought to make their empire free from harm (**to escape the clutches of ruin**). From the low-lying valley of their homeland, these conquerors used their illegal gain to build a towering world empire.

2:10. To elevate themselves, the Babylonians trampled others down. Their building plans included **the ruin** (lit., "cutting off") **of many peoples** (cf. "nations" in 1:17; "nations" and "peoples" in 2:5; and "many nations" in v. 8). But their plan to destroy others in order to make themselves secure failed. A **house** built of tortured bodies and stark skeletons is not too habitable. In the fray to erect a monument, they constructed their own shameful (cf. "shame" in v. 16) mausoleum. Death became their due.

2:11. Intriguing witnesses in the trial that would yield the eventual death sentence were **the stones of the wall . . . and the beams of the woodwork.** Even if every single enemy were exterminated, the very stones and lumber would testify against the rapacious and cruel hands of the Babylonians that had fashioned these building materials to show off their empire's strength and glory. The stones and timber with which the houses and palaces were built had been obtained through plunder and injustice.

The exalted nest (v. 9) would be knocked from its lofty perch and the lavish palace would seal the deaths of its builders. The proud, intemperate building plans only served as evidence of God's forthcoming judgment on wicked Babylon.

3. WOE FOR INIQUITY (2:12-14)

2:12. The plunder mentioned in the first woe (vv. 6-8) and the pride exposed in the second woe (vv. 9-11) were both fed by the sin-sick perversity revealed in the third woe (vv. 12-14). It is as though the stones and timbers of Babylon's vast building projects took up the song here. **Woe to him who builds a city with bloodshed and establishes a town by crime!** The cities of the Babylonian Empire were built by the blood and sweat of enslaved peoples. Murder, bloodshed, oppression, and tyranny were the tools employed in this building project. (The word trans. "bloodshed" is the pl. of the Heb. noun "blood" and always signifies the guilt of murder; cf. the Heb. "bloods" in vv. 8, 17.)

2:13. In each of the previous stanzas of this dirge, the sins introduced by the woe exclaimed in the first verse of each stanza were further exposed in the two verses that followed. Here, however, attention is diverted to **the LORD Almighty** and His penetrating assessment of the sordid scene. It is a welcome break in the midst of the five distressing stanzas. The Lord Almighty, the Sovereign of the universe, declared that their ambitious work had been done in vain: **the people's labor is only fuel for the fire** (cf. Jer. 51:58). Their carefully hewn stones would serve as the altar and their ornately carved wood as kindling for the giant sacrificial fire that would leave Babylon in ashes. Habakkuk added **that the nations exhaust themselves for nothing.** All their work—the labor of Babylon or any nation like it—is a waste if it is wrought with bloodshed and crime.

2:14. By contrast, **the** entire **earth will** one day **be filled with the knowledge of the glory of the LORD, as the waters cover the sea.** The wearisome toil of a whole generation of boasting Babylonians provided a little fire and ended up as a heap of ashes in one corner of the earth. But God's everlasting glory will fill the entire earth! This verse is based on the declaration in Isaiah 11:9 with only minor alterations. (The earth filled with God's glory is also spoken of in Num. 14:21; Ps. 72:19; and Isa. 6:3.) Isaiah closed his description of the messianic kingdom (Isa. 11:1-9) by stating that the earth would be full of the knowledge of *the Lord.* Habakkuk stated that the earth would be filled with the knowledge of *His glory.* Isaiah dealt with the essence of the kingdom, Habakkuk with the establishment of the kingdom. Isaiah presented the fact, Habakkuk the act. God will overthrow and judge future Babylon (Rev. 17–18) and all ungodly powers (Rev. 19:19) represented by Babylon. The Lord's glory (Matt. 24:30) and majesty (2 Thes. 1:9) will be made evident in the Millennium and thereby acknowledged throughout the earth.

When the Messiah rules in His kingdom, knowledge of the Lord will be worldwide. Everyone will know of Him (cf. Jer. 31:34). So extensive and abundant will be that knowledge that it will be like water covering the sea. The jagged rocks of injustice and the slimy seaweed of sin will be covered with the smooth surface of God's righteousness.

4. WOE FOR INDIGNITY (2:15-17)

2:15. The fourth woe turns back to the sordid scene of the Babylonians' barbaric actions. The focus here is on the inhumanity and the indignity of the conqueror to his subjects. He is pictured as a drunkard giving **his neighbors** wine to intoxicate them so that he may indulge in some evil wantonness and expose his victims to shame. So the Babylonians added lust to their violence and drunkenness. Such action is severely condemned by God (Gen. 9:21-25). An alternate rendering of the phrase **pouring it from the wineskin** is "joining (to it) your wrath." In other words the Babylonians poured out more than wine. With the wine they mixed "wrath," a word related to "heat," signifying any violent passion. This was indeed a "mixed drink." Hate and passion were poured out together. The nations that were enticed, or more often forced, to partake of the Babylonians' poisonous mix fell like drunks and lay prostrate in shame and subjugation.

2:16. Those who gloated over the shame of their drunken victims would someday **be filled with shame** (cf. "shaming" in v. 10). Their glory was their shame. This perverted "glory" of the Babylonians contrasted sharply with God's preeminent glory (v. 14). Far from glory, the Babylonians reveled in shame and soon they would **drink,** fall down intoxicated, **and be exposed** as one who is "uncircumcised" (literal Heb.). To be uncircumcised was, to the Jews, to be scorned. The Babylonians had caused others to drink and be shamefully exposed (v. 15); later the tables would be turned (cf. v. 7) and *they* would be drunk and naked.

The cup that they must drink was **from the LORD's right hand,** a figure of divine retribution (cf. Isa. 51:17-23; Jer. 25:15-17; Lam. 4:21). On drinking God's judgment, Babylon would be covered with **disgrace.** "Shame" in the first line of Habakkuk 2:16 and "disgrace" in the last line translate similar Hebrew words, but the second of these is in an emphatic form in Hebrew (used only here in the OT). It signifies extreme contempt. The once-glorious Babylon was pictured as a disgraceful, contemptible drunk.

2:17. The reason for Babylon's abject shame was her **violence** (cf. 1:9) **done to Lebanon.** Lebanon, a nation north of Israel, was known for its abundance of cedar trees and wild **animals.** It had suffered the ruthless removal of timber for Babylonian buildings and the destructive slaughter of beasts that lived in the forests. The violence done to the forests would weigh on Babylon and its senseless hunting and killing of the fauna would **terrify** it.

The worst charge, however, was that of human bloodshed, already leveled against the Babylonians twice (2:8, 12). They had not only wrecked the forests and ravaged the hillsides, but had also ruined **lands and cities** (cf. v. 8) **and everyone in them.** The indignities on God's creation and His creatures would bring Babylon from apparent world glory to everlasting shame. God's great judgment would **overwhelm** her.

5. WOE FOR IDOLATRY (2:18-20)

2:18. The final stanza does not open with the hollow and ominous "Woe!" (That comes in v. 19.) Rather it begins with the penetrating question, **Of what value is an idol?** The answer is obvious. An idol (lit., "graven image," i.e., an idol carved out of wood or hewn from stone) and **an image** (lit., "molten image," i.e., an idol made by melting metal and casting it into a shape of a false god) were of no benefit. Whatever form or seeming beauty those objects may have had, they were still only blocks of wood or masses of metal. To trust in such an idol was to trust in an object **that teaches lies,** for people were deceived and deluded by it, thinking it could help them. But **idols** and images were lifeless. Since they were the worshipers' own creations, idols could not aid them (cf. v. 19). **Carved** or cast, they were dumb objects. The oracles attributed to them were obvious lies, for idols **cannot speak.**

2:19. God expressed His condemnation of the insidious sin of idolatry. **Woe**

to him who says to wood, Come to life! Or to lifeless stone, Wake up! How absurd it is to stand before a piece of wood or some cold stone and cry out, "Arise! Awake!" The scene is like the prophets of Baal when they were taunted by Elijah (1 Kings 18:26-29).

No help or **guidance** comes from a lifeless object even if it is encased in **gold and silver** (cf. Isa. 40:19). It has **no breath** or spirit and therefore no life (cf. Gen. 2:7). Isaiah frequently taunted the Babylonians for their trust in numerous false gods, which were nothing but man-made idols (Isa. 41:7; 44:9-20; 45:16, 20; 46:1-2, 6-7; cf. Jer. 10:8-16). Idols are valueless for they cannot talk, come alive, guide, or breathe. And idolatry—worshiping man's carvings rather than the Creator—stands condemned under God's woe.

2:20. The last verse of this stanza is unique. In the other four "woe" stanzas each concluding verse starts in the Hebrew with "for" (*kî*, vv. 8, 11, 14, 17). However, verse 20 opens with "but." The contrast is marked and the climax is marvelous: **But the LORD is in His holy temple.** From dumb, man-carved idols, attention shifts to the living Lord, the self-existent, eternal (cf. 1:12; 3:6), holy (cf. 1:12; 3:3) Sovereign who rules the universe from His holy temple, that is, heaven (cf. Pss. 11:4; 18:6, 9; Micah 1:2-3). Instead of shouting, "Arise! Awake," the whole **earth** must stand in **silent** awe and worship **before Him.** The Hebrew word *hāsâh*, rendered "be silent," means "hush" (also used in Zeph. 1:7, "Be silent," and Zech. 2:13, "Be still").

For Habakkuk, the message was clear. Stop complaining! Stop doubting! God is not indifferent to sin. He is not insensitive to suffering. The Lord is neither inactive nor impervious. He is in control. In His perfect time Yahweh will accomplish His divine purpose. Habakkuk was to stand in humble silence, a hushed expectancy of God's intervention. The closing verse of this woeful dirge recorded by Habakkuk serves as a link to the song of worship that follows in Habakkuk 3.

III. A Doxology to God: Habakkuk Praised God's Design of Creation (chap. 3)

The distressed prophet, who complained over the unchecked sin in his country, was amazed at God's disclosure that He had already prepared an instrument to judge Judah, namely, Babylon. Habakkuk was shocked. He expressed his dilemma to God and waited for an answer. That answer came in the form of a dirge, or taunt-song, that Habakkuk was instructed to record. Learning of God's just plan to destroy Babylon, Habakkuk bowed in humble adoration. His majestic prayer and hymn of praise followed.

Chapter 3 is the culmination and climax of Habakkuk's book, contrary to the contentions of some scholars who would make this chapter a separate entity that he wrote much later. Others consider this chapter a document written by some other author, a second person also named Habakkuk or a second person who assumed Habakkuk's name.

Despite the arguments about change of style and a separate title, the third chapter fits well in the flow of the book. The new style fits the new subject, just as the shift from the dialogue in chapter 1 to the dirge in chapter 2 indicated a changing emphasis. Furthermore, the title in 3:1 provides a clear break in the change, as "the ramparts" announced the shift at chapter 2.

When the Dead Sea Scrolls Commentary on Habakkuk, which included only chapters 1 and 2, was discovered at Qumran, those who held to the disjointed theory felt they had won their case. But the issue is not so easily conceded. The ancient commentator may well have used only the parts of the book that suited his purpose. This scroll is not proof that a chapter 3 did not exist. It is more reasonable to see the thematic unity of Habakkuk. Chapter 3 is not a postscript; it is a pinnacle of praise. It is the mountaintop destination of a journey that began in a valley of distress.

A. Habakkuk's prayer for mercy (3:1-2)

3:1. At the opening of chapter 2, Habakkuk had positioned himself to await God's reply and to determine how he might respond to the Lord concerning his complaint (2:1). He then recorded God's extensive reply (2:2-20). Now the prophet gave his response to God. It was no protest, however. It was a prayer of praise as indicated by its simple title: **A prayer of Habakkuk the prophet.**

This heading resembles that of several psalms, in which the contents, the author, and the poetical character of the song are indicated (cf., e.g., Pss. 16; 30; 45; 88; 102; 142). Habakkuk again identified himself as a prophet, as he had done at the beginning of his book (Hab. 1:1).

The word *shigionoth* is somewhat obscure. In Hebrew it is the plural of the noun that appears elsewhere only in the title to Psalm 7 where it is in a slightly different form rendered *"shiggaion"* in the NIV. It seems to be related to a verb meaning "to reel to and fro." Thus some see this as an erratic song of enthusiastic irregularity sometimes used in songs of triumph or victory, or an elegy or plaintive song of variant chords. It is unlikely that it refers to the content of the song, even though the Hebrew root verb may also mean "to transgress or err." But the theme is not directed to the transgressions or wanderings of Babylon and Judah; the song centers on the majesty of God. Therefore it is much more reasonable to see *shigionoth* as having a musical-liturgical significance. Another musical notation is found at the end of Habakkuk 3. Possibly this song became a part of the temple worship.

3:2. Habakkuk had **heard** God's purposes to discipline Judah and destroy Babylon. The report filled him with **awe.** God's plans were beyond human understanding and God's preeminence beyond comprehension. The reaction to what he "heard" (lit., "Yahweh I have heard the hearing of You") was to fear God (lit., "I am afraid").

The prophet then expressed two petitions. He prayed for a fresh manifestation of God's power (**Renew them,** i.e., **Your deeds**) and a full measure of God's pardon. Both might and **mercy** were requested. These were the only petitions in his entire prayer.

The first request for renewal or revival of God's intervention was twice linked to time: **in our day** and **in our time** (lit., "in the midst of the years" on both occasions). It seems that the prophet desired a prompt fulfillment. God had, of course, already promised it (1:5).

The prophet's second request evolved from the first. In these acts of judgment (**wrath**; cf. 3:8, 12) Habakkuk pleaded for mercy.

After he expressed the two petitions

he wrote what is more appropriately considered a hymn of praise than a prayer (vv. 3-19). In it Habakkuk recalled the awesome deeds the Lord had performed in bringing His people from Egypt through the wilderness and into the Promised Land. Recounting those deeds gave the prophet confidence that God could also deliver His people from Babylon.

B. God's presence of majesty (3:3-15)

Habakkuk's telephone-like conversation with God in chapter 1 became more like a closed-circuit television hookup in chapter 2. The audio connection (chap. 1) was enhanced by visuals witnessed from Habakkuk's ramparts (2:1). Then suddenly the prophet was ushered into the very presence of the Creator with whom he had spoken so boldly from a distance. The prophet stood face-to-face, so to speak, with the sovereign Lord (cf. Job 42:5).

1. GOD'S ARRIVAL (3:3A)

3:3a. As God came down to His people at Sinai to establish His covenant with them, so He would come to liberate His people and reaffirm His covenant with them. Habakkuk wrote of God's earlier visitation at Sinai: **God came from Teman, the Holy One** (cf. 1:12) **from Mount Paran.** Moses had said the Lord's appearance was like a light shining "from Seir . . . and from Mount Paran" (Deut. 33:2).

Teman was a desert oasis in Edom but it might also represent the entire region south of the Dead Sea. "Seir," used by Moses, was a poetic name for the mountainous region referred to as Teman. Paran lies west of Edom across the valley Ghor, between the Sinai Peninsula to the south and Kadesh Barnea to the north, another mountainous area.

It may be of some significance that God's appearance to Moses was in the region south of Judah while the Babylonians invaded from the north. Furthermore, it was in this area to the south that God performed many wonders as He led His people into the Promised Land from Egypt.

The term normally used for "God," the plural 'ĕlōhîm, is used in this verse in the singular, 'ĕlôah, which may stress the

essential unity of the divine Deliverer, "the Holy One."

What is generally considered another musical notation, **Selah** (Hab. 3:3, 9, 13), probably indicates a pause in the song. (In the NIV "Selah" is in the right-hand marg., whereas in other versions it is within the verses.) "Selah" is used elsewhere only in the Psalms, where it occurs 71 times. The Hebrew verb from which the term comes means "to exalt, to lift up." It may mean a pause (a) to elevate to a higher key or increase the volume, (b) to reflect on what has been sung and exalt the Lord in praise, or (c) to lift up certain instruments for something like a trumpet fanfare. Whatever its meaning, an obvious break was intended in the middle of Habakkuk 3:3.

2. GOD'S APPEARANCE (3:3B-7)

3:3b. At Sinai God had come like an awesome thunderstorm sweeping down from the mountainous region in the south. As **His glory covered the heavens,** the sun and the moon appeared pale in comparison. God's shimmering glory not only filled the heavens but **His praise filled the earth.** "Praise" probably refers not to the response of mankind but to the reality of God's fame. God's revelation of Himself encompassed the heavens and penetrated to the uttermost parts of the earth.

3:4. The prophet indicated a progressive quality to God's appearance by comparing **His splendor** to a **sunrise.** The heavens are first tinted with early **rays** of the hidden sun, then the earth is illuminated as the ball of fire appears over the horizon, and finally everything is flooded with brilliant, glorious light. Just as rays of light streak across the morning sky, so rays **flashed from** God's **hand.** As God advanced, the all-pervading light was traced to its source, the hand of the Lord. The rays (lit., "horns") emanated from God as they do from the sun. People often illustrate a sunrise by drawing a circle surrounded by lines, cones, or horns, a rather crude but nevertheless effective way of depicting radiance. Interestingly the Hebrew verb "to send out rays," related to the Hebrew noun for "horns," was used to describe Moses' countenance after he had come down from Mount Sinai: "his face was radiant" (lit., "his face sent out rays of light," Ex. 34:29-30, 35). This accounts for the strange horns emanating from Michelangelo's famed statue of Moses.

God's radiance is both emanating and concealing. It reveals His glory but veils **His power.** It is easy to forget that the light and warmth which showers the earth with blessing comes from a ball of fire that could consume the globe in a moment. So God's power is **hidden** in His glory. His revelation is restrained lest it consume its beholders.

3:5. God is fully capable of exercising His might. He is a terrifying God to those who oppose Him. Habakkuk saw that as God moved across the land, **plague** preceded **Him** and **pestilence** (lit., "burning heat" or "bolts of fire") lay in **His** wake. At His will God can strike down His enemies with plagues (as in the 10 plagues on Egypt, Ex. 7:14–11:10) or with pestilence (cf. Deut. 32:24). The pestilence here may refer to some disease that is accompanied with a burning fever or to the charring of the earth by lightning bolts. God is not a little old man upstairs who dotes on people with sweetness and light. He is all-powerful as He is all-loving. His grace and glory are coupled with might and majesty.

3:6. Habakkuk's vision of God coming from the distance and marching across the land rose to a climax. Having reached the place from which He would execute judgment, God stopped, **stood, and shook the earth.** His very presence caused the earth to shake. Furthermore, by a mere glance at **the nations** He caused them to **tremble** (lit., "leap in terror") and even the framework of nature was shattered. **The** primeval **mountains** and **age-old hills,** the firmest constituents of the globe, **crumbled** into dust. He came down on Mount Sinai with thunder, lightning, and fire amidst shaking mountains (Ex. 19:16-19). Though the age-old (lit., "eternal") hills **collapsed,** God's everlasting ways go on. Here is a stark warning to those who honor the creation over the Creator! (Cf. Hab. 2:19-20.)

3:7. Witnesses to God's appearance at the Exodus and in the wilderness wanderings were **Cushan** and **Midian,** nations that lay on either side of the Red Sea (or Cushan may be another name for Midian). God's wondrous acts at the Red Sea (when He led His people from Egyp-

tian captivity) threw neighboring nations into terror and they experienced **distress** (fear) and **anguish.** Other nations too heard of God's mighty acts and were in fear (Ex. 15:14-16; Deut. 2:25; Josh. 2:9; 5:1). Reference to the people's **tents** and **dwellings** (lit., "tent hangings") seems to emphasize their precarious state. If the mountains melted away, what hope was there for those who huddled under canvas?

3. GOD'S ACTIONS (3:8-15)

Habakkuk's attention was now drawn from the awesome appearance of God to a description of God's acts on earth. This section of the ode is introduced in verse 8 by a series of questions that serve as a literary interruption to give life and vitality to the message and to provoke the reader to think about its implications. The questions are in a poetic style that expects no answer. They are thought-questions.

a. In nature (3:8-11)

3:8. Three questions center on God's motive for His appearance: Was God showing His wrath at **the rivers?** And at **the streams?** And at **the sea?** In other words, was God **angry** with nature? While direct answers are not given, a no answer was implied. God is not displeased with nature. He was using nature as a tool to demonstrate His power (cf. vv. 12-13). God had exhibited His power by smiting the Nile River (Ex. 7:20-21), the Red Sea (Ex. 14:15-28; 15:8-10; cf. Ps. 78:13), and the Jordan River (Josh. 3:14-17). Similarly God would smite the nations. His motive was to destroy His enemies and deliver His people. God was seen as a victor riding forth **with** His **horses** (cf. Hab. 3:15) and **chariots** in majestic power. What a contrast with the Babylonians' horses (1:8-9) that would eventually be stopped when Babylon fell a few decades later, in 539 B.C. (cf. 2:6-8).

3:9. God **uncovered** His **bow,** that is, He pulled it from its sheath for ready action. The statement translated **You called for many arrows** is an enigma in Hebrew. One scholar claimed he found more than 100 translations of this short phrase of three Hebrew words (*š^eḇu'ôṯ maṭṭôṯ 'ōmer*). The first word may be rendered "seventh" (related to Sabbath), "oath," or "sworn." *Maṭṭôṯ* may be "branches," "rods," "staves," or "tribes." (The NIV has "arrows," in parallel with the word "bow.") *'Ōmer*, a word used exclusively in poetry, denotes "a discourse," "a word," or "an affair or occasion." (NIV has "You called.") Perhaps a reasonable and somewhat literal translation is, "Staves [arrows] are sworn by a word." There is a certain seriousness about God's action here. By solemn oath He affirmed that His weapons were employed. The NIV captures this thought of God's confirming His use of arrows by saying He "called for" them.

The parallel between this verse and parts of Deuteronomy 32 is striking. The Song of Moses speaks of a consuming fire (Deut. 32:22), pestilence and plagues (Deut. 32:24), and arrows drunk with blood (Deut. 32:42) as part of His oath for vengeance against His adversaries (Deut. 32:41).

Whatever the translation of this rather minor phrase in Habakkuk's ode, there is another call by the word *Selah* to stop and meditate. God's motive and His majestic power were seen in His actions in nature, among the nations, and against His enemies. The effect of God's power is seen in the way He creases the earth's surface **with rivers.**

3:10. In personifying **the mountains,** Habakkuk said they added their reaction to God's presence and power, for they **saw** God **and writhed.** The Hebrew verb translated "writhed" depicts a person twisting or turning while seized with pangs like a woman in childbirth. Earlier (v. 6) the prophet had said that mountains crumble before God; now he said they writhe. Mount Sinai had quaked when God appeared to Moses (Ex. 19:18; Ps. 114:4, 6-7). To the witness of rivers (Hab. 3:9) and mountains (v. 10a), flooding waters moved in recognition of God's power. Underground waters of the abyss (**the deep**) were personified as speaking (**roared** is lit., "gave their voice"), and its high waves were personified as having hands: the deep **lifted its waves** (lit., "hands") **on high.** God's power can cause tremendous upheaval in nature! The Red Sea and the Jordan River had both responded to God's command (cf. Pss. 77:16, 19; 114:3, 5).

3:11. In the chorus of nature, the **sun and moon stood still** (cf. Josh. 10:12-13), eclipsed by the dazzling majesty of God. They were pictured as being **in the heavens** (lit., "high or elevated dwelling places").

While all nature shook, the **arrows** and spears of God's wrath (His flashes of **lightning;** cf. Pss. 18:14; 77:17) sped to their targets. Sun and moon paled before the brilliance of the lightning flashes, which perhaps accompanied the hail that destroyed Israel's enemies near Gilgal (Josh. 10:11). In His wrath God often used and controlled the forces of nature.

b. Among the nations (3:12-15)

3:12. Habakkuk envisioned God as being like a thundering giant who **strode through the earth.** God was hardly "tiptoeing through the tulips." **In wrath** (cf. vv. 2, 8) He had **threshed the nations.** As an ox treads the grain to beat out and crush the chaff, so God marched across the earth to crush sinful people and bring salvation to Israel. And the prophet was confident God would do it again.

3:13. The motive of God's judgment is clear. His anger was not vented toward nature (cf. v. 8) or against everybody. His purpose was to crush **wickedness** and **deliver** His own. Special deliverance was the goal behind God's destruction. Salvation was for God's people, but it was also for the **anointed One,** a term never used in the Old Testament for the nation Israel. The term probably refers to the coming Messiah (cf. Ps. 2:2; Dan. 9:26). By preserving the people of Israel (delivering them from Egypt and then later from Babylonian Captivity), God maintained the line for the Messiah.

God, Habakkuk said, **crushed the leader of the land** (lit., "head of the house") and **stripped him.** The figure in the Hebrew is that of a building from which the gable is ripped off and then the entire structure demolished, so that the foundations are laid bare. So God had destroyed Pharaoh's horsemen who pursued Israel (Ex. 14:23-28) and other leaders (Num. 21:23-25; Josh. 6:2; 8:28-29; 10–11). If God could do this, He could destroy Babylon. Belshazzar, also a "leader" in a "land of wickedness," was stripped of his power (Dan. 5:26-28, 30-31).

Again, the musical score of this dreadful ode called for a pause. The third and final *Selah* is inserted (cf. comments on Hab. 3:3). The utter and absolute ruin of those who oppose God elicits meditation. Before God charged in for the final slaughter of the wicked people, He called for a moment of reflection while the dust settled from the devastating blow that crushed the Babylonian fortress.

3:14. These final two verses of this ode on God's awesome self-revelation speak of the ultimate destruction of the enemy. Thrown into panic, those who sought to destroy Israel would destroy each other with their own weapons, as the **warriors** (lit., "village hoards") **stormed** into battle. Apparently the prophet had identified himself with those the Babylonians sought **to scatter,** for he referred to the enemies' target (Judah) as **us** (lit., "me").

The barbaric hordes were also described as bandits who were **gloating** (a word meaning "rejoicing or exulting," used only here in the OT) over the helpless, **wretched** victims they were about to rob. Their gloating would turn to gore, their pride to panic, and they would suddenly attack one another in deadly confusion. It is not clear which event in Israel's history this refers to.

3:15. The awesome recital of God's acts came to a crashing conclusion with a reference to one of the most spectacular of His miracles. He took His people through the Red Sea and then delivered the pursuing Egyptians to their watery grave (Ex. 14:15-18; 15:8-10). God's victory over Egypt's horsemen was pictured figuratively as if He Himself had **trampled the sea with** His own **horses** and chariots (cf. Hab. 3:8). In this victory God had churned **the great waters** (cf. v. 10).

C. Habakkuk's peace in ministry (3:16-19)

Obviously anyone who witnessed this amazing display of God's power would be left in awe. Habakkuk was no exception. He had asked for a show of God's might (v. 2). Little did he realize what a display it would be.

3:16. The prophet's **heart pounded,** his **lips quivered,** and his **legs trembled.** Habakkuk was about to collapse from this amazing encounter with God. He felt as though his **bones** were in a state of **decay** and his nervous system was all unraveled. In his weakened state, however, his confidence and hope were renewed. He found a new sense of peace and purpose in his prophetic ministry. He said he would **wait patiently** (lit., "rest") **for the day of calamity to come on the nation invading** Judah. The prophet was determined to wait for that day which would be filled with destruction and yet be a day of victory and vindication over wicked Babylon. God's deeds on Israel's behalf in Egypt, at the Red Sea, at Mount Sinai, at the Jordan River, and in the Conquest of Canaan were unquestionably awe-invoking. This review of God's power in the past assured the prophet that God would provide a similar deliverance for Israel from Babylon. Habakkuk was confident that someday God would again "renew" (v. 2) those acts of power, with "wrath" on Babylon and "mercy" (v. 2) on Judah.

3:17. The prophet's weakened physical state contrasted with his incredibly strong spiritual state. Habakkuk outlined the worst possible consequences: complete failure of crops (figs, **grapes,** olives, and grain—on which the nation depended for food) and total loss of **sheep** and **cattle.** Even in the midst of absolute ruin and abject famine (which came when the Babylonians captured Jerusalem, Lam. 2:12, 20, 4:4, 9-10; 5:17-18), the prophet was prepared to trust God. He realized that inner peace did not depend on outward prosperity.

3:18. Habakkuk did not state that he would merely endure in the hour of distress. He said he would **rejoice in the** Lord and **be joyful.** God is the inexhaustible source and infinite supply of joy. **God my Savior** is literally, "the God of my salvation" (*'ĕlōhê yiš'i*; the same Heb. words are in Pss. 18:46; 25:5). Far too many people keep trying to buy joy, but happiness is not found in circumstances. Joy is available to everyone, even to those stripped of every material possession, for joy is to be found in a Person. It comes through an intimate and personal relationship with the Lord, so that even those in the worst circumstances can smile.

3:19. The unfailing source of **strength** and confidence necessary to satisfaction and contentment is **the Sovereign** (*'ădōnāy*) Lord (*Yahweh*) Himself. The strength He gives is like the power found in **the feet of a deer,** a gazelle, or any active, swift-footed animal. Much as a deer can quickly bound through a dark forest, so the prophet said he could move joyfully through difficult circumstances. Though his legs trembled (v. 16) at the awesome theophany of God, that same Lord was His joy (v. 18), strength (v. 19), and assurance. Furthermore, God enabled the prophet to walk **on the heights.** Not only would he bound through trials; he would also climb to the mountaintops of victory and triumph. The poetic language of this verse is common in other passages (e.g., Deut. 32:13; 2 Sam. 22:34; Ps. 18:33). A deer or gazelle pictures strength, surefootedness, beauty, and speed.

The concluding words, **For the director of music. On my stringed instruments,** serve as an addendum and are related to the heading of the prophet's doxological ode (Hab. 3:1). They refer to the use of this song in worship. The prophet appointed his psalm for use in public worship accompanied by players with stringed instruments. The sour drone of Habakkuk's complaining (1:2-4, 12–2:1) was replaced by vibrant chords of hope and happiness.

The Sovereign Lord gives triumph over circumstances to those who trust Him. The way to get out from under the load is to get right under the Lord. To be under the Lord is to be over the circumstances. That lesson is worth the price of the book, especially when the world seems like a cesspool of quicksand.

Habakkuk was about to "go under" when he started this book. Destruction, violence, strife, conflict, injustice, and wickedness were all he could see. But he cried out to God and his cry did not go unheeded. The Lord not only answered his complaint but also provided the confidence needed to lift him from the quagmire. Habakkuk started in the pits, but ended on the mountaintop. His journey was not exactly an easy one, but it was certainly worth it.

God directed Habakkuk through the *dialogue* (chap. 1) in which He revealed His plans for disciplining Judah and destroying Babylon. Then at God's command Habakkuk recorded a woeful *dirge* (chap. 2) that further justified God's judgment on Babylon. Finally, the prophet reached a pinnacle of praise in which God revealed Himself in all His glory and power. The *doxology* (chap. 3)

concluded with Habakkuk's unwavering trust in the Lord.

The prophet's complaints were swallowed up by confidence. His fear turned to faith. Habakkuk was transformed from a sour, jittery prophet weighed down with burdens to a secure, joyous preacher bouyed up with blessing. The just, the upright, the happy, the contented, the victorious live by their faith. Yes, faith *is* the victory that overcomes the world! (1 John 5:4)

BIBLIOGRAPHY

Eaton, J.H. *Obadiah, Nahum, Habakkuk and Zephaniah.* Torch Bible Commentaries. London: SCM Press, 1961.

Feinberg, Charles L. *The Minor Prophets.* Chicago: Moody Press, 1976.

Freeman, Hobart E. *Nahum, Zephaniah, Habakkuk: Minor Prophets of the Seventh Century B.C.* Everyman's Bible Commentary. Chicago: Moody Press, 1973.

Fuerbringer, L. *The Eternal Why.* St. Louis: Concordia Publishing House, 1947.

Gaebelein, Frank E. *Four Minor Prophets: Obadiah, Jonah, Habakkuk, and Haggai.* Chicago: Moody Press,1977.

Gowan, Donald E. *The Triumph of Faith in Habakkuk.* Atlanta: John Knox Press, 1976.

Ironside, H.A. *Notes on the Minor Prophets.* Neptune, N.J.: Loizeaux Brothers, 1909.

Keil, C.F. "Habakkuk." In *Commentary on the Old Testament in Ten Volumes.* Vol. 10. Reprint (25 vols. in 10). Grand Rapids: Wm. B. Eerdmans Publishing Co., 1982.

Lloyd-Jones, D. Martin. *From Fear to Faith.* Reprint. Grand Rapids: Baker Book House, 1982.

Pusey, E.B. *The Minor Prophets: A Commentary.* Vol. 2. Grand Rapids: Baker Book House, 1950.

Stoll, John H. *The Book of Habakkuk.* Grand Rapids: Baker Book House, 1972.

Tatford, Frederick A. *The Minor Prophets.* Vol. 2. Reprint (3 vols.). Minneapolis: Klock & Klock Christian Publishers, 1982.

Ward, William Hayes. "Habakkuk." In *A Critical and Exegetical Commentary on Micah, Zephaniah, Nahum, Habakkuk, Obadiah, and Joel.* The International Critical Commentary. Edinburgh: T. & T. Clark, 1911.

ZEPHANIAH

John D. Hannah

INTRODUCTION

Title. The name "Zephaniah," which is also borne by three other men in the Old Testament, means "Yahweh hides," "Yahweh has hidden," or "Yahweh treasured." This may point to God's protection of His people during the impending difficulties in Zephaniah's day, or to God's protection of Zephaniah in his childhood during Manasseh's wicked reign (2 Kings 21:16).

Author. Beyond the information given in Zephaniah 1:1, little is known about this prophet. His ancestry is traced back four generations, which is unique among the prophets. This implies he was a man of prominence and even of royalty. As the great-great-grandson of Hezekiah, king of Judah, Zephaniah was the only known Old Testament prophet with such high social standing. He was thus a distant relative of King Josiah in whose reign he prophesied. Also the prophet may have been a resident of Jerusalem because of his words "from this place" (v. 4) and his familiarity with the city (vv. 10-11).

Date. According to 1:1, Zephaniah's ministry was during the reign of King Josiah (640–609 B.C.). Scholars differ on whether the prophet ministered before or after the recovery of the Law by Hilkiah and the subsequent religious revival in 622 B.C. (2 Kings 22–23; 2 Chron. 34). Probably Zephaniah's prophecy was given after Josiah's revival, for these reasons. (1) Cutting off the remnant of Baal worship (Zeph. 1:4) implied that a religious awakening was in progress. (2) Jeremiah, who prophesied long after 622 (as well as before), described Judah's religious and moral condition much as did Zephaniah (cf. Jer. 8:2; 19:13 with Zeph. 1:5; cf. Jer. 5:2, 7 with Zeph. 1:5b; and cf. Jer. 8:8-9 with Zeph. 3:4). (3) The fact that the king's sons wore foreign apparel (1:8)

suggests that they were old enough to make their own choices. (4) Zephaniah's frequent quotations of the Law suggest that he was using the sources discovered by Hilkiah (cf. v. 13 with Deut. 28:30, 39; cf. Zeph. 1:15 with Deut. 4:11; cf. Zeph. 1:17 with Deut. 28:29; and cf. Zeph. 2:2 with Deut. 28:15-62). (5) Zephaniah's message of impending judgment would be appropriate for those who spurned the religious revival under Josiah. Thus his prophecy was given sometime after the time of Josiah's revival in 622, but before the destruction of Nineveh in 612—which Zephaniah indicated was still in existence then (Zeph. 2:13) as the capital of the Assyrian Empire.

Setting. Politically Judah was benefiting from a power vacuum among the superpowers of the day, so much so that King Josiah extended his influence militarily as far north as Naphtali. At that time Assyria—which had carried off the 10 Northern tribes in 722 B.C., under Sargon II—was rapidly suffering eclipse. When Sin-shar-ishkun (623–612 B.C.), Ashurbanipal's son, was reigning over Assyria, the Neo-Babylonian Empire began to emerge under Nabopolassar in 626. Also the Medes, under Cyaxares II in 625, pulled out from under Assyrian authority. So Josiah was encouraged to remove Assyrian religious practices from Judah. As a result Judah prospered politically. The collapse of the Assyrian Empire was delayed as the Egyptians under Psamtik I (664–609) allied with them, but a coalition of Medes and Babylonians destroyed Assyria's capital city, Nineveh, in 612.

Before Josiah's reign, Manasseh (695–642) and Manasseh's son Amon (642–640) had introduced wicked practices into Judah. Manasseh built altars to Baal and worshiped the sun, moon, and stars. He built altars to these stellar objects and placed them in the temple courts (2 Kings 21:4-5) and he made a

161

carved Asherah pole (an image of the goddess Asherah) and placed it in the temple (2 Kings 21:7). Child sacrifice and astrology prospered (2 Kings 21:6; 23:10-11). King Amon, who may have been named after an Egyptian deity, continued his father's policies until his assassination (2 Kings 21:19-26; 2 Chron. 33:21-25). Josiah succeeded Amon in 640 at the age of 8. In 632, at age 16, Josiah began to seek after the God of his forefather David. In 628, Josiah started a reform movement in which much of the idolatry was purged from Jerusalem and Judah. About that time Jeremiah (627) commenced his ministry and Judah moved toward independence from Assyria with a possible revival of the idea of an undivided kingdom like that of David and Solomon. Then in the 18th year of Josiah's reign (622) a copy of the Law was discovered by Hilkiah the high priest (2 Kings 22:3-8). This accentuated the religious renewal including a new enthusiasm for celebrating the Passover (2 Kings 23:1-25). Unfortunately the promising reform movement was superficial for it did not deeply affect the politico-religious life of the nation. Worship of Yahweh was reestablished, but idolatry was not entirely removed. Both Zephaniah and Jeremiah prophesied to a politically prospering people of coming judgment because Josiah's reform movement still went unheeded.

Theme. "The day of the LORD" is an expression used more frequently in this prophecy than in any other Old Testament book. Thus the theme of the book is the impending judgment of God on Judah for its disobedience. A corollary of the judgment motif within Zephaniah and the other prophets is the preservation of the true remnant by the mercies of the covenant-keeping God. Though judgment was sure, God's promise to protect His people and fulfill His promises was steadfast and everlasting. The book's theme is capsuled in Zephaniah 1:7a: "Be silent before the Sovereign LORD, for the day of the LORD is near."

OUTLINE

I. Introduction (1:1)
II. The Day of Yahweh's Judgment (1:2–3:8)

A. Judgment on all the earth (1:2-3)
B. Judgment on Judah and Jerusalem (1:4–2:3)
  1. The objects of judgment (1:4-13)
    a. The idolaters (1:4-7)
    b. The princes (1:8)
    c. The oppressors (1:9)
    d. The merchants (1:10-11)
    e. The indifferent (1:12-13)
  2. The description of judgment (1:14-18)
    a. The nearness (1:14a)
    b. The horror (1:14b-18)
  3. The deterrent to judgment (2:1-3)
    a. A summons to the nation: Repent (2:1-2)
    b. A summons to the humble: Seek God (2:3)
C. Judgment on the surrounding nations (2:4-15)
  1. On Philistia (2:4-7)
  2. On Moab and Ammon (2:8-11)
  3. On Ethiopia (2:12)
  4. On Assyria (2:13-15)
D. Judgment on Jerusalem (3:1-7)
  1. The prophet's indictment (3:1-5)
  2. The Lord's judgment (3:6-7)
E. Judgment on all the earth (3:8)
III. The Day of Yahweh's Restoration (3:9-20)
A. The restoration of the nations (3:9-10)
B. The restoration of Israel (3:11-20)
  1. The redemption of the nation (3:11-13)
  2. The joy of the nation (3:14)
  3. The Ruler of the nation (3:15-17)
  4. The reward of the nation (3:18-20)

COMMENTARY

I. Introduction (1:1)

1:1. Zephaniah's introductory words, **The word of the LORD that came,** were also used by Hosea, Joel, and Micah at the beginnings of their books. (In the NIV Micah begins, "The word of the LORD given," but the Heb. is the same as in the other books mentioned.) This introduction along with the words **to Zephaniah** make the reader aware of both the Source of the message and the messenger; though the messenger is human, the message is from God and has His authority.

The biographical note on Zephaniah traces his lineage back four generations. Most prophets are traced only to their fathers (e.g., Jonah son of Amittai [Jonah 1:1]; Joel son of Pethuel [Joel 1:1]), though Zechariah's lineage is traced to his grandfather (Zech. 1:1). Zephaniah's careful delineation of his pedigree which included **Hezekiah** has led many scholars to assume Zephaniah's royalty (not all hold to this inference, however; cf. Laetsch, *The Minor Prophets*, p. 354).

II. The Day of Yahweh's Judgment (1:2–3:8)

Zephaniah's prophecy has two major themes: (a) the bold declaration of God's imminent wrath, which implies a serious call to repentance, and (b) the comforting words of the prophet that even in judgment God will not forget his covenantal mercies but will restore His people at a future time. In his initial section Zephaniah sounded a stern warning of doom. He began by pronouncing judgment on the earth (1:2-3) and concluded with the same theme (3:8). In the interim he dealt twice with Judah and/or Jerusalem (1:4–2:3; 3:1-7) and once with the surrounding nations (2:4-15). This is an interesting introversion pattern (*a*, *b*, *c*, *b¹*, *a¹*) illustrated in this way:

a Judgment on all the earth (1:2-3)
   b Judgment on Judah and Jerusalem (1:4–2:3)
      c Judgment on the surrounding nations (2:4-15)
   b¹ Judgment on Jerusalem (3:1-7)
a¹ Judgment on all the earth (3:8)

A. Judgment on all the earth (1:2-3)

1:2-3 With horrifying abruptness Zephaniah set forth the Lord's proclamation of universal judgment. Isaiah also wrote about God's worldwide judgment (Isa. 24:1-6, 19-23). In Zephaniah 1:2 the prophet spoke in general about judgment and in verse 3 he gave details of that judgment. God would bring about this judgment, in which He would **sweep away everything**. "Sweep away" (used three times in vv. 2-3) means "to gather

and take away, to remove, to destroy." This impending judgment on **the earth** would extend, Zephaniah said, to life on the land (**men and animals**), in the **air** (**birds**), and in the sea (**the fish**). Interestingly these four are in reverse order from Creation: fish (Gen. 1:20a), birds (Gen. 1:20b), livestock and wild animals (Gen. 1:24), and man (Gen. 1:26). So this destruction which Zephaniah saw is a kind of reversal of Creation. When God would **cut off** (cf. Zeph. 1:4; 3:6) **man,** the only thing left on **earth** would be ruins (**heaps of rubble**) of a once-prosperous past. Since Zephaniah later wrote that a remnant would be delivered (3:9-13), the universal destruction of mankind referred to in 1:2-3 would apparently be limited to **the wicked.** Jeremiah made this clear (Jer. 25:31-33).

B. Judgment on Judah and Jerusalem (1:4–2:3)

Having set forth in broad terms the major premise of impending doom, the prophet then focused on Judah and Jerusalem. In the Old Testament a generalized statement is often followed by detailed particulars (cf. Gen. 1:1 with Gen. 1:2-31).

This section (Zeph. 1:4–2:3) clearly indicates that Judah's wicked people would be destroyed at the Babylonian invasion of Jerusalem in 586 B.C. But how could Zephaniah at the same time write about *universal* judgment? (1:2-3) How could he turn so quickly from Judah's destruction in 586 to speak of the "day of the LORD" (v. 14), a yet-future event separated from that devastation in 586 by many centuries? When Babylon conquered Judah, judgment was not universal; so how could the two be related? One common answer is that every instance of divine judgment is called the day of the Lord. Another answer is that verses 2-3 and 3:8 refer not to universal judgment but to the Babylonian invasion described in words of hyperbole. Perhaps a better explanation is that Zephaniah saw Judah's destruction and universal judgment as *two parts of one grand event*, "the great day of the LORD" (1:14). The destruction of the prophet's own people would be so terrible that it was envisioned as ushering in God's day of wrath (v. 15; 2:2) on all the world's wicked. Later Zephaniah again associated God's judgment on the nations (3:6) and the whole world (3:8) with His judgment on Judah (3:1-5). The Babylonian destruction of Judah was thus a step in God's work of wrath on His people.

The day of the Lord (see comments under "Major Interpretive Problems" in the *Introduction* to Joel) was referred to by many of the prophets (Isa. 2:12; 13:6, 9; Jer. 46:10; Ezek. 13:5; 30:3; Joel 1:15; 2:1, 11, 31, 3:14; Amos 5:18, 20; Obad. 15; Zech. 14:1; Mal. 4:5). In several of these verses and in verses immediately before or after them the day of the Lord is associated with universal judgment (cf. Isa. 24).

1. THE OBJECTS OF JUDGMENT (1:4-13)

a. The idolaters (1:4-7)

1:4. The prophet informed his hearers that the Lord was about to **stretch out** His **hand** in judgment and wrath (cf. 2:13) on the Southern Kingdom and its capital, **Jerusalem.** Every aspect of **Baal** worship would be removed. Baal was the Canaanite god of fertility whom many in Israel had worshiped in the time of the Judges (Jud. 2:13) and in the time of Ahab (1 Kings 16:32). Baal worship involved terrible sexual acts. Manasseh, wicked king of Judah, had erected Baal altars (2 Chron. 33:3, 7), but his grandson Josiah destroyed them (2 Chron. 34:4). But this "revival" of Josiah's in 622 B.C. had no lasting effect. Baal was again being worshiped (cf. Jer. 19:5; 32:35). However, the time would come, Zephaniah wrote, when God would remove every last vestige of that pagan worship.

Zephaniah referred to two classes of priests. One group was **the pagan . . . priests,** non-Levitical appointees by the kings of Judah (2 Kings 23:5; cf. **idolatrous** "priests," the same Heb. word, in Hosea 10:5). The Hebrew word for "pagan priests" is *k*e*mārîm,* which means idol-priests, priests who prostrated themselves before idols. The other group was the idolatrous priests, Levitical priests who had defected from the worship of the true God to a superstitious faith.

1:5-6. After Zephaniah said that God would remove the false priests, he then referred to three forms of idolatrous worship, introducing each of them by the phrase **those who.** First, he noted the

worshipers of stellar bodies, people **who bow down on** flat **housetops** (cf. Jer. 19:13; 2:29) as star-worshipers—through which the powers of nature were supposedly harnessed. The sun, moon, and stars were regarded as deities. Though God had clearly warned against this practice (Deut. 4:19), Manasseh led the way in this perversion also (2 Kings 21:3, 5; cf. 2 Kings 23:4-5).

Second, Zephaniah mentioned **those who** attempted to combine the worship of Yahweh with the worship of **Molech,** a form of religious syncretism. Molech was the chief god of the Ammonites (1 Kings 11:33), a people east of the Dead Sea (cf. Zeph. 2:8-9). Jeremiah, a contemporary of Zephaniah, said the Jews were sacrificing children to Molech (Jer. 32:35; cf. 2 Kings 16:3; 21:6). The Hebrew *Malkām* (Zeph. 1:5, NIV marg.) is a variant spelling of "Molech." To **swear by** a deity meant to pronounce an oath under the threat of punishment by that deity if one failed to carry out his oath.

Third, the prophet spoke of others who were religiously indifferent and unconcerned about worshiping the true God (v. 6), though they may not have been worshiping other gods.

1:7. After citing three types of idolatry in Judah—the overtly pagan, the syncretistic, and the religiously indifferent—the prophet called on all of them to **be silent before** God (cf. Hab. 2:20) because of the imminence of **the day of the LORD.** This is the first of 19 references in Zephaniah to "the day," "that day," "a day," "the day of the LORD's wrath," and similar phrases referring to "the day of the LORD." (See comments on Zeph. 1:4–2:3 and 1:14.) Such impending judgment ought to evoke fear and silence. No more calling on Baal; no more invoking the stars; no more swearing by Molech—for now Yahweh, the only God, would act. They may have forgotten Him, but He would not forget them! In fact God **prepared** Judah like **a sacrifice,** that is, He prepared her for slaughter much as sacrificial animals were prepared to be eaten (cf. Isa. 34:6; Jer. 46:10). The **invited** guests, the Babylonians, were God's chosen instrument (cf. Jer. 10:25; Hab. 1:6) to eat the sacrifice; they had been **consecrated** or set apart to be the agent of God's judgment on His chosen nation.

b. The princes (1:8)

1:8. In addition to the idolaters (vv. 4-7) Judah's royalty were also the objects of God's scorn. They included **princes** (officers of the king's court; cf. Jer. 36:12; Hosea 8:4), Josiah's **sons,** and the aristocracy who evidenced their disobedience by wearing the latest fashions from Nineveh and Babylon (**foreign clothes**). Adopting foreign dress outwardly most likely implied that they also had absorbed foreign values and practices inwardly. Josiah's sons were certainly punished. His son Jehoahaz reigned only three months and then was captured by Pharaoh Neco II and taken to Egypt (2 Kings 23:31-34). Josiah's wicked son Jehoiakim, who reigned for 11 years (2 Kings 23:36), was defeated by Nebuchadnezzar (2 Kings 24:1-2). Jehoiakim's son Jehoiachin reigned only three months in 597 and was taken captive to Babylon (2 Kings 24:8-16). Then 11 years later Judah's last king, Zedekiah, another of Josiah's sons, was blinded by Nebuchadnezzar and taken to Babylon (2 Kings 24:18–25:7).

c. The oppressors (1:9)

1:9. God said He would **punish** not only false worshipers (vv. 4-6) and sinful political leaders (v. 8), but also those who plundered for material gain. **All who avoid stepping on the threshold** refers either to people who followed the Philistines' superstition about not stepping on a threshold (1 Sam. 5:5) or perhaps more likely to those who suddenly leaped into others' homes to pillage and steal. This is paralleled by the words **violence and deceit.** The gain of such robbery was then offered to pagan deities as objects of sacred worship. It was strange that pagan religious leaders condoned such violence and plundering.

d. The merchants (1:10-11)

1:10. To emphasize the thought that God's judgment would fall on every segment of Jewish society, Zephaniah noted that lamentations would arise from every quarter of Jerusalem (cf. the words "all who live in Jerusalem," v. 4). **The Fish Gate,** located in the northern sector, was the gate through which Nebuchadnezzar entered the city. It was given its name because of its proximity to the fish market. **The New Quarter** was northwest of

the temple area. The meaning of **the hills** is uncertain. They could refer to the whole city, or the hills on which Jerusalem was erected, or the hills surrounding the lower portion of the city (cf. Jer. 31:39). **A cry** and **wailing . . . and a loud crash** would go up from these areas because of the loss of lives as Nebuchadnezzar progressed through the city.

1:11. Zephaniah then singled out one area in the city—**the market** (or business) **district**—and said that those **who live** there would **wail** (cf. v. 10) because their businessmen (**merchants**) would **be wiped out** (lit., "will be silenced"). In the Tyropean Valley, running north to south and separating the city east and west, the merchants plied their **trade with silver** and grew rich through usury. Because they took advantage of others, God would judge them and they would **be ruined** (lit., "be cut off, killed"; cf. "cut off" in vv. 3-4).

e. The indifferent (1:12-13)

1:12. The Lord declared that He would make a diligent, comprehensive **search** throughout **Jerusalem** so that none would go unpunished. Josephus wrote about a later invasion in which the city's aristocracy were literally dragged from the sewer system where they hid for fear of death. Probably something like this also occurred when the Babylonians attacked Jerusalem. The analogy of **wine left on its dregs** suggests that the nation had become spiritually polluted. Wine allowed to ferment for a long time forms a hard crust and the liquid becomes syrupy, bitter, and unpalatable. Instead of removing the dregs of daily pollution, Judah had become hardened and indifferent to God. So great was her degeneration that the people did not even believe that Yahweh did as much as their self-made images. Pagan idolaters accorded their numerous deities the power of judging wrong and vindicating right. But the Jews at that time had such a low view of Yahweh that they believed He could not keep either His promises or His threats: He **will do nothing, either good or bad.** Their own spiritual complacency led them to think **the LORD** was complacent.

1:13. Zephaniah stated that Yahweh is not so weak and uninterested as the Jews thought because judgment is within both His power and His will. In this three-part verse the prophet first stated that God will cause the Jews' enemies to plunder the people's **wealth** and demolish **their houses.** This would be as God had predicted (Deut. 28:30). With both their money and their residences gone, they would have no physical security. God then stated that their effort to rebuild their **houses** and **plant** their **vineyards** would be futile. They would **not live** long enough to enjoy them.

2. THE DESCRIPTION OF JUDGMENT (1:14-18)

Having boldly pronounced Yahweh's impending judgment on the land of Judah by delineating the objects of His wrath, the prophet then described the devastation of that judgment.

a. The nearness (1:14a)

1:14a. To awaken the complacent (cf. v. 12) nation to its peril the prophet returned to the theme stated in verse 7, **the great day of the LORD.** Grammatically the verse stresses the word **near,** which is first in the sentence in Hebrew (cf. "near" in v. 7, where it also appears in this emphatic position). The fearful wrath of God was to come on the nation **quickly.** Since Zephaniah wrote shortly after 622 B.C., the year of Josiah's partial revival, the day of the Lord was in fact imminent. In 605, only 17 years after Josiah's revival, Judah under Jehoiakim became a vassal of Babylon and many of Judah's best young men were deported. Under Jehoiakim's equally wicked successor, Jehoiachin, the city was again besieged by Nebuchadnezzar in 597 and some 10,000 Jews were deported. Under Zedekiah the city was under a long siege by Nebuchadnezzar and was finally destroyed in the summer of 586. (For the relationship of this event to the day of the Lord see the comments under "B. Judgment on Judah and Jerusalem [1:4–2:3].")

b. The horror (1:14b-18)

Verses 14b-16 describe the physical characteristics of that awful day, while verses 17-18 describe the personal trauma of that judgment.

1:14b-16. The prophet began by calling the nation to hear his words (**Listen!**) for the **day** of Babylonian terror would cause the people to **cry** in bitterness and even the mighty Jewish **warrior** would retreat in fear and horror. The **wrath** of Almighty God on sinners (cf. v. 18; 2:2-3; 3:8) is depicted by such words as **distress . . . anguish . . . trouble . . . ruin . . . darkness . . . gloom . . . clouds, and blackness.** When the Babylonian soldiers did barge into the city, the Jerusalemites were distressed and in anguish; their houses were ruined, and the sky was dark from the smoke of the buildings set on fire. As the Babylonian hordes rushed to conquer, kill, and ravish, they sounded the **trumpet** and shouted in **battle** in their moves **against** not only Jerusalem but also other **fortified cities** in Judah. Soldiers at **the corner towers,** normally strongholds of defense against attacking enemies, were defenseless.

1:17. So great would be God's judgment, Zephaniah said, that the Jews in **distress** would wander about **like** helplessly **blind** people (cf. Deut. 28:28-29), unable to find any safe quarter. Such **distress** was not because of God's impersonal cruelty; it was retribution for their having **sinned against the LORD.** The inhabitants of Judah would be viciously killed; so much of **their blood** would be shed that it would be **like dust** on the streets. And their bodies would be cruelly ravished, with their innards piled up **like** the **filth** of dung piles.

1:18. They would have no hope of deliverance; their wealth (**silver** [cf. "silver" in v. 11] and **gold**) would not **be able to** buy off their attackers (cf. Ezek. 7:19). Zephaniah then returned to the theme of universal judgment (cf. Zeph. 1:2-3). **The whole world will be** destroyed and **all** its inhabitants will quickly (**He will make a sudden end**) be subjected to the wrath of God. All this will stem from **His jealousy,** His consuming passion and concern that His own people follow Him, not false gods.

3. THE DETERRENT TO JUDGMENT (2:1-3)

Having described the awful day of God's wrath on Judah, the prophet at last brought his readers to his purpose. His goal was not to bring the people to despair, but to repentance and obedience. As Matthew Henry so appropriately stated, Zephaniah intended "not to frighten them out of their wits, but to frighten them out of their sins" (*Commentary on the Whole Bible in One Volume,* p. 1168).

a. A summons to the nation: Repent (2:1-2)

2:1. Zephaniah urged the people, **Gather together,** perhaps to come collectively to repent as a nation. Repeating the command stressed the urgency of his appeal. The words **O shameful nation** are literally, "O nation not shamed." ("Shamed" is *niḳsāp,* from *kāsap,* "to be pale or white with shame." A related word *kesep* means "silver," the pale-colored metal mentioned in 1:11, 18.) Judah, because of her sin, was without shame (cf. 3:5); her face was not blushing or white or pale with embarrassment. Sin had hardened her sensitivity to sin (cf. 1:12).

2:2. The urgency of the prophet's summons is seen in this verse. The three phrases introduced by the word **before** emphasize the point. If the nation did not repent, it would soon be too late. The nation could prevent the impending judgment if their repentance, like that of Nineveh's, were immediate. The words **and that day sweeps on like chaff** function as a parenthesis to strengthen the first of the three clauses. Imminent repentance was imperative because the day of God's wrath was rapidly approaching, like light chaff driven forcefully by the wind. The words **anger** and **wrath** translate the same Hebrew word *'ap* (lit., "nostril," thus anger evident in hard breathing). **Fierce** (*ḥārôn*) means "burning," from *ḥārâh,* "to burn, to kindle" (cf. "fierce anger" in 3:8).

b. A summons to the humble: Seek God (2:3)

2:3. The prophet urged those who already know the Lord (as evidenced by their humble obedience to Him) to continue steadfast in their walk with Him. They were commanded to strive for three things: **the LORD . . . righteousness,** and **humility** (cf. 3:12). The last two result from following the Lord. If the remnant would seek the Lord, then they would **be sheltered** (lit., "hidden, concealed," from *sātar,* a synonym of *ṣāpan,* from which comes the name "Zephaniah") from the impending doom of God's **anger** (*'ap;* cf. 2:2). Though many died in the Babylonian invasions, others were spared and some were exiled to Babylon (2 Kings 24:14-16). God sheltered or protected His remnant.

C. Judgment on the surrounding nations (2:4-15)

Zephaniah turned from warning Judah to prophesy similar wrath on her equally idolatrous neighbors. God is the God of all the nations, and those nations that led Judah to stumble would not escape the fury of His wrath. Since He would punish Judah, He surely would not overlook the sins of others. Zephaniah began with the nation to Judah's west, Philistia (vv. 4-7), then moved east to Moab and Ammon (vv. 8-11), then south to Ethiopia (v. 12), and north to Assyria (vv. 13-15).

1. ON PHILISTIA (2:4-7)

2:4. The prophet predicted the destruction of four of Philistia's five major cities—**Gaza . . . Ashkelon . . . Ashdod,** and **Ekron,** mentioned in order from south to north (see the map "Israel and Surrounding Nations in the Days of the Prophets" before Isa.). The reason for Gath's being omitted is uncertain, but most scholars feel that the city had not recovered from Uzziah's devastation of it (2 Chron. 26:6). Or it may be that four rather than five are mentioned in order to maintain the literary symmetry of the verse's structure. (Amos 1:6-8 omits Gath also.) Fittingly the Hebrew words for "Gaza" (*'azzâh*) and **abandoned** (*'āzûḇâh*) are similar in sound, as are the words for "Ekron" (*'eqrôn*) and **uprooted** (*tē'āqēr*). Ashdod would be destroyed **at midday,** when many people would be eating or resting, not alert for an invasion.

2:5. The identity of the **Kerethite people** (cf. "Kerethites" in v. 6) is uncertain. The words are literally "nation of the Cretans," thus referring to some Cretans who migrated eastward and settled on the Mediterranean coastal plains, **by the sea.** (Kerethites are also mentioned in 1 Sam. 30:14; 2 Sam. 8:18; 20:23; 1 Chron. 18:17; Ezek. 25:16.) "Caphtor" in Jeremiah 47:4 and Amos 9:7 is another name for Crete. The name **Canaan** in the same verse also refers to the coastal plains. The Lord's pronouncement is as horrifying as it is clear—complete destruction was coming! **None** of the inhabitants on Palestine's coastal plain would **be left.** That destruction was initially inflicted by Pharaoh Neco II of Egypt (609–594), the succesor of Psamtik I, as he attempted to consolidate the area west of the Euphrates against the Babylonians (Jer. 47).

2:6-7. Zephaniah wrote that Philistia, **the land by the sea, where the Kerethites dwell,** would be so depopulated that it would become pastures for the herding of **sheep.** In fact it would be acquired by **the remnant of . . . Judah,** those whom God would rescue from the judgment (v. 3). The survivors of the day of wrath would become sheepherders, would occupy the land of their once-hated enemy, and would derive sustenance from it. The explanation for this gracious provision for God's remnant is given in the last sentence of verse 7. The remnant is the object of the love and providential concern of **the LORD their God** who cares for and restores His people. (**Restore their fortunes;** cf. 3:20, renders the lit. "bring back their captives"; cf. NIV marg.) Judah's future occupancy of this territory is guaranteed by the Abrahamic Covenant (Gen. 15:18-20).

2. ON MOAB AND AMMON (2:8-11)

2:8. Zephaniah turned from the Philistines in the west to the two tribes to the east, **Moab** and Ammon, that were descended from Lot's daughters (Gen. 19:30-38) and therefore were blood relatives of Judah. The sin of these tribes was their verbal hostility (**insults . . . taunts . . . threats**) toward God's Chosen **People** (cf. Zeph. 2:10). These tribes had consistently been Israel's enemies. The Moabite king Balak tried to destroy the nation with Balaam's curses (Num. 22), for which God pronounced extermination (Num. 24:17). In the era of the Judges both Moab and Ammon repeatedly attempted to subjugate Israel (Jud. 3:12-14; 10:7-9; 11:4-6). Both Saul and David defeated **the Ammonites** (1 Sam. 11:1-11; 2 Sam. 10:1-14), and Joram and Jehoshaphat routed the rebelling Moabites (2 Kings 3). Other prophets noted that Moab and Ammon haughtily violated Judah's borders and ridiculed their distant Jewish relatives (cf. Isa. 16:6; 25:10-11; Jer. 48:29-30; Ezek. 25:1-3, 6; Amos 1:13).

2:9. Following God's indictment (v. 8) His punishment was pronounced (v. 9), intensified by the twice-repeated word **surely.** The Almighty God made a solemn oath (**as surely as I live**) that those arrogant oppressors would **become like Sodom** and Gomorrah, key cities destroyed in the day of their ancestor Lot (Gen. 19:23-29). This analogy meant that those nations would be reduced to complete ruin. The **land** would be taken from them and would become so barren that it would grow only **weeds** (prickly plants) and be covered with **salt pits** (cf. Jer. 48:9). As a sterile **wasteland** it would no longer be fruitful. Being near the Dead Sea, much of Moab and Ammon is salty, barren land, though the final fulfillment of the prophecies in Zephaniah 2:8-10 is yet future in view of the words in verse 11.

Zephaniah added that the Moabites and Ammonites will be enslaved by the Jews and that the Jewish remnant (**the remnant of My people . . . the survivors**) will possess those territories (cf. Isa. 11:14).

2:10-11. Zephaniah repeated the reasons for the judgments described in verse 9. The sin of Moab and Ammon was **their pride** (cf. Isa. 16:6; Jer. 48:29), evidenced by their **insulting and mocking** of God's **people** (cf. Zeph. 2:8; Ezek. 25:5-6, 8). Again after the indictment God spelled out the penalty (cf. the similar pattern in Zeph. 2:8 followed by v. 9). **The LORD will** judge **them** with His power and will destroy all their idols. Then the prophet made another statement that awaits future fulfillment. In the Millennium people in all **nations . . . will worship** the true God (cf. Mal. 1:11), **everyone in his own land.** The removal of all idolatry will pave the way for worldwide worship when Christ rules as King on the earth.

In this section (Zeph. 2:8-11) the prophet repeated his message in a threefold argument: reasons for judgment (vv. 8, 10), nature of the judgment (vv. 9a, 11a), and the ultimate provision of blessing (vv. 9b, 11b).

3. ON ETHIOPIA (2:12)

2:12. The **Cushites** or Ethiopians are descendants of Cush, a son of Ham (Gen. 10:6; 1 Chron. 1:8). These people, residing in the upper Nile region (today's southern Egypt, Sudan, and northern Ethiopia), were the southernmost people known to Judah. Zephaniah's words concerning them were few and one wonders if his choice of them, rather than, say, the troublesome Edomites, was simply to stretch the points of the compass to the known extremes. Cushite kings dominated Egypt until their defeat by the Assyrian king Esarhaddon in 670 B.C. King Asa of Judah defeated a large Cushite expedition under Zerah that threatened Judah (2 Chron. 14:9-13). The Lord's judgment on Cushites is that they, like all Israel's enemies, would be killed in battle (**slain**). The fulfillment of this prophecy was at least partially realized by the Babylonians under Nebuchadnezzar in 586 B.C. (cf. Ezek. 30:4-5, 9). Since the Babylonians were God's instrument, God called the attackers' swords **My sword.**

4. ON ASSYRIA (2:13-15)

2:13. Though Assyria lay to the distant northeast of Judah, Zephaniah designated them as from **the north** because invaders from that area followed the Fertile Crescent westward and then proceeded southward. Zephaniah predicted that the Lord would **destroy Assyria** and leave **Nineveh,** Assyria's capital and a city well known for its impregnability, a wasteland. This was the nation that con- quered the Northern Kingdom of Israel in 722 B.C. Assyria was a much-feared nation because of its merciless atrocities on its captives. An alliance of Babylonians and Medes destroyed Nineveh in 612 B.C., with the Assyrian king Sin-shar-ishkun dying while trying to defend his city. A remnant of the Assyrians escaped the fall of the city under their new king, Ashur-uballit II. Though aided by an alliance with Pharaoh Neco II of Egypt, the Assyrian Empire was crushed in 609 B.C. Zephaniah's prediction was fulfilled. (Another prophetic description of the fall of Nineveh is given in Nahum 3.) Zephaniah's words that Nineveh would become **dry as the desert** were fitting because the city had many irrigation canals! Nahum's words were equally appropriate (Nahum 1:8; 2:6, 8).

2:14. Having stated the fact of Assyria's destruction (v. 13), Zephaniah then elaborated on the nature of that nation's utter demise (v. 14). **Flocks and herds** may refer to hordes of wild animals (cf. v. 15), not domesticated ones, that require extensive vegetation. Animals, the prophet said, would find their abode (**lie down**) in the city, and the noise of a busy city would be replaced by the sounds of the beasts and birds. Eerily, owls would occupy the **columns** and call **through the windows** of deserted

buildings. (The exact identification of the birds **desert owl** and **screech owl** is uncertain, as noted in the NIV marg. to Isa. 34:11.) **Doorways** of homes would be deserted; only **rubble** would lie there (cf. "rubble" in Zeph. 1:3). **The beams of cedar,** lying under more elaborate wall and ceiling coverings, would **be exposed** because of the soldiers' ransacking of homes. The image that emerges is one of depopulation, destruction, and ruin.

2:15. The picture of Nineveh's destruction is completed as the prophet reiterated that the city, though apparently quite secure, would be shamed. Its king was arrogant (cf. Isa. 10:12) because of its supposed impregnability. It was known as **the carefree city,** as its populace felt it **lived in** complete **safety.** The city was quite large, having with its suburban areas a circumference of 60 miles and a population of at least 120,000 (cf. comments on Jonah 3:3; 4:11). In addition to an extensive outer wall there was an inner wall with an 8-mile circumference, 50 feet thick and 100 feet high. Between the two walls was enough farmland to support the huge population. Nineveh's claim (**there is none besides me**) was no idle boast! For approximately 200 years she was superior in strength to any other city of her time.

An attack on the outer wall, begun in 614 B.C. by the Medes and Babylonians, was initially withstood by the Ninevites, but a combination of trickery by the attackers, carelessness by the attacked, and a natural disaster, finally brought victory to the attackers (cf. Nahum 1:10; 2:3-5; 3:11). The great inner wall collapsed because of an unexpected deluge that swelled the Tigris River in a normally dry season of the year and inundated the wall. Thus the city was unexpectedly defeated (cf. Nahum 1:8; 2:6-8; 3:12). The carefree boasting of the city was hushed by her enemies, and all who later saw its ruins scoffed at her former haughtiness (cf. Nahum 3:19). To **scoff and** to **shake their fists** were signs of contempt. God reduced the city miraculously and gave it to the **wild beasts!**

D. Judgment on Jerusalem (3:1-7)

Having described God's impending judgment on the countries surrounding Judah, the Prophet Zephaniah again re- turned to the theme of Jerusalem's doom (cf. 1:4–2:3). He emphasized the need for the wicked Jews to seek repentance. The prophet listed God's grievances against His people (3:1-5), and then pronounced God's inevitable judgment (vv. 6-7).

1. THE PROPHET'S INDICTMENT (3:1-5)

3:1-2. The prophet made a general statement about Jerusalem's wickedness: she had sunk to the level of the heathen nations (cf. Hab. 1:2-4). Though Jerusalem is not named in Zephaniah 3:1, verse 2 shows that it was meant. **Woe** was a pronouncement of an indictment, an indictment that was here threefold: a **city of oppressors** (cf. Nineveh, which Nahum called "the city of blood," Nahum 3:1), **rebellious and defiled.** This general threefold indictment was then elaborated in Zephaniah 3:2-5: they *oppressed* their own people (v. 3), were *rebellious* against God (v. 2), and were *defiled* religiously (v. 4). The Jerusalemites failed to heed the **correction** provided by the Law and the Prophets. Such rebellion was a failure to **trust in the Lord** and to be **near** Him in fellowship and worship (cf. 1:6).

3:3-4. The prophet then indicted both the civil leaders (cf. 1:8) and the religious leaders (cf. 1:4-5). The **officials** were compared to voracious, hungry **lions**; the **rulers** (judges) were insatiable **wolves** who completely devoured an evening prey by **morning** (cf. Ezek. 22:27; Micah 3:1-3). Judah's leaders robbed the citizenry in order to appease their own lust for power and plenty (cf. Micah 3:9-10).

Jerusalem's religious leaders were equally debauched! The **prophets** were self-styled, **arrogant** religionists who, with the treachery of the priests, twisted and perverted the Law of God in order to fill their bulging purses (cf. Ezek. 22:28; Micah 3:5, 11). The **priests** (cf. Zeph. 1:4) profaned **the sanctuary** probably by their idolatry and astrology (1:4-5) and by offering blemished animal sacrifices. Since they violated **the Law** by their disobedience (cf. Ezek. 22:26), no wonder their people were not teachable (Zeph. 3:2).

3:5. The **Lord**—in contrast with the people in general (v. 2), their civil leaders (v. 3), and their religious leaders (v. 4)— **is righteous . . . does no wrong,** exercises **justice,** and never fails. Certainly, then, He would uphold the oppressed

and punish the wicked! The nation evidenced the depth of its debauchery by its callous conscience: **the unrighteous know no shame** (cf. 2:1). The word "unrighteous" (*'awwāl*) is related to the word "wrong" (*'awlâh*) in the first part of 3:5. It means "to distort, to turn aside, to be wicked."

2. THE LORD'S JUDGMENT (3:6-7)

3:6-7. The Lord's words recorded in verses 6-13 point up Judah's dire situation. The Lord rehearsed His past actions against other **nations** (v. 6), and then cited both the reasons for and the actuality of a near-future judgment (v. 7). God had acted in conformity with His righteousness by judging nations for their wickedness, leaving them **demolished . . . deserted,** and **destroyed.** A classic example for Judah would be the 10 Northern tribes dispersed by Sargon II of Assyria in 722 B.C. God pleaded with His people to follow in His ways, accepting His **correction** (cf. v. 2) in order to avoid being **cut off** (cf. 1:3-4) and having to face His **punishments** (cf. 1:9-13; 2:1-3). The word **but** in the last sentence of 3:7 has a sad implication. Instead of responding to the Lord's unceasing mercies, Judah consciously and purposely repudiated Him and was even **eager** to continue in her corrupt ways. Complacency (1:12) and rebellion (3:1) led to an enthusiasm for corruption! (v. 7) What a cameo of human history!

E. Judgment on all the earth (3:8)

3:8. The prophet concluded the "judgments" portion of his prophecy by reverting to the universal theme with which he introduced the section. He began with a summary statement of universal judgment (1:2-3); then he delineated God's judgment on Judah and Jerusalem (1:4–2:3) and on other **nations** (2:4-15). Then for emphasis he repeated the judgment on Jerusalem (3:1-7). Now he ended this long section with another general summary of universal judgment. In the Lord's impending universal judgment on the nations, His cup of wrath was about to be poured out; at that time His grace would take second place to His anger! At the end of the yet-future Tribulation, God will cause the nations' armies to assemble toward Jerusalem, and in the Battle of Armageddon (cf. Zech. 14:2; Rev.

16:14, 16) He will **pour out** on them His **wrath** (*za'am*, from "foam"), **all** His **fierce anger** (cf. comments on Zeph. 2:2), and **the fire of** His **jealous anger** (lit., "jealousy").

III. The Day of Yahweh's Restoration (3:9-20)

The word "then" in verse 9 signifies a major pivot in the prophet's message both in tone and in content; he shifted from frightful predictions of destruction to prophecies of blessing and peace. After destroying the nations' armies, God will restore the nations to His favor. Instead of horrifying threats, here are comforting promises of love, mercy, and restoration. These promises look forward to the Millennium when Christ will rule as King on the earth.

A. The restoration of the nations (3:9-10)

3:9. Zephaniah predicted that the nations will be renewed both morally (v. 9) and spiritually (v. 10). The purifying of **the lips of the peoples** does not mean they will speak a new language (as the KJV seems to imply by its trans. "a pure language"). Instead it means the renewal of once-defiled speech. One's lips represent what he says (the words spoken by his lips), which in turn reflect his inner life (cf. Isa. 6:5-7). The nations, formerly perverted by the blasphemy of serving idols, will be cleansed by God for true worship. As a result the nations, turning to reverential trust in God, will **call on the name of the LORD and** will evidence their dependence on Him by their united service (**shoulder to shoulder**).

3:10. As an example of the unanimity of their spiritual service the prophet mentioned those **beyond the rivers of Cush** (the upper Nile region—southern Egypt, Sudan, and northern Ethiopia; cf. 2:12), the most distant land to his knowledge. In their converted state the nations, represented by Cush, **will bring . . . offerings** to the Lord in Jerusalem (cf. Isa. 66:18, 20). This will be a marvelous reversal of the Gentiles' policies during Zephaniah's day! This stream of **worshipers** going to Jerusalem will include Israel—**My scattered people.** Zephaniah then elaborated on this fact (Zeph. 3:11-20).

B. The restoration of Israel (3:11-20)

When God restores the nations to Himself, He will also turn from wrath to bless His chosen nation Israel. This grand prophetic theme is both the high point of prophetic promise for the nation and the climax of Zephaniah's message. Israel's regathering to Jerusalem was promised by God in words given to Moses (Deut. 30:1-10). Though God must punish sin, He is full of mercies and is always true to His promises. Though national judgment is assured, God will not forsake His people. He is the covenant-keeping Sovereign! This closing section of Zephaniah's message is comforting to Israel because of the reassurance of God's faithfulness to His promises.

1. THE REDEMPTION OF THE NATION (3:11-13)

3:11-13. At the beginning of the Millennium (**that day**) Israel will be cleansed and restored. She will have no **shame** before God because of her sins (**wrongs** renders a Heb. word that means "terrible deeds") for God will have removed **from the city** all **those** guilty of **pride** or haughtiness. This will occur in the judgment of Israel (Ezek. 20:34-38; Matt. 25:1-13). Evildoers, full of shame, will be judged, and God's **holy hill** (Jerusalem; cf. Pss. 2:6; 3:4; 15:1; 24:3; 78:54; Dan. 9:16, 20; Joel 2:1; 3:17; Obad. 16) will be inhabited only by a pure people—**the meek and humble** (cf. Zeph. 2:3)—those trusting **in the . . . LORD.** All iniquity—**wrong** (*'awlâh*, lit., "injustice"; cf. 3:5, God "does no wrong"), **lies,** and **deceit**—will be purged away, and in that cleansed condition they will find peace and security. The closing line of verse 13 brings to mind the promises of the shepherd psalm, Psalm 23. Israel, so long defiled, turbulent, and ravished, will at last be at rest among the nations and without fear (cf. Zeph. 3:15-16).

2. THE JOY OF THE NATION (3:14)

3:14. The tone of this verse is clearly that of exultation and joy: **Sing . . . shout aloud. . . . Be glad and rejoice.** Israel will be joyful in that millennial day because she will have been redeemed by God. Though the immediate prospect for the nation was one of sorrow and torment (vv. 1, 5-7), a day will come when the remnant's fears will give way to shouts of praise.

3. THE RULER OF THE NATION (3:15-17)

3:15. Shouts of joy will arise because Israel's Redeemer, the Messiah King, will be in her midst (cf. Isa. 9:7; Zech. 14:9). The long-promised Deliverer will protect them. Wrath from God's hand (Zeph. 3:8) and oppression by her **enemy** (cf. v. 19) will be gone, and **the LORD, the King of Israel,** will be **with** her (cf. v. 17), and she will have no **fear** (cf. v. 13).

3:16-17. Verse 16 amplifies the theme of calm from fear in the last line of verse 15. **They** (apparently converted Gentiles) will encourage Israel not to be fearful or in despair. **Hands** that **hang limp** picture despair through alarm and anxiety (cf. Jer. 47:3). Instead, Israel will lift her hands, symbolic of triumph, because of the Lord's presence (He will be **with you;** cf. Zeph. 3:15) and power (**He is mighty to save**). In addition to being with His redeemed remnant and delivering them, **He will . . . delight** in them. The nation will again be the object of God's great **love,** not His wrath. The Millennium will indeed be a time of peace for His troubled people; Israel will rejoice (v. 14). But more than that, *God* **will rejoice!** (v. 17) In fact He will be **singing** with delight and joy because His Chosen People will be in the land under His blessing.

4. THE REWARD OF THE NATION (3:18-20)

Seven times in these concluding verses, the Lord said, "I will." He wanted to place a strong hope before the believing remnant in Zephaniah's day, since His judgment was imminent and His restoration mercies remote. The prophet, in spite of dark days, wanted the repentant to grasp firmly God's promises for comfort and strength.

3:18. Many Jews, scattered from their homeland, had **sorrows** because they were unable to take part in **the appointed feasts.** But the Lord **will remove** those sorrows when He regathers His people to Jerusalem where they will enjoy His blessings. No longer will their feasts be **a burden,** something they hate to do, **and a reproach,** a cause for God's displeasure because of their sinful ways.

3:19. As Zephaniah had already stated (2:4-15; 3:8-15), God will remove Israel's foreign oppressors (cf. Gen. 12:3, "whoever curses you I will curse"), **gather** His people **scattered** in other lands,

and give them a favorable reputation (**praise and honor**; cf. Deut. 26:19; Zeph. 3:20) in all places where they are held in disrepute (cf. v. 11).

3:20. This verse summarizes Israel's yet-future blessings: regathering in the Promised Land (**home**), a favorable reputation (**honor and praise**; cf. v. 19) **among all the** nations, and a restoring of her **fortunes** (or a bringing back of her captives; cf. 2:7). This will all happen **before** her **very eyes.** In the Millennium, Israel will possess her land as God promised (Gen. 12:1-7; 13:14-17; 15:7-21; 17:7-8), and the Messiah, Israel's King, will establish His kingdom and will reign (2 Sam. 7:16; Ps. 89:3-4; Isa. 9:6-7; Dan. 7:27; Zeph. 3:15).

To emphasize the divine authority of his message as well as the certainty of God's comfort, Zephaniah ended his book with the words, **says the LORD!**

BIBLIOGRAPHY

Baxter, J. Sidlow. *Explore the Book.* Reprint (6 vols. in 1). Grand Rapids: Zondervan Publishing House, 1970.

Calvin, John. *Commentaries on the Twelve Minor Prophets.* Vol. 4. Grand Rapids: Baker Book House, 1981.

Fausset, A.R. "Zephaniah." In *A Commentary Critical, Experimental and Practical on the Old and New Testaments.* Vol. 2. Reprint (6 vols. in 3). Grand Rapids: Wm. B. Eerdmans Publishing Co., 1978.

Feinberg, Charles L. *The Minor Prophets.* Chicago: Moody Press, 1976.

Freeman, Hobart E. *Nahum, Zephaniah, Habakkuk: Minor Prophets of the Seventh Century B.C.* Chicago: Moody Press, 1973.

Henry, Matthew. *Commentary on the Whole Bible in One Volume.* Reprint (6 vols. in 1). Grand Rapids: Zondervan Publishing House, 1966.

Keil, C.F. "Minor Prophets." In *Commentary on the Old Testament in Ten Volumes.* Vol. 10. Reprint (25 vols. in 10). Grand Rapids: Wm. B. Eerdmans Publishing Co., 1982.

Kleisert, Paul. "The Book of Zephaniah." In *Commentary on the Holy Scriptures Critical, Doctrinal and Homiletical.* Vol. 7. Reprint (24 vols. in 12). Grand Rapids: Zondervan Publishing House, 1960.

Laetsch, Theo. *The Minor Prophets*. St. Louis: Concordia Publishing House, 1956.

Poole, Matthew. *A Commentary on the Holy Bible*. Vol. 2. 1685. Reprint. London: Banner of Truth Trust, 1979.

Pursey, E.B. *The Minor Prophets: A Commentary*. Vol. 2. Reprint. Grand Rapids: Baker Book House, 1950.

Tatford, Frederick A. *The Minor Prophets*. Vol. 3. Reprint (3 vols.). Minneapolis: Klock & Klock Christian Publishers, 1982.

HAGGAI

F. Duane Lindsey

INTRODUCTION

Significance. The Book of Haggai is the second shortest book in the Old Testament; only Obadiah is shorter. The literary style of Haggai is simple and direct. The content of the book is a report of four messages by a seemingly insignificant postexilic prophet whose ministry was apparently of limited duration.

Nonetheless the significance of his message and of his role in encouraging the rebuilding of the temple should not be underestimated. "The truth is that few prophets have succeeded in packing into such brief compass so much spiritual common sense as Haggai did" (Frank E. Gaebelein, *Four Minor Prophets: Obadiah, Jonah, Habakkuk, and Haggai*, p. 199). Notable in Haggai's ministry is his self-awareness of the divine origin of his messages. No less than 25 times in his two short chapters Haggai affirmed the divine authority of his messages. Not only did he introduce his sermons with, "This is what the LORD Almighty says," but also he concluded them with a similar formula ("declares the LORD Almighty"), and sprinkled those expressions throughout his messages. He was fully aware he was God's messenger (1:13).

Haggai the Prophet. The life and ministry of Haggai are wrapped in comparative obscurity. He was the first prophet through whom God spoke to the postexilic Judean community. His four messages are all dated in the second year of Darius I (520 B.C.). He was soon joined by the Prophet Zechariah who continued and completed the task of encouraging the people to rebuild the temple (cf. Ezra 5:1-2; 6:14). (See the chart in the *Introduction* to the Book of Zech. for a comparison of dates mentioned in the Books of Hag. and Zech.)

Haggai referred to himself simply as "the Prophet Haggai" (Hag. 1:1, etc.; cf.

Ezra 5:1; 6:14). Nothing is known of his parentage or genealogy. His name apparently means "festive" or "festival," derived from the Hebrew word *ḥāg* ("a festival"). A few scholars therefore suppose that he was born on a feast day, but nothing in the text supports this. Some believe his reference to the Solomonic temple in Haggai 2:3 shows he was one of the exiles who saw it destroyed in 586 B.C. If so, he may have been an elderly prophet.

It is interesting that some ancient versions of the Old Testament attribute the authorship of certain psalms to Haggai and/or Zechariah: Psalms 137 and 145–148 in some manuscripts of the Septuagint (Gr. trans. of OT); Psalms 125–126; and 145–147 in the Latin Vulgate. This probably erroneous tradition apparently arose from the close connection these prophets had with the temple where these psalms were sung.

Historical Background. The destruction of the temple in Jerusalem by the Babylonian armies in 586 B.C. marked the end of an era in Jewish national and religious life. As exiles in Babylon, the Jews were without a temple and without their sacrifices. Though they could direct their prayers toward Jerusalem (1 Kings 8:48; Dan. 6:10), it was only under the generous policies of Cyrus the Great, king of Persia, that almost 50,000 Jews were allowed to return to Jerusalem with Zerubbabel (Ezra 1:2-4; cf. Isa. 44:28), accompanied by Joshua the high priest and the Prophets Haggai and Zechariah. Levitical sacrifices were soon reinstituted on a rebuilt altar for burnt offerings (Ezra 3:1-6), and in the second year of the return the foundation of the temple was laid (Ezra 3:8-13; 5:16). However, Samaritan harassment and eventual Persian pressure brought a halt to the rebuilding of the temple. Then spiritual apathy set in; and for about 16 more years—until the rule of

175

the Persian king, Darius Hystaspes (521–486 B.C.)—the construction of the temple was discontinued. In the second year of Darius (520 B.C.) God raised up Haggai the prophet to encourage the Jews in the rebuilding of the temple (Ezra 5:1-2; Hag. 1:1). His task was to arouse the leaders and the people of Judah from their spiritual lethargy and to encourage them to continue working on the temple. The initial success of Haggai in his mission (cf. 1:12-15) was supplemented by the continued efforts of Zechariah until the temple reconstruction was finished in 515 B.C. (The critical problems relating to the Book of Hag. are minor and are reviewed by Hobart E. Freeman, *An Introduction to the Old Testament Prophets*. Chicago: Moody Press, 1968, pp. 330-2).

OUTLINE

COMMENTARY

Haggai, the Lord's messenger (1:13), delivered four dated messages from the Lord which encouraged the leaders and the people of Judah to rebuild the temple. (See the comments on vv. 12-15 for the view of some scholars that the book contains five messages.)

I. The First Message: A Judgmental Call to Rebuild the Temple (chap. 1)

A. The superscription (1:1)

1:1. This superscription identifies the date, the prophet, and the addressees. That the prophecy is dated **in the second year of** the Persian **King Darius** rather than in a regnal year of a king of Judah is a vivid reminder that Haggai was ministering during "the times of the Gentiles" when Israel had no king of her own (cf. Zech. 1:1; Dan. 2; Luke 21:24). In Judah's postexilic calendar, adopted from the Babylonian system of beginning the new year in the spring rather than in the fall (cf. Ex. 23:16; 34:22), this date was 1 Elul (August 29), 520 B.C. Since this was the **day** of the new moon, it was probably a holy festival day in Jerusalem (cf. Isa. 1:14; Hosea 2:11). This provided **the Prophet Haggai** with a ready audience to listen to **the** first **word of the Lord** that broke the postexilic prophetic silence. The instrumental role of Haggai as a prophet, "the Lord's messenger" (Hag. 1:13), is stressed throughout this brief book. The book is virtually punctuated with the "messenger formula" ("This is what the Lord Almighty says," and similar expressions, vv. 2, 7, 13; 2:4, 6-9, 11, 14, 23). In addition, each message is identified as "the word of the Lord" (1:1; 2:1, 10, 20). There is no doubt about the divine origin of Haggai's messages.

The people were included in the implied address of 1:3 but this first message is initially directed to the two leaders, **Zerubbabel** the **governor of Judah** and **Joshua . . . the high priest.** Zerubbabel was the heir apparent to the throne of David, being the grandson of King Jehoiachin (1 Chron. 3:17-19; cf. Matt. 1:12, where Jehoiachin is called Jeconiah). That Zerubbabel was called both the **son of Shealtiel** and the son of Shealtiel's brother Pedaiah (1 Chron. 3:17-19) is probably due to a levirate marriage (cf. Deut. 25:5-10). After Pedaiah died his brother Shealtiel may have taken Pedaiah's widow to be his wife and to them was born Zerubbabel. Joshua's father **Jehozadak** was the high priest who was deported to Babylon from Jerusalem in 586 B.C. (1 Chron. 6:15).

B. The accusation of procrastination (1:2-6)

1:2. Haggai's addressing the leaders first (v. 1) emphasizes their responsibility. The message is from **the LORD Almighty** (lit., "the LORD [*Yahweh*] of armies"). Haggai used this title of God, "the LORD Almighty," 14 times! The reference to Judah as **these people** rather than "My people" implies a divine rebuke because they did not act like the Lord's people. Their excuse for not building the temple (**the time has not yet come**) is laid bare in the next verses which describe their misplaced priorities.

1:3-4. The word of the LORD was now addressed to the people (**you** is pl.) mentioned in verse 2, and not just to the leaders. **Haggai** rebuked the people for their selfish indifference and negligence. They had built their own houses while neglecting to rebuild the **house** of God (cf. v. 9). The term **paneled houses** may only mean that they had roofs over their heads, though the word can also refer to luxurious paneling which may have adorned the houses of the leaders and the more well-to-do people.

1:5-6. The LORD exhorted the people to reflect on their conduct in view of their present poverty. **Give careful thought to your ways** is literally, "Set your hearts on your ways." Four other times Haggai wrote, "Give careful thought to" (v. 7; 2:15, 18 [twice]). They needed to reappraise their perverted priorities and give preeminence to God and their relationships with Him. What they had done was deplorable; and it was also fruitless. Their self-centeredness had not produced economic stability. Their abundant

plantings had resulted in only meager harvests (cf. 1:10-11; 2:15-17, 19). The simplest necessities of life—food, **drink,** and clothing—were not being met. The resulting inflation is pictured graphically: **You earn wages, only to put them in a purse with holes in it.** The implication is strong that these economic conditions were divine chastening for disobedience (cf. Lev. 26:18-20; Deut. 28:38-40). All their efforts at farming and wage-earning availed nothing because they had not put the Lord first. Their ancestors who had gone into captivity had experienced the same retribution (cf. Deut. 28:41), but God wanted better things of the returned exiles.

C. The exhortation to rebuild the temple (1:7-8)

1:7-8. The LORD again (cf. v. 5) exhorted the people to reflection and challenged them to action. Having rebuked them for what they had *not* done and having shown the fruitlessness of what they *had* done, **the LORD** challenged them concerning what they *should* do—rebuild the temple to the glory of God. The implicit message of verses 2-4 is now made explicit: **Build the house** (i.e., God's temple). The need for bringing **timber** down from the **mountains** may imply that they had used up for their own houses the lumber purchased for rebuilding the temple a few years before (cf. Ezra 3:7). Also it appears that sufficient stone was available from the desolated temple and that they needed only timber for finishing the walls and roof. The completion of the temple would be pleasing to God (**so that I may take pleasure in it**). It would also bring Him honor or glory, showing the nations that Israel's God was worthy of worship in such a place by His servants.

D. The explanation of the people's impoverishment (1:9-11)

The divine judgment referred to in verses 5-7 is now made more specific. Failure to do what they should—rebuild the temple—resulted in economic ruin and poverty.

1:9a. Two steps led them downward to poverty: (a) their harvest was much smaller than **expected,** for while their hopes were high, the yield was low, and (b) what they did receive appeared to vanish at once, graphically pictured as God's doing: **What you brought home I blew away.**

1:9b. God then explained that the reason for this chastening was their selfish neglecting to rebuild the temple. These words emphatically restated the thought in verse 4 (the temple remained **a ruin while** the people were **busy with** building their **own** houses). While laboriously involved with their own affairs the people were neglecting their spiritual responsibilities.

1:10-11. Their economic impoverishment resulted from a divinely designed drought. **Because of** their disobedience **the heavens . . . withheld their dew and the earth its crops.** In the dry season (April-October) morning dew, often heavy in Palestine, was essential to the growth of summer crops. So the absence of dew was devastating. The **drought,** brought about by God, affected the three basic crops of Palestine—**the grain, the new wine,** and **the oil** (from olive trees)—as well as **whatever** else **the ground** produced (cf. 2:16-17, 19). The absence of rain and dew indicates God's curse on the land and its people because of their disobedience to the covenant (cf. Lev. 26:19-20; Deut. 28:22-24). This in turn deprived **men and cattle** of food provisions. **The labor of** the people's **hands** in the fields would all be for naught.

E. The response of leaders and people to the prophetic message (1:12-15)

Because of God's word of encouragement in verse 13 and the mention of a different date in verse 15, some scholars regard this section (vv. 12-15) as a separate prophetic message, making five in all. However, the date in verse 15 relates to the actual resumption of construction which probably followed the word of encouragement, so the whole section best fits the structure of the book as the response motif within this first of four messages.

1:12. Haggai reported the obedient and reverent attitude of both the leaders and **the people.** It was rare for a prophet of God to receive rapid and favorable response to a message he had given them from God. But this was the case regarding Haggai's simple and straightforward message. The response of the leaders and **the people** was demonstrated in two ways: (a) they **obeyed the voice of the** LORD **their God and the message of the Prophet Haggai** (their recognizing the words of Haggai as God's word caused an effective change in their attitudes and actions), and (b) they **feared the** LORD (they had a new awe and reverence for God as they pondered the significance of their past disobedience and self-centeredness and their new sense of obedience to divine priorities). Haggai referred to the people as a **remnant** (here and also in v. 14 and in 2:2), not merely because they were survivors of the Babylonian Exile but also because they were becoming what the remnant of God's people should always be—those who are obedient within their covenant relationship to the Lord (cf. Isa. 10:21).

1:13. This verse, more than any other in his book, describes Haggai's role as **the** LORD'**s messenger** and his words as **the message of the** LORD. The divine origin of all Haggai's recorded words is affirmed throughout this prophetic book (cf. v. 1). Here Haggai conveyed a word of encouragement from the Lord **to the people** as they anticipated rebuilding the temple: **I am with you** (repeated in 2:4; cf. 2:5 and Isa. 43:5). This assurance of God's presence to guide and empower them should have cast out all fear and apprehension about accomplishing their designated task of rebuilding.

1:14. The LORD **stirrred up the spirit of Zerubbabel . . . Joshua . . . and . . . the whole remnant** to rebuild the temple, just as He had moved their hearts to leave Babylon about 18 years earlier (cf. Ezra 1:5). Thus aroused by God and enabled for the task, **they . . . began to work on the house of the** LORD **Almighty, their God.**

1:15. The date when the actual rebuilding was resumed was 24 Elul (September 21), 520 B.C. There had been a delay of 23 days between the original prophecy (v. 1) and the resumption of the work (v. 15). This delay is explained by two factors: (a) the harvest of figs, grapes, and pomegranates was in Elul, the same **sixth month,** and (b) a period of planning and gathering of materials probably preceded the actual reconstruction.

II. The Second Message: A Prophetic Promise of the Future Glory of the Temple (2:1-9)

A. The superscription (2:1-2)

2:1-2. Like the superscription of the first message (1:1), this superscription identifies the date, the prophet, and the addressees. The date of this message was 21 Tishri (October 17), 520 B.C. This was nearly a **month** after the people had resumed the rebuilding of the temple (1:15). In this period the progress in rebuilding was slow, no doubt because of the laborious task of cleaning up 60 years of rubble and the cessation of work during the numerous festivals **of the seventh month**—the weekly Sabbaths, the Feast of Trumpets on the first day, the Day of Atonement on the 10th, and the Feast of Booths (or Tabernacles) from Tishri 15 to 21, with Tishri 22 also being a rest day (Lev. 23). This second message by **the Prophet Haggai** was delivered on the last ordinary day of the Feast of Booths. It was addressed to those who had begun to rebuild: **Zerubbabel . . . Joshua . . . and . . . the remnant of the people** (cf. Hag. 1:12).

B. The promise of the Lord's enabling presence as an encouragement for rebuilding the temple (2:3-5)

2:3. The Lord surfaced their unfavorable comparison of the temple then under construction with the preexilic temple. Even in the initial stages of reconstruction the people were apparently making insidious comparisons between the restored temple and the glories of Solomon's temple which had been dedicated centuries before at the same time of year (1 Kings 8:2).

Before Haggai gave a solution to the people's discouragement, God told Haggai to ask three questions to surface the people's unfavorable comparison: **Who of you . . . saw this house in its former glory? How does it look to you now? Does it not seem to you like nothing?** These questions are essentially rhetorical, causing the people to face openly the fact that their temple was not going to be as splendid as Solomon's. Implied is the fact that some of those present, perhaps even Haggai himself, had seen the glories of the Solomonic edifice prior to its destruction 66 years before (in 586 B.C.). (A similar phenomenon occurred when the foundation of the temple was laid a few years earlier; Ezra 3:10-13; cf. Zech. 4:10.)

2:4a. The LORD then encouraged the people by urging the two leaders and their people to take firm action. The thrice-repeated exhortation, **Be strong** (or "Take courage"), is followed by the single command, **and work.** Interestingly David had used both expressions when he committed the original temple project to Solomon (1 Chron. 28:10, 20), along with the promise of divine enablement. God had motivated the people (Hag. 1:14) and now He strengthened them. The expression, **all you people of the land,** does not refer to the adversaries of Judah as in Ezra 4:4, but is synonymous with "the remnant of the people" (Hag. 2:2; cf. 1:12, 14).

2:4b-5. The LORD forthrightly reaffirmed His presence with them: **I am with you** (cf. 1:13). As the **Spirit** of God was with the Israelites **when** they **came out of Egypt** (cf. Isa. 63:11-14), so He would be **among** them in rebuilding the temple, a task associated with the "Exodus" from Babylon. The covenant relationship between God and His people was also recalled in order to encourage them in their rebuilding.

The Lord then reassured them by encouraging them not to be fearful. Since He was with them (Hag. 1:13; 2:4) and since His Holy **Spirit** was with them, they could be calm and assured. The expression, **Do not fear,** is a common motif in an oracle of salvation (e.g., Isa. 41:10; 43:1).

C. The proclamation of the future glory of the temple (2:6-9)

The people's unfavorable comparison of the restored temple with Solomon's temple (v. 3) was counteracted by God's assurance of ultimate success because of the future glory of the millennial temple. This proclamation about coming glory was given to encourage present success.

2:6-7a. The words **in a little while** suggest not chronological immediacy but the impending or imminent it-could-occur-anytime character of God's action indicated here. This future divine judgment (**I will once more shake the heavens and the earth, the sea and the dry land**) is depicted in terms of an earthquake as a symbol of God's supernatural intervention (cf. Isa. 2:12-21; 13:13; Ezek. 38:20; Amos 8:8; Hag. 2:21-22). When Jesus Christ returns to earth, "the earth and the sky will tremble" (Joel 3:16; Matt. 24:29-30). This event will affect not only the natural order (Hag. 2:6) but also people (**I will shake all nations**, v. 7). This "shaking" of the nations may refer to God's gathering the nations for the Battle of Armageddon (Zech. 14:1-4).

The writer to the Hebrews quoted Haggai 2:6 in Hebrews 12:26 and then added that the kingdom of God, which "cannot be shaken" (Heb. 12:28), will survive all divine judgments. This divine judgment was impending in Haggai's day since the Old Testament prophets did not see the valley of time lying between the First and Second Advents of Jesus Christ (cf. Isa. 61:1-2; Luke 4:18-21).

2:7b. The adornment of the future temple will be provided by the nations' wealth. **The desired of all nations** should probably be understood as a collective noun ("desirable things," i.e., treasures) to correspond with its plural verb (in the Heb.) **will come,** suggesting that surrounding nations will gladly give up their treasures to adorn the temple in Jerusalem (cf. Isa. 60:5; Zech. 14:14). The rendering, "the desire of all nations" (KJV), has been usually understood as a messianic prophecy referring to the coming of the One desired by all nations. The trend of recent translations and commentators has been away from this personal reference to the impersonal "desired things." However, the evidence is not all one-sided, and a case can be made for retaining a personal messianic reference. Perhaps Haggai deliberately selected a term that had exactly the ambiguity he wanted in order to include both an impersonal and personal reference (see Herbert Wolf, *Haggai and Malachi*, pp. 34-7).

2:7c. The future millennial temple (**this house**) **will** be filled **with glory.** This too could refer to material splendor (cf. Isa. 60:7, 13) but elsewhere the only "glory" that is said to **fill** the temple is the Shekinah glory of God's presence (cf. Ex. 40:34-35; 1 Kings 8:10-11). Though the ultimate reference is to the glory of God in the millennial temple (cf. Ezek. 43:1-12), Christ's bodily presence in the temple at His first coming may also be implied in Luke 2:32. Simeon referred to

Jesus as "the Glory of Thy people Israel" (NASB).

2:8. Some of the Lord's inexhaustible natural resources (**silver** and **gold**) will be available for use in constructing the temple, for He has ultimate providential control of the wealth of all nations.

2:9a. The restoration temple (**this present house**), Haggai said, would have a **glory** greater than the Solomonic temple (**the former house**) because during Herodian times the presence of the Messiah would adorn it (cf. Matt. 12:6; John 2:13-22). (The Herodian temple was a continuation, in a sense, of the postexilic "second" temple, not a "third" temple.) In addition, the ultimate fulfillment of this **greater glory** will be in the millennial temple. By building this postexilic temple the people would help advance God's program of manifesting Himself in a central place of worship: the Solomonic temple, and the yet-future millennial temple. So their work was more than merely constructing a building; it was a spiritual work which would ultimately culminate in God's millennial program.

2:9b. The blessings of the Messianic Age are summed up in a word—**peace.** **This place** probably refers to Jerusalem, not just the temple. Lasting peace in Jerusalem will result only from the presence of the Prince of Peace (cf. Isa. 9:6; Zech. 9:9-10).

III. The Third Message: A Priestly Decision to Illustrate the Present Blessings of Obedience (2:10-19)

A. The superscription (2:10)

2:10. The superscription of the third message specifies the date as 24 Kislev (December 18), 520 B.C., and once again **the Prophet Haggai** received **the word of the LORD.** During the two months since the second sermon (v. 1, "seventh month"; v. 10, **ninth month**), the Prophet Zechariah had begun his ministry (Zech. 1:1).

B. A ritual comparison showing the corrupting effect of sin (2:11-14)

2:11-13. The LORD commanded Haggai to **ask the priests what the Law says,** that is, he was to seek an official priestly ruling on a ceremonial matter. Haggai's question regarding the transmission of ritual holiness was answered in the negative by **the priests. Consecrated meat** was meat set apart for a specific sacrificial purpose (cf. Lev. 6:25; Num. 6:20). While the **garment** that might contain such meat would also be holy (cf. Lev. 6:27), that holiness of the garment could not be transferred to **bread . . . stew . . . wine, oil, or** any **other food.** But this is not true of ritual defilement, as indicated by the priests' positive reply to Haggai's question regarding the transmission of ritual uncleanness (Hag. 2:13). A person's ceremonial defilement (e.g., **by contact with a dead body**) is as transferable to other things as is a contagious disease (cf. Lev. 11:28; 22:4-7).

2:14. Haggai then applied to the **people** of Judah the priests' answer in verse 13—disobedience renders even sacrificial worship unacceptable. This defilement of the **nation** Israel probably looked back to the period before the temple rebuilding began (cf. 1:2-4), because the defilement contrasts with the changed situation "from this day on" (2:15).

C. A promise of present blessing in contrast with previous chastening (2:15-19)

2:15-17. Haggai called on the people to remember their previous economic disaster which came because they disobeyed by not rebuilding the **temple.** For the third of five times (1:5, 7; 2:15, 18 [twice]) the people were challenged to **give careful thought to** (lit., "set their hearts on") their disobedience (**before** they started rebuilding) and the consequences of their sins. As stated in 1:6, their harvests were again (2:16) said to be short in quantity. Grain had decreased 50 percent (from **20 measures** to **10**) and the grape harvest had decreased 60 percent (from **50** to **20** measures of juice in the **wine vat;** cf. 1:10-11; 2:19). Again God claimed responsibility for this condition: **I struck . . . the work of your hands** (cf. 1:9, "I blew [it] away"). **Blight** (crop disease) and **mildew** are linked in several passages that deal with divine judgment for disobedience (cf. Deut. 28:22; 1 Kings 8:37; 2 Chron. 6:28; Amos 4:9). **Hail** also occurs in many judgment passages (Ex. 9:25; Isa. 28:2; 30:30). For an agricultural society such punishments were catastrophic to the economy and to survival. **The LORD** reminded the nation of its

failure to respond to His chastening hand (**you did not turn to Me**) just like the failure of an earlier generation (Amos 4:9).

2:18-19. After citing God's present chastening on Israel for her past disobedience, Haggai urged the people to remember the renewed temple construction as the beginning of present blessing. They were to **give careful thought to** (lit., "set your hearts on"; cf. 1:5, 7; 2:15) **the day when** they laid the temple's **foundation.** From the day of this third message (in **the ninth month**) they were to look back three months ("the sixth month," 1:14-15). The drought of divine judgment had already affected the year's harvest so that their barns were already emptied of the sparse harvest. They had neither staples (**seed,** or grapes, or olives) nor luxuries (figs and pomegranates). To this too they were to **give careful thought.** But things would now be different, for the Lord promised, **From this day on I will bless you.** Their faithful obedience in continuing to rebuild would enable them to experience God's blessing.

IV. The Fourth Message: A Messianic Prophecy concerning Zerubbabel (2:20-23)

A. The superscription (2:20-21a)

2:20-21a. The final message begins with the mention of the prophet, the date, and the addressee. As in the previous messages, Haggai said he was merely the Lord's messenger bringing **the word of the LORD.** This message **came to Haggai** on the same **day** as the third message, that is, 24 Kislev (December 18), 520 B.C. This message, however, was addressed only to **Zerubbabel governor of Judah.** As the people had needed encouragement to rebuild, perhaps Zerubbabel needed encouragement to lead this seemingly insignificant group of Jews who resided in a corner of the vast Persian Empire.

B. A proclamation of the future overthrow of the Gentile kingdoms (2:21b-22)

2:21b. God told Haggai to tell Zerubbabel that He would **shake the heavens and the earth.** As in the second message (vv. 6-7), the earthquake motif highlights divine judgment and introduces the subject of God's judgment on Gentile world powers.

2:22. Zerubbabel learned from Haggai that God would **overturn royal thrones and shatter the power of the foreign kingdoms.** This is reminiscent of the destruction of Gentile world powers represented in the great image in Daniel 2. There the worldwide messianic kingdom will replace the Gentile kingdoms (Dan. 2:34-35, 44-45). The overthrowing of **chariots** and the **fall** of **horses and their riders** indicate that this change in world government will be military as well as political. In the confusion of this great Battle of Armageddon (Rev. 16:16-18) at the Lord's second coming (Rev. 19:11-21) many a man will turn **the sword** against **his** own **brother** (cf. Zech. 12:2-9; 14:1-5).

C. A proclamation of the restoration of the Davidic kingdom (2:23)

2:23. Three facts are prominent in this verse: (a) **the Lord** will fulfill this prophecy **on** the future **day** of Gentile judgment (cf. vv. 21-22); (b) the Lord will make **Zerubbabel . . . like My signet ring;** and (c) **the Lord** had **chosen** Zerubbabel as the channel of the Davidic line and therefore representative or typical of the Messiah. The title **My servant** frequently marked out the Davidic king (cf. the "Servant songs" in Isa. [42:1-9; 49:1-13; 50:4-11; 52:13–53:12] and also cf. 2 Sam. 3:18; 1 Kings 11:34; Ezek. 34:23-24; 37:24-25). Haggai's contemporary, Zechariah, used the messianic title "Branch" to refer to Zerubbabel (Zech. 3:8; 6:12; cf. Isa. 11:1; Jer. 23:5-6; 33:14-16).

The significance of comparing Zerubbabel to a "signet ring" (a seal of royal authority or personal ownership) is clarified by the imagery in Jeremiah 22:24-25. God said that if Jehoiachin (Zerubbabel's grandfather) were His signet ring, He would pull him off His hand and give him over to Nebuchadnezzar. Possibly Haggai was saying that in Zerubbabel God was reversing the curse pronounced on Jehoiachin. At any rate, Zerubbabel's place in the line of messianic descent (Matt. 1:12) confirmed his representative role in typifying the Messiah. Since the words "on that day" point to a yet-future fulfillment in the Messianic Age, it is wrong to suggest that Zerubbabel would actually rule as the anointed one on the Davidic throne in Haggai's day. This was not intended any more than the crowning of Joshua the high priest (Zech. 3:1-

10) indicated he would have political rule over Israel. The crowning of Joshua was clearly symbolic of things yet to be fulfilled by the Messiah (Zech. 6:9-15). Joshua was portrayed in Zechariah's vision in his official capacity as high priest rather than in his own person. Similarly Zerubbabel was owned as the Lord's "signet ring" in his representative position as the son of David, not for personal fulfillment in his own lifetime but for messianic fulfillment in the kingdom of the final Son of David (cf. Luke 1:32-33). An alternate interpretation sees Zerubbabel exercising delegated authority with David during the future millennial reign of Christ.

Appropriately the last words in Haggai's book are **the Lord Almighty** (cf. comments on Hag. 1:2). The sovereign covenant-God is able to bring about all He promised through Haggai. The temple will be rebuilt and filled with the glory of the Lord. The final Son of David will rule the earth in peace and righteousness. Therefore God's people are to be faithful now to the task to which He has called them.

BIBLIOGRAPHY

Baldwin, Joyce G. Haggai, Zechariah, Malachi: An Introduction and Commentary. Downers Grove, Ill.: InterVarsity Press, 1972.

Feinberg, Charles L. "Haggai." In The Wycliffe Bible Commentary. Chicago: Moody Press, 1962.

_____. The Minor Prophets. Chicago: Moody Press, 1976.

Gaebelein, Frank E. Four Minor Prophets: Obadiah, Jonah, Habakkuk, and Haggai. Chicago: Moody Press, 1970.

Keil, C.F. "Minor Prophets." In Commentary on the Old Testament in Ten Volumes. Vol. 10. Reprint (24 vols. in 10). Grand Rapids: Wm. B. Eerdmans Publishing Co., 1982.

Laetsch, Theo. The Minor Prophets. St. Louis: Concordia Publishing House, 1956.

Tatford, Frederick A. The Minor Prophets. Vol. 3. Reprint (3 vols.). Minneapolis: Klock & Klock Christian Publishers, 1982.

Wolf, Herbert. Haggai and Malachi. Chicago: Moody Press, 1976.

Wolff, Richard. The Book of Haggai. Grand Rapids: Baker Book House, 1967.

ZECHARIAH

F. Duane Lindsey

INTRODUCTION

In an often-quoted statement, George L. Robinson has called the Book of Zechariah "the most messianic, the most truly apocalyptic and eschatological of all the writings of the Old Testament" (*International Standard Bible Encyclopedia*. Grand Rapids: Wm. B. Eerdmans Publishing Co., 1956, 5:3136). The messianic emphasis of Zechariah accounts for its frequent citation by New Testament authors. Nestle and Aland list 41 New Testament citations or allusions to Zechariah's book (Eberhard Nestle and Kurt Aland, eds., *Novum Testamentum Graece*. New York: American Bible Society, 1950, pp. 670-1).

Zechariah the Prophet. The postexilic Prophet Zechariah was a Levite born in Babylon (Neh. 12:1, 16). He was the son of Berekiah and the grandson of Iddo the priest (Zech. 1:1). Ezra and Nehemiah referred to him as "a descendant of Iddo" (Ezra 5:1; 6:14; cf. Neh. 12:4, 16), implying perhaps that his father had died young and Zechariah became the successor of his grandfather (cf. Neh. 12:4, 16). So, like Jeremiah and Ezekiel before him, Zechariah was both a prophet and a priest. Zechariah's name, which he shared with about 30 other men in the Old Testament, means "Yahweh (NIV, 'the LORD') remembers."

Zechariah was a contemporary of Haggai the prophet, Zerubbabel the governor, and Joshua the high priest (Ezra 5:1-2; Zech. 3:1; 4:6; 6:11). Zechariah returned to Jerusalem from Babylon with almost 50,000 other Jewish exiles. He was probably a relatively young man at the beginning of his prophetic ministry (cf. 2:4) while Haggai might have been considerably older.

The Historical Background of Zechariah. The fall of Jerusalem to the armies of

Nebuchadnezzar in 586 B.C. marked the finale of the kingdom of Judah, much as the earlier defeat at the hands of the Assyrians in 722 B.C. brought to an end the Northern Kingdom of Israel. Most of Jerusalem's inhabitants were deported to Babylon for a period of about 70 years, as prophesied by the Prophet Jeremiah (Jer. 25:11; 29:10). During this Exile the Prophet Daniel received the revelation that Gentile kingdoms would be dominant over Judah and Israel until God would set up His kingdom on the earth under the rule of the Messiah (Dan. 2; 7). This period was referred to by Jesus Christ as "the times of the Gentiles" (Luke 21:24).

When the Babylonian Empire fell to the Persian Empire (539 B.C.), Cyrus the Great decreed that the Jews could return to Jerusalem to rebuild their temple (Ezra 1:2-4; cf. Isa. 44:28). However, only a small minority of about 50,000 Jews (including Haggai and Zechariah) returned under the leadership of Zerubbabel the governor and Joshua the high priest (Ezra 2). Levitical sacrifices were soon reinstituted on a rebuilt altar of burnt offering (Ezra 3:1-6), and in the second year of their return the foundation of the temple was laid (Ezra 3:8-13; 5:16). However, external oppression and internal depression halted the rebuilding of the temple for about 16 more years of spiritual apathy till the rule of the Persian King Darius Hystaspis (522–486 B.C.). In the second regnal year of Darius (520 B.C.) God raised up Haggai the prophet to encourage the Jews in rebuilding (Ezra 5:1-2; Hag. 1:1). Haggai preached four sermons in four months and then disappeared from the scene. Two months after Haggai delivered his first sermon, Zechariah began his prophetic ministry (cf. Hag. 1:1; Zech. 1:1), encouraging the people to spiritual renewal and motivating them to rebuild the temple by revealing to them God's plans for Israel's future. With this prophetic encouragement the people completed the temple reconstruction in 515 B.C. (Ezra 6:15). The dated portions of Zechariah's prophecy fall within the period of the rebuilding of the temple. The undated prophecies of Zechariah 9–14 were probably written much later in his ministry.

The following summary compares significant dates in the ministries of Haggai and Zechariah (cf. the chart "Chronology of the Postexilic Period," near Ezra 1:1):

Dates of Key Events in Haggai's and Zechariah's Time

August 29, 520 B.C.	Haggai's first sermon (Hag. 1:1-11; Ezra 5:1)
September 21, 520	Temple building resumed (Hag. 1:12-15; Ezra 5:2)
October 17, 520	Haggai's second sermon (Hag. 2:1-9)
October-November 520	Zechariah's ministry begun (Zech. 1:1-6)
December 18, 520	Haggai's third and fourth sermons (Hag. 2:10-23)
February 15, 519	Zechariah's eight visions (Zech. 1:7–6:8)
December 7, 518	Delegation from Bethel (Zech. 7)
March 12, 515	Temple dedicated (Ezra 6:15-18)

The Unity of the Book of Zechariah. The unity of the Book of Zechariah was first questioned by those who attributed chapters 9–14 to a preexilic writer such as Jeremiah (cf. Zech. 11:12-13; Matt. 27:9-10). However, the higher critical tradition has generally argued for a composition date for those chapters long after Zechariah (about the third century B.C.). The arguments for a later date generally emphasize stylistic differences and alleged historical discrepancies. Such arguments have been answered satisfactorily by conservative scholars who have demonstrat-

ed that the entire Book of Zechariah was indeed written by the prophet (e.g., Hobart E. Freeman, *An Introduction to the Old Testament Prophets*. Chicago: Moody Press, 1968, pp. 337-44; Merrill F. Unger, *Commentary on Zechariah*, pp. 12-4). The differences in subject matter, literary style, and probably a later period in Zechariah's life account adequately for the stylistic differences found in chapters 9–14. The reference to Greece in 9:13 does not require a late date if one accepts the reality of predictive prophecy.

The Style and Literary Genre of the Book of Zechariah. The style of Zechariah is characterized by epitome and also much figurative language. Zechariah showed much dependence on his predecessors and summarized many of their prophetic themes. However, he also displayed creative individuality of both thought and expression as the Spirit of God guided the recording of the divine revelation communicated to him.

Zechariah's prophetic book embraces several types of literary genres. Following the opening exhortation (call to repentance, 1:2-6), Zechariah gave a series of eight prophetic dream-visions he saw in a single night (1:7–6:8). These visions are in the form of apocalyptic ("revelatory") literature—highly figurative descriptions of eschatological encouragement. Chapters 9–14 are composed of two prophetic oracles (see comments on 9:1), which consist primarily of promises of Israel's future salvation.

OUTLINE

I. The Eight Symbolic Visions (chaps. 1–6)
   A. The introduction to the visions (1:1-6)
      1. Preface to the call to repentance (1:1)
      2. Particulars of the call to repentance (1:2-6)
   B. The communication of the visions (1:7–6:8)
      1. The vision of the red-horse rider among the myrtles (1:7-17)
      2. The vision of the four horns and the four craftsmen (1:18-21)

COMMENTARY

I. The Eight Symbolic Visions (chaps. 1–6)

A. The introduction to the visions (1:1-6)

This preface to the entire book appropriately introduces Zechariah's series of eight apocalyptic visions. Its clarion call to repentance establishes the prerequisite for the spiritual blessings promised to Israel in the eight visions to follow. God would not bestow comfort on unrepentant hearts. God's covenants with Abraham (cf. Gen. 12:2-3; 15:5-21) and David (cf. 2 Sam. 7:8-16) rendered certain the fulfillment of His purposes for Israel. But those covenants did not nullify the need for each generation of Israelites to be obedient to God in order to experience His promised blessings.

1. PREFACE TO THE CALL TO REPENTANCE (1:1)

1:1. This verse relates the time, source, and agent of the opening call to repentance. The specific day of **the eighth month** (which began October 27, 520 B.C.) is not mentioned as it is apparently unimportant. More significant is the fact that a Jewish prophet dated his prophecy according to the reign of a Gentile monarch. This was a vivid reminder to all of Zechariah's hearers that "the times of the Gentiles" (cf. Luke 21:24; Dan. 2; 7) were in progress and that no descendant of David was sitting on the throne in Jerusalem (cf. Hosea 3:4-5). (See the *Introduction* for a list of dates mentioned in Ezra, Hag., and Zech.)

Zechariah was merely the agent of this prophecy and not its source, for **the word of the LORD came to** him as it did to other true prophets before him (e.g., Hosea 1:1; Joel 1:1; et al.). As a **prophet** Zechariah was merely a servant and spokesman called to bring God's efficacious word to the people. Regarding Zechariah's lineage, the same three generations are mentioned in Zechariah 1:7, but in Ezra 5:1; 6:14, Zechariah is called the "descendant" (lit., **son**) of **Iddo.** (In Heb. the word "son" often means a descendant.) In this way the prophet was seen in relation to his better-known grandfather. (A comparison of Jehu's lineage in 2 Kings 9:2, 14 with that in

1 Kings 19:16 and 2 Kings 9:20 illustrates the same phenomenon.)

2. PARTICULARS OF THE CALL TO REPENTANCE (1:2-6)

This solemn warning not to repeat the errors of their fathers (cf. Paul's analogous warning in 1 Cor. 10:11) was intended to destroy any false security that Zechariah's contemporaries might develop in view of the great things God intended to do for Israel in the future. This warning for the present, which emphasized divine anger (Zech. 1:2) and extended divine grace (v. 3), drew its severity from a threefold lesson from the past—a warning against disobedience (v. 4), delay (v. 5), and doubt (v. 6).

1:2. Zechariah affirmed that the destruction of Jerusalem and the Exile experienced by the previous generations were an expression of divine anger. In fact **the LORD was very angry** (lit., "angry with anger"), a phrase indicating extreme displeasure. The Lord ("Yahweh"), who had entered into personal covenant relationship with the nation Israel, was intensely angry **with** their **forefathers,** especially the last generation before the Captivity (but cf. 2 Kings 21:14-15), because of their rebellion against Him.

1:3. Whereas the sins of their forefathers were responsible for the desolation of the temple, their own sins had resulted in delay in rebuilding the temple. Nevertheless **the LORD Almighty** now extended to them a gracious invitation to repent. The threefold repetition of the divine name stresses the divine imperative conveyed in this call to repentance. The condition for their receiving divine blessing was not simply to resume building the temple, but to **return to** Him—not just to the Lord's Law or to His ways but to **the LORD** Himself. Their repentance two months before (cf. Hag. 1:12-15) apparently involved an incomplete commitment, resulting in delay in rebuilding the temple. Now a complete return to **the LORD** would bring divine blessing, expressed by the words, **I will return to you.**

1:4. The warning against disobedience features the bad example of their **forefathers** who not only rebelled against the Lord but also refused to respond to the preexilic prophets' preaching. These **earlier prophets** were separated from Zechariah and his contemporaries by the years of Exile in Babylon. One major feature (but not the whole content) of the preexilic preaching was a call to repentance—**Turn from your evil ways and your evil practices.** This illustrates the *"forth*telling" aspect of a prophet's message to his own generation (cf. Jer. 3:12-13; 18:11; 25:5-6; Ezek. 33:11; Hosea 14:1; Joel 2:12-13; Amos 5:4-6). Another aspect of prophecy ("*fore*telling") is prominent in Zechariah's own ministry (cf. Zech. 9–14). The negative response of the forefathers (**they would not listen or pay attention to Me**) was already apparent to the earlier prophets (e.g., Jer. 17:23; 29:19; 36:31).

1:5. The warning against delay was conveyed by two striking rhetorical questions which call attention to the brevity of human life. Zechariah asked, **Where are your forefathers now?** They were dead from sword, famine, pestilence, and natural causes, as predicted by the earlier prophets. Zechariah's second question was, **The prophets, do they live forever?** The implied answer was, no; their ministries were also brief, so the opportunity for repentance which they offered should not be ignored.

1:6. A warning against doubt was implied in Zechariah's affirming the effectiveness and certain fulfillment of God's message of judgment. This message consisted of **My words** (of threatened punishment; e.g., Jer. 39:16) **and My decrees** (i.e., judicial decisions; e.g., Zeph. 2:2; Isa. 10:1). Though **the prophets** died, God's words live on to be fulfilled. The certainty of fulfillment is indicated in that God's words and decrees did **overtake** their **forefathers.** The Hebrew word for "overtake" is a hunting term implying that the threatened judgment of God pursued and caught the evildoers. "Overtake" is used in Deuteronomy 28 of both judgment (Deut. 28:15, 45) and blessing (Deut. 28:2), and is illustrated in the action of the avenger of blood (Deut. 19:6). That the forefathers **repented** does not necessarily mean that they returned to God, but perhaps only that they came to their senses and recognized that they deserved punishment and that God had justly accomplished what He had purposed in sending them into Exile (Lam. 2:17). On the other hand many could have repented sincerely dur-

Zechariah's Eight Night Visions

Vision	Reference	Meaning
The Red-horse Rider among the Myrtles	1:7-17	God's anger against the nations and blessing on restored Israel
The Four Horns and the Four Craftsmen	1:18-21	God's judgment on the nations that afflict Israel
The Surveyor with a Measuring Line	Chapter 2	God's future blessing on restored Israel
The Cleansing and Crowning of Joshua the High Priest	Chapter 3	Israel's future cleansing from sin and reinstatement as a priestly nation
The Golden Lampstand and the Two Olive Trees	Chapter 4	Israel as the light to the nations under Messiah, the King-Priest
The Flying Scroll	5:1-4	The severity and totality of divine judgment on individual Israelities
The Woman in the Ephah	5:5-11	The removal of national Israel's sin of rebellion against God
The Four Chariots	6:1-8	Divine judgment on Gentile nations

ing the Exile, resulting in the forgiveness and restoration to the land that followed.

Thus the prerequisite for experiencing the spiritual blessings revealed in Zechariah's further visions and prophecies was a genuine and wholehearted turning to **the Lord**. They were not to be disobedient as were those of the former generation who were taken into Exile as a result of God's certain judgment.

B. *The communication of the visions (1:7–6:8)*

In a single night Zechariah saw a series of eight visions which were interpreted by an angel and which described the future of the nation Israel. God's program of spiritual blessing set forth in the visions bridges the centuries from the rebuilding of the temple in Zechariah's day to the restoration of the kingdom to Israel under the Messiah (still future in Acts 1:6, to be fulfilled at Christ's Second Advent; cf. Acts 15:16). Joyce Baldwin has

correctly observed a "standard pattern" in the record of Zechariah's visions: (a) introductory words, (b) a description of the things seen, (c) a question by Zechariah to the angel for the meaning, and (d) the explanation by the angel. She also notes that four of the visions are accompanied by summarizing oracles which usually follow the vision (Zech. 1:14-17; 2:6-13; 6:9-15), except for one oracle within a vision (4:6-10) (*Haggai, Zechariah, Malachi,* pp. 92-3).

1. THE VISION OF THE RED-HORSE RIDER AMONG THE MYRTLES (1:7-17)

This vision established the general theme of hope for dispersed and downtrodden Israel. Gentile oppression was offset by comforting promises of divine blessing.

1:7a. The day the visions came was **the 24th day of the 11th** (Jewish) **month** of Darius' **second** regnal **year** (February 15, 519 B.C.). **Shebat** was the Babylonian name of the 11th **month,** adopted by the Jews after the Exile. This date was five months after the building of the temple was resumed (Hag. 1:14-15; 2:15), three months after Zechariah's first prophecy (Zech. 1:1), and two months after Haggai's last prophecy (Hag. 2:20—a prophecy regarding the destruction of world powers before the millennial rule of the Messiah; cf. Hag. 2:21-23).

1:7b-8a. The source of Zechariah's visions is clearly denoted by the clause **the Word of the Lord came** (cf. v. 1), a kind of prophetic "formula" indicating divine revelation. The visions, with partial interpretations, were seen in the spirit, had the significance of verbal revelation, and were supplemented by additional words of God. The words **I had a vision** (KJV, "I saw") denote the means by which divine revelation was conveyed to **Zechariah.** The expression does not refer to a dream, much less to a mere literary form. Zechariah was awake, as is apparent from his questions (e.g., v. 9) and interruptions (e.g., 3:5).

1:8b. The vision included three things: (a) a description of what Zechariah saw (v. 8), (b) an explanation of the same (vv. 9-11), and (c) intercession by the Angel of the Lord (v. 12).

Throughout the vision the primary focus on the **man riding a red horse** suggests that he was the leader of the horsemen. **He was standing** (i.e., astride his horse) as though stationed to await the report of his reconnaissance patrol. He is identified in verse 11 as "the Angel of the Lord." This Messenger (cf. comments on v. 11) was located **among the myrtle trees in a ravine,** possibly in the Kidron Valley east or southeast of Jerusalem where these fragrant evergreen shrubs were probably abundant. Riders sat on the horses **behind him** (because the riders were to report, v. 11), but the more important fact here is the colors of the horses: **red** (bay or reddish brown), **brown** (sorrel), **and white.** The significance of the colors is not stated, and this is complicated by the fact that the Hebrew word translated "brown" (NIV) or "speckled" (KJV) is found only here in the Old Testament, so that its meaning is not sure.

1:9-11. When Zechariah **asked** about the vision's meaning (**What are these?** cf. v. 19; 4:4, 11; 6:4; also cf. 5:6) an interpreting angel answered. In the fifth and sixth visions the angel asked Zechariah if he knew the meaning (4:2, 5, 13; 5:2). Apparently this was to rouse his curiosity. This angel referred to in the visions as **the angel who was talking with me** (1:11, 13-14, 19; 2:3; 4:1, 4-5; 5:10; 6:4), was not **the Angel of the Lord** (1:11-12; 3:1-6). The interpreting angel showed Zechariah the meaning of the vision by allowing its actors to speak. The first speaker was the central figure astride the red horse, who referred to the other riders as **the ones the Lord has sent to go throughout the earth.** The phrase "to go throughout" seems to be used here in the military sense of patrolling or reconnoitering. Just as the Persian kings had mounted messengers to send throughout the empire, so the Angel of the Lord had sent out angelic horsemen to reconnoiter the world scene. The patrol reported to their Leader, now called "the Angel of the Lord." That this "Angel" (lit., "Messenger") is a manifestation of the preincarnate Christ is established in chapter 3 where He is specifically called "the Lord" who yet refers to "the Lord" as another Person (3:2). Also He is seen exercising the divine prerogative of forgiving sins (3:4). (Cf. comments on "the Angel of the Lord" in Gen. 16:7.) The patrol had completed its assignment of searching **throughout the earth, and** had **found** the earth peacefully inhabited, **at rest** from war, but Israel was not at **peace** and rest. Was this report good news or bad news? If the reference is to the peace that existed during the second year of Darius, it was the result of Persian oppression and injustice, so this was bad news to Israelites who were under Gentile domination. Perhaps the vision has a more eschatological reference in anticipation of the worldwide kingdom of Messiah, since the patrol covered not only the vast Persian Empire, but also **the whole world**—though perhaps "the whole world" is a figure of speech (synecdoche) for the Persian Empire.

1:12. The intercession of **the Angel of the Lord** is unusual, for this divine Messenger is usually seen representing God to people rather than functioning in an intercessory role representing people to God. That the divine Messenger addressed the **Lord Almighty** in prayer supports a distinction of Persons in the Godhead, and contributes to the implicit doctrine of the Trinity in the Old Testament. The lament formula **How long?** expresses the deep need of Israel to have the Lord act on her behalf. The **70 years** of promised Captivity were over (cf. Jer. 25:12; 29:10), but the city was still not rebuilt.

1:13. The preceding vision unveiled God's controlling activity in the world, but a verbal message was now added to convey comfort to Israel. This message from **the Lord** (this may or may not be "the Angel of the Lord" of v. 12) was communicated to and through the interpreting angel to Zechariah so that he might proclaim it to the people. The message conveys (a) God's love for Israel (vv. 13-14), (b) God's wrath on the nations (v. 15), and (c) God's blessings on Israel (vv. 16-17).

The content of the **kind . . . words** which promised good and the **comforting** words which produced consolation is found in verses 14-17.

1:14. God's love for His people (**Jerusalem and Zion**) is expressed in the words **very jealous** (lit., "jealous with great jealousy"). This speaks of His burning zeal (cf. 8:2) to protect His covenant love with Israel. This burning zeal was expressed against Judah for 70 years (1:12), but His anger now turned toward the nations, which is the theme of the second vision (vv. 18-21).

1:15. God's anger with **the nations** was doubly emphatic (**very angry**; lit., "with great anger I am angry"; cf. v. 2) because of the false security which they so precariously enjoyed. His extensive wrath on the nations resulted from their immoderate, prolonged, and intensified punishment of Israel when God **was only a little angry,** that is, when He desired moderate punishment of His people. The nations **added to the calamity** by overstepping the limits God had intended for Israel's punishment (cf. Isa. 47:6).

1:16-17. Because of (**therefore**) God's love for Israel and His anger toward the Gentiles, He now promised six blessings for Israel: (a) the presence of God in **Jerusalem** (**I will return . . . with mercy;** cf. Ezek. 43:5; 48:35) in contrast with the departure of the divine glory from the preexilic temple (Ezek. 10:18-19; 11:22-23); (b) the rebuilding of the temple (**My house will be rebuilt;** cf. Ezek. 40–48); (c)

the rebuilding of the city (**the measuring line will be stretched out over Jerusalem;** cf. Jer. 31:38-40); (d) Israel will be enriched (**towns will again overflow** with the wealth of divine blessings which the city walls will be unable to contain; cf. Isa. 60:4-9); (e) the inhabitants of Jerusalem (**Zion**) will be comforted by the fulfillment of God's gracious promises (cf. Deut. 13:17; 30:3; Isa. 14:1; 49:15); and (f) they will be chosen (cf. Zech. 2:12; 3:2), referring to God's focusing His sovereign love on them and perhaps also referring to God's inaugurating the New Covenant with Israel (Jer. 31:31-40; cf. Rom. 11:26-27).

The complete fulfillment of these blessings from a New Testament perspective relates to the Second Advent of Christ, the millennial temple, and the blessings of the millennial kingdom, as suggested in the parallel Scripture passages mentioned above. Though the restoration temple was completed about four years after this prophecy (Ezra 6:15) and a partial rebuilding of the city about 80 years later (Neh. 6:15), the passages noted from Ezekiel indicate that the divine glory will be absent from the temple until millennial times. Nevertheless the Jews of Zechariah's day may have felt that those promised blessings were imminent, and this probably encouraged them in rebuilding the temple.

Several salient features from this first vision are elaborated on in the next two visions, in which God's displeasure with the nations is visualized in the second vision and God's causing Israel to prosper with the blessing of His presence is pictured in the third vision.

2. THE VISION OF THE FOUR HORNS AND THE FOUR CRAFTSMEN (1:18-21)

The consolation and comfort spoken of in verses 13 and 17 are displayed panoramically in the contrasting features of the second and third visions. The second vision on the one hand shows God's judgment on the nations that afflict Israel (vv. 18-21). The third vision on the other hand shows God's blessing in prospering Israel (chap. 2). The vision of the four horns and the four craftsmen shows *how* God will execute His displeasure, mentioned in 1:15, on the Gentiles. The nations that scattered Israel will themselves be crushed.

a. The four horns observed (1:18)

1:18. Zechariah **looked up** to see a new scene portrayed **before** his eyes (cf. 2:1; 5:1, 9; 6:1; Dan. 8:3; 10:5). He observed **four horns** such as those of a ram or a goat (cf. Dan. 8:3-8). However, since no reference is made to any animals their presence should not be presumed.

b. The four horns identified (1:19)

1:19. Again Zechariah asked, **What are these?** (cf. v. 9; 4:4, 11; 6:4; also cf. 5:6) A horn when used symbolically indicates invincible strength (cf. Micah 4:13) or often a Gentile king who represents his kingdom (Dan. 7:24; Rev. 17:12). Here the four **horns** symbolize proud Gentile powers ("horns of the nations," Zech. 1:21) **that scattered Judah, Israel, and Jerusalem** (an all-inclusive designation to denote God's people in Exile). Some writers understand these four horns to be the four Gentile empires envisioned in Daniel 2 and 7 (Babylon, Medo-Persia, Greece, and Rome). In that view the four craftsmen are the empires that succeeded them, respectively, with the fourth craftsman being the messianic kingdom from heaven (Dan. 2:44). However, in Zechariah's vision the angel said the horns "scattered" Israel (past tense, Zech. 1:19) and that was before any craftsmen arrived on the scene. It seems better either to regard the number four as a number of completeness, the totality of Israel's opposition, or to refer the four horns to four nations that had scattered Israel before Zechariah saw the vision (perhaps Assyria, Egypt, Babylonia, and Medo-Persia).

c. The four craftsmen introduced (1:20)

1:20. The Hebrew word for **craftsmen** (*hārāšîm*) indicates workmen skilled in wood, stone, or metal. Since the material of which the horns are composed is not mentioned, the general translation "craftsmen" is appropriate. (The RSV translates the word "smiths," apparently assuming the horns were iron.)

d. The four craftsmen explained (1:21)

1:21. The identity of **the craftsmen** depends on the identity of **the horns.** If the **horns** are the succeeding kingdoms in Daniel's visions (Dan. 2; 7), then the craftsmen are Medo-Persia, Greece, Rome, and the messianic kingdom. Oth-

erwise they were probably **nations,** including Persia, which God used to overthrow Israel's past oppressors (see comments on Zech. 1:19). In any case, the vision shows that God raises up instruments of judgment to deliver His people Israel from all her enemies.

3. THE VISION OF THE SURVEYOR WITH THE MEASURING LINE (CHAP. 2)

a. The content of the vision (2:1-2)

2:1. The expression, **Then I looked up** (cf. 1:18; 5:1, 9; 6:1) reflects not only the transition to a new vision, but also its continuity with the preceding one. The divine judgment on the Gentile nations will be followed by God's enlarging and protecting Jerusalem. This basic message of the vision is clear, but the details are less certain because of ambiguity in answering three key interpretive questions: Who are the persons mentioned in the vision? What is the position and movement of each person? Who is speaking in 2:4-13?

The man's occupation as a surveyor is identified by the **measuring line in his hand.** There is no necessary reason to regard this man as more than an unidentifiable man in the vision. Some interpreters, however, identify the "young man" (v. 4) with the "man with a measuring line" (v. 1). According to this view the "interpreting angel" left Zechariah's side and met another angel who urged him to recall the surveyor who had a mistaken notion about Jerusalem needing rebuilt walls. However, it seems better to regard this young man as Zechariah himself who was given the message of Jerusalem's enlargement (vv. 4-13) as an explanation of the surveyor's activity.

The identity of the surveyor is not given in the passage, but there is merit to the view which identifies him with the Angel of the Lord (1:11; 3:1; cf. Ezek. 40:3). Comparing this vision with Zechariah's first vision (Zech. 1:7-17) supports this view that the surveyor is the divine Angel of the Lord who is conveying divine revelation to Zechariah. At any rate the words in 2:4-13 are a message (or series of messages) from the Lord Himself, addressed first to the young man (vv. 4-5), then to Israel (vv. 6-12), and finally to "all mankind" (v. 13).

2:2. The surveyor's purpose, as indicated in his response to Zechariah's question, was to mark out the boundaries of **Jerusalem,** probably to indicate the present boundaries of the city from which the future overflowing would progress.

b. The communication of the message (2:3-13)

2:3-4a. Another angel, possibly coming from the surveyor, gave a message to Zechariah's interpreting **angel** to be conveyed to the prophet.

2:4b. That **Jerusalem will be a city without walls** indicates that the city will overflow its boundaries because of divine blessing. It will need no fortification or protection because of God's presence (cf. v. 5; Ezek. 38:11).

2:5. The LORD will be Jerusalem's protection without and **glory within** (cf. Isa. 60:19). This promise looks forward to the Lord's personal presence through the Messiah in the millennial kingdom on earth. Ezekiel envisioned the future return of the divine glory to the temple (Ezek. 43:2-5) but Zechariah was granted a vision of the glory extending to the entire city (Zech. 2:5) and to the whole land (v. 12; cf. 14:20-21).

2:6-9. This divine oracle seems to be a practical application of the preceding vision(s) addressed to Zechariah's contemporaries (**Zion** refers to Jews) who are still in **Babylon,** urging them to return to Jerusalem. The last part of verse 6 should probably be translated **I have scattered you**—not to **the four winds,** but—"*as the* four winds" **of heaven.** This may suggest a violent scattering, or it may be a figurative way of describing any significant dispersion of the Jews from their land. The exiles were intact in Babylon, **the land of the north,** so-called because invasions from Babylon came on Israel from the north. **The LORD** Himself (i.e., as the Angel of the Lord or as the Messiah) speaks in verses 8-9, though some interpreters refer parts of this statement to Zechariah's explanation of his prophetic call. **After He has honored Me and has sent Me** is the NIV translation of a difficult Hebrew phrase, translated in the KJV, "After the glory hath He sent Me." The idea seems to be that God will send the Messiah who will judge **the nations that . . . plundered** Israel and will display His glory. This will be fulfilled in the judgment of the Gentiles at Messiah's Second Advent (Matt. 25:31-46). The **ap-**ple of His eye** is a figure taken from Deuteronomy 32:10, the "apple" (lit., "gate or opening") probably referring to the pupil of the eye, that part of the eye most easily injured, the most demanding of protection. Here it symbolizes Israel under God's protective care.

2:10-12. This oracle is possibly aimed at the remnant which had already returned to Jerusalem. But again the reason for the call to praise is messianic, looking forward to the time when the earth will be prepared for the reign of Christ. **Shout and be glad** is a typical call to praise in songs and is linked with the rule of Yahweh (NIV, **the LORD**) as King in Jerusalem (cf. Pss. 93; 96; 98; Isa. 52:7-10; Zeph. 3:14-15). The Lord's **coming** to **live among** Israel is messianic, referring to the time when the Messiah will come to rule on the throne of David. Possibly, however, both of Christ's advents are in view here as in passages such as Isaiah 9:6-7; 61:1-2. But the emphasis here is on the Second Advent when God's blessings on Israel will overflow to the nations. **That day** is a shortened way of referring to the future "day of the LORD" when He will come to judge the nations and fulfill His covenants with Israel in the millennial kingdom. In the Millennium people from **many nations** will worship the LORD (cf. Zech. 8:20-23; 14:16; Isa. 2:3). **The holy land**—a phrase found only here in the Bible—will be the Lord's inheritance (cf. Zech. 8:3), and **Jerusalem** will be God's choice (cf. 1:17; 3:2) for the world's capital (Isa. 2:1-2).

2:13. The entire human race is to bow in silence and awe before the Almighty God.

4. THE VISION OF THE CLEANSING AND CROWNING OF JOSHUA (CHAP. 3)

Topographically the setting of Zechariah's visions apparently shifted from a valley outside Jerusalem (first two visions, 1:7-21) to an observation point within the city (third vision, chap. 2) to the courts of the temple itself (fourth and fifth visions, chaps. 3–4). Symbolically the first three visions pictured Israel's external deliverance from Captivity, her expansion, and the material prosperity of the land, whereas the fourth vision (chap. 3) sets forth Israel's internal cleansing from sin and reinstatement into her priestly office and functions.

a. The symbolic action (3:1-5)

The Lord introduced the vision to Zechariah ("He showed me"), who clearly perceived the identity of the actors in the vision and the significance of their actions. Therefore this fourth vision differs from the preceding ones by the absence of questions by Zechariah and explanations by the interpreting angel. The actors or participants are (a) Joshua the son of Jehozadak, the high priest of the restoration who returned with Zerubbabel from Babylon; (b) the Angel of the Lord, the preincarnate Christ, already introduced in 1:11-12; (c) Satan, the accuser (cf. Rev. 12:10); (d) attending angels ("those who were standing before" Joshua, Zech. 3:4); and (e) the Prophet Zechariah, who became a vocal participant in the vision (v. 5).

3:1-2. The first significant feature in the vision is the position of **Joshua . . . standing before the Angel of the Lord.** Here the word "standing" is practically a technical word for priestly ministry (cf. Deut. 10:8; 2 Chron. 29:11). This implication concerning the deity of the Angel of the Lord and His identity as the preincarnate Christ is more explicitly indicated in Zechariah 3:2 where He speaks under the title of "Lord" and yet distinguishes Himself *from* the Lord in addressing **Satan** (cf. comments on 1:11). This identification is further supported in 3:4 where His action is virtually that of forgiving sins.

Satan's resistance changed the scene from a priestly one to a judicial one where Joshua was the object of Satan's accusations. Then the Angel of the Lord rebuked **Satan** and proceeded to acquit Joshua, not because Satan's accusations were false, but because of God's gracious love for and choice of His people Israel. Joshua was functioning here in his high priestly capacity as representative of the nation Israel. God's choice of **Jerusalem,** not Joshua, was the basis of the **rebuke** (v. 2). Later the sin was removed from the land, not just from Joshua (v. 9). Joshua and his priestly companions were said to be "men symbolic of things to come" (v. 8). Therefore much as the high priest represented the entire nation on the Day of Atonement (cf. Lev. 16:1-10), so here Joshua the high priest was accused and acquitted on behalf of the nation Israel.

3:3-5. The acquittal took the form of removing Joshua's **filthy clothes,** representative of his sin and guilt and that of the nation. Joshua was then **clothed** with festal or **rich garments,** speaking of the purity associated with his forgiveness, and **a clean turban,** possibly suggesting the joy of his reinstatement into the priesthood. This symbolized the forgiveness and restoration of the nation Israel as a priestly nation (cf. Ex. 19:6).

b. The significant communication (3:6-10)

This communication includes a charge to Joshua (vv. 6-7) and an explanation of the vision's symbolism (vv. 8-10).

3:6-7. The **charge to Joshua** embodied two conditions and three results of divine blessing. To **walk in** God's **ways** describes the personal attitude of the priests (and ultimately the nation) toward God, and keeping God's **requirements** (cf. 1 Kings 2:3) refers to the faithful performance of priestly duties. If Joshua met these conditions he would enjoy three things: (a) **govern My house** —have continued service in the temple; (b) **have charge of My courts**—guard the temple from idolatry and other religious defilement; and (c) receive **a place among these standing here**—perhaps referring to Joshua's free access to God (cf. Zech. 3:1) comparable to that of the angels (those who are "standing" are distinguished from Joshua's fellow priests who are "seated," v. 8).

3:8-10. The Lord next affirmed the point of the vision—that **Joshua** and his priestly companions were **symbolic of things to come.** In their official priestly cleansing from sin they prefigured the future cleansing of the nation Israel. This future cleansing was linked with the coming of the Sin-Remover who was given three messianic titles—**My Servant, the Branch,** and **the Stone.** As the Servant of the Lord, Christ is the One who comes to do the will of the Father (Isa. 42:1; 49:3-4; 50:10; 52:13; 53:11). As the Branch of David, Christ is the Davidic Descendant who will rise to power and glory out of the humiliation into which the line of David had fallen (Isa. 4:2; 11:1; Jer. 23:5; 33:15; Zech. 6:12-13). As the Stone (cf. Ps. 118:22; Matt. 21:42; 1 Peter 2:6) He will bring judgment on the Gentiles (Dan. 2:44-45) and be a stone of stumbling for unbelieving Israel (Rom. 9:31-33). But ultimately He will bring cleansing to Israel and **remove the sin of this land in a single day.** Some say this refers to the day of Christ's crucifixion, but it is more likely a reference to the day of His Second Advent when at the end of the future Tribulation period the merits of His death will be applied to believing Israel (Zech. 13:1).

The **seven eyes** on the **stone** probably symbolize the Messiah's full intelligence with which He will judge. This may also allude to the Holy Spirit (Isa. 11:2; Rev. 5:6). **That day** (Zech. 3:10) seems to refer to the whole period of millennial blessing which will follow the return of Christ. Sitting under one's own **vine and fig tree** refers to conditions of peace and prosperity (1 Kings 4:25; Isa. 36:16; Micah 4:4).

5. THE VISION OF THE GOLD LAMPSTAND AND THE TWO OLIVE TREES (CHAP. 4)

a. The description of the vision (4:1-4)

4:1-4. The interpreting **angel** aroused Zechariah **from . . . sleep** and directed his attention (by a question; cf. vv. 5, 13; 5:2) to **a solid gold lampstand,** the exact appearance of which is subject to controversy. Appearing in a context of priestly temple ministry (cf. the previous vision), this lampstand was apparently similar to the lampstand placed in Israel's tabernacle (cf. Ex. 25:31-40), and the 10 lampstands of Solomon's temple (1 Kings 7:49). However, the tabernacle lampstand had to be filled with oil by the priests, but this lampstand was automatically filled with an endless supply of oil without human agency. This is indicated by three significant and peculiar features: (a) **a bowl** for storing oil was suspended over the lampstand (Zech. 4:2); (b) oil was transported by gravity from the bowl through **seven channels** or conduits to each of the **seven lights** of the lampstand, apparently 49 conduits in all (v. 2); and (c) the lampstand was flanked by **two olive trees** which were tapped by "two gold pipes" through which "golden oil" flowed constantly into **the bowl** (vv. 3, 11-12). (Baldwin gives an alternate description of the construction of this lampstand; *Zechariah,* pp. 119-20.) Zechariah's inquiry **What are these?** (cf. 1:9, 19; 4:11; 6:4; also cf. 5:6) possibly referred to the "seven lights" (i.e., lamps). (See com-

ments on 4:10b.) But, more likely, "these" referred to the two olive trees. The prophet's question was seemingly put off by the angel and repeated later by Zechariah (v. 12), when again the prophet received a delayed answer. The two delays by the angel focused attention on the answer which was finally given in verse 14.

b. The significance of Zerubbabel (4:5-10a)

4:5-10a. Before identifying the "two olive trees" (v. 3) with "the two who are anointed" (v. 14), the angel prepared for this conclusion by relating the vision **to Zerubbabel,** the governor of Judah (cf. Hag. 1:1, 12, 14; 2:21). The angel suggested that he would finish the **temple** (Zech. 4:9) through the abundant supply of the **Spirit** of God. Thus the oil for the lamp is associated with the Holy Spirit. By His enabling the temple would be completed (v. 6) and every obstacle (**mighty mountain,** v. 7) to rebuilding would be removed. Military strength (**might**) and human manpower (**power**) could not accomplish the task, but Spirit-empowered workers under the direction and leadership of **Zerubbabel** would do so.

The LORD explained to Zechariah (vv. 8-10) that Zerubbabel's finishing the restoration temple would drive the critics to silence for they would **know** God had **sent** the prophet and the reconstructionists (**God bless it!** [v. 7] **Men will rejoice** [v. 10]). (Because Joshua the high priest was the subject of the preceding vision, no specific mention is made of him in this vision, but the two visions go together).

As **Zerubbabel . . . laid the foundation of this temple** (v. 9; i.e., he began the work of rebuilding on the ancient foundations), so he would **also complete** it, epitomized by his laying **the capstone** (v. 7). The word translated **plumb line** (v. 10) is disputed and possibly refers to this final crowning stone (cf. Baldwin, *Zechariah,* pp. 122-3). Others say it symbolizes Zerubbabel's supervising the rebuilding project. Those who despised **the day of small things** may have been older Jews who thought this temple was insignificant compared with the former temple of preexilic times (cf. Ezra 3:12-13; Hag. 2:3).

c. *The interpretation of the two olive trees (4:10b-14)*

4:10b-14. The words about the **seven** being **the eyes of the LORD** are possibly a delayed answer to Zechariah's question in verse 4. Like "eyes" the seven lights (lamps, v. 2) symbolize God's worldwide scrutiny, for nothing is hidden from Him. Others understand the "seven" to refer back to the seven eyes in the previous vision (3:9).

The **two olive branches** and **two gold pipes** are mentioned for the first time in the vision in 4:12. The two branches with olives poured their oil into the gold pipes, which flowed into the bowl and then through the 49 channels to the seven lamps. The interpreting angel removed Zechariah's confusion regarding the **two olive trees** (vv. 3, 11) by indicating that their two oil-supplying branches represent **the two who are anointed to serve the LORD of all the earth** (v. 14). The branches refer to the anointing of priests and kings, with particular allusion to Joshua and Zerubbabel who typify the Messiah as both Priest and King. **The lampstand,** then, seems to represent Israel as a light to the nations (cf. Isa. 42:6; 49:6), potentially in Zechariah's time, but will be actually so during the millennial reign of Christ. Another fulfillment, partial at least, of Zechariah 4:11-14 is found in the two witnesses in the future Tribulation period (Rev. 11:3-6, esp. v. 4).

6. THE VISION OF THE FLYING SCROLL (5:1-4)

The last three visions have to do with the administration of judgment. This vision of the flying scroll is both simple and severe.

5:1. This vision is introduced with the words **I looked again** (cf. v. 9), similar to the second and third visions ("Then I looked up," 1:18; 2:1; cf. "I looked up again," 6:1).

5:2. Again (cf. 4:2, 5, 13) the interpreting angel asked Zechariah, **What do you see?** to bring out the features and to communicate the significance of the vision. Zechariah said he saw a huge **flying scroll, 30 feet long and 15 feet wide.** The scroll was not rolled up; it was spread out like a large sheet so it could be read on both sides (cf. 5:3). Its large size was coincidentally or intentionally the exact size of the tabernacle, perhaps suggesting that the judgments contained on the scroll were in harmony with God's holy presence in the midst of Israel. The suspended position of the scroll as "flying" or floating facilitates its function of rapid entrance into and judgment on the houses of thieves and perjurers.

5:3. That the scroll had writing **on one side** and **on the other** is reminiscent of language describing the two tablets of the Law (Ex. 32:15). In fact **the curse** of the scroll is directed toward violators of the middle command of each of the two tablets—the eighth commandment against stealing (Ex. 20:15) and the third commandment against swearing **falsely** by (misusing) the **name** of the Lord (Ex. 20:7). Thus the specified objects of the curse probably represent all those who violate the Law of God.

5:4. The severity ("banished," v. 3, purged out of the covenant community) and the totality (**remain in his house and destroy it**) of the judgments suggest a fulfillment in the Millennium because only then will divine judgment on sin be so rapid and so complete.

7. THE VISION OF THE WOMAN IN THE EPHAH (5:5-11)

a. *The appearance of the ephah (5:5-6)*

5:5-6. The interpreting **angel** directed Zechariah's attention to another object in flight, this time **a measuring basket** (Heb., 'êpâh, a large barrel or basket used for a common household measure). Estimates of the capacity of an ephah, the largest dry measure used by the Jews, range from approximately 5 to 10 gallons. Since this would be much too small a container to enclose a woman, the ephah was apparently greatly enlarged in the vision, as the scroll was in the previous vision.

The angel indicated that the basket represented **the iniquity of the people throughout the land.** The NIV marginal translation for "iniquity of the people" is "appearance," which is closer to the Hebrew word which is literally "eye." The clause could be translated, "This is the appearance (or resemblance, i.e., of the ephah) in all the land," which gives good sense. However, the term "iniquity" is attested by the Greek and Syriac versions and also makes sense in this passage (cf. Baldwin, *Zechariah*, p. 128).

The use of a measuring basket to

symbolize the corporate evil of the land of Israel was appropriate in view of the common perversity of making false measures (cf. Amos 8:5). The sins associated with commercial preoccupation were gripping Israel at this time (Neh. 5:1-13; cf. Mal. 3:8-9). However, it is probably too specific to identify the basket only with godless commercialism. The rest of the vision seems to include the concept of false worship.

b. *The woman in the ephah (5:7-8)*

5:7-8. The material of which the measuring **basket** was made is not identified, but it had a **cover of lead** to assure the security of its contents. When the cover was lifted, **a woman** was observed inside and was identified as **wickedness.** The woman (probably because the Heb. word for wickedness is in the fem. gender) was wickedness personified, a term denoting civil, ethical, and religious evil. The interpreting angel had to keep the woman (wickedness) in confinement. Not only must the wicked in Israel be punished (the vision of the flying scroll, vv. 1-4) but also wickedness itself must be removed from the land.

c. *The removal of the ephah (5:9-11)*

5:9-11. Two unidentified **women** with great **wings like those of a stork** transported the ephah of wickedness **to the country of Babylonia** (lit., Shinar), the recent place of Israel's Exile but also the site of ancient and future idolatry and rebellion against God (Gen. 11:2; Rev. 17:3-5). This lends support to the view that the city of Babylon on the Euphrates River will be rebuilt (cf. comments on Rev. 17–18). Unger identifies these women with demonic forces that seek to protect the woman of wickedness and enshrine her for worship in Babylon (*Zechariah,* p. 98). Others see them as agents of divine power or providence.

Israel's corporate sin, associated with idolatry, will be removed from her land. The phrases in Zechariah 5:11—**to build a house for it,** and **be set there in its place** (i.e., on an idol pedestal)—suggest that the ephah of wickedness will be erected in a temple as an idol. Such idols of Babylon were powerlessness personified, as indicated in Isaiah's many idol satires (Isa. 44:9-20; 46:1-2; etc.). Returning the wickedness of idolatry to its place

of origin in Babylon apparently will set the stage for final judgment on Babylon (Rev. 17–18). Its removal from Israel will prepare the way for Christ's second coming and millennial kingdom (Rev. 19–20).

8. THE VISION OF THE FOUR
   CHARIOTS (6:1-8)

This eighth vision concludes the messages which Zechariah saw in one night and which outline the future history of the nation Israel. It is reminiscent of the first vision, with horses going out from the presence of the Lord throughout the whole earth. However, these horses are harnessed to chariots and come on the scene from between two mountains of bronze. The judgment determined by God on the Gentiles in the first vision is executed by divinely commissioned war chariots in this final vision. No mention is made of any riders or charioteers. Except for the divine words in verses 7b-8, the conversation is limited to the normal dialogue between Zechariah and the interpreting angel.

a. *The description of the vision (6:1-3)*

6:1-3. The chariots' place of departure is identified as **two mountains** which were made **of bronze** (an alloy of copper and tin), the ancient counterpart to brass (an alloy of copper and zinc). Bronze seems to symbolize righteous divine judgment against sin (cf. Rev. 1:15; 2:18). Since the Hebrew text has the definite article ("*the* two mountains"), some see a reference to the two well-known mountains, Zion (cf. Joel 3:16) and Olivet (cf. Zech. 14:4). Though the association of Olivet with the second coming of Christ may support this view, it is doubtful that actual mountains are intended since these were made of bronze. The **four chariots** with different-colored **horses** speak of the universality of divine judgment which will go in all directions throughout the earth. If the colors are significant, perhaps **red** symbolizes war and bloodshed, **black** designates death and famine, **white** speaks of triumph and victory, and **dappled** denotes pestilence and plagues (see comments on Rev. 6:1-8). For a discussion on problems regarding the Hebrew words for the various colors of the horses in both this and the first vision see Baldwin, *Zechariah,* pages 138-40.

b. The explanation of the vision (6:4-8)

6:4-7a. At Zechariah's request (**What are these?** cf. 1:9, 19; 4:4, 11; also cf. 5:6) the interpreting **angel** explained the significance of the horses with their chariots. **The four spirits** (or "winds") **of heaven** may refer to angels of divine judgment or to the power of God to accomplish His judicial purposes (cf. Ps. 148:8; Jer. 49:36; Dan. 7:2; Rev. 7:1). The divine title, **the Lord** ('ādôn) **of the whole world,** is a millennial designation describing the universal rule of Messiah over the earth during the future Kingdom Age (cf. Micah 4:13, "Lord ['ādôn] of all the earth"). **The north country** refers to Babylon whose invasions came on Israel from the north. **The south,** of course, refers to Egypt. Rather than the NIV text, **the one with the white horses toward the west,** the Hebrew may read "the one with the white horses after them" (cf. NIV marg. and NASB), that is, after **the black horses** going to the north. If that translation is followed, then north and south are the only directions mentioned. This would be appropriate to Israel's location.

6:7b-8. The speaker in these verses is the Lord, introduced simply as **He. My Spirit** probably refers here to divine wrath (hence the NIV marg., "spirit"; cf. God's wrath subsiding, as recorded in Ezek. 5:13; 16:42; 24:13). God's wrath, after being executed on the wickedness transplanted to Babylon (Zech. 5:5-11; cf. Rev. 18:2, 10, 21; 19:1-3) will then come to **rest.** In the first vision God was angry with the nations that felt secure (Zech. 1:15); in this vision He was satisfied with their just judgment (cf. Rev. 19:2, 15-19).

C. The symbolic act concluding the visions (6:9-15)

The eight night visions were brought to a conclusion with a divine oracle to Zechariah. God instructed him to perform a symbolic act by crowning Joshua the high priest. Joshua hereby represented "the Branch," the Messiah, who will rebuild the future temple and will be both a Priest and a King.

1. THE SYMBOLIC CROWNING (6:9-11)

6:9-11. By **the word of the LORD** (this formula, indicating direct prophetic revelation, assumes that the night visions had terminated) Zechariah was instructed to crown **Joshua** the **high priest** with a **crown** made of **silver and gold.** The precious metals were received from a small, otherwise unknown delegation of Jewish **exiles** from Babylon—**Heldai** (the Heb. text calls him Helem in v. 14), **Tobijah, and Jedaiah**—who probably brought **the silver and gold to** aid in the rebuilding of the temple. They were apparently visiting at the home of an also otherwise unknown Jew—**Josiah son of Zephaniah** (nicknamed Hen, meaning "gracious one," in v. 14). The "crown" is singular though the Hebrew word for it is plural, perhaps indicating a "plural of majesty" or the fact that it might have had several parts, or tiers (made of *two* precious metals). The crowning of the high priest Joshua, rather than Zerubbabel the governor (Hag. 1:1, 12, 14; 2:21; cf. Zech. 4:6-10) safeguards the symbolic significance of the crowning. The crowning of Zerubbabel could have been misunderstood by some as the crowning of the messianic Son of David, since Zerubbabel, like the promised Messiah, was both a descendant of David and a political leader.

2. THE PROPHETIC MESSAGE (6:12-13)

6:12-13. God told Zechariah to convey to Joshua that he would represent or typify **the Branch** who will rebuild the millennial temple. The crowning had a typical significance pointing forward to the Messiah as King-Priest, like Melchizedek centuries earlier (Gen. 14:18-20; Ps. 110:4; cf. Heb. 7:11-21). The title "Branch" is a messianic title, as already indicated (Zech. 3:8). Since the promise to rebuild the postexilic temple in Zechariah's day was given to Zerubbabel (4:9), any role Joshua himself had was apparently minor. So the promise that the Branch will **build the temple of the LORD** is probably limited to Messiah's role in establishing the millennial temple (cf. Isa. 2:2-4; 56:6-7; Ezek. 40–46; Micah 4:1-2).

The messianic Branch **will be clothed with majesty**; this refers to Christ as the Bearer of the essential glory of God (cf. Isa. 4:2; John 1:14). Christ will also **sit and rule on His throne** (Isa. 9:7; Jer. 23:5; Micah 4:3, 7; Zeph. 3:15; Zech. 14:9) as a **Priest** (Heb. 4:15; 5:6; 7:11-21) **on His throne.** A Levitical priest could never become a king and sit on a throne. But Christ will unite in Himself the offices of priest and king, as also indicated in the statement, there will be harmony between the two (i.e., the two offices of priest and king).

3. THE VISIBLE MEMORIAL (6:14)

6:14. God told Zechariah to give **the crown** to the delegation from Babylon **as a memorial** of the significant and typical crowning of Joshua. Apparently after Joshua was crowned, the three were to place the crown **in the temple of the LORD,** after it would be built.

4. THE UNIVERSAL SIGNIFICANCE (6:15)

6:15. Imperceptibly the divine instructions to Zechariah to perform the symbolic crowning seem to have merged with a prophecy spoken by the Branch or the Angel of the Lord (who are One and the same), who is sent by the Lord (**the LORD Almighty has sent Me to you**). The deputation from Babylon, though consisting of Jews, appears to be typical of all **those who are far away** who will **help to build the** millennial **temple.** People from many nations around the world will bring their wealth for the temple (Isa. 60:5, 9, 11; 61:6b; Hag. 2:7-8).

II. The Four Explanatory Messages (chaps. 7–8)

A. The messages required by the question about fasting (7:1-3)

7:1-2. Nearly two years after the night visions (December 7, 518 B.C.; cf. v. 1 with 1:7) and about halfway through the period of temple rebuilding (520–516) **Zechariah** gave four messages. Three of the messages were introduced by the clause "the word of the LORD Almighty came to me" (7:4; 8:1, 18). The second message was introduced similarly: "The word of the LORD came again to Zechariah" (7:8). These messages were given in response to a delegation that came to Jerusalem to ask whether the nation should continue to fast in remembrance of Jerusalem's destruction. The delegates were evidently Jews (in spite of their foreign names, apparently acquired in Babylon) who came from **Bethel** (cf. Ezra 2:28), the Israelite city 12 miles north of Jerusalem that had been the center of apostate worship for the Northern 10 tribes of Israel (cf. 1 Kings 12:28-29; 13:1; Amos 7:13). (The KJV reads, "When they had sent unto the house of God Sherezer and Regemmelech." This trans. does not specify who sent them or where they came from. For a discussion of this and other views on the grammatical problem in the sentence, see Baldwin, *Zechariah,* pp. 141-3.)

7:3. The question raised by the Bethelites implied a desire to discontinue the self-imposed religious observance of fasting **in the fifth month** (July-August, the month Ab), which commemorated the burning to the ground of the city and the temple by Nebuchadnezzar (2 Kings 25:8-10).

B. The messages declared as the answer from the Lord (7:4–8:23)

1. A MESSAGE OF REBUKE (7:4-7)

7:4-7. The answer to the delegates' question was not given till the fourth message (8:18-19). Meanwhile the first divine message reminded the people that God warned their fathers **through the earlier prophets** that He wanted reality, not ritual (e.g., Isa. 1:11-17; Hosea 6:6; Amos 5:21-24). The question provided an occasion to rebuke self-imposed fasts that not only were antiquated by God's present blessing on the returned remnant but also were observed without proper motivation and spiritual attitude. Thus the rebuke was against empty formalism devoid of spiritual reality, for whether fasting or **feasting,** they were doing it not for the Lord (Zech. 7:5) but for themselves (v. 6).

The exiles had observed two fasts during the Babylonian Captivity, one in the **fifth** month (see comments on v. 3) and one in the **seventh** month. This seventh-month fast was not the divinely instituted fast on the annual Day of Atonement (Lev. 16:29, 31; 23:26-32), which was also in the seventh month, but a fast commemorating the murder of Gedaliah, governor of Judah, during a time of civil strife after the fall of **Jerusalem** (Jer. 41:2). The feasting probably included both the national feasts of Leviticus 23 and the family feasts associated with Levitical sacrifices (cf. Deut. 12:5-7).

2. A MESSAGE OF REPENTANCE (7:8-14)

7:8-10. The second message from **the LORD** centered on the conduct of the earlier generation that resulted in the Exile. In preexilic times, as in Zechariah's own day, God desired inner spiritual reality rather than external formalism. **True**

justice (cf. Isa. 1:17; Amos 5:24) along with **mercy and compassion** (cf. Zech. 8:16-17; Micah 6:8) should be demonstrated toward all, but especially toward **the widow . . . the fatherless, the alien,** and **the poor** (cf. Deut. 15:7-11; 24:14-15, 19-21; 26:12-13), who were in no position to stand up for themselves, and so are often mentioned in the Bible as objects of God's care. In addition God's people were not even to **think evil of each other.**

7:11-14. The previous generation had been disobedient; **they turned their backs** (lit., "shoulder") **and** plugged up **their ears** (cf. Isa. 6:10). **They made their hearts as hard as flint** (KJV, "an adamant stone," i.e., diamond) and neither listened to nor obeyed **the words that the LORD Almighty had sent by His Spirit through the earlier prophets.** This statement not only places the words of the preexilic prophets on a par with the Mosaic Law but also identifies the Spirit of God as the Source of prophetic inspiration who spoke through human agents (cf. 2 Tim. 3:16; 2 Peter 1:21). The people's disobedience to revealed truth resulted in divine anger, the results of which are indicated in Zechariah 7:13-14: (a) a denial of response to prayer (v. 13), (b) a dispersion **among . . . the nations** (v. 14a), (c) a desolation of the **land** (v. 14b).

3. A MESSAGE OF RESTORATION (8:1-17)

As chapter 7 resembles the call to repentance in 1:2-6, so chapter 8 reflects the promised blessings pictured throughout the night visions (1:7–6:8). Thus the third and fourth messages view the restoration from Exile in Zechariah's day as a precursor of future blessing and prosperity in the Millennial Age. They also place emphasis on that future time when righteousness, justice, and peace will fill the earth.

8:1. Zechariah again identified this message as a revelation from God (cf. 7:4, 8; 8:18). The message is divided into seven parts by the recurring phrase, "This is what the LORD Almighty [or LORD] says" (vv. 2-4, 6-7, 9, 14). Whether each of these sections summarizes more lengthy messages which Zechariah delivered orally but did not record cannot be determined from the passage.

8:2. God's zeal on behalf of **Zion**

(i.e., the people of Jerusalem) is affirmed in superlative terms (cf. 1:14; Joel 2:18).

8:3. God's resumed presence with His people when He will **return to Zion and dwell in Jerusalem** (cf. 2:12) anticipates millennial fulfillment through the personal reign of Christ on the throne of David. At that time His **truth** and holiness (cf. Joel 3:17; Obad. 17) will be imparted in **the city** and throughout the earth. Zion was originally the name of the mound where the Jebusites lived, whose fortress David conquered (2 Sam. 5:7). Later Zion (and Mount Zion) were names for the temple site in Jerusalem (Ps. 2:6; Isa. 8:18; Joel 2:1). Also Zion became a synonym for the entire city of Jerusalem (Isa. 2:3; 4:3; 33:20; Amos 1:2; Micah 3:10, 12). Zion and Jerusalem are mentioned together several times by Zechariah (Zech. 1:14, 17; 8:3; 9:9).

8:4-5. Jerusalem will be secure and safe for senior citizens and children alike (cf. Isa. 65:20-22).

8:6. Such future blessings **may seem marvelous to the remnant of this people at that time,** in contrast with the destruction that will precede it (cf. Matt. 24:15-25), but such miraculous performances are not difficult for God (cf. Gen. 18:14; Matt. 19:26).

8:7-8. Once again the LORD promised to regather Israel and Judah in the future. **The countries of the east and the west** is probably a merism for countries in all directions, all over the earth (cf. Isa. 11:11-12; 43:5-6). The worldwide scope of this restoration suggests that **Jerusalem** represents the land of Israel as a whole. This regathering will institute a restored relationship between God and Israel (**They will be My people;** cf. Zech. 13:9; Hosea 2:21-23) in which God's faithfulness and righteousness will be most evident (cf. Hosea 2:19-20).

8:9-13. The people who heard **these words spoken by the prophets** (Zechariah and Haggai) were to be encouraged (**let your hands be strong;** cf. Hag. 2:4) to complete the rebuilding of **the temple.** God's promises of future blessing should always encourage His people in their present tasks.

Before that time, when the people started to rebuild the temple, their work had little results (Hag. 1:6, 9-11; 2:16-19) and enemies kept them unsafe. Israel's future blessings relate not only to the productivity of the land (Zech. 8:12) but also to a reversed role among the nations (v. 13). Now an object of cursing among the nations (cf. Deut. 28:37), Judah and Israel . . . will be a blessing (cf. Micah 5:7; Zech. 8:22-23). Therefore the people should not be afraid (cf. v. 15).

8:14-17. The LORD then affirmed the certainty of the fulfillment of His divine purpose for future blessing. He contrasted that forthcoming blessing with the already fulfilled promises of disaster which He brought on their sinning fathers (vv. 14-15; cf. 7:11-14). In view of the options of disaster and blessing, God offered His people an agenda that reflected spiritual reality rather than the hypocritical formalism that had characterized their fathers and was threatening them. Truth, justice, mercy, and honesty should characterize them in both personal and civil spheres (cf. 7:9-10). In short, the message is, "Do the things God loves (cf. 8:19) and avoid the things God hates."

4. A MESSAGE OF REJOICING (8:18-23)

8:18. Like the preceding word of the LORD through Zechariah, this one is also divided into several sections by the repeated phrase, "This is what the LORD Almighty says" (vv. 19-20, 23).

8:19. The LORD waited till now to answer the question raised by the Bethel delegates (7:2-3) about the commemorative fasts. He said the fasts would become joyful and glad occasions and happy festivals. Two additional fasts are included which were not previously mentioned (cf. 7:3, 5)—one on the 10th day of the 10th month to remember the commencement of the siege of Jerusalem (2 Kings 25:1-2; Jer. 39:1), and one on the 9th day of the 4th month to recall the capture of Jerusalem by Nebuchadnezzar (the 9th day of the 4th month was the day the city wall was breached, 2 Kings 25:3-4; Jer. 39:2). These fasts were all self-imposed and had been observed for 70 years (Zech. 7:5) with sorrowful hearts and misdirected motives (cf. 7:5-7). These fasts are still observed by some Jews today. But at the Lord's Second Advent these fasts will be turned into feasts, symbolizing millennial joy. Therefore again the people in Zechariah's day were encouraged by their future hope to love

what God loves (cf. 8:16-17), in this case, truth and peace.

8:20-23. In the future day of blessing, peoples of the whole earth will join with Jews because of their relationship with the LORD. People will know that God is with Israel and that they are His people (v. 8). As a result, many nations will come to Jerusalem to worship during the Millennium (cf. 14:16-19; Isa. 2:3).

III. Two Revelatory Oracles (chaps. 9–14)

The final division of the book consists of two oracles (see comments on 9:1-8) that look forward to the messianic King and kingdom. Chapters 9–11 refer (for the most part) to the First Advent of Christ, stressing the theme of His rejection but also outlining Israel's prophetic history to the end times. Chapters 12–14 focus on Messiah's Second Advent and emphasize His enthronement as the commencement of the grand finale of Israel's history.

These two oracles contain numerous passages which are counterparts to major themes of the eight visions, thus giving testimony to the unity of the entire Book of Zechariah. The future prosperity of Israel and Jerusalem (first vision, 1:7-17) parallels 10:6-9 (in the first oracle) and 12:6-8 and 14:11 (in the second oracle). The destruction of the nations (second vision, 1:18-21) is reaffirmed in 9:1-8 (first oracle) and in 12:1-6 and 14:1-3 (second oracle). The divine protection and exaltation of Jerusalem (third vision, chap. 2) are further developed in 9:9-17 (first oracle) and in 12:7-9 and 14:4-11 (second oracle). The spiritual cleansing of Israel (fourth vision, chap. 3) is clarified in 10:2-3 (first oracle) and in 12:10-14 and 14:8 (second oracle). The divine enablement of Israel (fifth vision, chap. 4) is explained in 10:1-6 (first oracle) and in 13:1-6 (second oracle). Divine judgment on sinners (sixth vision, 5:1-4) is elaborated in chapter 11 (first oracle) and in 13:7-9 and 14:12-15 (second oracle). The removal of iniquity from the land of Israel (seventh vision, 5:5-11) results in a condition of holiness in Jerusalem and Judah (14:20-21, second oracle). God's judgment on and rule of the whole world (eighth vision, 6:1-8) are reflected in 14:16-19 (second oracle).

A. The anointed King rejected (chaps. 9–11)

1. THE INTERVENING JUDGMENTS ON NATIONS SURROUNDING ISRAEL (9:1-8)

The NIV regards the term "An oracle" ("burden," KJV) as a heading separated from verse 1, which begins with, "the word of the LORD" (cf. 12:1). This is probably more accurate than the redundant translation of the KJV, "The burden of the word of the LORD." The Hebrew word *maśśā'* ("oracle") is derived from the verb *nāśā'* which has two meanings—"to bear" and "to lift up." Though some translations (KJV, ASV) and scholars (e.g., Baldwin, *Zechariah*, pp. 162-3) have understood the word *maśśā'* to mean "burden," an ominous message of judgment which was borne by the prophetic messenger, the word is more likely based on the other nuance of the verb—"to lift up (the voice)" (cf. Jud. 9:7, "shouted"; Isa. 3:7; 42:2, "cry out"). The noun is used this way ("oracle," not "burden") in Numbers 23:7; 24:3, 15-16. So the noun in Zechariah 9:1 and 12:1 should be translated "oracle"—what is lifted up (by the voice), whether a threat or a promise. In this context in Zechariah the two oracles are primarily promises of salvation.

Most conservative commentators regard 9:1-8 as a prophecy of the conquests of Alexander the Great throughout the area of Palestine after the battle of Issus in 333 B.C. Zechariah, living in the days of the Medo-Persian Empire, predicted the coming Grecian Empire (9:1-8, 13), the Roman Empire (11:4-14), and Israel's future in the last days (chaps. 12–14).

9:1-2. Alexander the Great was probably the human cause of the destruction set forth in these and the following verses (the order of the cities seems to correspond generally with Alexander's line of march). But his involvement is bypassed in this prophecy to stress the ultimate divine cause of the judgment on certain cities and countries beginning north of Israel. The northernmost location, **Hadrach,** was probably Hatarikka, a city and country lying north of Hamath and mentioned in Assyrian cuneiform inscriptions. **Damascus** was the capital of Aram (Syria). The words, **the eyes of men and all the tribes of Israel are on the LORD** indicate the awe of all peoples at the divine judgment brought on their cities. **Hamath** was an Aramean (Syrian)

city north of Damascus on the Orontes River. Westward on the coast were the Phoenician cities of **Tyre and Sidon.**

9:3-4. **Tyre** was **a stronghold,** a citadel of defense which had withstood a 5-year siege by the Assyrians under Shalmaneser V and, years later, a 13-year siege by the Babylonian army of Nebuchadnezzar. Her commercial and economic self-sufficiency is reflected in figures of speech which speak of **silver** being as common as **dust and gold** as common as **the dirt** (cf. Ezek. 28:4-5; 27:33). Her impoverishment and destruction by Alexander's relatively brief five-month siege are ascribed to God's ultimate action in destroying **her power on the sea** (NASB, "cast her wealth into the sea"; cf. Ezek. 26:17-21; 27:27, 34).

9:5-7. Four of the five principal Philistine cities (Gath is omitted) are next on the judgment march (cf. Amos 1:6-8; Zeph. 2:4; Jer. 25:20). **The blood** and **the forbidden food** (from idolatrous sacrifices) removed from the very **mouths** and clenched **teeth** of some Philistines indicate their removal from idolatry to **belong** to the **God** of Israel and even **become leaders in Judah. Like the Jebusites,** they will be absorbed into the population of God's people. Since there is no evidence that this was fulfilled in the invasion of Alexander, it apparently awaits future fulfillment as part of the blessing that will result from the messianic rule (Zech. 9:10).

9:8. The Macedonian armies of Alexander passed and repassed the city of Jerusalem without laying siege to it. The ultimate cause of this was the divine protection of the city (**I will defend My house**). This defense foreshadows God's final protection of the city in the Millennium, when **never again will** enemies invade Jerusalem (cf. Joel 3:17).

2. THE BLESSINGS OF THE MESSIAH (9:9–10:12)

a. The coming of the Prince of Peace (9:9)

9:9. The inhabitants of Jerusalem were personified as the **Daughter of Zion** (cf. 2:10; Isa. 1:8) and the **Daughter of Jerusalem** who, representing the whole nation of Israel, were exhorted to welcome the coming King not with fear but with glad rejoicing. The announcement that **your King comes to you** refers to the long-awaited King and Messiah (cf. Isa. 9:5-7; Micah 5:2-4; Luke 1:32-33). **Righteous** describes both His character and His reign (cf. Ps. 45:6-7; Isa. 11:1-5; 32:17; Jer. 23:5-6; 33:15-16). The phrase **having salvation** denotes that He will come as a Deliverer, as One to give salvation to others (cf. Isa. 62:11). His peaceful entrance—**riding on a donkey**—was fulfilled when He presented Himself to Israel in the Triumphal Entry (Matt. 21:1-5). In the ancient Near East, if a king came in peace, he would ride on a donkey instead of on a war stallion. Christ rode **on a colt, the foal** (lit., "son") **of a donkey.** (On the question of whether Christ rode one or two donkeys see comments on Matt. 21:2.) Like some other Old Testament prophecies this one (Zech. 9:9-10) blends two events into one perspective—events that the New Testament divides into two distinct advents of Christ separated by the present Church Age (cf. Isa. 9:6-7; 61:1-2; Luke 4:18-21). In His First Advent He rode on a donkey and presented Himself to the nation Israel but they rejected Him as their King. So His universal rule (Zech. 9:10) will be established when He comes again.

b. *The kingdom of the Prince of Peace (9:10–10:12)*

(1) Messiah will establish peace. **9:10.** God's destruction of war instruments—removing **the chariots,** the **war horses,** and **the battle bow**—signifies the end of war in the Millennium (cf. Isa. 2:4; Micah 4:3). This peaceful **rule** of the coming messianic King **will extend from sea to sea and from the River** (the Euphrates; cf. Micah 7:12; Isa. 7:20) **to the ends of the earth.** These expressions clearly indicate the worldwide extent of the messianic kingdom.

(2) Messiah will deliver Israel (9:11-17). **9:11-12.** God's faithfulness to His covenants with Israel is His basis for delivering her from worldwide dispersion. The immediate addressees in these verses may have been Jewish exiles still in Babylon, but the covenant-fulfillment theme suggests an ultimate reference to Israel's end-time regathering. At least the nation's future hope (messianic deliverance) was the basis for contemporary encouragement in Zechariah's day. **The blood of My covenant with you** may refer to the sacrifices of the Mosaic Cove-

nant (cf. Ex. 24:8), but could as well relate back to the foundational Abrahamic Covenant which was confirmed with a blood sacrifice (Gen. 15:8-21). **The waterless pit** (an empty cistern used for a dungeon) is probably a figure for the place of exile. The **fortress** refers to Jerusalem. The exiles in Babylon were called **prisoners of hope** because they had God's promise of being regathered. God **will restore twice as much,** that is, His blessings in the Millennium will far exceed anything Israel has ever known.

9:13. At least this verse, and perhaps the rest of the chapter, refer to the conflict of the Maccabees (169–135 B.C.) with Antiochus IV Epiphanes (cf. Dan. 11:32; see comments on Dan. 8:9-14), Antiochus V Eupator, Antiochus VI, and Antiochus VII Sidetes, Greek rulers of Syria. This Jewish victory foreshadowed Israel's final conflict and victory when God will bring them into millennial blessing. As the **bow** and arrow (that which "fills" the bow) are each essential to the other, so **Judah** and **Ephraim** (Ephraim represents the 10 Northern tribes of Israel) will be reunited. The reference to these weapons of warfare (including the **warrior's sword**) indicates that God will empower His people to defeat the enemy, the **sons** of **Greece.**

9:14-15. The description of a thunderstorm controlled by God (v. 14) pictures poetically Israel's empowerment for victory over her enemies (v. 15). The divine appearance was through providential means in the Maccabean period but will be literal and visible when Christ appears victoriously at His Second Advent. The last part of verse 15 pictures Israel's unrestrained joy and fullness of rejoicing because of God's mighty deliverance.

9:16-17. The divine deliverance predicted here will come **on that day,** a reference to the end time. **God will care** for them as a shepherd cares for his **flock** (cf. 10:3). Then Israel **will sparkle in His land like jewels in a crown.** This is a beautiful cameo of the fulfilled promises concerning the people in the land (cf. Amos 9:11-15). They will be **attractive and beautiful** symbols of all God has done for them. Divine blessing on nature will produce conditions of plenty (cf. Joel 2:21-27) so that physical health will also be assured (Zech. 9:17).

(3) Messiah will destroy the false shepherds at His coming. **10:1-5.** The exhortation in verse 1 is transitional, indicating that the source of natural blessings (**rain and plants of the field**) is the LORD, not idolatrous and deceptive false **shepherds** (vv. 2-3). As a result of the deception by the false (and apparently foreign) prophets and **diviners**, God's **people wander like sheep.** Therefore God announced that He would bring wrath and judgment on the false shepherds and victory to **His flock** (cf. Micah 5:4). The remedy for the nation's deception focuses on the coming of the Messiah who is described in a fourfold way as **the Cornerstone** (cf. Isa. 28:16), **the Tent Peg . . . the Battle Bow** (cf. Ps. 45:5), and the **Ruler** (cf. Gen. 49:10; Micah 5:2). These terms emphasize the strong, stable, victorious, and trustworthy nature of Messiah's rule. The Lord will not do all the fighting but will empower His people to conquer **like mighty men.** His presence (He will be **with them**) will enable them to be victorious.

(4) Messiah will regather all Israel (10:6-12). The worldwide scope of this prophecy relating to both Israel and Judah and God's activity on behalf of His Chosen People indicate that the final regathering of Israel just before the Second Advent of the Messiah is in view.

10:6-7. God announced that He **will strengthen** (cf. v. 12) and deliver all Israel (**Joseph** was the father of two major Northern tribes, Ephraim and Manasseh). **Because** of His **compassion** they will be restored and reunited (cf. Hosea 1:11), with their sins forgiven and forgotten—**as though I had not rejected them,** enjoying communion with God (**I will answer them**). The name of the northern tribe of Ephraim was sometimes used for the Northern Kingdom (cf. Hosea 10:6; 11:8, 12). Israelites will **be glad** and **joyful** and will **rejoice in the LORD** because of God's blessings on them.

10:8-10. Israel will be regathered from present worldwide dispersion. God announced, **I will signal for them.** The term "signal" means "whistle" (as in gathering a swarm of insects; cf. Isa. 7:18) or "pipe" (as a shepherd using a reed pipe to gather his flocks; cf. Jud. 5:16). The latter meaning seems more appropriate in view of the shepherd/sheep imagery in the general context (Zech. 9:16;

10:2-3; 11:4-16; 13:7). Their regathering will be accompanied by redemption and multiplication (10:8b; cf. Hosea 1:10). On the human side their **return** will involve the fact that **they will remember** God. On the divine side God said, **I will bring them back. Egypt** and **Assyria** are representative of all the countries of Israel's dispersion (cf. Hosea 11:11; Zech. 10:11). **Gilead and Lebanon** are probably named to indicate the northern and eastern extents of Israel's occupancy of the land promised to Abraham (Gen. 15:18; cf. Deut. 30:3-5).

10:11-12. In regathering Israel to the land, God will remove every obstacle to restoration, pictured in terms of the ancient deliverance when He brought Israel **through the sea** on dry land. Again Assyria and Egypt were mentioned to represent all Israel's enemies (cf. v. 10). The prophecy closes with its opening phrase, **I will strengthen them,** so that Israel's behavior (**walk**) will be **in His name** (i.e., she will glorify Him by obeying Him).

3. THE REJECTION OF THE GOOD SHEPHERD AND ITS CONSEQUENCES FOR ISRAEL (CHAP. 11)

This dark chapter conveys the cause for the delay in Israel's realizing the blessings of chapter 10.

a. The coming of wrath introduced (11:1-3)

11:1-3. This lamentation portrays the impending devastation that will result from the people rejecting the Messiah as the True and Good Shepherd (vv. 4-14). The language obviously involves personification, but the references to the **cedars of Lebanon . . . oaks of Bashan,** and **lush thicket of the Jordan** suggest devastation of the entire land of Israel from the north to the south, including of course its inhabitants. All three areas—Lebanon, Bashan, and the Jordan—were heavily forested. **Shepherds** would **wail** because their **pastures** would be devastated. Even **lions** who lived in the thick woods around the Jordan River would **roar** because of the destruction of their living areas.

The general description of the devastation is to be taken literally. However, some writers have viewed the trees as representing the glory of Jerusalem, particularly the temple which was constructed, in part, of lumber. While this is doubtful, the general period of the destruction, whether literal or figurative, probably includes the destruction of Jerusalem by the Romans in A.D. 70.

b. The cause of devastation indicated (11:4-14)

In this difficult but messianically significant passage, Zechariah was directed by God to portray Israel's true Shepherd-Messiah. Then (vv. 15-17) Zechariah was required to portray the wicked shepherd, pointing to the end-time Antichrist. The passage (vv. 4-14) is probably not intended to be a strict dramatic portrayal, for this would require the unlikely cooperation of other actors in the narrative. The passage focuses attention on Israel's spiritual condition at the time of Christ's ministry and the consequences of her rejection of Christ, the True Shepherd.

11:4. God told Zechariah, **Pasture the flock marked for slaughter.** To "pasture" includes not only feeding but also directing and defending. The "flock" was the nation Israel which God had designated for slaughter by the Romans.

11:5. There is debate whether the **buyers** of the flock and **those who sell them** were Jewish leaders or foreign oppressors. However, **their own shepherds** are Jewish leaders who would fail in their responsibilities to care for their people (cf. 10:3).

11:6. The climactic phase of Israel's apparently pitiable condition was God's withholding of pity: **I will no longer have pity on the people of the land.** This divine withdrawal seemed to result from the people's rejection of their true Shepherd-Messiah, stated in verses 8-13. The **king** to whom God would hand over Israel was apparently the Roman emperor (cf. John 19:15, "We have no king but Caesar"). God would not deliver them from the Roman armies.

11:7. As commanded, Zechariah portrayed the work of a shepherd tending **the flock marked for slaughter** (cf. v. 4), especially **the oppressed of the flock.** This perhaps refers to the believing remnant at Messiah's First Advent. Like any good shepherd, Zechariah **took two staffs** to use in directing and protecting the flock. The staffs were given the symbolic names of **Favor** (or beauty, grace, pleasantness) and **Union** (lit., bands or

"ties"). They depicted God's gracious benefits toward His people (cf. 9:14-17) and the internal union of Israel and Judah as a nation (cf. Hosea 1:11).

11:8-9. The identity of **the three shepherds** disowned by the True Shepherd is not indicated (accounting for the more than 40 interpretations of v. 8!). Most likely, the shepherds refer to three kinds of Jewish leaders—prophets (custodians of the Law), priests, and kings (or civil magistrates)—all of them inadequate. Closely linked to the disowning of the three shepherds is the flock's disowning of their True Shepherd whom they **detested,** a word (used only here in the OT) that means to loathe to the point of nausea. The Messiah (portrayed by Zechariah) repudiated His role as Shepherd (**I will not be your Shepherd**), and He relegated the flock to their doom, involving foreign oppression (**Let the dying die and the perishing perish**) and internal civil strife (**Let those who are left eat one another's flesh**). An alternate interpretation sees this last clause as speaking of the cannibalism that occurred in the Roman siege of Jerusalem in A.D. 70.

11:10-11. The revoked **covenant** (symbolized by breaking the **staff called Favor**) had been **made with all the nations,** apparently to secure God's providential protection of Israel. The divine disfavor on Israel because of her rejection of the True Shepherd resulted in spiritual blindness (Rom. 11:25) and national destruction and dispersion. Only the believing remnant (**the afflicted of the flock**) who recognized Jesus as the true Messiah understood His true origin in God.

11:12-13. Israel's appraisal of the True Shepherd's worth was **30 pieces of silver,** the compensation price for a slave gored by an ox (Ex. 21:32). Baldwin thinks 30 pieces of silver for a slave indicates the "high value set on human life" in the Mosaic Law (*Zechariah,* p. 184). Whether or not this is correct, the choice of the slave price was probably intended as an insult to the Shepherd, worse than a direct refusal to pay Him any wage. Throwing this **handsome price** (an obvious use of irony) **to the potter** shows its trifling worth (**the potter** was one of the lowest of the laboring class). This prophecy was fulfilled in Judas' betrayal of Christ (Matt. 26:14-16; 27:3-10; for a survey of problems relating to Matthew's citation of this passage, cf. Hobart E. Freeman, *An Introduction to the Old Testament Prophets.* Chicago: Moody Press, 1968, pp. 340-2).

11:14. Zechariah then **broke** the **second staff called Union** to picture the dissolving of the national solidarity of **Judah and Israel.** Discord within the nation was one of the factors that led to the destruction of Jerusalem in A.D. 70 and a new wave of worldwide dispersion.

c. The consequences of rejecting the True Shepherd (11:15-17)

After rejecting the True Shepherd, the flock of Israel will accept a foolish and worthless shepherd. This is a prophecy of the end-time Antichrist who will do the very opposite of Christ the True Shepherd (cf. John 5:43).

11:15-16. Zechariah was called on to portray a second prophetic role, this time **a foolish shepherd.** The Hebrew word rendered "foolish" (*'ĕwîl*) suggests a person who is a coarse, hardened fool. This **shepherd** will have no concern for the flock and its needs; he will be interested only in his own gluttony. Instead of defending the flock, the foolish shepherd will destroy it (cf. Rev. 13:7).

11:17. Thus the foolish shepherd is also a **worthless shepherd who** rightfully deserves the condemnation pronounced (**Woe**). The **arm** indicates his strength and the **eye** his intelligence. The foolish plottings of the worthless shepherd will be annulled when the True Shepherd returns (cf. 12:10; Rev. 19:19-20).

B. The rejected King enthroned (chaps. 12–14)

Chapters 12–14 are one "oracle" (KJV, "burden"; cf. 9:1) concerning God's people Israel. The events predicted deal with one future time period (except for 13:7) and center in the city of Jerusalem. Thus the prophecies of these chapters rank among the most significant in the Old Testament.

1. THE REDEMPTION OF ISRAEL (CHAPS. 12–13)

Two conditions are necessary for the establishment of Israel's future messianic kingdom: (a) the overthrow of the Gentile world powers that oppose the establishment of this kingdom and (b) the regeneration of individual Jews who will constitute the nation when God fulfills the Abrahamic and Davidic Covenants. Both of these conditions will be accomplished by the Lord, as seen in chapters 12–13. He will deliver Israel physically from her enemies (12:1-9) and He will deliver her spiritually (12:10–13:9).

a. Israel's physical deliverance (12:1-9)

12:1-3. The future siege of **Jerusalem** by the nations (cf. 14:1-5) is revealed through **the word of the LORD,** who is identified as the great Preserver of His Creation (portrayed in 12:1 by **stretches out . . . lays . . . forms,** which are pres. participles in Heb.). This almighty power of the Lord is mentioned to confirm His ability to fulfill the deliverance predicted in the following verses.

An introductory summary is given in figurative language (v. 2) and a concluding summary is given in literal language (v. 9). God will destroy **the surrounding peoples** (i.e., **all the nations of the earth,** v. 3) who besiege **Judah** and **Jerusalem . . . on that day.** "That day" (mentioned five times in vv. 3-4, 6, 8-9, three times in chap. 13 [vv. 1-2, 4], and seven times in chap. 14 [vv. 4, 6, 8-9, 13, 20-21]) refers to the future Battle (or better, Campaign) of Armageddon, in which the nations' armies will gather against Jerusalem (cf. 14:1-3; Rev. 16:16; 19:19). Some think that Judah will be on the side of the nations till they recognize that God is empowering the Jerusalemites (Zech. 12:5). Two metaphors describe how God will use Jerusalem as a foil to destroy the nations: (1) Jerusalem will be **a cup** of **reeling** (v. 2). This common prophetic phrase describes divine judgment (cf. Isa. 51:17, 21-22; Jer. 25:15-28). (2) **Jerusalem** will be **an immovable rock** (Zech. 12:3). The defeat of the Armageddon armies is thus likened to a man who drinks more than he can hold, or tries to move a weight heavier than he can lift. Those who attack Jerusalem will do so to their own ruin.

12:4-5. In verses 4-9 Judah's future deliverance by the Lord is described more fully in terms not only of the defeat of the nations but also of the victories first for Judah and then for Jerusalem.

The characteristic chaos of a cavalry defeat is here ascribed to divine intervention. God will cause **every horse** to **panic** and every **rider** to go mad, and **the horses** will be blinded (cf. 14:15; see comments on Ezek. 39:9-11 on whether literal horses will be involved in battles in the last days). In contrast, God's protective care for **Judah** is anthropomorphically attributed to His **watchful eye.** The leaders of Judah will recognize in faith the divine source of the empowerment for victory, so they will be encouraged also to trust **God** for triumph over their enemies.

12:6-7. Judah's future military triumph is described in two similes: **like a firepot in a woodpile, like a flaming torch among sheaves.** The armies of the nations will be devastated quickly and thoroughly as **Jerusalem** watches (**intact in her place**). Elsewhere Judah's enemies are said to be consumed like stubble burned by fire (e.g., Isa. 47:14; Obad. 18; Mal. 4:1). Judah's victory will come from the Lord (**the Lord will save . . . Judah first**). The priority of Judah's deliverance over that of Jerusalem will assure the entire nation's unity with the inhabitants of the capital city.

12:8-9. God will protect Jerusalem like a **shield** and will also give divine enablement to all **those who live in Jerusalem,** from the weakest to the greatest. This empowerment will be so great that the most feeble weakling **will be** a great warrior **like David,** and the leaders of the city (**the house of David**) **will be** granted superhuman strength. Some scholars believe the reference to "the house of David" is a personal reference to Christ at His Second Advent, but this is not likely since "the house of David" in verse 10 and 13:1 apparently refers simply to the political leaders of Israel. So 12:9 is a concluding summary regarding the defeat of **the nations** gathered against **Jerusalem** (cf. the introductory summary in v. 2).

b. Israel's spiritual deliverance
(12:10–13:9)

Israel's spiritual deliverance at the Second Advent of Christ will be accomplished only by a divinely provided fountain of cleansing (13:1) and the outpouring of the Holy Spirit to lead individual Israelites to repentant faith in Jesus as their Messiah (12:10-14).

(1) The outpouring of the Holy Spirit. **12:10a.** Both leaders (**the house of David**) and commoners (**the inhabitants of Jerusalem**)—thus excluding no Israelites (cf. 13:1)—will be the objects of the outpouring of the divine **spirit of grace and supplication.** This is most probably a reference to the Holy Spirit (see NIV marg.), so called because He will minister graciously to Israel in her sinful condition and will lead her to supplication and repentance.

(2) The mourning of the nation Israel (12:10b-14). **12:10b.** Thus Israelites will receive divine enablement to **look on Me, the One they have pierced.** The Lord refers to the nation's action of piercing Him, a term usually indicating "piercing to death." The piercing evidently refers to the rejection of Christ (as God Incarnate) and crucifying Him, though the word does not specifically refer to the Crucifixion. The "looking" could be either physical vision (sight) or spiritual vision (faith). Probably it refers here to both, for this will occur at the Second Advent of Christ when Israel will recognize her Messiah and turn to Him. The change to the third person (**mourn for Him,** rather than "mourn for Me") is common in prophetic literature. The mourning for sin that is prompted by the outpoured Spirit is illustrated by a private act of mourning (v. 10) and a public act of mourning (v. 11). The loss of **an only child** or of **a firstborn son** was aggravated by the felt curse associated with childlessness and the lack of an heir to continue the family name and property.

12:11. The future mourning of Israel over her Messiah is likened, in the second place (cf. v. 10), to the **weeping** on the day when godly King Josiah, the last hope of the fading Judean nation, was slain by Pharaoh Neco II, **at Hadad Rimmon,** traditionally identified as a village near Jezreel, **in the plain of Megiddo** (cf. 2 Chron. 35:20-27). Thus the greatness of the mourning at this final outpouring of the Holy Spirit can be compared only to the weeping of a most extreme individual (Zech. 12:10) and to corporate (v. 11) catastrophes of the nation.

12:12-14. These verses picture the universality and intensity of the nation's future mourning. David had a son named Nathan (2 Sam. 5:14) and Levi had a grandson named Shimei (Num. 3:17-18). There was also a Nathan who was a prophet in David's time (cf. 2 Sam.

7:1-17). Thus the mention of **the house of David . . . the house of Nathan . . . the house of Levi,** and **clan of Shimei** may refer to the repentance (and guilt) of kings, prophets, and priests; or if the Nathan referred to is David's son, then just the royal and priestly families are specified. The phrase **each clan by itself, with their wives by themselves** seems to indicate the individuality and thus the sincerity of the mourning rather than a mere outward conformity.

(3) The cleansing of the nation Israel (13:1-6). This section discusses the provision for Israel's cleansing (v. 1) and the removal of idolatry and false prophecy (vv. 2-6).

13:1. **That day** refers to the future day of the Lord (cf. 14:1). The phrase "on that day" occurs 16 times in these three closing chapters (12:3-4, 6, 8-9, 11; 13:1-2, 4; 14:4, 6, 8-9, 13, 20-21). On the day of Christ's crucifixion the fountain was opened *potentially* for all Israel and the whole world. At the Second Advent of Christ, the **fountain will be opened** *experientially* for the Jewish nation. This spiritual cleansing of the nation is associated in other passages of Scripture with Israel's spiritual regeneration and the inauguration of the New Covenant (e.g., Jer. 31:31-37; Ezek. 36:25-32; Rom. 11:26-27). **The house of David** (political leaders) and **the inhabitants of Jerusalem** include all the people of the land (cf. Zech. 12:10) who need cleansing. The terms **sin and impurity** can refer specifically to idolatry (cf. "impurity" in 13:2; Ezek. 7:19-20 speaks of gold being "unclean" and of idols being "detestable"), but they probably have a broader reference here to the total sinful condition of the people.

13:2a. The LORD announced His intention to **banish the names of the idols from the land** (cf. Micah 5:13-14). He will overcome all factors that detract from His worship and all idolatry will become extinct. Idolatry near the time of the Second Advent of Christ will include worship of the image of the beast in the temple in Jerusalem (Dan. 9:27; 11:31; Matt. 24:15; 2 Thes. 2:4; Rev. 13:4), though other types of idolatry will also be present (Rev. 9:20).

13:2b-3. Associated with the extinction of idolatry will be the extinguishing of false prophecy, which includes human false **prophets** and the (superhuman)

spirit of impurity (cf. v. 1), probably to be understood as a personal agency of evil, in contrast with the Spirit of grace, that will inspire false prophets. The death penalty enjoined against false prophets in Deuteronomy 18:20 (cf. Deut. 13:6-11) will be exacted by the nearest of kin, one's **parents,** to remove false prophets **from the land.**

13:4-6. This prevalence of justice will cause false prophets to disavow all associations with their prophetic trade. They will forego the deception of wearing **a prophet's** garb. Some true prophets did wear a **garment of hair** (e.g., Elijah, 2 Kings 1:8, and later John the Baptist, Matt. 3:4). Also to avoid detection, the alleged prophets will claim to have been involved in the lifelong occupation of farming. Further, false prophets will lie about the source of **wounds** or scars on their bodies. This probably means on the chest (though the Heb. phrase, lit., "between your hands," NIV marg., could also refer to the back). These scars no doubt will be from self-inflicted wounds associated with idol-worship. To answer the accusation that they were involved in idol-worship, the false prophets will claim they were disciplined by those who love them, either loving parents or brawling companions. Some scholars relate Zechariah 13:6 to verses 7-9, and say that verse 6 refers to the Messiah. However, that makes the thought shift rather abruptly from verses 5 to 6. The thought in verse 6 fits better with the preceding verses on false prophets.

(4) The provision of the True Shepherd (13:7-9). In contrast with false prophets (vv. 2-6) the Lord presented His True Prophet, the Messiah, whom He calls My Shepherd. This poetic unit (vv. 7-9) highlights aspects of the *preceding* prophecy, including the piercing of the Messiah (12:10; cf. 11:7-8), the abandoning of the sheep (cf. 11:9), and the restoration of covenant relationship (13:1-2). This passage (vv. 7-9) speaks of the smitten Shepherd (v. 7a), the scattered sheep (vv. 7b-8), and the saved remnant (v. 9).

13:7a. This highly poetic utterance by the LORD Almighty combines a number of figures of speech. The abrupt turning aside to address a nonpresent agent (**Awake, O sword**) combines two figures of speech—apostrophe (a direct address to an impersonal object as if it were a person) and personification. These words ascribe to an inanimate object the ability to hear, respond, and arouse out of sleep. The "sword," as a synecdoche (mention of a specific object to represent the more general), represents any instrument causing death (cf. 2 Sam. 11:24; 12:9 where Uriah's death by arrows is ascribed to the sword). The basic idea, then, is that the Lord will direct the death of His **Shepherd**. He is the True Shepherd, the Messiah (cf. Zech. 11:4-14; John 10:11, 14, "the Good Shepherd"; Heb. 13:20, "the Great Shepherd"; 1 Peter 5:4, "the Chief Shepherd").

The Lord added that this Shepherd is **the Man who is close to Me.** The Hebrew word translated "who is close to Me" is found elsewhere only in Leviticus (6:2; 18:20; etc.) where it refers to a "near relative" (though it is trans. "neighbor" in the NIV). In Zechariah 13:7 the Lord is claiming identity of nature or unity of essence with His Shepherd, thus strongly affirming the Messiah's deity.

13:7b-8. Calling on the wielder of the sword to **strike the Shepherd,** the Lord then indicated the consequences: **the sheep will be scattered.** In His crucifixion Christ was smitten (Isa. 53:4, 7, 10). His own disciples abandoned Him like scattered sheep (Matt. 26:31, 56). The reference to God's turning His **hand against the little ones** may refer to His allowing the persecutions against Jewish Christians in the Book of Acts. The scattering of the sheep also seems to refer to the scattering of the Jewish nation when Jerusalem was destroyed by the Romans in A.D. 70. Just as the Olivet Discourse (Matt. 24–25; Mark 13; Luke 21) telescopes prophecies of the scattering of the Jewish nation fulfilled in A.D. 70 with those to be fulfilled in the last half of the future Tribulation period, so Zechariah here combines into one focus the same two periods and scatterings of the Jewish nation. Thus Zechariah 13:8-9 probably will see its final and complete fulfillment in Israel's dispersion in the Tribulation (cf. Rev. 12:6, 13-17). At that time **two-thirds** of the Jewish nation **will be struck down and perish,** but the surviving remnant will be restored, at least for the most part, to their covenant relationship with the Lord.

13:9. The surviving remnant will have been purged and purified by the persecutions in the Tribulation, as well as by God's judgment on living Israel at the Second Advent (cf. Ezek. 20:33-38; Matt. 25:1-30). They will **call** on the **name** of the Lord in faith (Zech. 12:10–13:1) and become a restored nation (Rom. 11:26-27). Their renewed covenant relationship with the Lord (Hosea 1–2; Jer. 32:38-41; Ezek. 37:23-28) will be reflected in God's words, **They are My people** (cf. Zech. 8:8), and the people's response, **The LORD is our** (lit., "my") **God** (cf. Hosea 2:21-23).

2. THE RETURN OF THE KING (CHAP. 14)

This chapter pictures the triumphant return of Israel's Messiah as the divine King. Thus it portrays the fulfillment of eschatological psalms—such as Psalms 93, 96–97, 99—which envision the universal earthly reign of the Lord. This reign is known from other Scriptures as the personal reign of the Messiah on the throne of David. Zechariah 14 progresses from the initial plundering of Jerusalem near the end of the future Tribulation, through the catastrophic judgment on the Gentile armies at Messiah's Second Advent and the establishment of His millennial reign, to a description of the worship in Jerusalem during the Millennium. The fact that these events have not yet occurred points to a premillennial return of Christ, that is, His return *before* the Millennium.

a. The deliverance of Jerusalem from the nations (14:1-3)

14:1. This summary verse announces the sack of Jerusalem in the **day of the LORD,** a theme occurring many times in the Old Testament, in relation to the severe judgments in the Tribulation period (e.g., Zeph. 1:14-18), as well as those accompanying the Second Advent (as here). The New Testament (2 Peter 3:10) makes it clear that the Millennial Age is also included within "the day of the LORD." The **plunder** which **will be divided** refers to the valuables in Jerusalem that will be taken and shared by the Gentile armies "in your midst" (better than NIV's **among you**), that is, within the city itself. This speaks of the self-assurance and seeming security of the conquerors.

14:2. This siege of **Jerusalem** by **all the nations** (i.e., their representative armies) is an early stage of the siege by the confederated Gentile armies described in 12:2-9 (cf. Isa. 34:2; Obad. 15; Rev. 16:14, 16) and known as the Battle (or better, Campaign) of Armageddon. Before the peoples of Judah and Jerusalem will be empowered for victory (Zech. 12:6-8; 14:14) and before the Lord brings about the destruction of the Gentile armies (12:9; 14:12-15), the Gentiles will at first obtain an initial but fleeting taste of victory in Jerusalem, including the typical characteristics of conquest described in verse 2. Either **half** of the population of Jerusalem will be left in **the city** (perhaps under occupational troops), or the Lord will return to destroy the enemies before their job is more than half completed.

14:3. Concerning the military intervention of the Messiah, Zechariah announced that **the LORD will go out and fight against those nations.** In military context the term "go out" is a technical term for a king going out to **battle,** which is the clear meaning here. The Lord will "fight" as a warrior (cf. Ex. 15:3; Isa. 42:13; Rev. 19:11-21).

b. The return of the Deliverer (14:4-5)

14:4-5. After affirming the fact of Messiah's military intervention, Zechariah explained the details of its accomplishment. It will begin with the personal appearance of the Messiah when **His feet will stand on the Mount of Olives,** the very place from which He ascended (Acts 1:11-12). Interestingly God's glory in Ezekiel's vision (Ezek. 11:23) departed from Jerusalem at a mountain **east of Jerusalem.** The apparent earthquake which will **split the Mount of Olives . . . in two from east to west** seems to be a direct intervention by the divine King. It will form **a great valley** eastward from Jerusalem as far as **Azel,** an unknown location, through which the remnant of Jews **will** flee. This may be the Valley of Jehoshaphat, spoken of by Joel, where God will judge the Gentiles (see comments on Joel 3:2, 12). The Lord will call the valley **My mountain valley.**

The **earthquake in the days of Uzziah** is mentioned in Amos 1:1 but not in the historical books. Josephus regarded it as a divine judgment on Uzziah for his intrusion into the temple to assume the priest's function (2 Chron. 26:16). When **the LORD** returns He will be accompanied by **all the holy ones,** probably angels as well as the souls of the redeemed (cf. 1 Thes. 3:13).

c. The establishment of the messianic kingdom (14:6-11)

At the heart of this section is the affirmation that "the LORD will be King over the whole earth" and that He will be accepted as the "one LORD" (v. 9). This great pronouncement is set in the context of changes in illumination, climate, and topography which God will bring on Jerusalem, Palestine, and no doubt the whole earth during the Millennium.

(1) The phenomena in the kingdom (14:6-8). **14:6-7.** The **unique day, without daytime or nightime,** may refer to the actual day of the Lord's return when celestial darkness accompanying the divine judgments will be replaced by light **when evening comes.** At any rate the time of Christ's Second Advent will be accompanied by unparalleled natural phenomena (Isa. 13:10; 34:4; Joel 2:10, 30-31; 3:15; Matt. 24:29).

14:8. A perennial spring of water (**living water** as opposed to rainwater) will erupt in **Jerusalem** dividing its water flow between **the eastern sea** (the Dead Sea) and **the western sea** (the Mediterranean). This year-round provision apparently will promote unsurpassed fertility throughout the land (cf. Isa. 27:6; 35:1-3, 6-7; Amos 9:13-14).

(2) The absolute lordship of the Messiah-King. **14:9.** The Messiah will not only reign as King of Israel but He **will** also **be King over the whole earth.** The worldwide scope of His reign is supported by Zechariah's description of Him elsewhere as "the LORD of all the earth" (4:14; 6:5; cf. Micah 4:13). This is confirmed by the Apostle John's identification of Him as the "Lord of lords and King of kings" (Rev. 17:14; 19:16). He has always been the one Lord (Deut. 6:4) in His unique, solitary, incomparable Being (cf. Isa. 37:16; 45:5-6, 14, 18, 22; 46:9). When He establishes His millennial kingdom, He will be universally recognized as such and worshiped as the one true God (Rev. 21:3). With idolatry and false worship cut off from the land (Zech. 13:1-2) **His name** will be **the only name** (cf. Acts 4:12) recognized in worship by people.

(3) The renovation of Judah and the

security of Jerusalem. **14:10-11. The whole land** of Judah—**from Geba** on its northern border (Josh. 21:17) **to Rimmon,** probably on its southern border, 35 miles southwest of **Jerusalem** (Josh. 15:32)— will be miraculously leveled to a broad valley **like the Arabah,** the low plain stretching from below Mount Hermon down the Jordan River Valley and the Dead Sea on to the Gulf of Aqabah. This will help make **Jerusalem** more prominent (cf. Isa. 2:2), as the capital city of the great King. Mention of the city's gates indicate the whole city. **The Benjamin Gate** (cf. Jer. 37:13; 38:7) may have been near the east part of the northern wall; **the site of the First Gate** is unknown; **the Corner Gate** was on the west wall; and **the Tower of Hannanel** (cf. Neh. 3:1) was on the north wall (see the map "Jerusalem in the time of Nehemiah," near Neh. 3:1-5). **The royal winepresses** were probably south of the city. Not only will **Jerusalem** be fully **inhabited** (cf. Joel 3:20); it will also be free of the curse or ban to destruction associated with holy war. It **will be** eternally **secure** (cf. Isa. 32:18; 33:20; Amos 9:15; Micah 4:4; Zech. 3:10).

d. The destruction of Israel's enemies (14:12-15)

14:12-15. In this parenthetical flashback (the words **the nations that fought against Jerusalem** look back to v. 2), Zechariah described the second phase of the invasion of Jerusalem by the confederated Gentile armies. In this phase the Gentile armies will be destroyed around Jerusalem (as previously described in 12:2-9). This section in chapter 14 summarizes: (a) the divine **plague** on the enemies, both man and beast (vv. 12, 15; cf. 12:4); (b) the **panic** from **the Lord** (14:13); and (c) the plunder taken from the Gentile armies (v. 14), much of which no doubt will be plunder that the Gentiles have just taken from Jerusalem (vv. 1-2).

e. The worship of Messiah-King by the nations (14:16-19)

14:16. After **Jerusalem** becomes secure and Messiah's worldwide reign has been established (vv. 9-11), **then the survivors from all the nations** will **worship** annually in Jerusalem. "The survivors" are not the Jewish remnant that had been scattered among "all the nations," for the Jewish remnant will already have been

regathered to the land at the time of the Second Advent. Rather, these survivors are from nonmilitary personnel of those nations whose armies were destroyed by Messiah in the attack on Jerusalem (vv. 1-5; cf. Rev. 19:19). The armies in the Campaign of Armageddon will be destroyed, but not the people of the nations they will represent. Futhermore, they will be the survivors of the divine judgment on the Gentile nations who will enter the kingdom of Christ as "sheep," the "goats" having been barred from entrance into the Millennium (Matt. 25:31-46).

That Gentiles will go to Jerusalem (cf. Isa. 2:2; 14:1; 66:23; Zech. 8:23) to worship does not mean they will become Jewish proselytes, as in Old Testament times. Millennial religious worship will not be a restored Judaism but a newly instituted worldwide religious order embracing both Jews and Gentiles. It will center in Jerusalem and will incorporate some features identical with or similar to certain aspects of Old Testament worship. One of these aspects is the annual celebration of **the Feast of Tabernacles** (cf. Lev. 23:33-43; Zech. 14:18-19). The need to go to Jerusalem is partially explained by the presence there of the object of worship—**the King, the Lord Almighty,** that is, Jesus Christ who will be ruling on the throne of David (2 Sam. 7:13, 16; Luke 1:32) in Jerusalem (Isa. 24:23).

14:17-19. Worshiping annually in Jerusalem will be necessary for the people to enjoy fertility of crops. Those nations that neglect or refuse such opportunities for **worship** will forfeit their water supply. For most nations this simply means **they will have no rain.** But **Egypt,** whose irrigation depends not on rain (at least not directly) but rather on the flooding of the Nile, will still experience **the plague** of drought as **punishment** from **the Lord,** as will **all the nations that do not go up to celebrate the Feast of Tabernacles.**

f. The holiness of Judah and Jerusalem during Messiah's reign (14:20-21)

14:20-21. In **that day** holiness will characterize millennial life (cf. 8:3) whether it be in public life (**the bells of the horses**), religious life (**the cooking pots in the Lord's house,** the millennial temple, Ezek. 40–43), or private life (**every pot in Jerusalem and Judah**). Perhaps the general thought is the removal of a dichotomy between secular and sacred. In the Old Testament **a Canaanite** had become symbolic of anything ceremonially unclean and ungodly (the dishonest "merchant" in Hosea 12:7 is lit., "the Canaanite"). In the millennial temple no such defilement will occur. Thus Zechariah's prophetic book which began with a call to repentance (Zech. 1:2-6) concludes with an affirmation that all will be **holy to the** Lord (14:20-21). Because He is **the** Lord **Almighty** and the Holy One, He will establish holiness throughout the glorious Millennium!

BIBLIOGRAPHY

Baldwin, Joyce G. *Haggai, Zechariah, Malachi: An Introduction and Commentary*. The Tyndale Old Testament Commentaries. Downers Grove, Ill.: InterVarsity Press, 1972.

Baron, David. *The Visions and Prophecies of Zechariah*. Reprint. Grand Rapids: Kregel Publications, 1972.

Feinberg, Charles L. *The Minor Prophets*. Chicago: Moody Press, 1976.

Keil, C.F. "Zechariah." In *Commentary on the Old Testament in Ten Volumes*. Vol. 10. Reprint (25 vols. in 10). Grand Rapids: Wm. B. Eerdmans Publishing Co., 1982.

Laney, J. Carl. *Zechariah*, Everyman's Bible Commentary. Chicago: Moody Press, 1984.

Leopold, H.C. *Exposition of Zechariah*. Grand Rapids: Baker Book House, 1965.

Luck, G. Coleman. *Zechariah*. Chicago: Moody Press, 1969.

Moore, T.V. *A Commentary on Haggai, Zechariah, Malachi*. London: Banner of Truth Trust, 1960.

Robinson, George L. *The Prophecies of Zechariah*. Chicago: University of Chicago Press, 1896. Reprint. Grand Rapids: Baker Book House, 1926.

Tatford, Frederick A. *The Minor Prophets*. Vol. 3. Reprint (3 vols). Minneapolis: Klock & Klock Christian Publishers, 1982.

Unger, Merrill F. *Commentary on Zechariah*. Grand Rapids: Zondervan Publishing House, 1962.

MALACHI

Craig A. Blaising

INTRODUCTION

Historical Setting. Malachi ministered in the fifth century B.C., about 100 years after Cyrus had issued the decree in 538 B.C. which permitted Jews to return from exile to Judah. In response to the prophetic ministries of Haggai and Zechariah, the repatriated Jews had rebuilt the temple, completing it in 515 B.C. Houses had been reconstructed. Most likely in Malachi's day the wall of Jerusalem was being rebuilt or had been completed (by Nehemiah's crew).

Life was not easy. The Jews were under the political dominion of Persia (*peḥâh,* "governor," Mal. 1:8, was a Persian title, also used in Ezra 5:3, 6, 14; 6:6-7, 13; Dan. 3:2-3, 27; 6:7). Harvests were poor and subject to locust damage (Mal. 3:11). Most hearts were indifferent or resentful toward God. Both the priests and the people were violating the stipulations of the Mosaic Law regarding sacrifices, tithes, and offerings. The people's hope in God's covenant promises had dimmed, as evidenced by their (a) intermarriages with pagans, (b) divorces, and (c) general moral ambivalence.

Date. Malachi's reference to a Persian governor (Mal. 1:8) shows that the book was written *after* 538 B.C. Most scholars agree that the Book of Malachi was written around 450–430 B.C., for these reasons: (1) Malachi's rebuke of the priests' malpractice in the temple shows that the temple had been rebuilt and the priesthood reestablished. (2) The moral and spiritual conditions Malachi addressed were similar to those encountered by Ezra, who returned in 458, and Nehemiah, who returned in 444. These included intermarriages with Gentiles (2:10-11; cf. Ezra 9:1-2; Neh. 13:1-3, 23-28), lack of the people's support for the Levites (Mal. 3:10; cf. Neh. 13:10), and oppression of the poor (Mal. 3:5; cf. Neh. 5:4-5). Either

Malachi was addressing the same generation that Ezra and Nehemiah spoke to, or Malachi spoke to a later generation some time after Ezra's and Nehemiah's corrections.

Author. Traditionally Malachi (*mal'āḵî,* lit., "My messenger") has been viewed as the last prophet of the Old Testament period before John the Baptist, whose ministry Malachi predicted (Mal. 3:1). Many, however, have argued that the word *mal'āḵî* is an anonymous designation, not a personal name. They give four reasons to support that view: (1) *Mal'āḵî* is not properly a name form. However, no other prophetic book in the Bible is anonymous. Possibly *mal'āḵî* is a contraction of a longer form *mal'āḵiyyâh* (cf. *'ăḇî* in 2 Kings 18:2, NIV marg. with *'ăḇiyyâh* in 2 Chron. 29:1, and *'ûrî* in 1 Kings 4:19 with *'ûriyyâh* in 1 Chron. 11:41). (2) The Targum (Aram. trans. and paraphrase of the OT) does not consider "Malachi" in Malachi 1:1 as a personal name. However, the Targum adds that this messenger was Ezra, a view that has little support. (3) Since *mal'āḵî* is an anonymous designation in Malachi 3:1 it therefore ought to be the same in 1:1. However, it is more likely that the anonymous *mal'āḵî* in 3:1 is a wordplay on the name of the prophet in 1:1.

(4) Another suggestion by some scholars is that the Book of Malachi was one of three anonymous oracles (the other two being Zech. 9–11 and 12–14) appended to the end of the Minor Prophets. The basis for this view is that the word *maśśā'* ("burden or oracle") introduces each of these three portions of Scripture (Zech. 9:1; 11:1; Mal. 1:1). However, the way Malachi introduces his book (lit., "The oracle of the word of the LORD to Israel by the hand of Malachi") differs from the way Zechariah introduced his two oracles (see Brevard Childs, *Introduction to the Old Testament as*

211

Scripture. Philadelphia: Fortress Press, 1979, pp. 489-92).

The contents of the Book of Malachi clearly indicate that it was written by a prophet. Nothing is known of his family line and he is not mentioned by name elsewhere in the Bible.

Style. Malachi's style differs from that of the other writing prophets. Rather than making direct proclamations, Malachi used a dialectical or disputational style. In this style he introduced each of his six messages (see points II–VII in the *Outline*) by a charge or command addressed to the people. Malachi then characterized the people as questioning five of the six charges (each one except the third one, point IV in the *Outline*). Then he offered proof that each charge was correct. This style was an appropriate way to confront the apathetic Israelites.

Message. Malachi's message is similar to that of the other prophets: covenant blessing requires covenant faithfulness. As people in each generation obeyed the requirements of the Mosaic Covenant, they participated in the blessings founded in the unconditional Abrahamic Covenant. Obedience to the Law was rewarded with blessing in the land of promise. Disobedience, on the other hand, brought a curse on the people and eventually exile. This covenant regulated Israel's relationship with God throughout the old dispensation.

Malachi's message applied the Mosaic Covenant to the problems of postexilic Israel—problems of neglect, expediency, and outright disobedience. Underlying these problems was a lack of proper perspective on God's covenant faithfulness, and the loss of the hope that the kingdom would be established. This led to widespread unfaithfulness, affecting the people's worship in the temple and marital relations in their homes. Malachi pointed to God's past, present, and future dealings with Israel in order to renew their perspective, reestablish their hope, and motivate them to proper covenant faithfulness.

OUTLINE

I. Introduction: The Burden of Malachi (1:1)

II. First Oracle: Respond to God's Love (1:2-5)
   A. The claim of God's love for Israel (1:2a)
   B. Israel's question of the claim (1:2b)
   C. The vindication of God's claim (1:2c-5)
      1. The election of Israel over Edom (1:2c-3a)
      2. The judgment of Edom (1:3b-5)

III. Second Oracle: Honor God (1:6–2:9)
   A. The charge of disrespect (1:6a)
   B. Israel's question of the charge (1:6b)
   C. The proof of God's charge: Contemptible sacrifices (1:7-14)
   D. A warning to the priests (2:1-9)
      1. The warning stated (2:1-4)
      2. The standard for priests (2:5-9)

IV. Third Oracle: Be Faithful as God's Covenant People (2:10-16)
   A. The charge of unfaithfulness (2:10)
   B. The first evidence: Illegal intermarriage (2:11-12)
      1. The sin (2:11)
      2. The consequence (2:12)
   C. The second evidence: Divorce (2:13-16a)
      1. The consequence (2:13)
      2. The sin (2:14-16a)
   D. The charge to faithfulness (2:16b)

V. Fourth Oracle: Hope in God (2:17–3:6)
   A. The charge of wearisome speech (2:17a)
   B. Israel's question of the charge (2:17b)
   C. The proof of the charge: No hope for God's justice (2:17c)
   D. The warning by God (3:1-5)
      1. The coming of the messenger in preparation (3:1a)
      2. The coming of the Lord in judgment (3:1b-5)
   E. The basis for hope in God (3:6)

VI. Fifth Oracle: Obey God (3:7-12)
   A. The charge of disobedience (3:7a)
   B. Israel's question of the charge

COMMENTARY

I. Introduction: The Burden of Malachi (1:1)

1:1. The word *maśśā'* ("burden"), with which the book begins, sets a sober mood. The NIV translates this word **An oracle.** In the prophetic books *maśśā'* introduces messages of a threatening nature 27 times (e.g., Isa. 13:1; 14:28; 15:1; Nahum 1:1; Hab. 1:1; Zech. 9:1; 12:1). (See comments on *maśśā'* at Zech. 9:1-8.) Standing alone at the beginning of Malachi, the word *maśśā'* gives this prophet's entire message a sense of anxiety and foreboding.

The phrase **the word of the LORD** frequently appears as an introduction to a prophecy, to identify it as a revelation from God that carries His authority. "The LORD" (*Yahweh*) is of course the name of God which recalls His association with the covenant He made with Israel at Sinai. Since the word is addressed **to Israel,** the burden of this discourse concerns problems in the covenant relationship between God and Israel. And since Yahweh is the faithful, loyal, covenant-keeping God, trouble in the covenant relationship can only be because of *Israel's* unfaithfulness. The fact that this burden from the

Lord came **through Malachi** must have heightened the sense of imminent rebuke in the minds of the original readers. The priests were supposed to be God's messengers (cf. Mal. 2:7), but now *they* were to listen to one whose name means "My messenger."

II. First Oracle: Respond to God's Love (1:2-5)

People who read these verses today may feel a little uncomfortable and yet somewhat fascinated, like one who is in the presence of an intensely personal conversation between two parties who have long known each other. By introducing the prophecy as a burden (v. 1) Malachi had already prepared his readers to anticipate accusation and rebuke. However, this first oracle begins not with a charge of wrongdoing but with a claim of God's unrequited love.

A. The claim of God's love for Israel (1:2a)

1:2a. The words **I have loved you** are not a general statement about God's love for all people. The God of *Israel* was speaking: He is the One who called her into existence and who ruled over her and raised her (cf. v. 6) for more than 1,000 years on the basis of His covenant with her. And she was the object of His love (v. 2c).

Considerable pathos is in the words, "I have loved you." This was not the first time the LORD had said this. One is reminded of Hosea 11:1, 3-4, 8-9, and God's tender words in Isaiah 43:4. But His love for Israel antedated her existence; He loved her in that He sovereignly and graciously elected her to be His own possession. This was clearly revealed at the time He gave the covenant (Deut. 4:37; 5:10; 7:6-9). Love was the heart of this covenant relationship. This is clear from the exhortations that follow these declarations of divine love (Deut. 4:39-40; 7:9-15). Acknowledging God's love for her, Israel should have responded by loving Him and obeying His commands (Deut. 6:4-9).

B. Israel's question of the claim (1:2b)

1:2b. Israel asked God, **How have You loved us?** (Cf. Israel's similar questioning in vv. 6-7; 2:17; 3:7-8, 13.) By questioning God's claim, Israel was betraying a distrust of God, a lack of faith in His Word—not only a lack of trust in Malachi's statement (1:2a) but also a distrust of God's faithfulness to His covenant. Israel's failure to believe God's Word caused her to fail to love Him and also caused her to be hostile toward Him.

Perhaps Israel thought her complaint was legitimate. After all, about 100 years had passed since the people had returned from the Exile; yet the kingdom predicted by God's prophets had still not come. Instead the people continued to be dominated by foreign governors (v. 8) and experienced hard times economically (2:2; 3:9, 11). If they had carefully read the covenant in Deuteronomy they would have known that such misfortunes were the *result*—not the *cause*—of their disobedience. While Malachi later indicated that a righteous remnant, which feared God, did exist at that time (3:16-18), the nation as a whole needed to repent from the sin of unbelief and fall in love wholeheartedly with the Lord.

C. The vindication of God's claim (1:2c-5)

1. THE ELECTION OF ISRAEL OVER EDOM (1:2C-3A)

1:2c-3a. The Lord's claim over Israel was vindicated by two considerations. First was His love expressed in His free choice, His election of **Jacob** and his descendants (including this generation which had questioned Him) to inherit the promise. This was contrary to the normal practice of choosing the oldest son. **Esau,** also named Edom and the father of the Edomites (Gen. 36:1), was the firstborn of the twins. Yet even before birth God freely elected Jacob, later named Israel, as the heir (Gen. 25:21-34; Rom. 9:10-13). The Hebrew words for **loved** and **hated** refer not to God's emotions but to His choice of one over the other for a covenant relationship (cf. Gen. 29:31-35; Deut. 21:15, 17; Luke 14:26). To hate someone meant to reject him and to disavow any loving association with him (cf. Ps. 139:21). Nor do these words by themselves indicate the eternal destinations of Jacob and Esau. The verbs refer to God's acts in history toward both of the two nations which descended from the two brothers.

2. THE JUDGMENT OF EDOM (1:3B-5)

1:3b-4a. The verbs "I have loved" and "I have hated" (vv. 2b-3a) are in the perfect tense and therefore express not only God's past relationship with Israel and Edom but also His historical and present dealings (in Malachi's day) with these peoples. This provided the second consideration which vindicated God's claim. Israel needed to consider what her lot would have been if she, like Edom, had not been elected to a covenant relationship with Yahweh. Both Israel and Edom received judgment from God at the hands of the Babylonians in the sixth century (Jer. 27:2-8). Yet God repeatedly promised to restore Israel (because of His covenant promises, Deut. 4:29-31; 30:1-10), but He condemned Edom to complete destruction, never to be restored (Jer. 49:7-22; Ezek. 35).

Thus the Lord **turned** Edom's **mountains into a wasteland** and only **the desert jackals** would have that land to pass on to their "descendants." Even Edom's greatest efforts to **rebuild** its **ruins** would be frustrated by **the Lord Almighty** (a title Malachi used 24 times in his short book). In the fifth century, the Nabateans, an Arabian tribe, occupied Edom (located south and east of Judea) and forced the Edomites westward into a desert area later known as Idumea. In the fourth century, the Nabateans took over Idumea as well.

1:4b-5. The Wicked Land contrasts with "the holy land" (Zech. 2:12) so that Israel's borders were also the borders of blessing. On the one side was Israel whom God loved and chose to set apart ("holy" means set apart) for covenant blessings. On the other side was Edom whom God had not chosen. Rather she would be destroyed by Him in His **wrath.** (On Edom's wickedness, see Obad. 8-14.) Israel, seeing God's sovereign dealings with Edom, would have a better understanding not only of God's love for her, but also of His greatness over all the earth: **Great is the Lord—even beyond the borders of Israel!**

III. Second Oracle: Honor God (1:6–2:9)

The first oracle ended with a statement about God's greatness both in and beyond Israel. In sharp contrast the second oracle addressed Israel's failure to honor God properly. Since Israel was supposed to love God wholeheartedly (Deut. 6:5) and to fear Him (Deut. 6:3), the seriousness of her condition was clear.

A. The charge of disrespect (1:6a)

1:6a. Malachi spoke of proper relationships in society, relationships Israel certainly would have insisted on. **A son honors his father, and a servant his master.** The question follows, Which set of relationships would Israel have considered comparable to her relationship with the Lord? Some Israelites might have suggested that God was like a father to Israel, for this analogy had been used before (Ex. 4:22; Isa. 63:16; 64:8; Hosea 11:1). The fifth of the Ten Commandments states that children are to honor their parents (Ex. 20:12; Deut. 5:16). Disobedient children who rebelled against discipline were to be stoned (Deut. 21:18-21).

Therefore should the nation which considered itself a "son" of the Lord be less obedient? So God's question was sharply presented, **If I am a Father, where is the honor** or glory **due Me?** (Cf. Isa. 1:2.) The Hebrew word for "honor" (*kābôd*) also means "glory." The glory of God is spoken of frequently throughout the Scriptures (He is even called "the King of glory," Ps. 24:7-10), and the fact that glory and honor are due Him is beyond dispute.

Perhaps some Israelites might consider the Lord the Master of Israel. Certainly Scripture presents Israel as the Lord's servant (Isa. 44:1-2). Therefore how could the nation that was the Lord's servant be disrespectful to Him? The Lord's second question was ominous, **If I am a Master, where is the respect due Me?** The word "respect" may also be translated "fear." There is no contradiction between the admonition to love God (implied in the first oracle, Mal. 1:2-5) and the exhortation to fear Him. Both appear together in the covenant (cf. Deut. 6:5 with Deut. 6:13). Fear of God does not mean being terrified of Him; it means a proper respect and reverence for Him, a reverence that leads to worship and obedience.

It is you, O priests, who despise My name. This charge is doubly sad because after the return from the Exile, the priests were responsible to teach the people God's covenant and turn their hearts to God (Neh. 9:38–10:39; cf. Ezra 6:16-22; 7:10). If the *priests* failed to honor God, what could be expected of the people? The words "My name" stand for God Himself. (In Mal., reference to God's "name" occurs 10 times: 1:6 [twice], 11 [thrice], 14; 2:2, 5; 3:16; 4:2.) They despised *Him*, the One who is **the LORD Almighty.**

B. Israel's question of the charge (1:6b)

1:6b. Malachi cast the priests in the rhetorical role of questioning God: **How have we despised Your name?** From the specific nature of the charge that follows (vv. 7-14), the priests were extremely insensitive to their sin, seemingly—and surprisingly—unaware that they had despised God.

C. The proof of God's charge: Contemptible sacrifices (1:7-14)

1:7. The Lord's reference to **defiled food** should have been enough to cause the priests to repent. They had specific instructions on what constituted defective sacrifices (Lev. 22:17-30). They were warned against offering such sacrifices lest the priests thereby profane and defile God's name (Lev. 22:2, 32). Yet the priests were guilty of that very sin—despising His name (Mal. 1:6) by offering "defiled food" (v. 7). But why did Malachi call the sacrifices "food"? Because all the offerings were called "the food of . . . God" (Lev. 21:6).

The priests asked, **How have we defiled You?** They did not say "We have not defiled You," for they could not really plead ignorance of the Law. So they asked *how* they had profaned the Lord. The fact that they saw the charge of improper sacrifices as a defilement of God Himself showed that they were familiar with Leviticus 22:2, 32. Apparently they had become so hardened and had so rationalized their sin that Malachi could portray them as daring God to spell out their wrongs.

Malachi answered that they had defiled God **by saying that the LORD's table is contemptible.** Malachi 1:7, 12 are the only two verses in the Old Testament where the phrase "the LORD's table" is found. It probably does not refer to the table on which the bread of the Presence was placed (Ex. 25:23-30; 1 Kings 7:48; 2 Chron. 13:10-11). Possibly it refers to the altar of burnt offering (cf. Ex. 38:1; 40:6) because Malachi had already mentioned it (Mal. 1:7) and he spoke of animal sacrifices (v. 8). Or the table may refer metaphorically to the whole spread of offerings sacrificed on the altar (cf. Ezek. 44:15-16).

The charge that the priests were calling the Lord's table contemptible was substantiated by their actions (Mal. 1:8). They were treating it with contempt by disregarding God's requirements concerning the kinds of sacrifices that should be placed on it. This made them guilty, deserving of death (Lev. 22:9). Also their contempt was deepened as they ate some of those unacceptable sacrifices (the priests received their food from the offerings, Lev. 24:5-9).

1:8-10. Malachi pointed out that the priests brought **blind animals** and **crippled** and **diseased animals** as sacrifices (cf. v. 13). He asked if **that** was **wrong.** Their answer, according to Leviticus 22:18-25 and Deuteronomy 15:21, should have been yes. It was to their shame that these things had to be pointed out to them. Ironically Malachi suggested, **Try offering them to your governor!** The governor's "table" was a lavishly prepared banquet (cf. Neh. 5:17) including "offerings" from the people. Certainly the governor (*peḥâh*, a Persian title) would not have been **pleased with** the meat of blind, crippled, or diseased animals; in fact he would not have accepted it. How much more absurd it was to expect the favor of **the LORD Almighty** (cf. Mal. 1:4) with such offerings. He did not accept such sacrifices, nor did He **accept** (vv. 8-9) the priests. To emphasize this point, Malachi said the whole **temple** service might as well be **shut** down. It was even useless to light the **fires on** the **altar** of burnt offering. God was **not pleased**; He would **accept** no **offerings from** them.

1:11. In the Hebrew, this verse begins with *kî* ("for, because"), not translated in the NIV. It indicates that what follows is the reason the Lord refused to accept the priests' offerings (v. 10). Scholars differ on whether the Hebrew passive participle *mûggāš* should be rendered **will be brought** (future tense, as in KJV, NASB, NIV or "is brought" (pres. tense as

in RSV and many commentaries). If the present tense is followed, then Malachi was referring to practices in his day. In that case the offerings refer either to those brought by Jews who were still dispersed among the nations or to offerings made by Gentiles. The first of these is rejected because the phrases **from the rising to the setting of the sun** and **in every place** indicate a practice more universal than the limited extent of the Jewish dispersion. Also the sacrifices given by Jews in the Dispersion could not be called **pure offerings** since they could be made only in Jerusalem. (Furthermore there is no evidence that Jews in the Dispersion offered any sacrifices.)

Those who accept a present-tense rendering of the verb *mûggāš* usually choose the second of the options just described. In this view God was endorsing pagan worship. However, this view must be rejected for several reasons. If it were adopted, it would be the only place in the Bible where pagan worship is considered legitimate, which would directly contradict numerous references that specifically condemn such worship (e.g., Ex. 23:24, 32-33; Deut. 13:6-11; 29:17; 1 Kings 18:19-46; Ps. 96:5; Isa. 48:5; 66:3; Hab. 2:18-20). Not even Paul's reference to the Athenean worship of an unknown god (Acts 17:22-31) supports this interpretation that pagans worship God's "name" with "pure offerings." Also such an interpretation does not accord with the rest of Malachi, which strongly emphasizes strict obedience to the Mosaic Covenant.

Taking *mûggāš* as future ("will be brought"), however, corresponds with other Old Testament prophecies and with the Book of Malachi itself. The prophets predicted a time when Gentiles will see the light and become worshipers of the Lord (Isa. 45:22-25; 49:5-7; 59:19). The Messiah will become King over the entire earth. Believers in all nations will worship Him (Isa. 11:3-4, 9; Dan. 7:13-14, 27-28; Zeph. 2:11; 3:8-11; Zech. 14:9, 16). Malachi also spoke of the coming of the future day when the Lord will return and will bring about pure worship in Israel (Mal. 3:1-4). It seems preferable then to associate the "pure" Gentile worship mentioned in 1:11 with Israel's pure worship. But will Gentiles in the kingdom give offerings "in every place"? No. This problem is alleviated if the preposition *bᵉ* (usually meaning "in") before "every place" is rendered "from," as in Isaiah 21:1 (cf. *Theological Wordbook of the Old Testament*. 2 vols. Chicago: Moody Press, 1980, s.v. "*b^e*," 1:87).

1:12-13. After speaking of the pure offerings in the future kingdom (v. 11), Malachi referred again to the immediate condition of the priests in his day. He repeated the charge that they were profaning God's name (cf. v. 6). In verses 7-8 the *actions* of the priests were condemned; here their *attitude* was condemned. Their attitude was one of contempt. Apparently the priests recognized that these sacrificial practices were irregular, for they said that **the LORD's table** (cf. v. 7) **is defiled** and that **its food . . . is contemptible.** But they did not care to take the trouble to set things straight. Being involved in offering the sacrifices was just **a burden.** Such a response was a form of contempt (cf. James 4:17).

That the priests brought unacceptable **animals** was repeated in Malachi 1:13 (cf. v. 8), and God's refusal to **accept them** was repeated from verses 8-10.

1:14. Here Malachi moved from speaking of sacrifices in general to discussing the payment of vows. Making a vow to the Lord was not mandatory, but if a person did so he was required to pay it (Deut. 23:21-23). Moses (Lev. 22:17-25) gave the priests specific instructions about the kinds of sacrifices acceptable for payments of vows. The vow to give an **acceptable** animal and then bring a **blemished animal** was wrong. Certainly no one would try to cheat a king or governor, for fear of being reprimanded and punished by that authority. Nor should one try to cheat *the* **great King,** the One whose **name is to be feared among the nations.** Malachi 1 ends by emphasizing God's supreme authority.

D. A warning to the priests (2:1-9)

1. THE WARNING STATED (2:1-4)

2:1-2. After giving and substantiating a charge against the priests, Malachi gave them a command (**admonition**; cf. v. 4): they were to **honor** God (**My name** stands for **Me**). How they were to honor Him is clear from the ways they had failed Him (1:6-14) and from the portrayal of a true priest (2:7). Failure to honor Him would result in their experiencing **a curse** (hardships). The Mosaic Covenant

had included curses for those who disobeyed the Law (see Deut. 27:15-26; 28:15-68). These curses were concerned with the people's physical, mental, and material welfare. The curse Malachi referred to would affect the priests' **blessings,** either their own blessings (as income from people's tithes and offerings) or blessings they pronounced on the people (Num. 6:22-27). Because of their hearts' condition, the curse was **already** in effect.

2:3-4. The priests were then warned of a rebuke that would fall against their seed. *Zera'* ("seed") refers to grain (NIV marg.) or to physical **descendants.** The following threat of the removal of the priests from office makes the latter option more probable. Some have suggested that instead of *zera'*, the text should read *z^{e}rōa'* which means "arm." To rebuke one's arm was a metaphor for rendering one powerless (1 Sam. 2:31, "strength" in the NIV is lit., "arm"). This would correlate with the interpretation (cf. Mal. 2:1-2) that the curse concerned the blessings pronounced by the priests on the people.

The Lord said He would **spread on** their **faces** the waste matter **from the sacrifices,** which ironically were described as festive. "Spread," from the verb *zārâh*, is a pun on the word *zera'* ("seed"), the descendants who were the object of God's rebuke (v. 3). The priests would be made as unclean as **the offal.** Much as it was discarded, so they would be disposed of as well. In other words they would be cast out of service. Then they would realize that **the LORD** was speaking to them. His purpose in admonishing them was to purify the priesthood so that His **covenant with Levi** could **continue.**

2. THE STANDARD FOR PRIESTS (2:5-9)

2:5-6. The **covenant** with Levi (v. 4), is now discussed in more detail. The tribal name Levi is used for the descendants of Levi who made up the priestly class. The covenant mentioned here refers to what may be called a covenant of grant (Num. 18:7-8, 19-21), a covenant made with an individual (and sometimes his descendants) because of some service the recipient performed. God made a similar covenant of grant with Phinehas (Num. 25:10-13). The phrase **a covenant of life and peace** seems to recall how Phinehas' zeal for the Lord turned away God's wrath from the people (cf. Num. 25:11 with Mal. 2:6, **He . . . turned many from sin**). Most important, **he revered** God (v. 5), the point of exhortation in this oracle. Besides, Levi's teaching was **true**, and his conduct was in **uprightness**.

2:7-9. The word **instruction** is *tôrâh*, also the word for "Law." The priests were to teach the Law (Deut. 33:10). As teachers, each priest was to be a **messenger** (*mal'ak*). However, since they were not giving true instruction, they were rebuked by the prophet whose very name, ironically, means "My messenger." Their **teaching . . . caused many to stumble** because they themselves had **turned from the way.** Saying that defiled sacrifices were accepted **violated** God's **covenant with Levi** (see Num. 18:19, 21). So the priests were **despised and humiliated before all the people.** This actually was a light sentence, for their penalty should have been death (Num. 18:32).

IV. Third Oracle: Be Faithful as God's Covenant People (2:10-16)

A. The charge of unfaithfulness (2:10)

2:10. The style of the third oracle differs from the others. Instead of an initial statement or charge followed by a question of feigned innocence, this oracle begins with three questions asked by the prophet. However, as at the beginning of each of the other oracles, the point is presented at the outset. The reference to **one Father** is probably parallel to **one God** so that "Father" refers to God (cf. 1:6), not to Abraham, as some suggest. Israel was like God's firstborn son (Ex. 4:22; Hosea 11:1). The fact that God had created Israel to be a distinct people on the earth (cf. Amos 3:2) formed the background for the problem Malachi now discussed (Mal. 2:10-16).

Breaking faith (cf. vv. 11, 14-16) renders the word *bāgad*, "to act unfaithfully with respect to a prior agreement or covenant." This word is often translated "to act treacherously." The concern of this oracle is the people's unfaithful activity in their relationships **with one another.** This activity was another way (in addition to the charge in the previous oracle) in which **the covenant** was being profaned.

B. The first evidence: Illegal intermarriage (2:11-12)

1. THE SIN (2:11)

2:11. What had been charged in the form of a question (v. 10) was then stated as a fact and explained. The unfaithfulness Malachi had in mind (v. 10) is called **a detestable thing** (lit., "an abomination"), something abhorrent to God. Furthermore this abominable unfaithfulness involved a profaning of holiness. The word for "holiness" (*qōḏeš*, "apartness, separateness") may refer to **the sanctuary** (as in the NIV), the covenant, the people, or simply the quality of holiness itself. Since the concern of this oracle was the uniqueness and unity of the people ("Did not one God create us?" [v. 10]), holiness may refer here to the quality of distinctiveness or separateness that the Lord desired **in Israel.**

The abominable unfaithfulness that profaned Israel's holiness was intermarriage with pagans. **Daughter of a foreign god** refers to pagan women who worshiped false gods. (If *qōḏeš* refers to the "sanctuary," then possibly the profanation referred to the involvement of these women in temple worship.) Such marriages had been expressly forbidden because they would lead the people into idolatry (Ex. 34:11-16; Deut. 7:3-4; Josh. 23:12-13). Intermarrying was a big problem after the return from the Exile (cf. Ezra 9:1-2, 10-12; Neh. 13:23-27). The Jews were supposed to marry within their own nation. Failures to do so were acts of unfaithfulness among themselves as well as to God. They involved both a disregard for the nation's corporate nature and disobedience to God.

2. THE CONSEQUENCE (2:12)

2:12. The prophet invoked a curse on any Jew who had committed or would commit this sin of marrying a pagan. To be **cut . . . off from the tents of Jacob** meant either that **the man** would die or that his line would cease and he would have no descendants in Israel. The phrase *'ēr wᵉ'ōneh* is difficult to translate. The NIV translates it **whoever he may be.** The NASB, which is more literal, reads, "everyone who awakes and answers," and the KJV has "the master and the scholar." Some translate it "who gives testimony" (NIV marg.). Perhaps this was a proverbial expression, whose meaning is not clear today.

The last clause—**even though he brings offerings to the LORD Almighty**—emphasizes the hypocritical and insensitive attitude of those who committed this sin of intermarrying. One is shocked to read that despite the abomination such a person committed he still brought offerings to seek the Lord's favor.

C. The second evidence: Divorce (2:13-16a)

1. THE CONSEQUENCE (2:13)

2:13. The two lines of evidence in this oracle are arranged chiastically so that the sin-consequence structure in the foregoing (v. 12) is reversed here. The consequence or symptom of the sin is presented first (v. 13); then the sin is stated (vv. 14-16a). Malachi said some people **flood the LORD's altar with tears.** Whose tears do these refer to? Some have suggested that these were the tears of divorced wives who were seeking justice from the Lord. But the second half of verse 13 indicates that these were the tears of the men who (after divorcing their Israelite wives to marry pagans, v. 14) found that the Lord **no longer** received their **offerings.** This fits naturally with verse 12.

2. THE SIN (2:14-16A)

2:14. Again Malachi stressed the Israelites' spiritual insensitivity. Since they—surprisingly—could not imagine what the problem was (**You ask, Why?**), the prophet had to spell it out for them. **The LORD** was **acting as the witness between** such a man **and** his **wife** with whom he had **broken faith** (cf. vv. 10-11, 15-16), that is, whom he had divorced. This "witness" may have been in a legal sense or in a general sense, depending on the covenant referred to. If it is to be taken in a legal sense, then the Lord was called on to be a witness and a judge in a legal agreement, as was sometimes done among the ancients (cf. Gen. 31:50, 53). If b^{e}rîtekā means **your marriage covenant** (NIV) then the Lord's witness would have this legal sense. He was the witness of the marriage covenant between the man and woman.

However, the word b^{e}rîtekā (lit., "your covenant") could conceivably refer to the covenant between God and Israel (cf. Mal. 2:10). In that case the Lord was a witness in the general sense that He knows all that happens. Then "the wife of your marriage covenant" would refer to the fact that she was chosen from among the covenant people. While the preceding context seems to support this second interpretation, the statement **she is your partner** (v. 14) seems to emphasize the marriage relationship itself (cf. Prov. 2:17). Most likely the word "covenant" (Mal. 2:14) refers to both the national covenant between God and Israel and the marriage covenant of individuals.

2:15. This is the most difficult verse in Malachi to translate. The first phrase could be either, "Did not One make them?" or "Did not He [the LORD] make one?" The first rendering emphasizes the creative and sovereign work of the one God (v. 10). The second has several possibilities. It may refer to one wife, one child of Abraham (Isaac), one flesh (man and woman made one in marriage), or one covenant nation.

The second sentence in verse 15 is even more difficult. Literally it reads, "And a remnant of the Spirit [or spirit] to him." The NIV follows the view of many commentators and reads **flesh** in place of remnant. However, the primary motivation for this is the opinion that the first phrase alludes to Genesis 2:24, which speaks of man and woman becoming one in marriage. This view is possible because marriage is being discussed in Malachi 2:10-16.

Probably a better view is that the prophet was contrasting the Lord's faithfulness to Israel (His one covenant people) with the marital unfaithfulness of individual Israelites. This contrast had already been drawn in verse 10 and was involved in the discussion of the sin of intermarriage (v. 11).

In this view the **one** in the first clause in verse 15 refers to Israel as one people. The stress on oneness would have special significance in the postexilic period, as the former division between Israel and Judah was removed. (In v. 11 "Judah" and "Israel" are used interchangeably.) Therefore the first phrase might have an intended double reference: "Has He not made one people?" *and* "Has He not made the people one?" The second phrase could read, "and made them His spiritual remnant." They could be His "spiritual" remnant only because He would fill them with His Spirit. Though Judah and Israel were united in Malachi's day, the granting of the Holy Spirit to the remnant is still future (Ezek. 37). But it was described from God's standpoint as if it had already taken place. Why was God concerned about the unity of His people? (**And why one?**) God is **seeking** a **godly offspring** (lit., "a seed of God"). "Seed" refers to the people corporately as the heir of His covenant promise (cf. Gen. 17:7) and parallels the phrase "spiritual remnant."

Malachi's command, **So guard yourself in your spirit** (repeated in Mal. 2:16) means to have the same desire for covenant unity that the Holy Spirit seeks, which would mean **not** violating the marriage covenant. Because the nation is one, no husband, Malachi said, should **break faith** (vv. 10-11, 14, 16) **with the wife of** his **youth** (cf. v. 14) by divorcing her (cf. v. 16).

2:16a. Malachi used strong language to emphasize God's displeasure with divorce. He said, **I hate divorce.** "Hate" (from *śānē'*) means to detest. (This differs from the Heb. word for "hate" used in 1:3.) To underscore his point, Malachi said that this pronouncement was made by **the LORD God of Israel.** This recalls the fact that He is the sovereign Lawgiver and Judge of Israel. If God despises a practice, certainly it ought not be done.

A man's covering himself . . . with his garment symbolizes marriage (cf. Ruth 3:9; Ezek. 16:8). But covering himself **with violence** describes violating the marriage relationship, which is what divorce does. The fact that this is the Lord's view is repeated for emphasis (**says the LORD Almighty**).

This verse is the most explicit statement in the Old Testament on God's feelings about divorce. Divorce was allowed but actually the instructions in that passage (Deut. 24:1-4) were given to protect the wife if a divorce should occur. Jesus taught that those concessions by Moses were given because of the hardness of people's hearts, but He emphasized that God does not approve of divorce (Matt. 19:7-9), though some Bible scholars see some bases for exceptions to this ideal. (Cf. comments on Matt. 5:31-32; 19:1-12; Mark 10:1-12; and 1 Cor. 7:10-24.)

D. The charge to faithfulness (2:16b)

2:16b. The charge in verse 15b is repeated in verse 16b: **So guard yourself in your spirit, and do not break faith** (cf. vv. 10-11, 14). The Israelites were not to break faith with one another by divorcing their Jewish wives and intermarrying with pagans (v. 11). Such activity profaned the covenant promise God gave to Israel. By guarding their spirits they would be acting in accord with God's purpose and would help preserve the unity of the nation as well as their individual marriages.

V. Fourth Oracle: Hope in God (2:17–3:6)

A. The charge of wearisome speech (2:17a)

2:17a. This oracle has a striking contrast between its first and last verses. Though the people had changed in their views on God's justice (2:17) God Himself had not changed (3:6). Because He does not change, neither do His covenant promises. Therefore Israel's faith and hope should have been stabilized. However, she was acting and talking as if she had no God to believe in or hope for. Therefore, ironically, the God whose word to people of faith is that He does not change or grow weary (cf. Isa. 40:28) is now said to be wearied with this people's faithless and hopeless **words** (cf. Isa. 43:24).

B. Israel's question of the charge (2:17b)

2:17b. Again the people were portrayed as being oblivious to their sin (cf. 1:6-7; 2:14): **How have we wearied Him?** (cf. Isa. 44:24)

C. The proof of the charge: No hope for God's justice (2:17c)

2:17c. The apparent prosperity of the wicked (**All who do evil are good in the eyes of the LORD**) and the suffering of the righteous is an age-old problem. In the Old Testament the problem was more pronounced than it is today because God promised Israel material prosperity as a reward for obedience to His Law (Deut. 28). However, many of these promises were intended for the entire nation, and in a society in which the righteous and wicked were mixed, there was opportunity for confusion and misunderstanding in individual cases. Added to this is the fact that God in His providence blesses the wicked as well as the righteous as a testimony to Himself (Matt. 5:45; Acts 14:17). Also the righteous as well as the wicked suffer because of the Fall (Gen 3:16-19; Ecc. 2:17-23). The Book of Job adds to the dilemma of human suffering the extra dimension of God's dealing with Satan. All of this makes it difficult, apart from known sin in one's life, to determine why a righteous person suffers.

The prosperity of the wicked was equally perplexing and was discussed by at least five biblical writers (Job 21:7-26; 24:1-17; Ps. 73:1-14; Ecc. 8:14; Jer. 12:1-4; Hab. 1). Though answers to this problem are not given in these passages, in each case questions about God's justice are removed by a futuristic perspective: God will come in judgment and punish the wicked (Job 24:22-24; 27:13-23; Ps. 73:16-20; Ecc. 8:12-13; Jer. 12:7-17; Hab. 2:3; 3:2-19) and establish the righteous in His kingdom forever.

The Jews in Malachi's day had failed to learn such hope from the Scriptures. They questioned God's justice by saying that He delights in evil people and by asking, **Where is the God of justice?** Yet *they* were the guilty ones; they were the ones who were unfaithful to Him. Here too God responded by referring to His forthcoming judgment (Mal. 3:1-5). However, unlike the answers by the righteous biblical writers mentioned earlier, the judgment which Malachi referred to was to be against the hypocritical questioners as well.

D. The warning by God (3:1-5)

1. THE COMING OF THE MESSENGER IN PREPARATION (3:1A)

3:1a. Malachi directed the attention of the faithless and hopeless questioners (2:17) to the future. Though some have taken **My messenger** (*mal'ākî*) as the writer of this book or as an angel, it seems best to see him as a future prophet. Jesus explicitly identified this person as John the Baptist (Matt. 11:7-10). The fact that this messenger will prepare His way harmonizes with Isaiah 40:3 (cf. John 1:23). The coming of this messenger was to be the first of a twofold eschatological event. The second step would be the coming of the Lord in His day.

2. THE COMING OF THE LORD IN JUDGMENT (3:1B-5)

3:1b. After the preparation by God's messenger, **suddenly the LORD . . . will come to His temple.** The coming of the Lord in His day is a much-discussed theme among the prophets. Zechariah said He will come to Zion and dwell there (Zech. 8:3). Ezekiel predicted the return of the glory of God to the temple (Ezek. 43:1-5). Malachi's two preceding oracles identified serious problems in the practice of temple worship, so the coming of the Lord to His temple would answer the questions about His justice (Mal. 2:17) and would have an ominous significance for the priests.

The title **the messenger of the covenant** occurs only here in the Bible. This individual is not the same as "My messenger" in 3:1, for the messenger of the covenant comes *after* the earlier messenger. Most likely the messenger here should be identified with **the LORD** Himself. The word "messenger" can be translated "angel," and the Angel of the Lord, a manifestation of God Himself, had been quite active in Israel's earlier history (cf. Gen. 16:10; 22:15-18; Ex. 3:2; 33:14 with Isa. 63:9; and Jud. 13:21-22). The parallel phrases, **the LORD you are seeking** and **whom you desire,** reflect the general expectation of the Lord's coming, as predicted by many other prophets. But these phrases also carry a note of sarcasm. That Israel's hope was superficial was indicated by her question (Mal. 2:17). However, though their hope was superficial, He **will come.**

3:2-4. The day of the Lord will be a day of judgment on the whole world, a day of disaster and death (Isa. 2:12; Joel 3:11-16; Amos 5:18-21; Zech 1:14-18). Later Malachi spoke of this day as coming like fire to burn up the wicked (Mal. 4:1). So the answer to both questions, **Who can endure the day of His coming?** and **Who can stand when He appears?** is that none of the wicked will endure. The Lord's coming will **purify** Israel by purging out the wicked.

Often the prophets spoke of the day of the Lord in connection with the judgment that would be poured on the nations and would effect Israel's deliverance (see comments under "Major Interpretive Problems" in the *Introduction* to Joel; and cf. Zech. 14). Malachi, however, made no mention of the other nations. He concentrated on this day as a time of judgment on Israel and especially on the Levites, her leaders and teachers.

The figures of **a refiner's fire** (that burned out the dross from metal ores) and **launderer's soap** emphasize the effectiveness of God's spiritual purging of the nation (cf. Isa. 1:25; Jer. 6:29-30; Ezek. 22:17-22). The result would be a pure class of **Levites.** Refined **like gold and silver, they will bring offerings in righteousness . . . as in days gone by.** This will contrast with Israel's unacceptable offerings of which Malachi wrote (Mal. 2:12-13). Following the return of **the LORD** and the judgment of Israel, **offerings** will be sacrificed in the kingdom (cf. Isa. 56:7; 66:20-23; Jer. 33:18; Ezek. 40:38-43; 43:13-27; Zech. 14:16-21).

3:5. The judgment of Israel will not be limited to Levites; it will include the whole nation (cf. Ezek. 20:34-38). God **will come near** Israel **for judgment.** He will purge the nation of those who are involved in sorcery (cf. Micah 5:12), adultery, perjury, depriving workers **of their wages,** oppressing **widows** and orphans, and mistreating **aliens**—all those who **do not fear** Him. All these crimes were prohibited in the Mosaic Law. God's removing these sinners from Israel will be His answer to the nation's question about His justice (Mal. 2:17).

E. The basis for hope in God (3:6)

3:6. But will this judgment bring about the end of Israel? Will the people be consumed by the refiner's fire? No, for as other prophets had predicted, Malachi stated that Israel will be delivered in the day of **the LORD.** The **descendants of Jacob** will **not** be **destroyed.** This is because of God's covenant promise. A promise is only as good as the person who makes it. God will keep His promise to the nation of Israel—it will **not change**—because His Word, like Himself, is immutable. This is the basis for Israel's hope (cf. Deut. 4:31; Ezek. 36:22-32). Significantly the Apostle Paul gives the same reason for expecting a future for national Israel (Rom. 3:3-4; 9:6; 11:1-5, 25-29).

VI. Fifth Oracle: Obey God (3:7-12)

A. The charge of disobedience (3:7a)

3:7a. Malachi's fifth oracle begins with a blanket condemnation of Israel's

disobedience to God's **decrees** throughout her history. (This contrasts with the positive note of God's unchanging faithfulness which concluded the preceding oracle, v. 6.) This calls to mind God's comments about Israel's stubbornness at Sinai (Ex. 32:7-9), which Moses repeated before the nation entered Canaan (Deut. 9:6-8, 13, 23-24; 31:27-29). Certainly the history of Israel from that day to Malachi's substantiated the prophet's charge. Malachi then voiced the Lord's appeal and a promise. If Israel would **return to** Him (in faith and obedience), then He would respond and would **return to** her. This promise was based on the covenant God made with Israel (cf. Deut. 4:30-31; 30:1-10).

B. Israel's question of the charge (3:7b)

3:7b. Again Malachi placed Israel in the rhetorical role of questioning God's charge: **How are we to return?** Only one who is aware of the path he has taken can retrace his steps. But Israel pretended to be ignorant of her waywardness.

C. The specification of the charge: Robbery (3:8a)

3:8a. Bluntly stated, Israel was accused of being a thief. Thievery against people was bad enough, but only a fool would try to **rob God. Yet** this was the charge against Israel.

D. Israel's repeated question of the charge (3:8b)

3:8b. The fifth oracle is parallel to the second, having two questions, "How are we to return?" (v. 7b) and **How do we rob You?** (v. 8) This literary device helped represent the general and the specific natures of the charge.

E. The proof of the charge (3:8c-9)

1. THE SIN: FAILURE TO GIVE TITHES AND OFFERINGS (3:8C)

3:8c. Again, the nation's problem had to do with offerings. The second oracle (1:6–2:9) dealt with the attitude of disrespect (1:6) which led to a profaning of the offerings (1:7-14). There the *quality* of the sacrifices was in question. Here the *quantity* was the issue (cf. "the whole tithe," 3:10).

The nation, God answered, was robbing God by not bringing **tithes and offerings.** The tithe was literally a 10th of all produce and livestock which the people possessed (Lev. 27:30, 32). A tithe was to be given to the Levites who in turn were to give a tithe of the tithe to the priests (Num. 18:21-32). The Israelites were also to bring a tithe of their produce and animals and eat it with the Levites before the Lord in Jerusalem as an act of festal worship (Deut. 12:5-18; 14:22-26). Also every third year a tithe was to be stored up in the towns for Levites, strangers, widows, and orphans (Deut. 14:27-29). While the word "offerings" may refer to offerings in general, it seems to refer here (Mal. 3:8c) to those portions of the offerings (as well as those portions of the tithes) designated for the priests (*Theological Wordbook of the Old Testament*, s.v. "tᵉrûmâh," 2:838). If the Levites and priests would not receive the tithes and offerings, they would have to turn to other means of supporting themselves. As a result, the temple ministry would suffer.

2. THE CURSE (3:9)

3:9. Since the temple was God's house (v. 10), failure to support its ministry was considered equal to **robbing** God Himself. The nature of the **curse** on the **nation** can be determined from verse 11: famine due to pests (locusts) eating the vegetation, and vines without grapes (cf. Deut. 28:38-40).

F. The promise of blessing (3:10-12)

3:10-12. This promise was a reaffirmation of the obedience-blessing relationship specified in the Mosaic Law (Deut. 28:1-14). What the people were experiencing was the disobedience-curse arrangement also given in that covenant (Deut. 28:15-68). This covenant was a gracious provision for Israel. No other nation had such promises from God. Since the Word of God is sure, God's part of the covenant arrangement would definitely be carried out. Israel could attest to this because she was experiencing certain curses in return for her disobedience to God's Law about the tithe. The Lord then appealed to His covenant promises in challenging Israel to **bring the whole tithe into the storehouse** so there would be adequate **food** for the priests. "Storehouse" refers to a special room or rooms in the temple for keeping tithed grain (cf. 1 Kings 7:51; Neh. 10:38; 13:12). By doing

this, the people would see that God would **open** heaven's **floodgates** and **pour out . . . blessing** on them. These blessings would include agricultural prosperity—good **crops** not destroyed by **pests,** and undamaged **vines** (Mal. 3:11) —and a good reputation among **all the nations** (v. 12). These blessings simply awaited their obedience.

One must be careful in applying these promises to believers today. The Mosaic Covenant, with its promises of material blessings to Israel for her obedience, is no longer in force (Eph. 2:14-15; Rom. 10:4; Heb. 8:13). However, the New Testament speaks about generosity and giving. While not requiring a tithe of believers today, the New Testament does speak of God's blessing on those who give generously to the needs of the church and especially to those who labor in the Word (Acts 4:31-35; 2 Cor. 9:6-12; Gal. 6:6; Phil. 4:14-19).

VII. Sixth Oracle: Fear God (3:13–4:3)

A. The charge of blasphemy (3:13a)

3:13a. In contrast with the blessings the Lord extended to Israel (v. 12), the sixth oracle charged the people with speaking **harsh things against . . . the LORD.** This was more than a contrast in tone, for the people's harsh words contradicted the promises reaffirmed in verses 10-12.

B. Israel's question of the charge (3:13b)

3:13b. Again, typical of Malachi's style, the spiritually insensitive people were portrayed as ignorant of the sin. They asked God, **What have we said against You?**

C. The proof of the charge: The endorsement of evil (3:14-15)

This sixth oracle is parallel in many respects to the fourth one (2:17–3:6). Questions concerning God's justice, because of the suffering of the apparently righteous and the seeming prosperity of the wicked (cf. 2:17), now reached a climax.

3:14. The people **said, It is futile to serve God.** "Futile" (šāwᵉ') may also be translated "vain." Ironically the people, in a sense, were indicting themselves, saying their own worship and service of the Lord was empty, useless, and without result. Hence they felt they gained no benefits from serving Him. They asked, **What did we gain. . . ?** They presumed they had been faithful to God, **carrying out His requirements.** And they presumed they had repented of their misdeeds, **going about like mourners before the LORD Almighty.** They thought all that remained was for God to fulfill His part of His bargain and bless them. They were subtly suggesting that God was *not* keeping His promises.

The problem, of course, was not on God's side. Malachi had already demonstrated that God was responding to them in accord with the covenant. However, His response was not in the form of blessing, which they desired. Two reasons explain this: (1) The people's hearts were not right with God; they were disobedient. (2) Some of the people who made the complaint (3:14) were guilty of the myopic legalism that eventually led to Jewish pharisaism in the first century A.D. This legalism concentrated on performing certain rigorous activities and not doing other things as the means of vindicating themselves before God. But this actually stifled the full expression of inner righteousness required by God (Matt. 5:20-48; 23:1-36). Thus their works would not be accepted as proper covenant obedience. God requires external obedience, but it must stem from the heart, and this obedience is not to vindicate one's own righteousness but to manifest God's righteousness. Believers today are in a much better position than Old Testament saints because those in the body of Christ have received the permanently indwelling Spirit who can overcome the flesh in manifesting the righteousness of God (Rom. 8:1-17; Gal. 5:16-26; Phil. 2:12-13).

3:15. Israel was still concerned that sinners were not punished. **The arrogant were blessed. . . . evildoers** were prospering, and those who confronted **God** escaped judgment. However, as Malachi pointed out later (4:1), the arrogant and the evildoers **will** be punished. (On this problem of the prosperity of the wicked, see comments on 2:17c.)

D. *The response of the believing remnant (3:16)*

3:16. The word **then** ('āz) is emphatic, indicating that the action described in

this verse was a consequence of the preceding confrontation. It is difficult to tell whether this remnant (**those who feared the LORD**) differs from the preceding questioners (vv. 13-15), is the same, or is a part of them. If the two groups are in some way identical, then the righteous repented of their harsh words and were then strengthened in their faith. But if they are unrelated, then their attitude and speech contrasted with the people in verses 13-15. What they said to **each other** is unknown, but it probably concerned a renewed perspective of God's faithfulness as was true in other similar struggles over these issues (cf. Ps. 73; Ecc. 12:13-14). Their fear of God exemplifies the response which God desired from this oracle. The **scroll of remembrance** means that a permanent remembrance of their faithful and reverent response is kept in heaven. This provides assurance that when God deals with these individuals He will not forget their submission to Him.

E. *The warning and promise of God (3:17–4:3)*

3:17-18. Those who fear the Lord (v. 16) will become His **in the day** He makes **up His treasured possession.** "The day" (also mentioned in 3:2 and 4:1; cf. "that . . . day" in 4:5) is the day of the Lord. It will be a day of judgment on the wicked and of deliverance for the righteous (God **will spare them**). As a result Israel **will again see the distinction between the righteous and the wicked.** In previous times Israel had seen God intervene decisively in judgment and deliverance (e.g., the Exodus, the Exile, and the return). Those events pointed up a distinction between the righteous and the wicked. The future day of the Lord, however, will bring about a much more extensive judgment on the wicked, and through physical deliverance and bodily resurrection, the righteous will be His "treasured possession" in the kingdom, fulfilling God's original intention for Israel (Ex. 19:5-6; Deut. 7:6; 14:2; 26:18; Ps. 135:4). This hope renews the righteous and strengthens their fear of God.

4:1. Malachi here elaborated on **the day** of the Lord. As in 3:2-3, the judgment on that day is described as a judgment of **fire.** The fact that **it will burn like a furnace** stresses not only its intensity but also its judgmental purpose; it is not a fire that burns out of control. Unlike 3:2-3, which emphasized the purification of Israel (in particular, the Levites), this passage emphasizes the destruction of the wicked (cf. Isa. 66:15; Zeph. 1:18; 3:8). So complete will be the judgment that the wicked (**the arrogant and every evildoer**; cf. Mal. 3:15), compared to **stubble**, will **not** have **a root or a branch** remaining. This does not mean annihilation in the sense of cessation of being (the wicked will be resurrected, Dan. 12:2), but rather the complete exclusion of the wicked from God's kingdom (cf. Matt. 25:46).

4:2. The day of the Lord, which will be like a fire to the wicked, will in contrast be like sunshine to God's people. The phrase **the sun of righteousness** appears only here in Scripture. Though many commentators have taken these words to refer to Christ, the phrase seems to refer to the day of the Lord in general. In the kingdom, righteousness will pervade like the sun. **Healing** (*marpē'*, "health or restoration") **in its wings** (or rays) refers to the restorative powers of righteousness, which are like the healthful rays of the sun. God's people will be spiritually restored and renewed.

The righteous are described as **you who revere My name** (cf. comments on "My name" in 1:6). "Revere" translates the same Hebrew word rendered "fear" in 3:5 and "feared" in 1:14; 3:16. Revering God contrasts with saying "harsh things" against God (3:13). The fact that the righteous rather than the wicked are personally addressed indicates the Lord's contempt for the wicked as much as His love for His own. The figure of **calves** enjoying open pasture after being cooped up in a pen (**stall**) expresses the future satisfaction and joy of the righteous (cf. Isa. 65:17-25; Hosea 14:4-7; Amos 9:13-15; Zeph. 3:19-20).

4:3. The righteous will **trample down the wicked,** who **will be** like **ashes under the . . . feet** of the righteous. This not only indicates the finality of the judgment on the wicked, but it also brings to a sharp conclusion the answer in this oracle to the cynical question asked by the unfaithful Israelites, "What do we gain by carrying out His requirements?" (3:14)

VIII. Conclusion: Be Prepared for God's Coming (4:4-6)

A. The present preparation (4:4)

4:4. In light of all that has been said about the Mosaic Covenant and Malachi's concern for the people's covenant faithfulness and obedience, this concluding exhortation was appropriately direct and to the point. The verb **remember** (*zākar*) is used 14 times in Deuteronomy as an exhortation to Israel concerning this covenant **Law.** This command can refer to: (a) mental acts of remembering or paying attention to something, or to (b) mental acts combined with appropriate external actions (in other words, recalling and obeying), or to (c) acts of reciting or repeating something verbally (*Theological Wordbook of the Old Testament*, s.v. "*zākar,*" 1:241). In light of Malachi's insistence on obedience, meaning (b) seems to be the force of this command: "Recall it to mind and do it!"

The reference to **My servant Moses** not only speaks of Moses' faithfulness (Heb. 3:5) but also reminds the reader that the Lord Almighty (Mal. 4:3) is the same God who powerfully displayed His judgments and His salvation at the time of the Exodus. And He is the Living God who gave the Ten Commandments to the people **at Horeb** (the ancient name for Mount Sinai; Ex. 3:1; Deut. 5:2; Ps. 106:19). He graciously accepted Moses' role as prophetic mediator in the giving of the entire Law (Deut. 5:23-31). The people in Malachi's time needed a renewed fear of God; they needed to repent and be faithful to God's covenant. Such repentance would cause them to benefit from rather than suffer in the coming day of the Lord.

B. The future preparation (4:5-6)

4:5-6. God promised through Malachi that **the Prophet Elijah** would come and minister **before** the day of the Lord. (See comments under "Major Interpretive Problems" in the *Introduction* to Joel.) This is the only passage in the Prophets that speaks of a future ministry for Elijah. Many commentators have linked this prophecy to 3:1 which speaks of a messenger who prepares the way for the Lord's coming. However, Matthew (Matt. 11:7-10) specifically states that John the Baptist was the messenger (Mal. 3:1) who prepared the way for the Lord.

But should John the Baptist also be considered the fulfillment of the prophecy about Elijah? (Mal. 4:5-6) Before John the Baptist was born an angel of the Lord predicted that he would minister "in the spirit and power of Elijah, to turn the hearts of the fathers to their children and the disobedient to the wisdom of the righteous—to make ready a people prepared for the Lord" (Luke 1:17). This would seem to put together the two prophecies (Mal. 3:1 and 4:5-6) and to see John as fulfilling both of them.

However, while he freely admitted that he was the one who prepared the way for the Lord (Isa. 40:3; Mal. 3:1), John expressly denied that he was Elijah (John 1:21-23). Even when Jesus called John "the Elijah who was to come," He conditioned that designation with the phrase, "if you are willing to accept it" (Matt. 11:14). A solution to the problem seems to be offered in Matthew 17. After Elijah appeared with Christ in His transfiguration, the disciples asked about Elijah's future coming. Jesus, speaking apparently after John's death (cf. Matt. 14:1-2), affirmed that "Elijah comes and will restore all things" (Matt. 17:11). This future expectation indicates that Malachi 4:5-6 was *not* fulfilled in the ministry of John. Israel did not accept John the Baptist as the Elijah-like restorer of all things, so another Elijah-like forerunner is yet to come before the day of the Lord.

However, Jesus went on to say, "Elijah has already come, and they did not recognize him" (Matt. 17:12), and the disciples understood He was talking about John the Baptist (Matt. 17:13). The solution to all this seems to be that though John did not fulfill Malachi 4:5-6 (for Elijah is yet to come), Elijah was a type of John in that there is a great deal of similarity between Elijah in 4:5-6 and the messenger (John the Baptist) in 3:1.

It is difficult to determine whether the Elijah to come is Elijah himself (as possibly indicated in Matt. 17:11) or someone in the spirit and power of Elijah (as John was, so that Christ referred to him as simply Elijah, Matt. 17:12). The latter seems preferable. The most likely New Testament reference to this future Elijah-like ministry is Revelation 11:1-13, which speaks of the two witnesses in the Tribulation. Possibly the Apostle John was expanding the Elijah expectation

into an Elijah-Elisha ministry (cf. comments on Rev. 11:3-6.) As a result of the ministry of the two witnesses many people will repent, thus uniting **the hearts of . . . fathers** with **their children.** This repentance will mean that they will not experience God's judgment in the day of the Lord.

The last words of the Old Testament are Malachi's ominous anticipation of the **great and dreadful day of the Lord.** This event of judgment, a climactic event in history, was a major theme of the prophets. The force of the warnings and appeals in Malachi's book hinges as much on the certainty of this coming judgment as on the covenant-based offer of grace. The Book of Revelation renders the same expectation of judgment and repentance at the end of the New Testament (Rev. 22:12-17) but with greater details about the One who will return.

BIBLIOGRAPHY

Baldwin, Joyce G. *Haggai, Zechariah, Malachi.* The Tyndale Old Testament Commentaries. Downers Grove, Ill.: InterVaristy Press, 1972.

Feinberg, Charles L. *The Minor Prophets.* Chicago: Moody Press, 1976.

Freeman, Hobart E. *Introduction to the Old Testament Prophets.* Chicago: Moody Press, 1968.

Isbell, Charles D. *Malachi: A Study Guide Commentary.* Grand Rapids: Zondervan Publishing House, 1980.

Kaiser, Walter C., Jr. *Malachi: God's Unchanging Love.* Grand Rapids: Baker Book House, 1984.

Keil, C.F. "Minor Prophets." In *Commentary on the Old Testament in Ten Volumes.* Vol. 10. Reprint (25 vols. in 10). Grand Rapids: Wm. B. Eerdmans Publishing Co., 1982.

Morgan, G. Campbell. *Malachi's Message for Today.* Reprint. Grand Rapids: Baker Book House, 1972.

Oswalt, John. *Where Are You, God?* Wheaton, Ill.: SP Publications, Victor Books, 1982.

Smith, J.M.P. *A Critical and Exegetical Commentary on the Book of Malachi.* The International Critical Commentary. New York: Charles Scribner, 1912.

Tatford, Frederick A. *The Minor Prophets.* Vol. 3. Reprint (3 vols.). Minneapolis: Klock & Klock Christian Publishers, 1982.

Wolf, Herbert. *Haggai and Malachi.* Chicago: Moody Press, 1976.

At David C Cook, we equip the local church around
the corner and around the globe to make disciples.
Come see how we are working together—go to
www.davidccook.com. Thank you!